COMPUTER GRAPHICS
APPLICATIONS

COMPUTER GRAPHICS APPLICATIONS

An Introduction to Desktop Publishing & Design

Presentation Graphics

Animation

E. KENNETH HOFFMAN, Ph.D.
Seton Hall University

with Jon Teeple
Calibre Five, Inc.

WADSWORTH PUBLISHING COMPANY   BELMONT, CALIFORNIA

Senior Editor: Rebecca Hayden
Editorial Assistants: Tamiko Verkler and Nancy Spellman
Production Editor: Vicki Friedberg
Text and Cover Designer: James Chadwick
Print Buyer: Randy Hurst
Copy Editor: Evelyn Mercer Ward
Art Editor: Irene Imfeld
Technical Illustrators: E. Kenneth Hoffman and Irene Imfeld
Compositor: Jonathan Peck Typographers
Cover Art and Opening Art for Unit One: Chris Murfitt, Electraslide, Calgary, Canada. Pansophic StudioWorks software
Opening Art for Unit Two: Robert R. Weekes, HECSA. Pansophic StudioWorks software
Opening Art for Unit Four: Brilliant Image, New York
Opening Art for Unit Five: Still frame from "Snoot and Muttly," Susan Van Baerle and Douglas Kingsbury, Ohio State University, Computer Graphics Research Group

Unless otherwise credited, all photos by E. Kenneth Hoffman.

Printed in the United States of America   85
1 2 3 4 5 6 7 8 9 10 – – – 94 93 92 91 90

Library of Congress Cataloging in Publication Data
Hoffman, E. Kenneth.
   Computer graphics applications : an introduction to desktop publishing and design presentation graphics animation / E. Kenneth Hoffman with Jon Teeple.
     p. cm.
   Includes bibliographical references.
   ISBN 0-534-12200-0
   1. Computer graphics. 2. Desktop publishing. I. Teeple, Jon.
II. Title.
T385.H638 1990   89-70558
006.6—dc20   CIP

For Candyce
and for Faith

About the Authors

E. Kenneth Hoffman, MFA and Ph.D from New York University, is an Associate Professor of Communication at Seton Hall University, where he supervises the curriculum in computer graphics—a program he initiated in 1984. He teaches a variety of media-related courses including motion picture production, still photography, and computer animation. He has lectured on computer graphics at professional and academic conferences, and his computer graphics images have been published in *Computer Pictures Magazine* and the *Webster's New World Dictionary, School Edition*. Before coming to Seton Hall University, he was an Associate Producer at Channel Thirteen, the PBS affiliate in New York City, and has directed films for the Department of Defense in Vietnam. His animated film "Leaves in Space" was selected for screening at the New York Film Festival, and a documentary film, "Treasures of the Past: Archaeology in New Jersey," which he produced for New Jersey Public Television, was shown on Channel Thirteen. Among his publications is *Legacy Through the Lens: A Study of Mendham Architecture*, for which he was photographer. He and his wife reside in northern New Jersey, where they are active in historic preservation.

Jon A. Teeple, BA in English from Fairleigh Dickinson University, is a partner in Calibre Five, Inc., a New Jersey–based advertising and design agency. Teeple has been involved in all aspects of advertising and design for more than 20 years, working with a daily newspaper, business-to-business marketers, a nation-wide consumer financial services organization, and consumer package goods concerns. He has been responsible for all types of business communications including broadcast and print advertising, annual reports, house organs, newsletters, flyers, promotional material, catalogs, product sheets, publicity programs, instruction manuals, and corporate identity programs. Today he is very much involved in desktop publishing for business communication and computer graphics in advertising. Mr. Teeple and his wife reside in northern New Jersey.

PREFACE

Today's new graphics tools—computer hardware and software—have transformed the image-making process. Corporations use personal computers to create colorful presentations for sales meetings. Desktop publishing is revolutionizing prepress operations, affecting everything from newsletters to technical manuals and even books. Using personal computers, advertising artists create full-color advertisements for magazines and newspapers and can design television logos with sophisticated solid modeling, simulated environments, and animation. Filmmakers create television advertisements, station identification (ID) spots, and motion picture segments using computer animation. Computer graphics have moved from novelty to necessity, and *Computer Graphics Applications* explores this change.

Divided into five logical units, *Computer Graphics Applications* starts with a foundation of microcomputer fundamentals written for artists and designers rather than programmers. In turn, each commercial application is covered from the artist's particular perspective: jobs (existing and emerging), work environment, software, typical assignments, design considerations, and examples. An article by a well-known authority introduces each applications unit, giving the reader a good overview of the application. Highlighting the units on desktop publishing and animation are case studies featuring a prominent company in the forefront of those industries. Included throughout the book are many diagrams and illustrations reflecting the importance of communicating ideas visually.

Units 1 and 2 introduce the important microcomputer fundamentals, with the understanding that an artist prefers creating to computing. In consideration of the range of work environments an artist may encounter, Unit 1 compares graphics on the microcomputer to graphics on the micro's faster and more powerful relative, the minicomputer workstation. The artist learns not only about the basic components of a computer graphics system but also about how to modify a generic microcomputer for high-performance graphics. The artist who doesn't believe it's art until it's off the screen and in hand will appreciate the discussion of such output devices as color thermal printers and color film recorders. A complete look at the lexicon of the budding industry is presented in Unit 2, where the reader gains familiarity with the terms and procedures used by computer graphic artists. The building blocks of bits, bytes, and baud rates are explained. Vector and raster systems are compared and related to the relevant projects an artist wants to undertake in three-dimensional drawing programs, and special features, such as texture mapping, ray tracing, and multiple light sources, are discussed. With this background, the artist is ready to enter individual commercial applications.

Unit 3 explores the world of prepress—desktop publishing. Providing examples and a step-by-step description of the production process, the unit enables the artist to successfully bridge the differences between manual and electronic layout and design operations. Because desktop publishing is usually a group effort, the unit introduces the artist to all the potential group members, along with a description of their responsibilities and how they impact the prepress process. The specialized terminology of design studios, advertising agencies, and print shops is presented and integrated with the new vocabulary of on-screen page design. The unit prepares the artist to step into the prepress environment comfortably and confidently.

Unit 4 examines the production of business graphics for marketing and managerial presentations. Here the artist gains an understanding of the proper visualization of numeric data. The relationship between the graphic artist and the presenter is explored at length, with the objective of producing presentations that are not only graphic but visually succinct. A complete range of chart examples taken from actual presentations is provided. The unit prepares the artist to create presentation graphics using an approach that considers appropriateness of the graphic to the application, continuity of style, and creative visual problem solving.

Unit 5 introduces the artist to computer animation. Beginning with a discussion of traditional animation techniques and film theory, the artist then explores the different types of computer animation used today. Three-dimensional computer animation is covered in depth. The artist gets to look over the shoulder of a designer creating an animated station ID—from concept, to storyboard, to wireframe models, to the completed visual sequence.

For the artist, the comprehensive glossary provides a ready resource of computerese and applications terminology. Special terms important for comprehension and understanding are previewed at the beginning of each chapter. A bibliography at the end of each chapter provides a list of additional references and resources.

While the text is directed toward the needs of first-year computer graphics students, other students will derive equal benefit. Business students will gain needed knowledge and experience for presentations, an important ingredient in communicating ideas in both sales and management meetings. Computer science students will gain a thorough insight in the fast-growing area of graphics applications. Fine art students can explore a new creative medium that will quickly be taking its place alongside the traditional art forms of photography, painting, and sculpture. In addition to students, such professionals as advertising art directors, film- and videomakers, and those connected with prepress operations, graphic design, and publishing can gain insight in how computer graphics are being used in their industries.

The text has been planned so that it can be used for an individual course in introductory computer graphics, or for a sequence of courses. Units One and Two will introduce students to computer fundamentals and to computer graphics terminology and procedures common to all computer graphics applications. Units Three through Five will then expand their knowledge of these basic concepts, with emphasis on individual applications such as desktop publishing, advertising (electronic layout and design), business applications, or computer animation.

Among the many people who assisted us in the writing of this book, we would like to thank especially the instructors who read drafts of the manuscript and offered helpful suggestions: Ronald Coleman, Bowling Green State University; Sharon Ford, Rancho Santiago College; Peter Haberman, Florida International University; Craig Johnson, Bucks County Community College; John Schnell, Fashion Institute of Technology–New York; Jon W. Sharer, Arizona State University–Tempe; John Snyder, Pratt Institute; Deborah Sokolove, George Mason University; Robert W. Stowers, University of Wisconsin–Stevens Point; and Ruth West, University of Massachusetts–Amherst.

We would also like to thank the students, staff, and faculty at Seton Hall University, Department of Communication, for their assistance, especially Donald McKenna for his critical reading of the manuscript at several stages. We would also like to thank Robert Allen, Paul Murtha, Peter Rosenblum, Christopher Sharrett, and Albin Wicki for their contributions; and from the Department of Academic Computing Services, Thomas Burtnett and Nancy Mustachio. Many others have offered their time and expertise. We particularly want to thank Jerry Cahn of Brilliant Image, Robert Long of Travelong; Thomas Weisz of Weisz Yang Dinkleberger, and Dean Winkler of Post Perfect for allowing us to feature their facilities in the book. We would also like to thank James Aneshansley, Oxberry; Susan Bickford, Sun Microsystems; Chuck Chulvick, University of Scranton; David Gieselmann, Station KSDK; David Gillespie, Pansophic; George Goodwin, photographer; Steven Sarafian, Lyon Lamb Video; Charles Schoettler, Silicon Graphics; and Lisa Smith and Chris Woods of R/Greenberg Associates for their assistance.

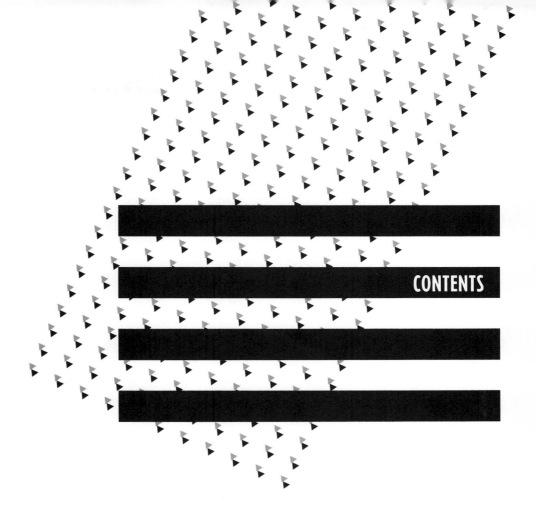

CONTENTS

Chapter Two   21

Hardware in the PC Environment—The Computer

Chapter Three   41

Hardware in the PC Environment—Peripherals

UNIT TWO   67

COMPUTER GRAPHICS CONCEPTS

The New Paint: Color from a Different Kind of Tube, by John Derry   69

Chapter Four   71

The Paint Programs

Chapter Seven

141

The Prepress Process

Chapter Eight

161

Page Composition and Design

UNIT FIVE

COMPUTER GRAPHICS ANIMATION

Animation's New Generation, by Beth Anderson   227

Chapter Thirteen   277

Video/Computer Graphics Interface

COMPUTER GRAPHICS
APPLICATIONS

Unit One

ELEMENTS OF

COMPUTER GRAPHICS

SYSTEMS

Before we begin studying microcomputer graphics applications for design, desktop publishing, business graphics, and animation, we will set the stage by investigating how computers create graphics—both from the programming side and from the point of view of computer graphics hardware. The first chapter in this unit introduces you to computer graphics programming in BASIC and compares PC-based systems to more powerful minicomputer graphics workstations. In the next two chapters, you explore computer graphics hardware and components, learning how the computer works and how various computer peripherals are used by graphics artists.

After reading each chapter, look at the end-of-chapter exercises. These exercises reinforce your understanding of computer graphics concepts and terminology, introduce you to the capabilities of the software your school is using, and give you practical experience with the computer graphics techniques discussed in the chapters. Further reading material can be found in the Bibliography at the end of each chapter, where you can find books and articles for areas of special interest to you.

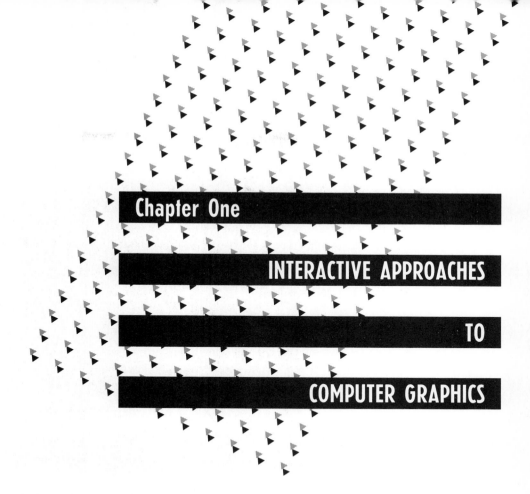

Chapter One
INTERACTIVE APPROACHES
TO
COMPUTER GRAPHICS

In this chapter you learn how computers can be programmed to create graphics. You compare batch processing, where you design now and view later, with interactive systems, where you see your designs emerge on screen as you create them. You next see how microcomputer (desktop) computer graphics fit into the larger family of computer graphics on minicomputers and mainframes. You investigate the operational differences between high-end workstations and microcomputer graphics systems. Finally, you examine three ways of communicating with the graphics program and discover the advantages of each in computer graphics design.

USING A COMPUTER TO CREATE GRAPHICS

Computer software contains instructions written by a computer programmer so the computer will do what you want. Computers may be programmed to do many different kinds of operations, from word processing to payroll accounting to painting and drawing. In each case the program supplies the instructions the computer needs to perform the specific task the user wants. Programs are usually written in high-level languages like Pascal, Fortran, and C, which use more-or-less recognizable words and phrases that are later translated into

Relevant Terminology

Batch processing

High-level language

Interactive program

Interface

Menu

Microcomputer

Minicomputer

PC-based

RAM

Workstation

machine language instructions—a series of 1's and 0's used by the computer. High-level languages like BASIC and Logo are easily learned by the programmer. In addition to commands that call for a knowledge of mathematics, these languages provide a vocabulary of graphics statements that helps the user create graphic designs easily, without extensive mathematics or computer knowledge. The following BASIC program tells the computer, in step-by-step instructions, how to draw an equilateral triangle[1]:

10 PSET (360,170)	Positions the cursor
20 DRAW "E25;F25;L50;"	Creates a line connecting the three points on the triangle
30 END	Concludes the program

The PSET statement establishes the point where the triangle is to be drawn on the screen. The DRAW statement tells the computer what kind of design to draw. E25 begins drawing a line at a 45-degree angle up and to the right for a distance of 25 units. F25 brings the line back down and to the right at a 45-degree angle for the same distance. L50 (which stands for left 50 units) brings the line back to the starting point (see Figure 1.1). Knowing the conventions of the language (that is, what the letters E, F, and L stand for) enables the programmer to use the DRAW statement as a form of shorthand to communicate to the computer.

BASIC DRAW statement movement commands allow the programmer to use powerful graphics functions built into the BASIC language (see Figure 1.2).

BASIC DRAW Statement Movement Commands
(n = distance)

U n	Move up n units.
D n	Move down n units.
L n	Move left n units.
R n	Move right n units.
E n	Move diagonally up and right n units.
F n	Move diagonally down and right n units.
G n	Move diagonally down and left n units.
H n	Move diagonally up and left n units.[2]

(Check the Exercises section at the end of this chapter for additional information about making graphics with BASIC.)

FIGURE 1.1

Equilateral triangle. This triangle was created using the BASIC DRAW statements in Figure 1.2. The letters E, F, and L refer to the direction and angle an imaginary pen will follow to create the triangle.

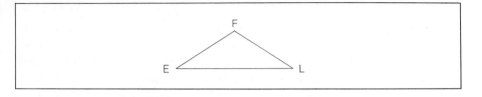

---

[1] There are several dialects of BASIC, some of which use slightly different commands. This BASIC program is written in IBM BASIC for the personal computer.

[2] *BASIC Reference*, IBM Personal Computer Hardware Reference Library (Boca Raton, Fla.: IBM, 1984), 73.

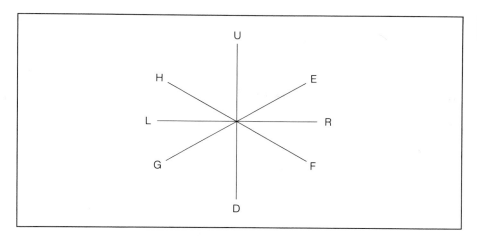

Lower-level languages have fewer shorthand commands, and one must use a combination of commands to accomplish the same task. For example, the triangle program in the assembly language, not having built-in graphics statements, is considerably longer. Programs written in lower-level languages generally run faster because they use a syntax more directly understood by the computer.

Interactive Programs

The triangle drawing program in BASIC shown above is an example of a program that does not allow user interaction. However, if the program were to stop and print the question "Length of first line?" and then wait for your response, it would be an interactive program. With an interactive program, you can create a triangle of any size, color, location, and so on, depending on the variables you are asked to specify.

Interactive programs contain many built-in subsections or functions in a complete drawing software package. An artist who wants to change a circle into a three-dimensional globe can invoke such a subsection, which will accomplish the conversion. These subsections take the form of menu options that can be selected when needed. Learning the capabilities of a program and the full range of menu options available is akin to becoming fluent in a foreign language. Remembering the syntax and vocabulary may be difficult at first, but once learned, the process becomes almost automatic.

Batch Processing

Programs that do not allow participation by the user while the program is being run are said to run in batch-processing mode. With batch processing, a program is run on a computer in its entirety, and the user has no opportunity to make modifications until the program is finished. This procedure is more suited to the mainframe environment of past years, where computer users (usually programmers and scientists with programming backgrounds) wrote specific programs and then waited for time on a mainframe computer to try them out. A programmer would sometimes wait until the next day or following week to see the results if the project was low priority. The introduction of less expensive minicomputers in the late 1960s brought relief from the hierarchy of mainframe computing. Minicomputers permitted decentralization, and more computers meant that users spent less time waiting for the results of a particular run.

Decentralization did not eliminate batch processing, however. Batch processing is still used in computationally intensive applications in business, science, and engineering. Batch processing is used whenever instructions can be programmed in advance to accomplish a discrete task—for example, as in the preparation of hundreds of payroll checks complete with deductions. In computer graphics animation, batch processing is used when hundreds of individual frames for a scene in a movie or television commercial must be computed from beginning to end.

TYPES OF COMPUTERS

In the broad field of graphic communication, and in the wider context of data processing, the use of computers can be divided into three hardware categories: mainframe computers, minicomputers, and microcomputers. The choice of hardware used is based on the scope and complexity of the computing project.

Mainframe Computers

At the high end of the scale are large mainframe computers used in government, science, and commercial data processing. These computers cost hundreds of thousands of dollars or more. They are found in general computing departments of large corporations and institutions or in computer service companies that rent time to clients with diverse computing applications. Their time-sharing and multitasking capabilities allow them to serve many people at the same time. When you use an automatic bank teller machine or when a travel agent types a request into a reservations terminal, a mainframe computer at the other end receives the communication. Mainframes are capable of storing and retrieving large amounts of information. Access to mainframes for programming purposes, however, is limited to people with extensive programming skills and a background in computer science.

Mainframe computers process information at roughly 25 times the speed of the average desktop computer (25 million instructions per second for the average mainframe versus 1 million instructions per second for a slow PC). They also process larger pieces of information at a time, making them even faster than their processing speed indicates. Supercomputers are a special class of mainframes, with processing speeds greater than 75 million instructions per second.

In the specialized area of computer graphics, mainframe computers have an important, though limited, role. Institutions and corporations began using mainframes for the production of slides and other graphic hard copy when desktop computer systems and desktop computer graphics software were not available. These companies still produce graphics on mainframe computers because the tradition, once established, has not yet ended. Other companies having extensive accounting and scientific databases stored in mainframe computers find it easier to produce graphics directly on mainframes rather than downloading summary data to PCs for production of slides and other business graphics.

For computationally intensive scientific and business applications, mainframes are the computers of choice. Their processing speed and huge memory capacity also make them capable of producing high-quality three-dimensional animation. Even so, high-quality animation can take anywhere from 30 seconds to 25 minutes per frame to generate. Thirty individual frames are required per second of video, so computing is usually done overnight. Complicated animations can sometimes take days to complete, even on the largest computers. The 25 minutes of computer animation in the feature film *The Last Starfighter* required more than a quadrillion calculations.[3] Each single frame took from 1 second to 20 minutes to generate (depending on its complexity) on a Cray supercomputer.[4] By comparison, the production of one slide for a business presentation does not require significant computer time and can easily be accomplished on a desktop computer.

Minicomputers

In contrast to the hundreds of thousands of dollars for a mainframe computer, minicomputers cost $25,000 and up. Their processing speed and memory storage capacity fall somewhere between that of mainframe and desktop computers. Minicomputers have replaced mainframe computers for data processing in medium-sized companies and are used extensively by engineering and research departments.

For several years there has been a trend away from mainframe computers toward minicomputer "turnkey" systems for many computer applications. These systems are termed *turnkey* because you buy the entire system, monitors to peripherals, from the same source. Turnkey systems are custom designed to accomplish specific tasks and have much the same speed and flexibility as a mainframe (see Figure 1.3). Included in turnkey systems are custom-designed hardware and VLSI (very large scale integrated) computer chips; these act to speed up repetitive graphics tasks, which on a general processing mainframe computer would take considerable computing power. The introduction of VLSI technology has made it possible to use minicomputers for computer animations that at one time had to be created on mainframe computers. Each frame in the Oscar-winning computer animation *Tin Toy* required 12 trillion calculations, in part because of the shiny surfaces, self-shadowing, and considerable amount of detail (see Color Plate 13).[5]

Microcomputers

Microcomputers (desktop computers) are at the low end of today's computing hierarchy. They are often called desktop computers because they fit conveniently on top of your desk and are sometimes referred to as personal computers (PCs) because they are used by one person at a time. They are slower than their larger relatives and access smaller amounts of information; however, they are becoming more and more powerful.

To comprehend how swiftly the microcomputer has evolved from the home hobbyist high-tech toy of the mid 1970s to the powerful productivity tool of today, it is useful to compare the capability of today's microcomputers

---

[3] Cynthia Goodman, *Digital Visions* (New York: Harry N. Abrams, 1987), 12.
[4] Mike Tyler, "3-D Images for the Film Industry," *Computer Graphics World* (July 1984): 64.
[5] Philip Elmer-Dewitt, "Through the 3-D Looking Glass," *Time* (May 1, 1989): 65.

FIGURE 1.3

Silicon Graphics' minicomputer
animation workstation. (Courtesy
Silicon Graphics.)

with that of mainframe computers just 10 years ago. In 1978 the average
mainframe computer could compute at the rate of 5 million instructions per
second. Today's fastest microcomputer easily surpasses that speed. For less
than $5000, you can purchase a microcomputer with the equivalent processing
power of a 10-year-old mainframe—a computer originally costing hundreds
of thousands of dollars!

> If automotive technology had advanced at the same pace as computers during
> the past two decades, a Rolls-Royce car theoretically might cost around $3,
> it might get around three million miles to the gallon, and might deliver
> enough power to drive an ocean liner.[6]

Microcomputers may be at the low end of today's computing hierarchy, but
when considered in perspective, they don't seem slow at all (see Figure 1.4).

MINICOMPUTER VERSUS MICROCOMPUTER GRAPHICS WORKSTATIONS

The emphasis in this section is on graphics systems developed for mini- and
microcomputers, even though mainframe computer graphics continue to be
an important source of innovation. Workstations are specially equipped com-

---

[6] F. X. Millor, "Using Your PC to Generate Graphic Slides That Tell the Story," *Computer Pictures* (July/
August 1985): 28.

FIGURE 1.4

Cubicomp microcomputer animation workstation. (Courtesy Cubicomp.)

puters designed to be used by one person and containing an input device (keyboard, mouse, or drawing tablet), a monitor, memory, disk storage, and an output device such as a printer or slide recorder. They are usually used for a specific task but can be used for any application from architectural design to programming. At one time graphics workstations consisted only of the input and output devices; design work was done at the workstation, but computing was done at a host computer connected to the workstation. Because of advances in miniaturization and computing power, workstations now do their own computing. They can be found at the minicomputer and microcomputer level. In the following subsections, we consider the operational differences between high-end minicomputer graphics workstations costing $100,000 or more (for software and hardware) and low-end microcomputer graphics workstations ranging in price from about $20,000 to $45,000.

Minicomputer Workstations

Minicomputer graphics workstations contain custom-designed hardware and software and use state-of-the-art high-speed microprocessors that are especially good for graphics computations. Dedicated graphics chips are used that speed the creation of images by doing operations in hardware that would normally be done in software if computed on general purpose machines. These systems are expensive because of their customized hardware and software and are often found in companies that specialize in computer animation, molecular modeling, visual simulation, and so forth.

Software development for minicomputer graphics workstations is a cottage industry—that is, small companies in this industry serve a relatively small and specialized market. Software is designed with specific hardware capabilities in mind and will run only on systems equipped with that hardware. Many companies writing graphics software are computer graphics service bureaus—that is, they create animation for clients using the same software they sell separately to other production companies. In this way the software benefits from constant improvement and additions. If a client asks for a graphic effect not currently available, the software is modified to permit the new effect. This modification becomes part of the software package sold to other computer graphics companies. Because of the proprietary nature of this type of computer graphics software, it can cost anywhere from $10,000 to $150,000 per station.

Several companies are now producing workstations for animation, business graphics, broadcasting, and engineering. AT&T Pixel Machines, Pixar, Quantel, and Computer Graphics Laboratories supply integrated software/hardware turnkey systems in the $100,000 price range. In addition, hardware-only systems can be purchased from Silicon Graphics, Hewlett-Packard, DEC, and Sun MicroSystems. Software for these hardware-only "graphics engines" can be obtained from Wavefront Technologies, Alias Research, Symbolics, Vertigo, and Intelligent Light, to name a few. Competition among these companies is intense, and every year animation produced on one or more of these systems is showcased at the SIGGRAPH (Special Interest Group on Computer Graphics of the Association for Computing Machinery) and NCGA (National Computer Graphics Association) conventions. The advantages and disadvantages of minicomputer workstations follow:

Advantages

1. Minicomputer workstations are designed as stand-alone graphics systems. Software, computer, and peripherals make an integrated turnkey package.

2. Software is usually developed by companies to meet the needs of the graphics artist. The software evolves as additional functions are needed.

3. Minicomputer workstations run at least 20 times faster than PC-based systems. One hardware manufacturer claims two to three orders of magnitude improvement in graphics performance over microcomputer systems. Where it will take five minutes to compute a single frame of complex graphics on a PC-based system, a minicomputer workstation can let you see the image in less than ⅓ second.[7]

4. Turnkey suppliers offer on-site support and considerable "hand holding."

5. Minicomputer workstations use high-resolution graphics monitors.

6. Minicomputer workstations readily support networking with other stations.

7. Minicomputer workstations are capable of accessing 16MB (megabytes) or more of RAM (random access memory) to allow manipulation of large graphics files.

Disadvantages

1. Minicomputer workstations have a high initial cost ($60,000 or more, including software).

2. Minicomputer workstations often require knowledge of the less-known UNIX operating system.

Microcomputer Graphics Workstations

Microcomputer graphics workstations run on specially equipped general purpose microcomputers. Because of the millions of desktop computers already

---

[7] Charles Schoettler, Silicon Graphics Company. Interview with the author, Nov. 30, 1987. One order of magnitude is a 10-fold improvement; three orders of magnitude would be 1000 times faster.

in use, the cost–performance ratio is very good. Models with the latest generation of high-speed microprocessor (the computer chip that does the actual calculating; see Chapter 2 for a full discussion) and several megabytes of memory sell for $5000 to $8000. However, adequate performance can be achieved with slower and less costly models that sell for about $2000.

Graphics systems developers have not lost sight of the advancing power of the personal computer. As personal computers have become more powerful, programmers have begun pushing the capabilities of such systems to the limit. PC-based graphics systems are now being used to create charts, diagrams, and other business presentations and also are used in advertising, animation, and the fine arts. This revolution in personal computing power is dramatically changing the way everything, from newspapers to television logos, is designed and produced. The revolution in desktop publishing has resulted from the advent of PCs with the power of mainframes and of software written to take advantage of that power. The personal computer has helped take computing out of the laboratory setting and sterile mainframe environment and place it in the more informal surroundings of the modern office and design studio. Instead of working through computer specialists and programmers, artists can create graphics directly on their own screens. "Dedicated" personal computers (that is, computers that are outfitted with special hardware and which are usually used for only one task such as business graphics or animation) are design tools and are as much a part of the design studio as shadow boxes, T squares, and artists' drawing boards.

Microcomputer graphics are created in a user-friendly environment. The software does not require extensive computer training or programming knowledge to operate. However, as with many complicated systems, there is usually a learning curve. You begin by learning the capabilities of the system, studying the documentation, and exploring the software menus and submenus. Most software is extensively documented and includes training exercises for the beginning user. Software capability is excellent, though performance can be much slower on microcomputer systems. The range of capabilities is very wide, including sophisticated paint and solid modeling, animation, automatic charting for business presentations, desktop publishing, and image capture and enhancement.

Microcomputer workstations use the same film recorders, videotape recorders, laser printers, and pen plotters found in minicomputer and mainframe computer installations. Since the technical quality of the final image is dependent on the capability of the recording equipment, an image created on a microcomputer can equal the quality of an image created on a minicomputer or mainframe computer.

Microcomputers are ideal for business graphics, illustration, and computer painting programs and are the functional equivalent of minicomputer workstation systems. However, computationally intensive applications, such as solid modeling and animation, are slower on a microcomputer. For this reason, users consider throughput when purchasing a graphics system. Throughput is the total time it takes to design, revise, and record an image on a given computer system. Higher initial cost of a minicomputer may be justified by its speed and production efficiency. The details of such decisions are always in a state of flux, owing to rapidly changing prices and capabilities of graphics systems. The advantages and disadvantages of microcomputer systems are as follows:

Advantages

1. Microcomputer systems have lower initial cost.
2. Competitive atmosphere in the microcomputer marketplace fosters rapid advances in software capabilities.
3. Microcomputers have lower maintenance costs.
4. Microcomputers have user-friendly menu systems; no programming skills are required.
5. There are extensive libraries of software for graphics and other applications.
6. Previous user familiarity with widely known operating systems, such as DOS (disk operating system used for the IBM PC and compatibles) and the icon system (found on Macintosh computers), makes learning microcomputer graphics systems easier for the artist.
7. There is a wide variety of software available for computer graphics and general business applications.

Disadvantages

1. Microcomputers are slower than minicomputer workstations.
2. Software and hardware come from different sources, and software upgrades are not always compatible with installed hardware.
3. Limitations in database size (the size of the graphics files) may limit microcomputer solid modeling systems to the creation of logos and simple 3-D objects.
4. Microcomputer systems are less likely to have advanced imaging features such as ray tracing and specular highlights.

GRAPHICS SOFTWARE INTERFACE

The software interface is what you use to give instructions to your graphics program. It is at the boundary between two components of a computer system—in this case the user and the software. The software interface includes menus, which list commands that access the interactive software, and the work area in which to draw or construct objects.[8] Menus can be pull-down windows that disappear when not needed or on-screen menu commands that are always available. Pull-down menus are popular because they are out of the way until needed. The Windows Presentation Manager from Microsoft Corporation and the Apple Macintosh menu system are two examples of a pull-down menu software interface.

In addition to how they display the menus, software interfaces use either text or graphic icons to represent the commands. We will investigate both approaches by examining three software interfaces.

---

[8] Graphics interfaces are becoming important tools in text-oriented programs as well. WYSIWYG (what you see is what you get) desktop publishing screens employ pixel-oriented dot matrices to display exact typefaces, kerning, charts, and other graphics.

Types of Interfaces

Icon Approach   Icons are probably the easiest of all interface tools to learn. Commands are represented by small pictures, or icons, that look like the function they represent. A garbage can on the Apple Macintosh system represents an option that discards the screen image or a file. A pencil represents the draw mode. Scissors represent cut and paste (see Figure 1.5).

FIGURE 1.5

Videoworks menu on the Macintosh II computer. Icons in the upper-left-hand corner provide access to magnification, draw, typesetting, and other features. Pull-down menus provide additional options, such as background patterns and additional colors.

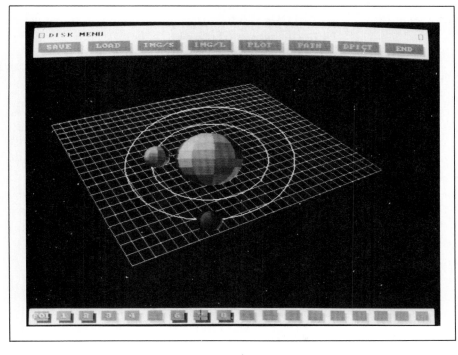

FIGURE 1.6

On-screen artwork menu from Pansophic, Inc. There are abbreviated menu commands at the top of the screen and folios for storing graphic objects at the bottom of the screen.

FIGURE 1.7

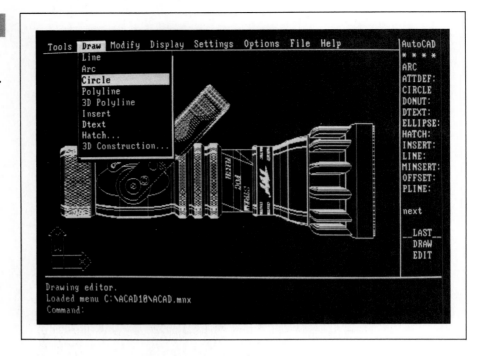

AutoCad command menu. Commands are typed on the command line at the bottom left of the screen. Many of the same commands can also be selected from the menu at the right or from the pull-down menu at the top of the screen.

Acronyms, or Abbreviated Menu Command Approach   Other programs use letter abbreviations to represent menu commands. The acronym IMG/S allows you to save a screen image; RUB, to rubber stamp a section of the screen; and X-R, to rotate an object on its x axis (see Figure 1.6).

Command Approach   The command interface approach uses keyboard commands to access the desired options, which can be found on a separate text monitor. This approach is very fast because commands can be stacked sequentially and executed quickly by typing the commands on the computer keyboard (see Figure 1.7). Many seasoned computer users prefer this approach. However, the beginner usually finds it more difficult to learn.

The Ideal Interface

The following are characteristics of an ideal interface:

1. Menu commands should be organized logically to facilitate work flow and should be intuitive to the user.
2. The software should have a hierarchical command structure with submenu headings that appear at the main menu level (see Figure 1.8).
3. The interface should be easily learned (have a short learning curve), but seasoned users should be able to take keyboard command shortcuts to other options.
4. On-line help should be readily available to the user.
5. The interface should be fun to use.
6. The artists should be able to terminate any command with the keyboard escape key.

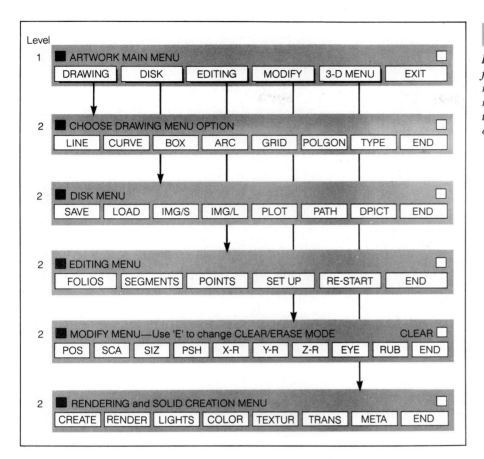

FIGURE 1.8

Hierarchical command structure from the Pansophic artwork main menu. Selecting an option in the main menu will open up an additional submenu having more specific commands.

7. All commands should be accessible from the screen; there should be no hidden commands accessed only from the keyboard unless they are duplicated on the screen.

8. There should be separate drive paths for program access and for saving images (data files).

PURCHASING GRAPHICS SOFTWARE

The variety of software for graphics applications, especially desktop publishing and presentation graphics, has increased tremendously. Every few months there are new releases of established software and completely new packages to consider. When purchasing software, first determine your graphic needs. Questions you might ask include:

1. What type of output will be required—videotape, 35mm slide, laser printer, or other?

2. What type of graphics applications will be used in the laboratory—illustration, package design, presentation graphics, desktop publishing, animation?

3. Who is going to use the software—artists, managers, clerical assistants?

4. What software features are needed to meet graphics requirements—freehand drawing, business charting, picture scan-in capability, 2-D or 3-D animation?

5. Must the software run on existing computers designed for normal office productivity programs (spreadsheets, word processing), or will additional hardware components be necessary for graphics?

6. Are there budget constraints? You may wish to devise a segmented purchasing plan in which critical elements of the system, such as the computer and software, would be purchased first. Slides and other graphics output could be created by service bureaus (see Chapter 9) from your data files.

Every department has its own particular environment and operating needs. Your specific needs will vary from those of others, so look at the unique requirements of your department and create a graphics software profile that prescribes the ideal system for your needs. Look for file compatibility between different types of programs. Paint programs should be able to "speak" with business charting programs, and vice versa. Many software packages support the computer graphics metafile (CGM) file standard. With CGM, files can be easily transferred between different types of graphics programs. An image created using a computer-aided design (CAD) program can be added to a chart for a business presentation. If the graphics program is for the art department, you might check for compatibility with programs used by other departments in the organization. Outside work should be performed on programs compatible with the graphics program used by the art department.

Learn as much as possible about available software. Read reviews in trade magazines. Go to regional and national graphics conventions. Look for featured "shoot-outs" (product comparisons) among competing software packages. These live, on-the-convention-floor comparisons are becoming more and more popular at trade shows. Talk to as many vendors as possible. Take a test run on the software, applying it to your particular graphics need or problem. Above all, don't take anything for granted. Be skeptical of "gee whiz" features and impressive output. If you haven't done it yourself, don't believe it, even when features are shown to you. Ease of use and the ability to move quickly from menu to menu is more important than fancy options that may get little use or are difficult to use. Go to "boutique" shops (value-added retailers [VAR]) that configure graphics stations specifically for your needs. Talk to graphics systems consultants. Find out what they recommend. You may want to pay their prices if continued support is an important consideration.

Don't rule out investigating software beyond your budget or needs. High-end software can be used as a yardstick to judge the features of lower-priced software. By looking at high-end systems, you can draw up a list of features you would like to have in your system and then look for these features in lower-priced software. Just because a package sells for $5000 doesn't mean that it is 10 times better than one selling for $500. High-end features can be found in less expensive software.

When you have narrowed your choices to one or two packages, ask the supplier to give you the names of companies using their product. Talk to the artists and managers using the software and find out if they have had any problems. Ask them if the program lacks any important features. Finally, consider purchasing additional peripherals that are needed to fully support the software. Digitizing cameras that bring video images into the program, high-resolution film recorders for creating 35mm slides, and laser printers may be needed before the software is fully up and running.

SUMMARY

Interactive graphics programs have enabled noncomputer programmers to create sophisticated computer graphics. Computer costs have fallen sharply, while computer capabilities have increased dramatically. It is now possible to create computer images on inexpensive microcomputers that a few years ago could only have been created on large minicomputers and mainframe computers. (See Appendix A for a full list of paint and 3-D programs for minicomputer workstations, Macintosh, and IBM compatible computers.)

The graphics interface is the means by which the user interacts with the computer software. Just as in word processing or other interactive programs, the user must learn the capabilities of the software and work within those limits. If additional capabilities are needed, and if time permits, an end user can usually ask the software developer to include specific functions in the next software upgrade. Software developers writing professional-level graphics software encourage dialogue of this type, but implementation can take 6 months or more to reach the end user.

Exercises

1. Using your own words, define the terms in the Relevant Terminology section at the beginning of the chapter.

2. If you were designing a PC computer graphics workstation, what would be some of the considerations you would have when buying the basic computer?

3. Perform the following BASIC graphics tutorial by doing the examples:

    If you have an IBM-compatible computer with a color graphics card or a Hercules monochrome graphics card, work through the following tutorial. (When using the Hercules card [this procedure will not work with Hercules clones], follow the "Getting Started" instructions in the Hercules manual before doing the exercises.) The tutorial will show you how computers create graphics by introducing you to graphics programming in BASIC. Use the BASIC interpreter program that came with your computer, either BASICA, if it is an IBM, or GWBASIC, if it is an IBM-compatible. Type the name of the BASIC program interpreter you are using. When BASIC interpreter interface is on the screen, type SCREEN 2 to enter graphics mode.

BASIC graphic statements use x and y coordinates to position lines, circles, and polygons on the viewing screen. Starting in the upper-left-hand corner of the screen, the x axis goes across the screen and the y axis goes down. The number of units across and down varies depending on the resolution (degree of sharpness) of the screen. For the purposes of these exercises, it is assumed that your screen has a resolution of 640 pixels across (pixels are tiny dots, the smallest units on the screen) $\times$ 200 pixels down (Screen 2 mode). Type in the commands as they are shown. When you hit the ⟨enter⟩ key, the graphics will appear on the screen. This is "direct" mode. Later you will want to work in indirect, or program, mode. Put line numbers next to each line that you type in; be sure to hit ⟨enter⟩ after each line. The F2 key will run the program— that is, draw the graphics. The F1 key will bring the program back to the screen. F4 will save the program to disk. F3 will load the program back from the disk.

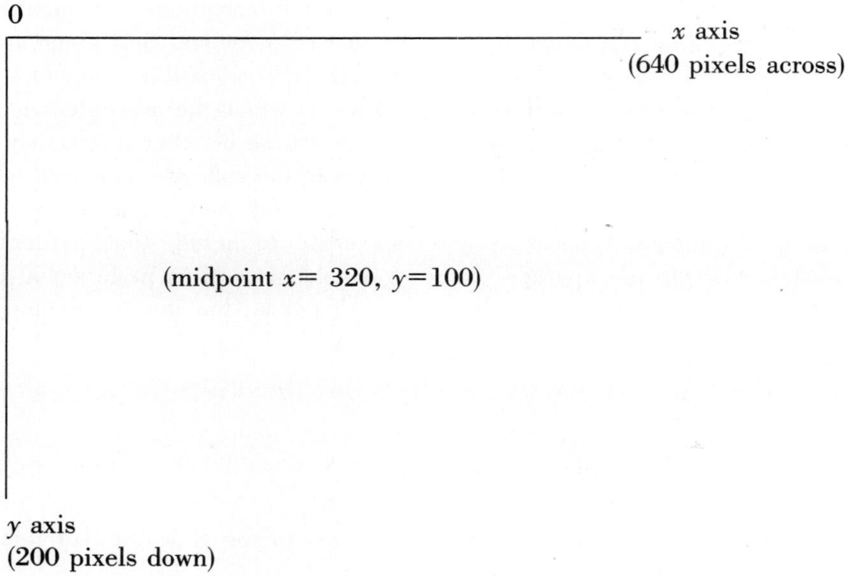

0

————————————————————————— x axis
(640 pixels across)

(midpoint $x = 320$, $y = 100$)

y axis
(200 pixels down)

PSET   Allows you to draw a point at a specific position on the screen.
> *Example:* PSET (320,100)

PSET is also used to note a position on the screen for a later graphics command to start from.

LINE   Provides the ability to draw a line between any two points on the screen.
> *Example:* LINE (320,100)−(200,175)
> Tells the computer to connect the first specified point to the second.

LINE statements can be used to draw a box.

Example: LINE (320,100)−(200,175),,B
> The points specified describe two opposite corners of the box. The B tells the computer to calculate and draw the four sides rather than a straight line.

LINE statements can be used to draw *and* fill a box.

    Example: LINE (320,100)−(200,175),,BF[9]

CIRCLE   Provides the ability to draw a circle on the screen.

    Example: CIRCLE (300,100),150

        The last number specifies the radius. The plot points position the center.

    Example: CIRCLE (300,100),150,,,,1/2

        Where 1/2 is used as a scale factor to compensate for the fact that the screen is more units wide than it is high. The scale factor will make the circle look round. Try different scale factors, such as 4/3 or 1/3.

VARIABLES   Just as in algebra, letters can be given numerical values. You can begin a program by saying A = 30, then substitute the letter A instead of using the number 30. With the substitution of letters, computers begin to show their real power of calculation.

    Example: 10 A=30
               20 DRAW "U=A;R=A;D=A;L=A;"

RUN the program by hitting the F2 key. Why isn't the box square? Save the program by hitting F4, typing a name (no more than eight characters, no spaces), and hitting return.

Additional DRAW statement commands:

N   Will return the cursor to the beginning of a line just drawn before beginning a new line. If you were drawing the spokes of a wheel, the N command would bring you back to the hub before going out on a new spoke.

TA   Turn angle (TA) makes it possible to turn an angle of a specified number of degrees before drawing a new line. The following program will draw the spokes of a wheel with spokes at 20-degree intervals around in a circle.

    Example: 5 'SPOKES
               10 FOR Q=0 TO 360 STEP 20
               20 PSET (200,100)
               30 DRAW "TA=Q;NU200":NEXT Q
               40 END

Q is a variable used to specify the amount of degrees between lines. TA=Q means turn an angle the value of Q. Because of the FOR and NEXT statements on lines 10 and 30, the program will continue to loop back to line 10 until the value of Q has reached 360. Each time it will draw a line at a 20-degree interval. Try changing the STEP value to 90 or 2. Use different x and y coordinates in the PSET statement. You will see a big difference in the image. Why?

---

[9] The area inside an object can also be filled using the PAINT statement [PAINT (x, y)]. Be sure that the x and y coordinates are inside the object and not on a line.

4. Using the BASIC DRAW commands on page 4, draw the outline of a house. Use LINE statements to put a sidewalk or fence in the foreground. Use program mode so that you can save the picture on your disk when you are finished.

5. **a.** Draw a box with equal sides using DRAW commands.

   b. Using the SPOKES program above, spin the box around in a circle, repeating it several times. Substitute your BOX instructions for the NU200 in the program. Be sure to include a line before the DRAW statement that assigns a value to A.

6. Type the following program into your BASIC interpreter and run it. Look at the graphics on the screen and explain why the program creates lines of different length.

```
5 'SNAIL
10 SCREEN 2
20 CLS 'Clears the screen first
30 FOR A=0 TO 360 STEP 5
40 Q=Q+5
50 DRAW "TA=A;NR=Q;"
60 NEXT A
70 FOR A=0 TO 360 STEP 15
80 Q=Q+1
90 DRAW "TA=A;NR=Q;"
100 NEXT A
110 END
```

Try different step factors and different values for Q—for instance, Q=Q+10.

Bibliography

Bates, William. *The Computer Cookbook.* Garden City, N.Y.: Quantum Press/Doubleday, 1984.

Deken, Joseph. *Computer Images: State of the Art.* New York: Stewart, Tabori & Chang, 1983.

Greenberg, Donald, A. Marcus, A. Schmidt, and V. Gorter. *The Computer Image: Applications of Computer Graphics.* Reading, Mass.: Addison-Wesley, 1982.

Lien, David A. *Learning IBM Basic for the Personal Computer.* San Diego, Calif.: Compusoft Publishing, 1984.

McGregor, Jim and Alan Watt. *The Art of Graphics for the IBM PC.* Reading, Mass.: Addison-Wesley, 1986.

Marshall, George R. *Computer Graphics in Application.* Englewood Cliffs, N.J.: Prentice-Hall, 1987.

Masterson, Richard. *Exploring Careers in Computer Graphics.* New York: Rosen Publishing Group, 1987.

Prueitt, Melvin. *Art and the Computer.* New York: McGraw-Hill, 1984.

Walter, Russ. *The Secret Guide to Computers.* 3 vols. Somerville, Mass.: Russ Walter, 1986–87.

Chapter Two

HARDWARE

IN THE PC ENVIRONMENT—

THE COMPUTER

In this chapter you will learn about the major types of desktop computers used for graphics—the IBM PC, the Apple Macintosh, and the Amiga. You will learn about computer system components such as hard drives, graphics cards, and random access memory (RAM). And you will see how PC computers are modified with special components for high-performance graphics.

The desktop computer is not only a widely accepted productivity tool in the business community and in education, it is also used in filmmaking, dance, music, fashion design, painting, sculpture, and other creative arts. Personal computers have become so pervasive in the arts that they are destined to influence the way we create in all media. To the extent that you understand the capabilities of computers—what they can do and what they cannot do—and the many types of software tools available, you will be better prepared as a computer graphics artist.

> Artists will be pleasantly surprised to discover that "computer literacy" is a goal well within their abilities. More good news is that opportunities for hands-on training in computer graphics applications are gradually becoming available across the country.[1]

---

[1] Susan Bickford, " 'User Friendly' Allies," *Audio-Visual Communications* 23 (November 1983): 40.

OPERATOR INVOLVEMENT

There are some popular misconceptions about the involvement of the graphic artist with the computer:

> "Most graphic artists may never need to see the inside of a computer."
>
> "The computer and its peripherals make up a complicated and mysterious system that no artist can hope to understand."
>
> "After all, the artist's job is to create images and meet the graphic needs of the client—a service technician is just a phone call away."

It is true that it is the nature of machinery to break down and that the more complicated the machinery, the greater the chance of breakdown. It is also true that every artist should understand the tools of the craft. While car owners don't have to know the inner workings of their automobiles, in the absence of a mechanic, it's good to know how to put on a spare tire or change the oil. Likewise for the graphic artist, many day-to-day problems can be solved with minimal computer knowledge, saving the considerable time and expense involved in waiting for a technician. There are generally three levels of operator involvement in computer graphics systems: the apprentice, the journeyman, and the craftsman.

Level 1: Apprentice

The apprentice knows where to find the computer power switch and how to boot the software. No use other than graphics is contemplated, so the apprentice never has to switch to a different program or use the disk operating system (DOS) commands if working on an IBM compatible. All interaction with the computer is done from inside the graphics software. All the aprentice's energy is devoted to creating images, and any problems are directed to someone else. Operator maintenance of the machine is limited to cleaning the monitor screens when they become dirty.

Level 2: Computer Journeyman

The journeyman sometimes uses the computer for word processing and other programs in addition to graphics and understands how to get from one program to the other. Occasionally, simple DOS commands are used to copy files from one disk to another or to clean up directories that are cluttered with files no longer needed. The journeyman understands how to use file conversion programs so that images created in one program can be transferred to another. If a problem with the hardware develops, the journeyman can describe the malfunction to a service technician, who then makes the repair. Operator maintenance at this level includes attaching peripherals to the computer, installing new software, running utility programs periodically to see if the hard drive is functioning properly, and maintaining peripherals that use expendables such as toner, color film, pens, ribbons, and so on.

Level 3: Computer Craftsman

The craftsman is willing to learn about the inside of the computer and to make educated guesses about the cause of a malfunction. The craftsman reads the manual packed with the computer and understands how the computer can be modified to create high-resolution images. After watching a technician replace an add-in card or install memory chips, the craftsman remembers how to do this next time, instead of calling a technician. On the software side, level 3 involvement includes creating customized commands (batch files) to speed up access to various programs and modifying the system at the DOS level so that the computer best matches the personality and style of the user. The craftsman isn't afraid to learn a programming language like BASIC or another easy-to-use programming language and considers such endeavors fun. Preventive maintenance includes occasionally cleaning the disk drive heads, isolating problems as to origin (for example, hardware or software), and finding the specific plug-in component or software configuration problem that is causing the difficulty.

Graphic artists exist and flourish at all levels. Those who attain the craftsman level are naturally of more value to their employers because they understand the graphics system as a whole, not just from the isolated perspective of a user. These operators are more autonomous and work well in offices where there is limited technical support. Level 3 involvement is essential for the free-lance computer graphics artist who works with many different software packages under varying support conditions. It is the objective of this book to make a level 3 operator out of you!

THE COMPUTER

Most professional graphics software is written for the IBM PC or PC clone. This might sound strange, since the Apple Macintosh is known for desktop publishing and the Amiga for great graphics. But the IBM PC was the first computer chosen in large numbers by corporate America, and because of its almost universal availability, third-party manufacturers have found ways to beef up its limited graphics abilities. (The Apple II computer came out first but wasn't a serious contender in corporate installations after IBM introduced the PC.) Today, with the proper graphics expansion cards and other add-on products, the PC and its derivatives are the most prevalent microcomputers used in professional graphics.

Desktop computer graphics systems include the basic microcomputer and several other devices used to create graphics. It is not unusual for graphics systems to include two monitors (one for graphics and one for text), a digitizing tablet or mouse to draw images on the graphics screen, a copy stand with television camera, and one or more output devices such as a digital film recorder or videotape recorder (see Figure 2.1).

FIGURE 2.1

Microcomputer graphics workstation and peripheral equipment.

IBM PC

There are four generations of PC family computers. First came the IBM PC and PC-XT. Even though considered slow today, they set the standards for features in later generations. They originated an open architecture design— meaning that other manufacturers could add products to the basic computer. PC computers use software compatible with the disk operating system (developed by Microsoft and known as MS-DOS) and use the Intel family of microprocessors (the central part of the computer system). Next came the PC-AT, performing seven times faster than the original PC. The AT is the first generation of microcomputer to adequately support professional graphics. The most recent additions to the PC family are the 386- and 486-level computers, named for the microprocessor that they use. They will prove to be the most versatile of all PC computers and clones.[2]

Each generation of computers is differentiated by the type of microprocessor used. The microprocessor is a small integrated circuit inside the computer and does the actual computing. It is also called the CPU (central processing unit) and is contained in a small ceramic case with two rows of tiny "legs." The ceramic case is about the size of a domino. Inside the case is a much smaller integrated circuit called a microchip. The microchip is smaller than your smallest fingernail and contains the equivalent of hundreds of thousands of tiny transistors and other components. Some of these components contain instructions that give the microprocessor the ability to do computational tasks such as adding numbers together and comparing numeric

---

[2] Clones are microcomputers made to work like (and sometimes to look like) computers manufactured by companies like IBM or Apple. Clones are cheaper than the name brands they imitate and are usually manufactured in Asia (Taiwan, Korea, Singapore, Hong Kong, or Japan) and imported as complete units or in separate parts to be assembled in this country. Most clones work well and should be seriously considered when purchasing a computer. Clones are sometimes referred to as work-alikes because they imitate all the major functions found in the name brand computers and run the same software. Virtually all IBM computers discussed here have clone counterparts.

values to see if they are equal or different. Instruction sets such as these give the chips limited intelligence—they can do extraordinarily "dumb" things astoundingly fast.

Microprocessors perform three basic functions. They fetch information from random access memory (RAM), perform arithmetic operations such as adding or comparing numbers, and go back to the program to get the next instruction. The slowest PC microprocessor executes 1 million instructions per second and can access 640 kilobytes of computer memory. The fastest microprocessor executes 6 million instructions per second and can access 16 megabytes, or 25 times the amount of computer memory. A byte is a unit of computer memory. It can store the equivalent of one alphabet character, encoded as a series of bits—8 bits to the byte. A kilobyte equals about 1000 bytes—technically, 1024 bytes. For comparison, the text in this chapter equals about 40,000 bytes (40 kilobytes, or 40K for short). The chapter contains about 6000 words, not including featured topics. (See Chapter 4 for a further discussion of bits and bytes.)

Apple Macintosh II

Based on research conducted by Xerox in the mid 1970s at its Palo Alto Research Center in California, Apple introduced graphics menus as a way of communicating with the computer in 1984, when Apple marketed the first Macintosh computer.[3] In place of the familiar MS-DOS screen prompt C>, the Macintosh uses a menu of options, each depicted by a graphics icon and window that can be selected with a mouse pointing device (see Figure 2.2). Many DOS computers will eventually use a Windows screen that functionally duplicates the icon approach used on the Macintosh. Likewise, desktop publishing became widely possible with the introduction of the Apple LaserWriter in 1985. Another plus for the Apple Macintosh is its Motorola M68000 series CPU, designed to facilitate high-resolution graphics. The only thing that held the first Macintosh back as a major player in the desktop graphics marketplace was its closed architecture. Third-party manufacturers couldn't add graphics enhancements to the computer because no expansion slots were provided. It was easier for graphics hardware enhancements to be developed for the open architecture of the IBM PC.

In 1986 Apple introduced the Macintosh II. Because it was designed for graphics from the ground up, it has many advantages over systems that considered graphics only as an afterthought. The Macintosh II is meant to be a serious competitor in the office computer marketplace, where desktop publishing and presentation graphics are becoming essential tools for business communication. Its open architecture, fast Motorola M68030 processor, high-resolution graphics monitor, and integrated desktop publishing and graphics software make it the ideal microcomputer-level graphics system. Its ability to display 256 simultaneous colors and its moderately priced professional-level

---

[3] The Xerox system is based on several key innovations now popular in desktop computing. Their computer stations can display several variable-sized overlapping windows, each with a program running simultaneously so that information can be copied from one window to the other. They use a mouse as a pointing device, and several computer stations can be linked together with a high-speed cable network called Ethernet so that data files can be shared by many users. (See J. D. Foley and A. Van Dam, *Fundamentals of Interactive Computer Graphics* (Reading, Mass.: Addison-Wesley, 1984).

FIGURE 2.2

Apple Macintosh icon approach. Programs are selected by clicking the icon with a mouse pointing device.

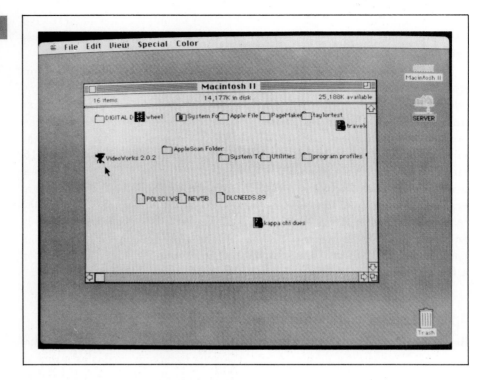

graphics and animation software make the Macintosh II a formidable competitor at both the micro- and minicomputer levels.

Amiga 2000

The Amiga 2000 from Commodore is a descendent of the Atari 800 computer, which was marketed as a home entertainment center.[4] Both computers were designed by Jay Minor. With graphics in mind, he designed the Amiga 2000 around the Motorola M68000-series CPU. The computer also has three additional chips to handle graphics, sound, and 2-D animation separately, without tying up the microprocessor. The Amiga easily outperforms off-the-shelf PC-level computers in graphics applications. Unlike the first Macintosh, which was limited to monochrome images, the Amiga supports a color monitor capable of 4096 simultaneous colors (see Figure 2.3). The Amiga's low price (less than $1000 for the entry model), video-capture capabilities, and video output make it ideal for independent video artists and home computer graphics enthusiasts. To tap into the vast amount of business software written for PC-compatible computers, Commodore developed special hardware and software to turn the computer into a PC-compatible machine. Unfortunately, even though it can run IBM PC software with a special add-in card, performance of PC software on the Amiga is poor when compared with the same software running on the AT or 386/486-level IBM computers.

---

[4] The Atari 800—a milestone in microcomputer graphics—produced graphics and animation for the then-considered modest price of about $1000. In graphics mode it allowed four colors at a time, at a screen resolution of 160 × 80. Its special graphics chips meant it could produce real-time animation. Hundreds of computer games were marketed for the Atari 800.

FIGURE 2.3

Amiga 2000 computer. (Courtesy Commodore.)

System Unit Components

Whether you are using an IBM compatible, Macintosh, or Amiga, there are several computer components you should know about. The system unit is the box on which the monitor sits and is what we generally think of as the computer. The unit houses the central processing unit (CPU), computer memory (RAM and ROM), the disk drives, and various other support components (see Figure 2.4). Hardware components controlled by the central processor but distinct from it are called peripherals. Monitors, printers, keyboards, videotape recorders, and joysticks are examples of peripheral devices.

System Board The system board (also called the mother board) usually rests at the bottom of the computer chassis. All components are connected to this board. Data travels to and from the CPU and other components along an electronic highway known as a bus. Besides a bus, there are support chips to keep the microprocessor going, a clock crystal to keep the computer in electronic step, and chips for read only memory (ROM) and random access memory (RAM).

FIGURE 2.4

Inside view of MS-DOS computer showing the (a) power supply, (b) hard disk drive, (c) floppy disk drive, and (d) system board, into which are plugged the CPU, RAM, ROM, and add-in cards.

Random Access Memory (RAM)   RAM is the physical place where programs and data are stored. The CPU looks in RAM when it needs additional programming information or when it must find specific data. For example, if you create a circle on the graphics screen with a graphics program and want to reshape it into an oval, the CPU reads the program instructions in RAM for making an oval, takes the data representing the circle out of another place in RAM, processes this data according to the program instructions, and returns the new data to RAM. Your screen now displays an oval (see Figure 2.5). The CPU can access all the data stored in RAM directly rather than having to read through the data serially as would happen if the data were stored on magnetic tape. Data stored in RAM is volatile, however. When you turn off the computer, your data disappears forever. Images not saved to the floppy disk or hard drive are lost; thus it is important to save your images often. Even an accidental power interruption will cause all data (programs and images) in RAM to be lost.

Read Only Memory (ROM)   ROM is special memory inside the computer that cannot be erased and will not go away when the computer is turned off. The CPU reads ROM instructions when the computer is first turned on. ROM instructions in the form of the power on system test (POST) tell the computer to do certain checks on system components. Control of the CPU is then given to the computer's operating system, which is automatically loaded from the

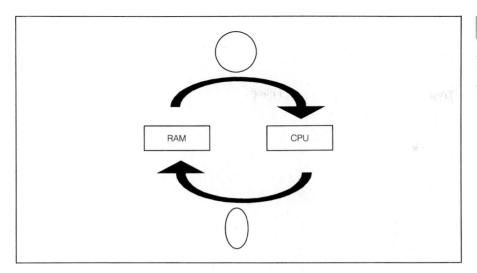

FIGURE 2.5

Flow diagram showing how the CPU acts on data according to program instructions.

floppy disk or hard disk. ROM memory is not volatile but neither can you add information to it. ROM instructions are burned into the chip at the factory and cannot be altered.

Memory Cards   Graphics applications are memory intensive. Since a single image can easily fill one floppy disk at professional-level resolution, computers that come with limited memory have to be beefed up to store and display all of this data. AT and XT compatible computers are modified for high-performance graphics by adding an additional memory card. When the memory card is used to store images, it is called a frame buffer (*frame* as in a film frame, *buffer* meaning a temporary place to store data waiting for processing). Most systems have two or more frame-buffer areas—a front buffer and one or more back buffers. The front buffer stores the image that is being sent to the color monitor. The front buffer is sometimes called the refresh buffer because it "refreshes" the image on the monitor screen. It is found on the graphics card, which is connected to the display monitor.

   The back buffer(s) can be found on the memory card or in reserved sections of RAM. The back buffers are used like clipboards, where images are stored and then quickly taken to be combined with other images. The memory card may also be used as a *z*-buffer card for displaying three-dimensional databases.

Monochrome Display Adapter   The monochrome display adapter plugs into the mother board and is connected to the text monitor. The adapter converts electronic signals representing the letters of the alphabet into the actual letters seen on the screen. This adapter differs from graphics adapters in that it cannot control (*address* is the computer term) individually the smallest dots seen on the screen. (Squint at a monitor and note the tiny dots that make up the text characters.) Rather, it sends each alphabet character to the monitor as a single matrix of dots known as a character box. This box is 14 units high and 9 units wide on the IBM PC-AT (see Figure 2.6). Some monochrome display adapters, such as the Hercules card and compatibles, have a graphics

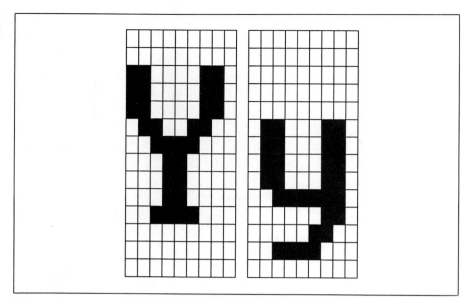

mode that can address individual dots and can support monochrome graphics in addition to text. These monochrome graphics cards are ideal for word processing and other programs that use graphics icons to select menu options.

Power Supply   In most IBM PCs and PC clones, the power supply is contained in a shiny box in the upper-right-hand corner of the computer. The power supply converts standard AC house current into the DC voltages used by other components in the computer. The power supply also contains a fan that circulates air throughout the computer. RAM chips get very warm and must be constantly cooled with circulating air or they will momentarily fail, causing serious problems with the operation of the computer. For this reason, it is important to keep your computer at about 72 degrees or less. Temperature is particularly critical in graphics computers because of the large number of memory chips heating up the inside of the computer.

Hard Disk Drive   Because RAM storage only works when the computer is running, programs and images must be permanently stored on magnetic disks. The hard drive contains several magnetic storage disks that can hold data to be saved. Space on the hard drive is measured in megabytes (1 million bytes of data). Most hard drives store from 10 to 80 megabytes of data. Some can store 800 megabytes or more.

Floppy Disk Drive   Floppy disk drives provide an alternative and readily portable means for storing data. Diskettes are placed inside the floppy disk drive unit and information is then recorded on the diskette. Standard 5¼-inch disks store from 360,000 bytes (360K) to 1.2 megabytes of information, depending on the type of disk. The 1.2MB disks are called high-density disks and are used in the PC-AT and 386/486-level computers. Surprisingly, smaller 3½-inch disks store more information—either 720K or 1.4MB. They are used in the IBM PS/2 and in the Apple Macintosh computers. When you use laboratory computers at school, it is better to store images on removable disks so they can be taken home when you leave.

Communication Ports An important feature of every computer is its ability to communicate with other computers and equipment. Computers send information to printers and other pieces of equipment through what are known as communication ports. The parallel port (usually found on the text monitor adapter card) enables the computer to be connected to most text and graphics printers. Parallel communications allow the full 8 bits of information in each byte to be transmitted simultaneously. A parallel communications cable, sometimes called a Centronics cable, is used for this purpose.

Serial ports transmit information more slowly, 1 bit at a time. Each of the 8 bits of data per byte must wait its turn to travel sequentially to the peripheral. Serial transmission is slower, but information can travel over longer distances. Serial interfaces are used for communication between computers, either through direct connections or over telephone modems. Most input devices, such as a mouse or digitizing tablet, use serial ports. The serial port is found on a separate serial add-in card or is part of the mother board.

Modems The term *modem* is an acronym for modulate/demodulate. Modems allow computers to communicate with other computers over telephone lines by converting the digital data of bits and bytes into analog form, like a voice, suitable for telephone transmission. At the other end of the telephone line, modems convert the analog data back into digital form. Analog signals and recordings have an *analogous* relationship to the original sound or image from which they were created. For example, when you speak on the telephone, vibrations in electrical energy carry your voice along telephone lines to a telephone receiver, where the electrical vibrations are converted into magnetic vibrations. These vibrations cause a diaphragm in the receiver to vibrate; the surrounding air molecules also vibrate generating sound waves that are carried to the listener's ears. Digital signals encode the sound by assigning numbers to correspond to the pitch and volume of our voices. Digital transmission and recording (as in laser discs) is more efficient because it is less likely that the encoded information will be lost or corrupted in transmission or recording. Digital signals must be converted back to analog signals with digital-to-analog converters (DAC) before the sound can be heard or the images seen. Record albums and sweep-hand wristwatches are examples of analog devices that have digital counterparts. Modems can either be separate devices that sit on your desk next to the computer or plug-in cards that connect to the mother board inside the computer. There are several speeds at which modems transmit data, the most common being 2400 baud (the amount of computer information communicated per second). Graphics files are usually very large, so it is wise to buy the fastest modem compatible with the system to which you are sending files. Special communication software is needed to facilitate modem communication.

Hardware Interfaces

By definition, a computer interface is the boundary between two components of a computer system. Often, the interface refers to the boundary between computer operator and computer hardware and software. The hardware interface includes input devices, such as the keyboard or mouse, and display

FIGURE 2.7

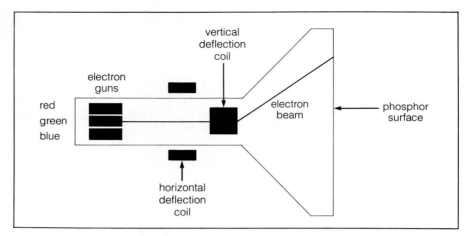

electron
guns

red
green
blue

vertical
deflection
coil

electron
beam

phosphor
surface

horizontal
deflection
coil

Cathode ray tube. At the back of the tube, inside the neck, are three electron guns, one for each component color—red, green, blue. Between the guns and the phosphor screen are deflection coils—a pair on each side and a pair top and bottom—that direct the stream of electrons leaving the guns and paint the image on the phosphor surface. Note that in magnetic deflection systems the beam is deflected at right angles to the magnetic field.

devices, such as the monitor (color or monochrome). Most text-oriented applications (word processing, accounting) use the keyboard or a mouse as the input device. Graphics programs use a digitizing tablet, mouse, or joystick.

Monitors

Keep in mind that PC graphics workstations usually come with two monitors: monochrome for text and color for graphics. The monochrome monitor is sometimes used to display the menu options for the graphics programs, and it is the sole monitor for text-oriented programs in word processing and accounting. Text monitors are usually capable of higher resolution than color monitors.

Cathode Ray Tube (CRT)   *Cathode ray tube* is the generic term for all monitors. The tube contains three basic components. In the front of the tube is the flat surface where the images are formed. The surface is coated with phosphors that glow when struck by a beam of electrons. At the back of the tube, inside the neck, are three electron guns, one for each component color— red, green, blue. Between the guns and the phosphor screen are deflection coils, a pair on each side and a pair top and bottom, that direct the stream of electrons leaving the guns. The top and bottom coils control horizontal movement, and the side coils control vertical movement. The electrons scan the phosphor screen, "painting" the color image a line at a time (see Figure 2.7).

Home television sets receive composite video signals, where all the electronic picture information is sent as a single video signal. Luminance (brightness) and chrominance (color) are sent as one package. Instead of composite signals, computer monitors use component video signals, where the red, green, and blue components of the signal are sent to the monitor over three separate wires. Each color has its own luminance level. When the three signals hit the phosphor screen, each affects a dot corresponding to its own color. A single grouping of red-green-blue dots is called a triad. The perceived color of each triad will vary as each color component of the triad changes in intensity. Maximum intensity of all three will produce a triad that looks white. A triad without any blue component and medium intensity of red and green appears yellow (see Color Plate 1).

FIGURE 2.8

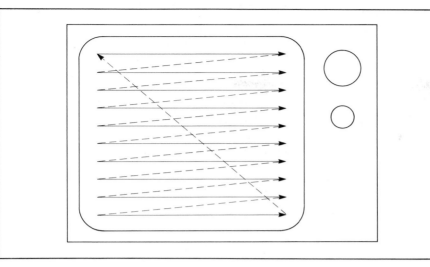

Raster Display   A raster display works much like a normal television screen.[5] The image is sent to the monitor from the display adapter, and the electron beam paints the image on the screen back and forth, a line at a time until the full raster has been scanned (see Figure 2.8). Raster displays are capable of subtle shading and can produce screen resolutions up to about 1500 lines. Most professional microcomputer graphics applications use 482-line monitors. Higher-resolution monitors require more computer memory to hold the image and as a result more time to generate each picture. This makes them too slow for the PC environment. They are usually found on more powerful minicomputer workstations, which generally use 1024-line monitors.

   Interlaced monitors first scan the even lines on the screen, then go back and scan the odd lines to create a full picture. Interlacing helps prevent flicker and makes the image easier on the eyes, because as the even lines fade, the odd lines are being refreshed. When interlacing is not practical, long-persistence phosphors are sometimes used to reduce flicker. The lines they create stay on the screen longer so that the screen does not appear to vibrate. Long-persistence phosphor monitors are not good for real-time animation, however, because the images tend to smear as they move.

Vector Display   This type of monitor is specific to computer graphics, computer-aided design (CAD) or computer-aided manufacturing (CAM), and scientific applications. Vector monitors differ from normal television monitors because they do not require the normal back-and-forth scanning of the whole picture in raster fashion. Instead, line segments are drawn individually where they are needed, based on their x and y coordinates. For this reason, vector monitors are sometimes called stroke monitors. Since most of the screen isn't affected when the individual lines are drawn, the pictures are drawn much faster (see Figure 2.9). Vector monitors are not capable of drawing shaded areas or of displaying halftone pictures or a wide variety of colors. Like the

---

[5] A display device can be called the CRT (cathode ray tube). It can also be called the color or text monitor (depending on which is referred to), the RGB monitor (red, green, blue) for the color monitor, or the video display. The terms *TV*, *TV set*, or *TV screen* should be avoided, since they imply that there is a television receiver attached.

FIGURE 2.9

Comparison of raster and vector monitors. The vector monitor on the left creates an image by connecting any two points on the screen with a line called a vector. The raster monitor on the right creates an image by scanning back and forth and intensifying the pixels that are closest to the outline of the object (in this case a house). The raster monitor has the advantage of being able to create shaded areas and is the predominant monitor used in computer graphics. (From "Computer Software for Graphics," by A. Van Dam. Copyright 1984 by Scientific American, Inc. All rights reserved. Used with permission.)

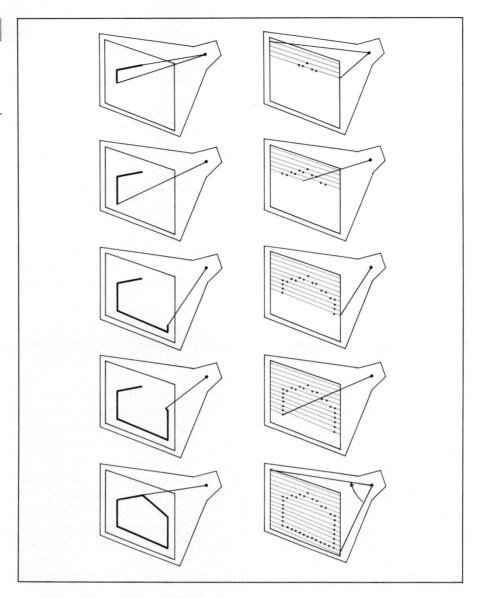

pen plotter—which uses a pen instead of an electron beam—the vector monitor displays its line drawings in high resolution (up to 4096 lines per screen).

TTL Monitor TTL stands for transistor-to-transistor logic. The image is sent to the monitor as a digital signal from the display adapter inside the computer. A TTL monitor is used for text and graphics. It comes standard on most PC computers. It usually allows a maximum of 16 colors on the screen at one time, so it is not ideally suited for professional graphics applications. Because it is standard equipment on most computers, most PC business graphics programs run on TTL monitors. For this reason it is a good idea to use a TTL color monitor as the text monitor on a graphics workstation. That way, you can use the station for commercially available business graphics packages that run only on standard monitors. The other color monitor is almost always a high-performance analog RGB monitor.

Analog RGB Monitor   This monitor has the greatest color capability. Analog color signals—one each for red, green, and blue—are sent to the monitor by the display adapter. Because the signals are transmitted in analog form, each color signal has an infinite number of intensity levels. The monitor can reproduce any color of the spectrum by combining various intensities of the RGB color components. The IBM PS/2, the Macintosh II, and the Amiga use analog RGB monitors for normal text requirements and for graphics. As more software is written for these computers, the analog RGB monitor will become popular for general computing in addition to being used as a specialized monitor for graphics. As a general rule vector, TTL, and analog monitors are not interchangeable. You must match the monitor with the specific type of display adapter you are using.

Graphics Adapters and Other Special Features

Graphics cards are a special type of display adapter capable of creating point-addressable images and are connected directly to the graphics monitor. They convert electronic signals created by the computer into images that can be seen on the color monitor.

By way of comparison, think for a moment how color images look on older PC-compatible color monitors. The first IBM color graphics adapter, called the CGA card, boasted a resolution of 320 × 200. That is, 320 dots horizontally and 200 lines down. By comparison, most monochrome text-only adapters operate at the equivalent of 720 × 350 resolution. The higher the resolution, the sharper the image (see Figure 2.10). The CGA card could display all of 4 colors out of a palette of 16. Later, IBM came out with the EGA (enhanced graphics adapter) card. It operates at a resolution of 640 × 200 and produces 16 colors at one time. The limited number of colors was a product of the times. Graphics require a considerable amount of random access memory, and in 1981 memory was expensive. After memory prices began to fall, third-party manufacturers began developing add-in products that boosted the graphics capabilities of the PC. These add-in products are also used on AT and (sometimes) 386/486 level machines.[6]

High-Performance Graphics Cards   It's not hard to imagine how difficult it would be to create professional-quality computer graphics on the standard 320 × 200 line, four-color graphics adapter. Two hundred lines of resolution and four available colors aren't nearly enough to meet professional graphics requirements. For this reason, several companies developed high-performance graphics cards. At this writing the most popular cards are the Revolution card from Number Nine Computer Corporation and the TARGA card from Truevision, Inc. These cards transform the standard PC or equivalent into a graphics workstation capable of producing professional-level graphics.

One of the first high-performance cards was introduced in 1983. Hailed as a major breakthrough in PC graphics, it was called the Revolution

---

[6] IBM has since come out with the VGA (video graphics array) graphics adapter. It operates at a resolution of 640 × 480 and displays 256 simultaneous colors out of a palette of 262,144. This card is used on the PS/2 line of computers.

FIGURE 2.10

How resolution affects the quality of the image. (a) An image displayed on a CGA card at a resolution of 320 × 200, with 4 shades of gray. (b) The same image displayed on a Revolution card at a resolution of 512 × 482, with 256 shades of gray. (c) The image displayed on a TARGA card at a resolution of 512 × 482, with 32,000 shades of gray. Because (b) and (c) are the same resolution, they show that the number of gray levels (or number of colors) is an important factor in creating a realistic image.

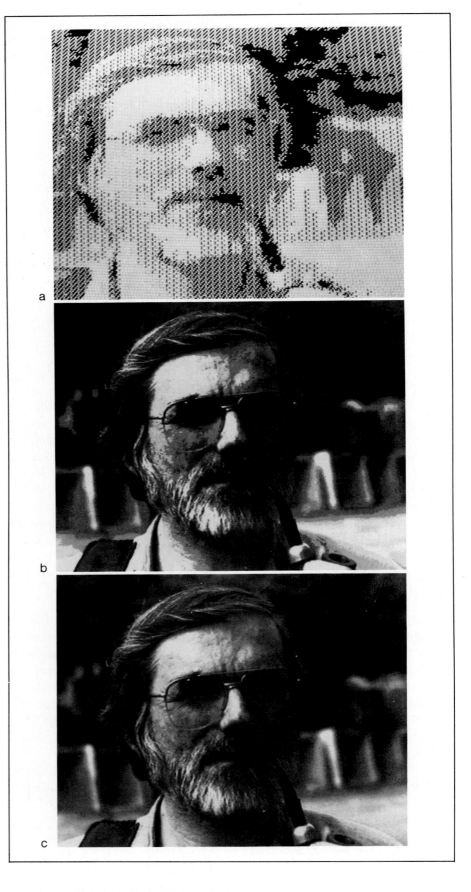

a

b

c

card by its Boston manufacturer. The card allows 256 colors to be displayed simultaneously, out of a palette of 16.8 million. By comparison, remember that the original IBM CGA card allowed 4 colors simultaneously out of a palette of 16; and at considerably less screen resolution. In addition to the increased resolution and color capability, the Revolution card converts computer images to standard video signals using an on-board video adapter called a genlock circuit. This capability enables the recording of computer animation on videotape, with resolution and colors acceptable to television audiences. Software developers began writing professional graphics software for the Revolution card immediately. Time Arts of California introduced Lumena, a paint system software with literally hundreds of options for the artist.[7] Artronics, a New Jersey company, introduced Artron, a paint system with similar capabilities, and West End Film of Washington, D.C., introduced Artwork, one of the first comprehensive solid modeling programs written for the PC environment. Software updates for these products are released frequently, and competition for new capabilities is intense. Recently, West End Film and Artronics were purchased by larger software companies (see Box 2.1).

Video Digitizing Cards   Digitizing cards convert normal analog television signals into digital representations that encode the continuous shades of light and color intensity as a series of numbers. The process operates much the same as compact disc recorders, which encode music as a series of numeric values and then convert those numeric values for pitch and loudness back into analog signals that we hear as music. Digitizing cards plug into the mother board and are connected to standard video cameras. Normal television images are converted into digital format so they can be used in paint and solid modeling programs. The digitizing card can be a separate unit, such as the PC-EYE card from Chorus Data Images, or part of a high-performance graphics adapter, such as the TARGA card.

[7] Prior to introduction of the Revolution card, Time Arts was running an earlier version of Lumena, called Easel, on the Scion card. This card allowed 16 colors on the screen at one time.

Unlike artists in other electronic environments such as television studios, the computer graphics artist usually works without close technical support. It is important, therefore, to become self-sufficient. Start by reading the hardware and software documentation. Subscribe to at least one computer graphics magazine. (Check the Bibliography at the back of this chapter for books that address both the Apple and DOS hardware environments and computer hardware.)

It is useful to learn a programming skill. Programming knowledge makes it easier to talk to graphics programmers about features you might need. You might also want to write specific routines for your graphics software if it accepts commands at the programming level. Both BASIC and Logo programming languages are easily learned and will produce intricate graphic patterns. Join the local chapter of SIGGRAPH (Special Interest Group on Computer Graphics of the Association for Computing Machinery) or the NCGA (National Computer Graphics Assocation). Both organizations have chapters in practically every state and hold national conventions where you can see the latest graphics systems and learn new computer graphics skills. If this is not possible, then join a local computer club. These clubs offer forums in which you can participate and where you can share your computer problems. Electronic bulletin boards communicate information on special interest forums on graphics and a variety of other topics and are a place where people can leave messages or post questions that others may be able to answer as well as a source of user-supported software that can be tried out before purchasing.

Don't be turned off by new terminology and working methods. Computer graphics started less than 40 years ago in science and engineering. Artists have only recently entered the field in large numbers, literally combining the fields of computers and graphics. Artists will eventually find as much familiar turf in this new field as the engineers, scientists, and programmers who prepared the way.

Exercises

1. Using your own words, define the terms in the Relevant Terminology section at the beginning of the chapter.

2. If you were purchasing a PC computer graphics workstation, what would be some of your considerations when buying the basic computer?

3. Why is it essential for you to save your computer images on floppy disks or on the hard drive inside of the computer?

4. What is the essential operational difference between display adapters that display text only and those that display text and graphics?

5. Explain the difference between analog RGB monitors and TTL monitors. Which monitor is better suited for graphics applications? Why?

Bibliography

Apple Computer, Inc. *Macintosh II Owner's Guide.* Cupertino, Calif.: Apple Computer, Inc., 1988.

Held, Gilbert. *IBM PC User's Reference Manual.* Hasbrouck Heights, N.J.: Hayden Book Company, 1984.

Norton, Peter. *Programmer's Guide to the IBM PC.* Bellevue, Wash.: Microsoft Press, 1985.

Norton, Peter. *Inside the IBM PC.* New York: Simon & Schuster, 1986.

Sargent III, Murray and Richard L. Shoemaker. *The IBM PC from the Inside Out.* Reading, Mass.: Addison-Wesley, 1986.

Chapter Three

HARDWARE

IN THE PC ENVIRONMENT—

PERIPHERALS

In this chapter you will discover peripherals, a group of input and output devices you can connect to your computer to perform a variety of specialized functions, such as translating an image to the computer screen as you draw it. You will also be introduced to simple microcomputer maintenance and troubleshooting and learn a variety of DOS commands to keep your computer files in order.

PERIPHERALS

A peripheral is a separate hardware device connected to and controlled by the computer. Peripheral devices play an important role in computer graphics. Input peripherals allow the artist to easily draw images into the computer memory and capture still photographs. Output peripherals enable you to create hard copy of your computer images—that is, color prints, slides, and pen drawings.

Input Devices

Digitizing Tablet   The most common graphics input device used by artists is a stylus connected to a digitizing tablet (see Figure 3.1). As you draw an image with the stylus, it appears in the work area on your graphics monitor.

Relevant Terminology

Bit pad

Digitizing tablet

DIP switches

DOS

Film recorder

Frame buffer

Hard copy

Inkjet printer

Joystick

Laser printer

Light pen

Mouse

Pen plotter

Peripherals

PostScript page description language

Scanner

Screen shooter

Stylus

Thermal printer

Tracking ball

Video still camera

The digitizing tablet (also called a bit pad or drawing tablet) translates stylus movements into cursor coordinate positions on the monitor, using an electronic web inside the tablet. This web can be either electromagnetic or electrostatic. In recent years the more dangerous electromagnetic webs have been replaced with the electrostatic variety. If your tablet is using electromagnetic means to translate stylus movements into cursor position, be careful not to place magnetic media (floppy disks or tape backup cartridges) on or near the tablet.

Mouse   The mouse does much the same thing as the tablet, but instead the cursor moves as a ball inside the mouse revolves. As you slide the mouse across the table, it translates your hand position into cursor position by measuring distance traveled as you move the mouse. The disadvantages of a mouse are (1) if the mouse is lifted while drawing, the cursor will stop moving; (2) the mouse has no absolute position relative to the drawing table, which makes it difficult for drawing; and (3) artists claim that drawing with a mouse is like drawing with your feet—not at all like holding a pencil! The mouse cannot be used to trace drawings into the computer because there is no way to see its exact position when it is on top of the artwork. The mouse is inexpensive, however, and works well when selecting screen options and when using presentation graphics and CAD programs (see Figure 3.2).

Tracking Ball   The tracking ball is seldom used in professional graphics programs. It does have an advantage over the mouse, however, in that it requires less space to operate and does not require a smooth surface to work on. The device is similar to a mouse except it is turned upside down—that is, the ball faces up instead of down. You turn the ball with your fingers in the direction you want the cursor to go (see Figure 3.3).

Joystick   Joysticks are typically used for controlling icons in computer games. Because of their lack of precision, they are not used as input devices for professional graphics programs.

Light Pen and Touch-Screen Devices   Light pens translate hand movements into cursor coordinates by noting the position of the light pen in relation to the monitor scan beam. Since the scan beam travels at a set speed, it is possible to compute the exact position of the light pen when it is pointed at the monitor. Light pens have not gained acceptance in the graphic arts and are usually found where limited interaction is necessary, such as at point-of-sale displays where the customer selects options directly from a computer screen with the light pen (see Figure 3.4).

Touch screens are also used with point-of-sale displays. The monitor has a touch-sensitive plastic cover that notes your finger position when the screen is touched. A typical application will ask the user to pick a category of interest from an on-screen list. The program will then search its database and display all books, toys, widgets, and so on in that category. Light pens and touch screens are intuitive. It's natural to point your finger or pen at the screen, but, if you had to do it continually, it would soon become tiring. For this reason, light pens and touch screens are not used with most graphics programs (see Figure 3.5).

FIGURE 3.1

Artist using a digitizing tablet. Also called a bit pad or drawing tablet, the digitizing tablet translates stylus movements into cursor coordinate positions on the monitor.

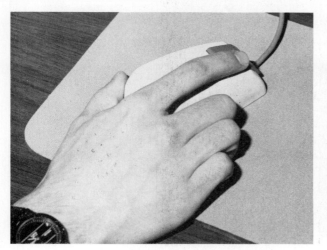
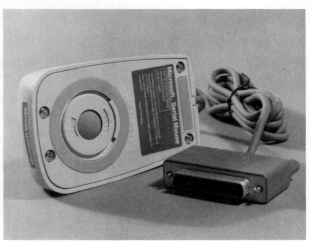

a   b

FIGURE 3.2

Video Cameras Video cameras are often used to import still images such as line drawings, flat art, and photographs. Usually the camera is attached to a copy stand so you can raise or lower the camera to reduce or enlarge portions of the artwork. Cameras that produce RGB signals are preferred to cameras that produce only composite video signals. (Professional video cameras divide the signal up into red, green, and blue components. Pictures from

(a) Top and (b) bottom views of a mouse pointing device.

FIGURE 3.3

Tracking ball input device used with Macintosh SE computer. (Courtesy Kensington.)

FIGURE 3.4

Light pen. (Courtesy Inkwell Systems; photo by Tom Netsel.)

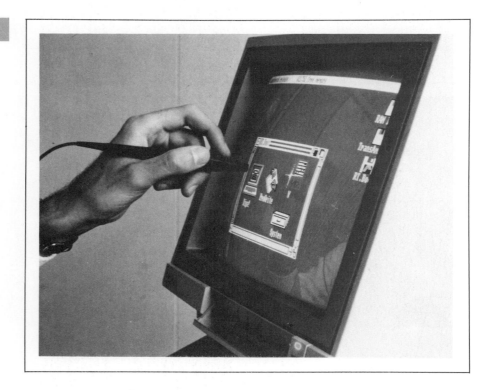

these cameras are better than those from cameras that do not separate the signals.) A recent innovation in video photography is the video still camera, which takes color images and stores them on a 2-inch disk that fits inside the camera. The disks will store 25 broadcast quality video images, which are played back on a separate record/playback unit. The unit conveniently sits on top of a PC computer and connects to the RGB input of the graphics

FIGURE 3.5

Touch-screen monitor. (Courtesy Virtual Prototypes.)

FIGURE 3.6

Sony Pro-Mavica video still camera with 2-inch disk capable of holding 25 broadcast quality color images.

digitizing card, such as the TARGA card or other graphics card with RGB compatibility. The camera is about twice the size of a 35mm still camera (see Figure 3.6).

FIGURE 3.7

Apple desktop scanner.

Desktop Scanners Scanners are similar in function to video digitizing cameras, but they look like desktop copiers. Flat artwork (photographs, news clippings, original art, and so on) is placed on a glass platen or sheet-fed into the scanner and "scanned" by a photoelectric imaging device that detects variations in light and dark. The image is then converted into digital form and transmitted to the computer. Unlike with a video camera that is raised or lowered to enlarge specific details of the original, cropping is done by selecting the area to be scanned from a quick low-resolution scan of the whole document. After the area to be scanned is marked, a full resolution scan is made, which is later sized to fit the document (see Figure 3.7). Special tracing software will permit the enlarging of specific areas of artwork without loss of detail by converting digitized images into vector form (line art images, no shades of gray). The software "traces" the outline of a raster image by sensing adjacent areas of similar contrast and then connects these like areas into vector lines that can be enlarged or reduced (see Figure 3.8). Scanners are primarily used in desktop publishing, where their ease of use makes them ideal for incorporating existing artwork and text into desktop publishing documents.

Output Devices

Output devices convert computer images into hard copy—slides, pen plots, video, and so on. These devices are connected to the computer and are usually accessed through the graphics software. It is important for the artist to understand how images will look when printed. Colors, in particular, never look quite the same when they are reproduced as hard copy. Since most images

Calibre five

a

Calibre five

b

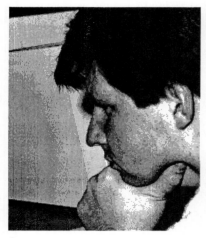

c

FIGURE 3.8

Comparison of vector and halftone enlargements. Figures (a) and (b) show the same line drawing at different sizes, with no loss of detail. Figures (c) and (d) show a halftone image cropped from a larger document and enlarged to approximately four times its size. Some loss of detail is noticeable. (Logo courtesy Calibre Five.)

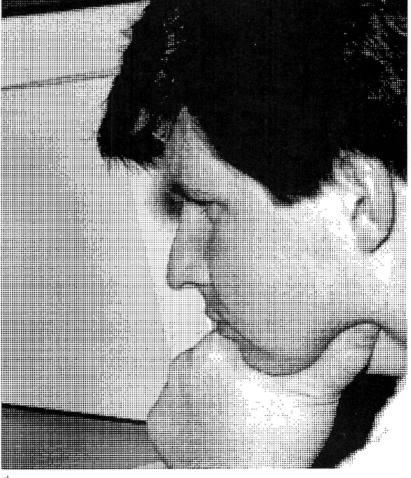

d

will be seen as hard copy, you must keep the limitations and capabilities of the output device in mind. The following sections describe several types of output devices.

Pen Plotter Like vector monitors, pen plotters are good at reproducing high-resolution line images. They cannot reproduce shaded images, however, because they are limited to what a pen can draw. They can fill in solid areas of one color, but this is time consuming. Pen plotters are used in architecture and engineering (computer-aided design programs), presentation graphics, and sometimes in traditional cell animation, where computer-generated line art is added to hand drawings (see Figure 3.9).

Laser Printer The Hewlett-Packard LaserJet printer and the Apple LaserWriter were introduced in 1984 and 1985, respectively. These printers and others like them use an office copier–type technology. Like office copiers, text and images are transferred to plain paper by using heat-sensitive plastic powder ink called toner. A laser beam "writes" the image to a positively charged drum, giving those areas on the drum a neutral charge. The drum, similar to an old-fashioned cylinder press, is then "inked" by rotating it through positively charged powder. Because opposites attract, the powder sticks to the neutral areas of the drum. The drum is then rotated over negatively charged paper, and the ink powder is attracted to the paper. The toner is fused to the surface of the paper by very hot rollers through which the paper passes on its way out of the printer (see Figure 3.10).

Laser printer images are reproduced in 300-dot-per-inch resolution. This resolution is much better than graphics monitor resolution but not quite as good as typeset resolution. Laser printers reproduce gray scale pictures and a wide variety of font styles, making them ideal for desktop publishing. More expensive models are capable of higher resolution, and some can reproduce color as well.

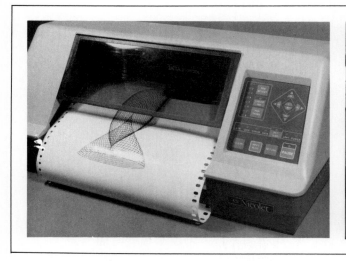 

FIGURE 3.9

Bruning eight-pen plotter.

FIGURE 3.10

Apple LaserWriter II.

The PostScript page description language from Adobe Systems is a popular graphics language developed for desktop publishing. It uses simple commands such as "rotate" and "repeat" to create intricate designs from a wide variety of fonts. It can also re-create gray scale images like photographs and images created in paint programs. PostScript-compatible laser printers are the printers of choice for desktop publishing.

Film Recorder   Film recorders reproduce computer graphics images on color transparencies, negatives, motion picture film, or prints. The transparencies can be of any size up to 8 × 10 inches but usually are the standard 35mm variety. The film recorder unit consists of a high-quality monochrome video display tube and a built-in still camera. Images are sent to the video display as monochrome RGB components. A color wheel inside the film recorder rotates into position for each separate exposure, one each for red, green, and blue. Film recorders can record animation on motion picture film when a motion picture camera is substituted for the still camera.

There are two types of film recorders. Analog recorders are hooked up to the back of the color monitor and record what is seen on the graphics screen at the existing screen resolution. Digital recorders are more expensive but produce higher-resolution images. These recorders can read data files and convert them into film images, using special software for that purpose. If the data file contains vector information (see Chapter 5), the images are recorded in extremely high resolution, limited only by the capabilities of the film recorder. Most digital film recorders are capable of 4000-pixels-per-line resolution, and some go as high as 8000 pixels per line. These images are not recorded in real time, however, and can take several minutes to compute and record. High-resolution digital images do not show the video scan lines and are ideal for presentation graphics (see Figure 3.11).

Color Thermal Printer   One of the most useful output devices is the color thermal printer. Color images are output to specially coated glossy paper at either 200 dots per inch or 300 dots per inch, depending on the printer. Some models can reproduce over 4000 simultaneous colors, making these printers ideal for reproducing scanned-in video images at near-photographic quality. Thermal printers are ideal for creating quick color proofs of computer artwork and are also a good medium for portfolio images (see Figure 3.12).

Thermal printers use special heat-sensitive ink coated on thin sheets of clear plastic. The ink is transferred to the glossy paper when it comes in contact with a heat bar inside the printer. Each image requires three passes over the heat bar, one for each of the primary colors. Since the final image is still heat sensitive, you must be careful *not* to use a dry-mount press or other heat source to mount the image. Dust and small particles of dirt quickly accumulate on the heat bar, so it must be cleaned often, otherwise long streaks mar the final image.

Inkjet Printer   Inkjet printers electronically direct ink from four nozzles (cyan, yellow, magenta, and black) in the print head onto the paper, forming color dots that make up the image. They are commonly used for both text and graphics applications and are ideal for creating printed reports that combine

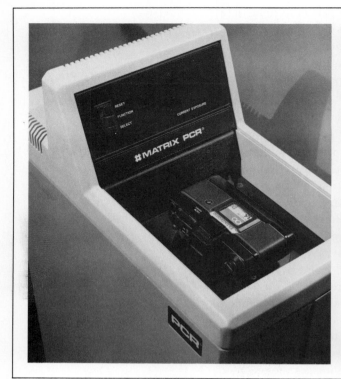

FIGURE 3.11

Matrix digital film recorder.

FIGURE 3.12

Matrix thermal color printer.

color charts and other graphics with text (see Figure 3.13). Because the ink is in liquid form, inkjet printers require frequent maintenance. The operator should clean nozzles often and refill or replace reservoirs when needed.

Low-cost one-color inkjet printers are now competing with laser printers in the desktop publishing market. They offer many of the same capabilities as laser printers (multiple fonts and 300 DPI graphics) but at a significant initial savings.

Dot Matrix Printer   The dot matrix printer has been a mainstay in the spectrum of output devices since the early days of microcomputing. Improvements in dot matrix technology make these printers ideal for text and medium-resolution graphics applications. Some dot matrix printers will print color images, but color fidelity is only fair to poor. These printers should not be used for the final image but are fine for proofs (see Figure 3.14).

Videotape   It would seem that videotape output would be a cinch, given that computers use video monitors as display devices. However, RGB computer monitors are not compatible with standard NTSC[1] broadcast signals. Special video conversion boards, which modify the digital RGB signals and

---

[1] National Television Systems Committee. This committee set the specifications for broadcast television in the United States. All television sets sold in the United States are capable of receiving NTSC signals.

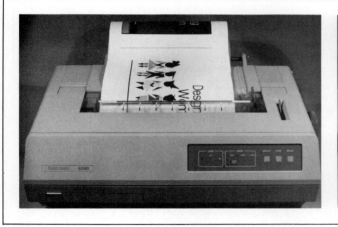

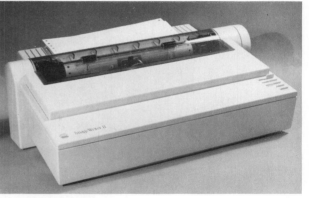

FIGURE 3.13

Tektronix inkjet printer.

FIGURE 3.14

Apple dot matrix printer.

make them compatible with NTSC recorders and monitors, must be added to the system. Standards conversion is not always perfect, and videotaped images will sometimes vibrate when seen on a television screen. Frame-by-frame animation requires an additional piece of equipment called a frame controller to stop and start the videotape recorder. Individual frames are recorded on videotape as they are created by the computer (see Figure 3.15). (See Chapter 12 for film and video animation.)

Screen Shooter   Images can be photographed directly from the graphics monitor using a 35mm or instant film camera. The screen shooter is a device that can quickly and cheaply capture screen images of works in progress on 3½ × 3½-inch Polaroid instant color prints. The screen shooter consists of a Polaroid camera attached to the back of a cone-shaped plastic hood that rests against the color monitor (see Figure 3.16).

Digital Typesetters   Digital typesetters are special printers used in the printing industry. They create extremely high-resolution typeset quality output and are used for typesetting text and graphics. Output resolution is 1200 dots per inch or higher. They are similar in function and application to laser printers used in desktop publishing but cost considerably more. Digital typesetters use photographic paper and wet chemistry processing, rather than plain paper, as used with laser printers (see Figure 3.17).

Interactive 3-D Displays and Other Exotica   Solid modeling programs simulate three-dimensional environments inside the computer. However, projections of these environments can only be seen on the computer monitor. True three-dimensional viewing is possible only with special viewing devices such as 3-D glasses and other viewing systems that project a different image to each eye. With these devices and special software it is possible to experience three-dimensional reality when looking at images created with 3-D drawing programs. (See Chapter 5 for more on 3-D drawing programs.)

FIGURE 3.15

Lyon Lamb Vas IV frame controller (used in conjunction with a Sony VO 5850 3/4-inch video cassette recorder).

FIGURE 3.16

Using a Screenshooter. Images are photographed directly from the monitor with an instant camera connected to the cone. (From NPC Photo Division, Newton Upperfalls, Mass.)

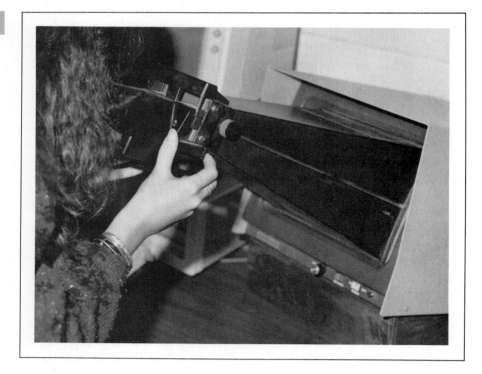

Three-dimensional helmets project a computer generated world in three dimensions on the helmet window. The pilot interacts with this environment as though it were real. Flight and target data can be superimposed over computer-generated images so that the pilot sees everything without looking away from the target. Such display helmets are used in flight simulators

FIGURE 3.17

Linotronic 300 digital typesetter with PostScript Rapid Image Processor (RIP) interface for accepting PostScript format graphics and text.

and may eventually be used in aircraft, where computer-simulated images will be replaced with computer-enhanced images of target areas, showing the best path around enemy radar and other obstacles (see Figure 3.18).

A special input device called the DataGlove is now being tested for applications in design engineering, space science, medicine, robotics, architecture, and animation. When wearing the DataGlove one can freely interact with computer-generated objects by grasping, rotating, and repositioning them as though they were real objects. The DataGlove has special sensors that transmit movement data to the computer and instruct the software to manipulate objects in the database. When worn with a device called the Eyephone, the user experiences a virtual reality that exists only in the computer. The Eyephone sends a separate video image of the database to each eye, stereo-optically, similar to Vu-Master slides and the 3-D helmet mentioned above. When the viewer turns his head to the right or left the image changes accordingly (see Figure 3.19). Also under development is the DataSuit, which is a further extension of the DataGlove.

Laser holographic projection of computer images can also create the illusion of three-dimensional reality. The illusion can be projected in space

FIGURE 3.18

Experimental display helmet. The display helmet projects computer-generated images of the terrain in front or behind the aircraft into the pilot's eyes using fiber optic bundles and combines these images with flight and target data generated by instruments in the aircraft. Movement of the pilot's head left or right triggers a change of scene in the helmet display. (Fred Ward, "Images for the Computer Age," National Geographic, June 1989, p. 724.) (Courtesy United States Air Force Human Resources Laboratory, Williams Air Force Base, Arizona.)

or printed out on paper as a color photograph. When the viewer moves to the left or right, the illusion appears to change perspective, suggesting a change in viewing position. Special glasses are not required for laser holographic images.

Computer-driven milling machines create physical objects from data supplied by computer-aided design (CAD) and three-dimensional modeling programs. Milling machines are used in computer-aided manufacturing (CAM) applications for creating machine parts and other objects from three-dimensional computer-generated models. Using such a device, we can create a physical goblet or three-dimensional gear mechanism from a computer graphics model. Not all computer models convert directly to physical objects. Complex moving parts, like a ball inside a box, for instance, might have to be milled as two separate units and assembled later.

INSTALLATION AND MAINTENANCE OF PC SYSTEMS

Designing a PC Graphics System

Microcomputers are modular in design. That is, major subsystems are self-contained units that can easily be attached to the mother board. Major components can be taken out or installed with little or no training. Disk drives,

FIGURE 3.19

(a) DataGlove used to interactively manipulate computer-generated objects in three-dimensional drawing programs. (b) EyePhone, which enables the wearer to see a three-dimensional view of the objects being manipulated. (Courtesy VPL, Inc.)

a

b

power supplies, memory and graphics cards, and even the mother board can be replaced or upgraded. A novice can build a computer from a box of parts (in reality, fewer than a dozen major plug-in components) in less than an hour after reading a short set of instructions. Kits can be purchased from mail-order distributors.

The complex technology on which PC computers are based is nicely hidden in microscopic circuitry contained in microchips that dot the mother board and other components. When a chip goes bad, a service technician can find the chip and replace it with a new one. In some cases the whole circuit

FIGURE 3.20

Inserting an add-in expansion card into an expansion slot on the mother board.

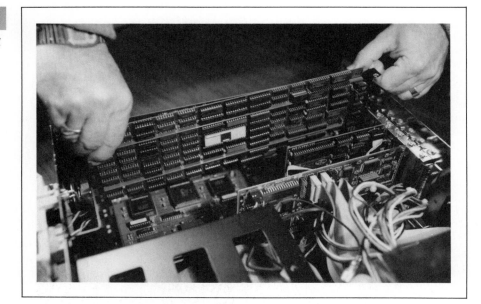

board is replaced. The old board is serviced at the factory or thrown away. Most parts are interchangeable, and you can add disk drives, memory boards, and math coprocessing chips when needed. A bank of 256K RAM memory chips (a row of nine chips) from one manufacturer can usually be replaced with a similar bank from another manufacturer.

Installation

The modular construction of microcomputers makes the installation of additional components a matter of opening the cover of the computer and plugging in the new component (see Figure 3.20). Microcomputers have several expansion slots that can be used for additional expansion cards. The AT is shipped with a total of eight slots, only two of which are used by the basic equipment. The Macintosh II is shipped with six expansion slots. Expansion slots can be used to add more memory, special graphics cards, video digitizing cards, modems, serial and parallel cards, network interface cards, and special interface cards for graphics components such as digital film recorders and videotape recorders. Some graphics cards are too wide to fit in one expansion card space, so it's easy to fill up the additional slots.

As a general rule, disconnect the computer and all peripherals before installing or removing expansion cards. Also, computer chips are extremely sensitive to static electricity, so always discharge static electricity from your body by touching a lamp or switchplate or computer chassis before working on the computer.

When installing a new card, be sure that the card is firmly seated in the expansion slot. Rock it back and forth end for end as you put it in, and *never* force it if it doesn't seem to want to go in at first. Sometimes the slot will not line up with the card connectors (gold colored contacts at the bottom of the card), and you may have to gently angle the card connectors over to the slot before pressing the card in.

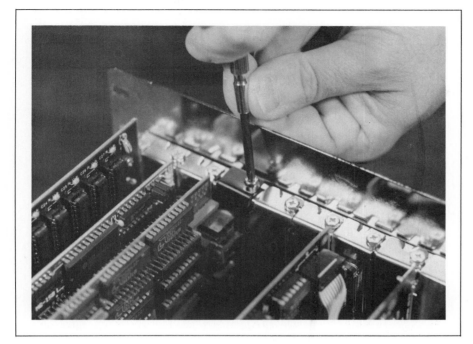

FIGURE 3.21

Attaching an add-in card.

Place add-in cards that use ribbon cables (flat flexible cables used to connect pieces of hardware) close to the components they are connected to. Respect the polarity of ribbon cable connectors—they can sometimes be plugged in two ways (only one is correct). Before disconnecting a cable from a component, mark the connector with a felt marker showing the way it was originally plugged in. Check to see if any of the cards are too close to each other. Electronic components on adjacent cards should not touch. Sometimes it is necessary to use a piece of paper or cardboard to tell if there is space between two cards (don't leave the paper inside the computer). Always screw down the metal flange at the back of the card that holds it in place (see Figure 3.21).

Peripherals   Connect peripherals such as printers and digital film recorders to their respective add-in cards at the back of the computer. Always turn the power off before connecting or disconnecting a peripheral. If there are several card cable connectors that match the one leading from the peripheral, be sure to plug the peripheral into the proper card.

RAM Chips and Coprocessors   RAM chips contain the random access memory used to hold programs and store data. PC- and AT-level computers can use a maximum of 640K of RAM without modification. 386/486-level PC computers and the Macintosh II come with a minimum of 1 megabyte and can be upgraded to 16 megabytes and 8 megabytes, respectively. When purchasing a PC or AT computer, ask that it be equipped with the maximum amount of RAM allowed on the mother board. If you already have a PC computer and want to check if it has the maximum amount, turn on the computer and note the amount of RAM displayed on the monitor during the ROM POST check, prior to seeing the C> or A> prompt. If it says "640K

bytes total base memory," then the XT/AT compatible computer is fully equipped. If the amount is less, you will have to install additional RAM chips. Consult the manual that came with the computer. Be doubly sure that you have discharged any static electricity by touching a switchplate before installing RAM chips.

A coprocessor is a microchip that will speed up certain mathematical calculations. Usually math-intensive programs like computer graphics programs and programs used in accounting, engineering, and the sciences will benefit from coprocessors. Check the software documentation to see if the software supports a coprocessor. If it does, then have one installed or install it yourself. Installation is not difficult; check the computer documentation for the type of coprocessor to use and for installation instructions (see Figure 3.22).

After installing new equipment, double-check to see that all cards are seated properly, peripherals are reconnected, and that dip switches (small switches on the mother board that tell the computer what kind of display adapter you have and how much RAM is installed, and so forth) reflect the addition of new cards or equipment. Some computers, such as the AT, use "soft switches" to set the system configuration settings. Run a special set-up program to change the settings. The Macintosh II and PS/2 can automatically tell what the hardware configuration is and will change the settings to reflect the new cards you have placed in the computer.

A Word About the Operating System

Computers use software called the operating system to manage the hardware components (system unit and peripherals) and logical reasoning of the computer. In PC-compatible computers, the disk operating system (DOS) is a

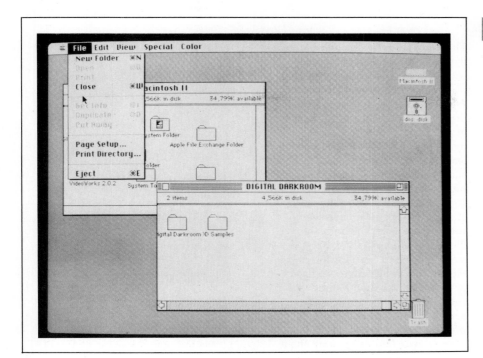

FIGURE 3.23

Macintosh pull-down menu system.

programming environment that interfaces with the application program and the various computer hardware components. At this level, most users will never notice the operating system. When you are working with a graphics or other application, the operating system is transparent to the user. Programmers, on the other hand, use DOS commands to manage computer memory, access drives, printers, and so forth. In addition to serving as a programmers' tool, DOS provides a collection of commands that are very useful to the average computer user. These commands let you organize computer files and do various housekeeping chores, such as formatting disks, making backup copies, and showing disk directories. On the Apple Macintosh, file access and management are handled by a menu of screen icons and pull-down window commands (see Figure 3.23). Both the DOS and Macintosh systems provide important tools for the computer user. It is important to learn the operating environment of your particular system (see Box 3.1).

Software Installation

When you buy a computer you must format the hard disk drive (as you would a floppy disk) so that it can store data.[2] The formatting process prepares the disk so that it can be used by the computer. It analyzes the entire disk for defective sectors, initializes the directory, sets up space for the file allocation table, and does other housekeeping chores.[3] When using an IBM compatible, put a copy of the DOS operating disk containing the DOS commands discussed earlier in drive A and turn on the computer. Enter the time and date when

---

[2] This discussion assumes that the dealer has performed low-level formatting and run the FDISK program. Low-level formatting is required prior to DOS-level formatting and FDISK creates partitions for different operating systems if they are needed. Ask the dealer if these procedures have been performed.

[3] Tim Duffy, *Four Software Tools Plus* (Belmont, Calif.: Wadsworth, 1989), 96.

BOX 3.1

COMMONLY USED DOS COMMANDS

There are a few DOS commands that everyone should be familiar with. You will use them every day, over and over again. For instance, to see what files are on a particular floppy disk you can call a directory of that disk. When you see the disk prompt A>, type DIR [enter], and the list will appear on your screen. (Note that [enter] means to hit the return key after typing the command.) It will show the name of the file (maximum eight letters with a three-letter extension after the period), the date the file was made or revised, and the size of the file. To switch from one drive to the other, type the letter designation for the new drive. If the active drive is currently C: and you wish to change to A: type A: [enter]. Detailed instructions about DOS commands can be found in the DOS manual that comes with your computer.

CD\   Allows you to move to another directory.

CHKDSK   Prints a status report of the disk, showing the amount of room left and whether there are any problems with the disk or its files.

CLS   Clears the monitor screen and moves the prompt up to the top of the screen.

COPY   Enables you to make copies of important files onto a second disk. Copy A:*filename.ext.* B: [enter] will copy a specific file from drive A to B. Copy A:*.ext.* B: will copy all files with the same extension from A to B. Copy A: *filename.** B: will copy all files with that name and different extensions from A to B. The * is a wild card. Use it to save typing the name of every file with the same extension. If the source file is located on the current active drive, you can eliminate the first drive letter designation. For example, if

Directory as seen on monitor.

the active drive is C: the command Copy *filename.ext.* A: will copy a file on C: to drive A:.

DEL   Will remove files that you no longer need from the disk. DEL A:*name.** will delete all files with a particular name but different extensions from your disk.

FORMAT   Will prepare a new disk for use. Use it before storing data on a disk for the first time. FORMAT A: will prepare the disk in drive A. Formatting will erase any data on a disk, so don't format any disks containing important data. All data will be lost!

MKDIR   Creates a new directory, MKDIR *name.* Use CD\ to enter that directory.

PATH   Path statements tell DOS what directories to look in when you type the name of a program at the C> prompt or try to use a batch file that is hidden in a separate directory. Check the DOS handbook for PATH statements if you use separate directories for your different programs.

PRINT   Will print a copy of the text file on a printer attached to the computer. PRINT A:*filename.ext.*

asked to do so. When you see the A>, type FORMAT C:/S[enter]. /S copies the system files over to the hard drive so that the computer will boot (load its operating system software) without using the DOS diskette. When the format process is complete, copy the contents of the DOS disk over to drive C:. Now the computer will boot from drive C every time the computer is turned on. You may want to configure the disk with special directories and other features to simplify and organize file management. The files contained on the DOS diskette can be put in a separate directory so they can be updated quickly when a new operating system is installed. Be sure to use the PATH command if you put the DOS software in a directory other than the route directory. See the DOS manual or consult one of the supplemental texts listed in the Bibliography. On the Macintosh computer, the hard disk is formatted as part of the install procedure; directories are automatically created when you open new folders.

After you have formatted the hard disk, you may want to create an AUTOEXEC batch file to customize your IBM-compatible computer for your specific programs and preferences. (Batch files execute a series of DOS commands or other programs every time the file is called. They end in the extension .BAT.) The AUTOEXEC batch file is read each time the computer is turned on. It changes system parameters such as the C> prompt (notice, for example, the directory shown in Box 3.1, where the C> prompt is preceded by the letters "shu"), specifies the directories it will search automatically with the PATH statement when you type the name of a DOS command or a program you want to use, and invokes other features, such as displaying a list of your applications programs. See the DOS manual for the proper way to create an AUTOEXEC.BAT file. Be sure to place the file in the root directory.

Application software is installed according to the procedures described in the software documentation. Many programs come with install programs that prompt you to insert disks containing the program, utilities, or printer drivers. Install programs will configure the software for your specific hardware, memory limitations, and peripherals. Software may not work properly if the install procedures are not followed, so use the install program that comes with the new graphics software (see Box 3.2).

Setting Up a Graphics System

Since everyone likes to save money when buying a graphics system, there is a temptation to purchase major parts independently (computer, printer, graphics boards, and so on) and hook them up yourself, thereby eliminating the middleman who specializes in total PC graphics systems. In fact, with some knowledge of the equipment and software, and with a clear understanding of your needs and objectives, it is possible to design a PC graphics system from off-the-shelf components. No background in computer science is necessary.

A case in point is the computer graphics laboratory at Seton Hall University. Working with clear educational objectives in mind, a microcomputer graphics laboratory for film and video production, desktop publishing, and advertising art was designed. The integrated facility will run a variety of basic and advanced software packages. Each graphics station is configured as follows:

> IBM PC-AT equivalent computer (640K), monochrome monitor
>
> Hercules monochrome graphics adapter
>
> Number Nine (Revolution) graphics card (256 colors) or Truevision TARGA card (32,000 colors)
>
> JRAM-2 frame buffer card (512K)
>
> Ayden analog RGB color monitor
>
> Kurta digitizing tablet
>
> Software:
>> West End Film/Pansophic (solid modeling, paint, animation, business graphics, and pagination software)
>>
>> Time Arts (Lumena paint software)

In addition, one station is equipped with a PC-EYE video digitizing card from Chorus Data, and two stations are capable of sending video signals to a Lyon-Lamb animation controller. Animation is recorded on a Sony VO-5850 ¾-inch videotape recorder.

> Additional peripherals and other items added the second year include:

> IBM AT-compatible computers (2)
>
> Matrix PCR film recorder (4000 × 3000 line resolution)
>
> Matrix TT200 thermal color printer (200 dots per inch)
>
> Apple LaserWriter printer
>
> Nicolet Zeta 8 pen plotter
>
> Iomega dual 20MB removable hard disk storage

Software:
  Time Arts (special effects and 2-D animation software)
  Autodesk (Autocad drafting software for Scenic Design)
  Cubicomp (PM-30 solid modeling/animation hardware and software)

The disadvantage to designing your own system is that if the system doesn't work or functions poorly, you are responsible for determining which component is causing the problem. An additional complication is the industry compulsion for passing the buck—the software people blame the hardware and the hardware people blame the software when something doesn't work properly.

If you do decide to set up a system using individual components, hardware/software compatibility should be thoroughly checked out in advance. A good approach is to select the software first. (See the section in Chapter 1 on purchasing graphics software.) Then ask the software supplier what hardware works best with their specific software, what additional memory cards and graphics cards are needed, and which computer is best for the application. See Appendix A for a list of hardware and software vendors.

Maintenance by the Operator

Clean the CRT screens occasionally with premoistened antistatic towels to prevent dust from accumulating on the surface. Vacuum the keyboard and inside of the computer about once a year. Clean the floppy disk drive heads under heavy use with a cleaning disk about every 6 months or otherwise about once a year. Keep the air intake holes in the front of the computer free of lint and accumulated dust and always listen for strange sounds coming from the floppy disk or hard drives. Disk drives will eventually fail. The only question is when. Always backup important files on floppy disks or on backup tape cassettes.

Computer Do's and Don'ts

Equally important is a short list of do's and don'ts. The list is self-evident but worth mentioning.

▸ Be careful not to place water or liquid beverages near the computer keyboard. (A small amount of liquid spilled on the keyboard will cause major problems.)

▸ Open the floppy drive door slowly.

▸ Never shove a disk into the drive if it meets with resistance.

▸ Try not to smoke in the computer room. (A smoke-filled environment will eventually cause the hard drive to malfunction. A particle of smoke is larger than the space between the disk surface and the read/write head.)

▸ Never move the computer while it is running. (The read/write heads in the hard drive unit are like the pick-up arm on a phonograph. You don't want the heads skipping on top of the hard disks.)

► Always run the hard drive head parking program before moving the computer. (This program puts the read/write heads in a safe place so that they will not knock around inside the hard drive and cause damage to the disks.)[4]

With specific reference to the care and treatment of floppy disks, remember the following:

► Keep them away from sources of magnetic energy such as magnets, monitors, telephones, radios, airport security checking equipment, and electromagnetic digitizing tablets.
► Never leave them out in the sun or in a warm place for long periods of time.
► Keep the disks in the protective envelope when not in the computer and never touch the disk surface through the little windows on each side of the envelope casing.
► Store disks vertically.
► Never bend a disk.
► Keep disks away from excessive moisture.
► When preparing a peel-off label, write on the label before affixing it to the disk. (If the label is already on the disk, use a felt-tipped pen.)
► Always make backup copies of your images on separate disks, just in case the first disk is damaged, lost, or the file is accidentally erased.

Troubleshooting

Using a computer is really a state of mind. Remember that it is not an intelligent machine, just a complex one. It cannot do what it has not been programmed to do. Conversely, if it does something unexpected, it is because the specific circumstances were not anticipated by the programmer. The program follows a logical path based on what it has been programmed to do. Aberrant behavior is often common in new software that is still being perfected. If a program has trouble with too many unanticipated circumstances, it is said to have bugs. If the program is buggy, the program developer should make major revisions.

Occasionally, one encounters problems in a computer system that cannot be blamed on the program. The program may be functioning properly, but the results may be less than anticipated. If a program runs fine one day and doesn't run the next, chances are that there is a hardware malfunction affecting the performance of the system. Any number of hardware problems can crop up. Memory chips may go bad with a surge in electrical power, or a poor electrical connection inside the computer may only work when the computer has warmed up. Also, the motors in a hard drive can wear out (see Box 3.3).

---

[4] The head parking program can be found on the utilities disk that comes with the computer. It is found under "Preparing the hard drive for travel" on the IBM utilities disk. Newer hard drives will automatically park the drive heads every time the computer is turned off, so this procedure may not be necessary.

BOX 3.3

Lack of compatibility between hardware components on MS-DOS computers can sometimes cause serious problems with I/O (input/output) devices like modems, disk drives, and printers. The cause of the problem may be an add-in expansion board (card) that is not compatible with cards already in the system. If you suspect a card incompatibility, take out one at a time the cards that did not come with the computer. Turn on the computer and check for the problem. If the problem goes away with a card missing, you have isolated the problem. Many card compatibility problems can be corrected with a change in settings on the problem card. Look for a system settings chapter in the documentation that comes with the card. Often, two devices will be assigned to the same serial port. A mouse, modem, or laser printer may be in conflict because two of them are assigned to COM1. Inventory all of your serial devices and be sure that they are directed to different serial ports.

Individual memory chips sometimes malfunction and must be replaced. There are utility programs that check the functioning of memory chips. One very good program is available from Tall Tree Systems Inc. Memtest can be run overnight if necessary, until the chip malfunctions. When you find a bad chip, take it out and replace it with a new one of the same type and manufacturer.

Every time the computer is turned on, the initial ROM check looks for problems in RAM and with other components in the system. If you see an error message at boot-up time, call a service company and give them the code number of the error message. These code numbers isolate the problem and make fixing the computer much easier. Sometimes the problem can be as simple as a dead system configurations battery.

Because graphics programs use extensive amounts of RAM, both for executing the program and for storing images in the frame buffer, they are more sensitive to hardware incompatibility problems and malfunctioning RAM chips. A word-processing program may run fine, but a graphics program may not boot, or images produced in a graphics program may show distortion lines when seen on the color monitor.

It is good to have a close working relationship with the local computer service company. Service contracts are expensive and may not be needed, but you should find a good service company and establish a relationship with them by calling them for all of your service needs.

SUMMARY

There is an old saying that artists should be in control of their tools. Just as one paintbrush is not like another and different weights and types of paper will influence how colors look when they dry, so the computer artist should understand the requirements of the computer hardware. The system unit that sits on top of your desk should not be a mysterious box of equipment that works only by chance. Learn about the machine—maintenance and operation. Anticipate hardware problems before they cause major work interruptions.

Each output device (laser printer, inkjet printer, film recorder, and so on) will produce slightly different results from the same screen image. The output device governs how your client sees your work, so be sure you understand how it works. There should be no surprises. Work within the capabilities of the hardware and software system and turn limitations into advantages when you can.

Exercises

1. Using your own words define the terms in the Relevant Terminology section at the beginning of this chapter.

2. What additional hardware and peripherals would you buy after selecting the computer? Explain what each add-in card or peripheral does and why it is needed.

3. List five DOS-level commands and explain how you use them as a computer graphics artist.

4. Compare the funtionality of a PC computer (which uses a keyboard and possibly a mouse pointing device) with a Macintosh computer (no keyboard commands, only icons selected with a mouse). Run the Introduction to the IBM PC program and compare it to the same type of program written for Macintosh users. Which computer interface do you like better? Why?

5. If you were designing a system primarily used for paint applications, would you choose a raster monitor or a vector monitor? Why? What are the advantages to using each? Explain.

6. How would you go about purchasing a graphics workstation for your office and graphics needs? Would you specify a minicomputer system or a PC-based system? Why? What are some of the considerations when buying software? Is it better to buy the hardware first or the software first?

Bibliography

Jamsa, Kris. *DOS: The Complete Reference*. Berkeley, Calif.: Osborne McGraw-Hill, 1987.

Williams, Gene B. *How to Repair and Maintain Your IBM PC*. Radnor, Pa.: Chilton, 1984.

Unit Two

COMPUTER

GRAPHICS

CONCEPTS

The personal computer is a revolutionary, creative, and productive tool for today's graphic artist. High-performance desktop systems display over 16 million colors at one time. Slide recorders create high-resolution, photographic-quality color slides. Paint programs not only reproduce the look of watercolor, oils, or charcoal but can modify, stretch, and transform these images while incorporating existing art or photographs. Solid modeling programs automatically construct three-dimensional objects in perspective from artists' initial sketches. Objects are positioned and lighted, textures (drawn or captured with video digitizing equipment) are applied to the objects' surfaces, and the reality of illusion is complete. As a graphic artist with a microcomputer, a new era of design is now at your fingertips.

To begin exploring this new horizon, this unit begins with an article by John Derry, a computer graphics artist. He explains what makes up a computer graphics system, describing the hardware and software and how the computer is used as a versatile graphics tool. Here you can start to discover the scope of computer graphics applications in the graphic arts and how electronically mediated art is related to traditional art forms.

What if I told you there was a new type of paint available that would dry instantly and precisely at the moment you specify, permanently preserving the subtle nuances of your work? This new kind of paint could be returned to a wet state at any time, allowing you to make any changes you desired. The new medium would let you do this as many times as you wished without ever desaturating the original colors or lowering the quality of the image. You could even change the colors on the canvas after they had been applied. Furthermore, this new "miracle" medium would come from a tube that never ran out of paint. You would probably be both skeptical and amazed at the same time, right? Well, this "super-medium" exists and is rapidly becoming available to a growing enthusiastic audience. It's called computer graphics, and the new "tube" this amazing medium comes from is the display tube of a color monitor.

SHOOTOUT AT THE PAINTBRUSH CORRAL

An ungrounded fear of artists in the skeptical class is that computer graphics is going to somehow "do away" with traditional fine arts media. Nothing could be further from the truth. In fact, the addition of computer graphics to the pantheon of fine arts media would serve to make the other expressive forms all the more unique. The subtleties of nuance present in media such as pencil, oil paint, pastels, and the like cannot be duplicated by one another. Oil painting, for example, has unique plastic qualities not found in other media: the record of the brush stroke, the texture of the canvas.

These are the qualities that make oil painting what it is. Computer graphics has its own unique qualities just waiting to be exploited by creative minds.

An important distinction between computer-mediated imagery and the traditional plastic arts is the very fact that computer imagery emphasizes content rather than plastic form. Viewed in this context, it has a close relationship to music. In the plastic arts, there is a physical end result. Something you can touch. (Unless it's in a museum!) Music, and computer graphics to an extent, is ethereal. Its end result is fleeting and transitory. A Bach concerto can be recorded on a compact disc, but the disc is not the art. Likewise, a computer graphic image can be recorded on a diskette, but the diskette is not the "art." In both cases, specific equipment, or "hardware," is required for correct reproduction.

WHAT MAKES UP A COMPUTER GRAPHICS SYSTEM?

Obviously, a computer is a major part of a computer graphics system, but there are some specialized pieces of hardware supplementing the computer that allow it to perform its image-making wonders. A graphics adapter, or "frame buffer," is necessary to produce the fineness of detail and richness of color required for high-quality image creation and manipulation. An input device, such as a digitizing tablet or mouse, is necessary. These devices allow the artist to treat the color monitor's screen much like a canvas. And a good quality monitor is necessary upon which to create an image.

Even with all these electronic components, it would be difficult, if not impossible, to create images

THE NEW PAINT: COLOR FROM A DIFFERENT KIND OF TUBE

JOHN DERRY

John Derry is Director of Creative Services for Time Arts, Inc., Santa Rosa, California. This article was originally published in *Art Product News*.

on the screen without the proper software. Software is a set of specific instructions that tells the computer what to do. In the case of a paint system, the software is telling the computer to act like paint! The critical link between the artist and the computer is the software "interface." This is the method the software uses to allow the artist to control the computer and its special hardware to react precisely to his or her eye/hand coordination. The sophistication of the software and its interface will dictate how rich and subtle an image an artist can create. As a general rule, the more complex the hardware/software combination is, the more robust the image-making possibilities are for the artist. A simple analogy might be magic markers. This particular medium is capable of a few image-making techniques, but it doesn't hold a candle to a complete airbrushing studio.

MAKING A COMMITMENT

How difficult is it to learn and use a high-quality computer graphics system? I don't think it is too far a stretch of the imagination to say that a professional-quality graphics system is not unlike learning to play a musical instrument such as the piano. This is definitely not intended to scare you off. However, many computer graphics systems have tended to be sold by the "so simple a child can do it" school of thought. If it is indeed so simple, then it probably has all the music-making potential of a whistle. Conversely, a computer graphics system will not turn a nonartist into the next Michelangelo. I can take an orange and roll it on the black keys of a piano. It may sound pretty, but it is definitely not music.

How long does it take to master a paint system? That tends to be a rather subjective question. As stated earlier, it has a lot to do with how rich a set of tools the software contains. But it also has a great deal to do with the skills and talent the artist brings to the computer graphics environment. There is probably a grain of truth to the notion that a paint system, or any artistic medium, for that matter, will cause the artist's imagery to have a particular look during the early stages of learning the medium. The notion of mastery involves the artist's ability to become intimate with a particular medium to the point that his ideas and the subtleties of the medium become one, each complementing the other in an equal balance. As Marshall McLuhan succinctly put it, "The Medium is the Message." Many of the current paint systems available are so complex in their image-making possibilities that one could explore them for years and never uncover every possible tool combination. But one could say that of many existing traditional fine arts media. Which is just the point I'm trying to make: computer graphics is at the stage where it has as much validity as a fine arts form as the media that has preceded it.

BUT IS IT ART?

There are those of the opinion that computer graphics should already be installed as a full-fledged member of the "Fine Arts Club." Several galleries and museums around the country sponsor juried competitions and display computer graphics. I constantly approach [computer graphics] with the same aesthetic concerns and point of view associated with painting and drawing. These are all healthy signs that computer graphics is gaining acceptance within the art community. To call it "Art" with a capital A at this point may be a bit premature. It took decades of daily interaction on the part of countless photographers before photography became a fine arts medium unto itself. I agree that many practitioners within the medium of computer graphics have invested a great deal of time and talent with the intention that the end result should be considered fine art. My own personal preference is that it be referred to as *computer imagery* rather than *computer art*. This term, at least for the time being, relieves the novice from having to bear too strong a responsibility to create "Art." Computer imagery is currently at the stage of its development where it fits in nicely with graphic design and illustration. No one will deny that pieces produced in these venerable crafts can sometimes rise to fine art status. The same can be true of computer imagery. Maybe calling it art is, in the final analysis, too confining.

Hopefully, I've been able to at least partially convince you that computer graphics has much to offer the artist. Continuing improvements in software interface design have served to assist artists in minimizing their fear of computers in general. You should, however, approach the medium realizing that it is a major undertaking to fully master a computer graphics system and use it as an instrument of your own expression. This is true of all sophisticated, expressive media. Consider the priceless musical contribution we all would have been deprived of if the young Mozart had found the piano keyboard too difficult an interface to deal with. While his rare musical genius allowed him to highly accelerate his integration of technique and personal expression, he still had to learn and master the keyboard before going on to fully exploit it.

Computer graphics really is a different kind of paint tube with a new supermedium flowing from it. And, yes, there is a special magic in it, but you're already familiar with it. It's that unique interaction between artist and tool that combines to create an individual artistic expression. It's not always easy to achieve, but it is certainly worth the effort.

Chapter Four

THE

PAINT

PROGRAMS

n this chapter you will be introduced to the theory and practice of computer graphics as applied to paint systems. The chapter will discuss digital notation, graphics screens, color look-up tables, file formats, and graphics databases. You will begin to see the links between the computer's ability to manipulate data and the visualization of that data on your screen as graphics.

FROM SCIENCE AND ENGINEERING

The first electronic computers were invented to save time and were primarily applied to long repetitive calculations, such as determining the trajectory of artillery shells in the military. Electronic computers shaved weeks from lengthy manual calculations, generating preprinted trajectory reference tables so that soldiers could aim their artillery weapons more accurately. Outside of the military, computing speed was also important, as well as the ability to file and retrieve massive amounts of information. Insurance companies, corporations, and government agencies used computers to calculate and keep track of their essential and massive databases.

The computer graphics area of computing evolved from computer applications in science. The artists were, for the most part, computer programmers and engineers who created computer art in their spare time on the same equipment used for science and engineering. With simple modifications, programs used for engineering could be used to create designs and other graphic images. In one of the earliest applications of computer graphics for animation, scientists at Bell Telephone Laboratories in New Jersey created a visual simulation of an earth satellite tumbling in space. It was art in the service of science. Individual line drawings of the satellite were sent to a high-resolution television screen one image at a time and then photographed on motion picture film frame by frame (see Figure 4.1).

LEARNING THE MEDIUM BY BITS AND BYTES

No matter how smart they may appear, computers are essentially dumb. Their seeming intelligence is limited by what they have been programmed to do. Computers use numbers to represent the letters and pictures on the screen so that the objects created with computer graphics programs can just as easily be output as a column of numbers filling many typewritten pages. The numbers are codes representing the lines, surfaces, 3-D shapes, and even the colors on the screen.

Binary Notation

Computers use a binary system of notation for remembering numbers. That is, computers can only count from 0 to 1 instead of 0 to 9. The computer tracks the thousands of pieces of information by assigning a binary code to each character we type or dot we create on the computer graphics screen. The code collects a series of 0's and 1's in an 8-digit series called a byte (see Figure 4.2). Technically, the 0's indicate that there is no electronic charge at a given spot in the computer memory, and the 1's indicate that there is an electronic charge present. Each digit in the code is called a binary digit (bit). Electronically, the computer must be able to store the code in its random access memory (RAM). To do so, it assigns to each memory location the condition of being on or off. If the location is on, it has an electrical charge (signified by 1); if it is off, it does not (signified by 0).

The 8-bit code (one byte of information) tells us which bits are on and which are off. If the computer checks its memory at a given location and finds 01000011, this binary code translates into the number 67. The number 67 in the ASCII (pronounced "ask-ee," an acronym for American Standard Code for Information Interchange) extended character set conversion table equals the letter C (see Appendix B). The computer display adapter (card connected to the monitor) translates the code into the letter we see on the screen. On the same ASCII table, we find that the number 64 (01000000) represents the character @. Other characters use different combinations of 1's and 0's. It is important to remember that a byte can represent anything we want it to represent. The number 128 (10000000) can be a letter of the alphabet or a color value at a given spot on the color monitor.

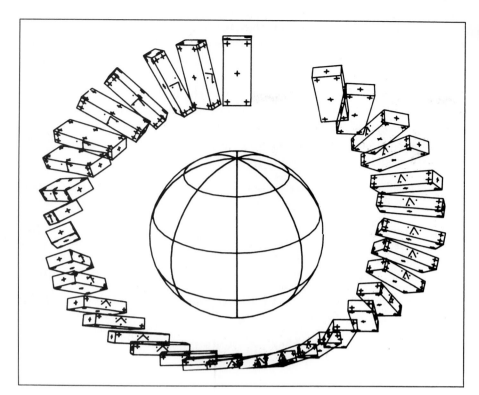

FIGURE 4.1

Still frame from 1963 Bell Laboratories animation by Edward E. Zajac. (Courtesy AT&T Archives, a unit of the AT&T Library Network.)

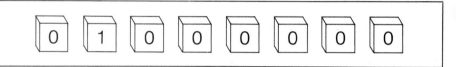

FIGURE 4.2

This 8-bit binary code equals 1 byte of information.

Computer Simulation and Modeling

Science experiments like the one at Bell Telephone Laboratories can be simulated on a computer—that is, artificially tested inside the computer using a mathematical model of actual phenomena. The experiment can be conducted as though it were happening in real life, and the model can be subjected to changes it could encounter in a real environment. Computer modeling is used in physical science disciplines for modeling real objects, such as bridges, or theoretical objects, such as the structure of molecules. In the social sciences, modeling is used for studying demographic patterns and forecasting political elections. Computer modeling has been used extensively in marketing and business management for testing "what if" hypotheses and alternative courses of action. The important thing to remember is that computer models in any discipline are soft representations of projected or actual phenomena. That is, the models exist only in the computer database.

Databases are organized collections of information pertaining to a particular project. An artist's database holds pictures and objects drawn on the computer screen. In 3-D mode, for example, letters of the alphabet can be extruded, rotated, and manipulated inside the computer, thereby creating a database of geometric coordinates. From this database, the letters can be assigned motion paths and can be animated and recorded on videotape or motion picture film.

Computer models don't have to obey the laws of nature. In computer animation, for instance, computer-generated models can easily defy the laws of gravity. Lance Williams, formerly of the New York Institute of Technology, describes some of the advantages of computer-generated animation using computer models.

> The models in computer animation are much less restrictive than the models filmed conventionally. When models are used to represent large scale objects there are severe problems of depth of field. There are optical problems. There are physical problems filming them. Computer controlled servo-mechanisms have been used to animate models like the model space ships in *Star Wars*. These models suffer from the ordinary limitations of the optical devices used in the filming process and the mechanical devices used to move the models. The models themselves are not unrestricted. It is very difficult to develop a physical model that can change its shape freely. [Computer] models don't use any supporting wires. They can defy gravity with ease. They don't require maintenance. They never get dirty. You can collect a million of them in a filing cabinet. They enjoy the advantages of fantasy over reality.[1]

The trend in motion picture production is toward more computer-generated animation. The film *Close Encounters of the Third Kind* used physical models for its spaceships. *The Last Starfighter*, created several years later, used computer models.

FROM NUMBERS TO PIXELS

Two-dimensional images are also based on numbers. The images we paint on the screen are really a series of dots that make up a fine grid of addressable points across and down the screen. The points are called picture elements (pixels) and are the smallest unit on the graphics monitor. The pixels are located by counting over and down a specific number of units. Each pixel occupies a discrete location in a two-dimensional coordinate system. We use the Cartesian system—named after the seventeenth century French philosopher and mathematician René Descartes, who introduced modern philosophy and scientific thought (see Figure 4.3). Figure 4.3a shows the origin of the coordinate system in the upper-left-hand corner. This is the system used for pixel images. The coordinate system can also have its origin in the center of the screen, as shown in Figure 4.3b, or in any of the other corners. Later, you will see how we use a similar system for defining the location of objects in our three-dimensional geometric work space.

---

[1] Lance Williams, research associate, New York Institute of Technology. Interview with the author, Feb. 11, 1981.

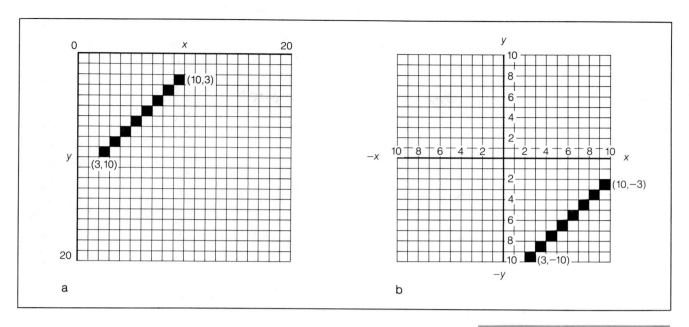

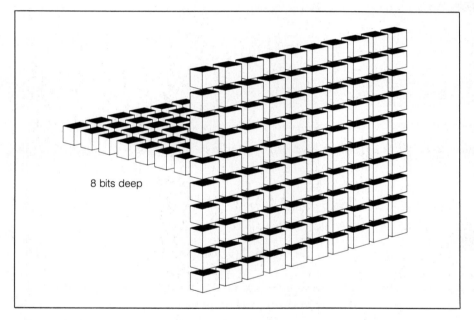

8 bits deep

Paint Systems

Paint systems allow artists to create electronic images directly on the screen by controlling the colors and intensities of each pixel. As an artist, this is your canvas. It is helpful to think of the graphics screen as a series of pigeonholes, one pigeonhole representing each pixel. Most professional PC graphics screens have 482 horizontal lines of information, with 512 pixels on each line. A number is assigned to each pixel across and down the screen, representing an intensity or color. A pixel 8 bits deep can hold any of 256 different colors, with a numeric value from 0 to 255 for each pixel (see Figure 4.4). The complete screen image, called a bit map, is stored in a place in computer memory known as the frame buffer, where the screen image is kept while it is being sent to the monitor. Buffers temporarily hold data en route to a peripheral so that the data can be quickly accessed when needed. A frame buffer is specifically reserved for holding screen information. (Printer buffers hold text and other printer information waiting to be printed, and keyboard buffers temporarily hold keystrokes.)

Pixels may have several levels of intensity (gray scale) or be one of several colors, depending on how much information is stored in the frame buffer for each pixel. For example, if the amount of memory available for each pixel is only 1 bit deep, the pixel can only be on or off—like the letters on a monochrome text monitor; there are no shades of gray. If there are two bits of memory for each pixel, the pixel can be 1 of 4 shades. Four bits of memory per pixel allow 16 shades or colors. The amount of information doubles for each additional bit of memory.

Bits	Colors
2	4
3	8
4	16
5	32
6	64
7	128
8	256
9	512
10	1024
11	2048
12	4096
15	32,768
16	65,536
24	16,777,216
32	4,294,967,296

Eight-bit systems are capable of remembering only 256 different colors for each pixel. Twenty-four-bit systems divide the frame buffer up into three sections, eight bits for each of the primary colors—red, green, and blue—for a total of almost 16.8 million possible colors per pixel. Often, color cards do not use all of the pixel memory for colors. Sometimes the extra bits per pixel are used as an overlay channel (also called the alpha channel) for live video special effects. The 32-bit TARGA card displays 16,777,216 colors plus overlay and blend. "Each pixel is represented by 24 bits of color specification, 1 overlay bit, and 7 bits (128 levels) for analog blend control."[2] The overlay bit allows the program to display the cursor over live video images. The blend capability allows you to anti-alias (see Chapter 5) the edges of text over live video.

---

[2] *Truevision Technical Guide* (Indianapolis, Ind.: Truevision, Inc., 1986), 5–3.

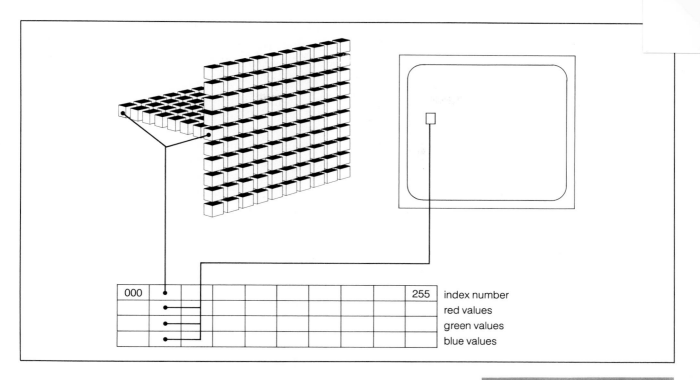

000							255	index number
								red values
								green values
								blue values

FIGURE 4.5

Color look-up table. Each memory location in the frame buffer indexes a different color in the look-up table. That color is made up of different intensities of red, green, and blue. Because the system uses the additive color model, black would be represented in the look-up table as 0, 0, 0; pure red would be stored as 255, 0, 0; and so on. These values can be customized by the artist so that the same frame buffer values will produce an image with different colors, such as warm tones for spring and blue tones for winter.

Color Look-Up Tables   A pixel with 8 bits of color information stored in the frame buffer can be set to any of 256 different colors. However, if these colors are referenced in a look-up table (see Figure 4.5), you are not limited to a fixed palette of 256 colors. Your palette can be customized from a rainbow of color possibilities. Many systems offer you 16.8 million theoretical colors, 256 of which can be displayed at one time using an 8-bit frame buffer. Look-up tables hold the RGB (red, green, blue) information for each color. The numbers in the frame buffer reference the 256 places in the look-up table. Each place holds information about a different color. Changing the colors in the look-up table means changing the colors on the computer screen.

Most paint systems use the HLS (hue/luminosity/saturation) color-modifying system, which lets you independently control the hue, luminosity, and saturation of each color in the look-up table. Hue is the actual color you select from the spectrum of colors available—red, orange, yellow, green, blue, indigo, violet, and shades in between. Luminosity is the brightness of the color. Too much luminosity will wash out the color so that it looks white. Saturation is the amount of color in the shade you have selected. Fully saturated colors are vivid. Colors with less saturation show more gray and look colorless. With the HLS system, you customize colors by mixing the amount of hue, luminosity, and saturation (see Color Plate 2). In some cases, the software will allow you to "ramp" a series of eight or more colors at once by selecting the first and last colors. The palette editor then automatically creates the in-between shades and stores the new color values in the look-up table. Once stored, you can use this special palette with later images. Systems that use a look-up table are called look-up table systems and offer flexibility for quick palette changes. If a different look-up table is substituted after a picture is drawn, all the colors in the drawing change to match the colors in the new look-up table. Systems with 15 bits or more of color per pixel do not use look-up tables because each pixel has enough memory in the frame buffer to store an ample variety of colors. They are true color systems and no look-up table is needed.

Pixel-based images, sometimes called raster images because of the raster of lines that make up a television screen, can be saved by remembering the numeric codes for each pixel location in that image. Recall the image from the computer memory, and the numeric codes will be converted back into the actual colors by the look-up table stored in the computer. If a different look-up table has been substituted for the original, then different colors will appear on the screen. For this reason, look-up tables are also called color maps. An artist can create a different color map for each picture or many color maps for a single picture, each color map being a different interpretation (see Color Plate 3). If you want to change a spring scene into a winter scene, no need to redraw it; simply create a new color map with winter colors replacing the spring colors.

Resolution-Dependent Images

Raster images are resolution dependent. That is, the resolution of a given raster image is dependent on the screen resolution of the system being used. If a 512 × 482 raster image is sent to a film recorder capable of creating images with a resolution of 4096 × 2732, the raster image will still be in the original resolution when seen on a color slide. Raster images are locked into the bit map of the original screen. They occupy a two-dimensional work space and are analogous to flat art—painting, watercolor, or photography. Similarly, a three-dimensional image created with a paint system is typically called pseudo 3-D because it is drawn in forced perspective. Later, we will see how 3-D programs create computer-generated, resolution-independent objects that interact in virtual three-dimensional environments.

Paint Systems versus Traditional Media

Paint systems are very similar to traditional media. Colors can be pushed from one image into another. You can mix colors on the screen and save them as a custom palette. Watercolor bleed effects can be created at the boundary of two images. Edges can be softened, dissolved into the background, or given a cartoon-like hard-edged look. Any style of brush can be created, saved, and modified as needed. Computer painting can take you far beyond traditional painting techniques. Your images can be rotated, scaled, duplicated, and combined (superimposed or cut-and-pasted) with other images. Colors can be changed even after they appear on the screen simply by changing the look-up table. The spectrum of colors in a given look-up table can be cycled so that all color areas on the screen cycle through the full palette. Color cycling is a form of animation and is often used in point-of-sale advertising.

Sections of the screen can be saved in a special buffer and used as the tip of a paintbrush or duplicated anywhere they are needed. Recurring texture patterns appear in an instant. Forced perspective can be added to an

FIGURE 4.6

Artist using a video camera to scan in flat art for manipulation in the computer. (Courtesy Seton Hall University.)

existing image so that it looks like a billboard viewed from a 45-degree angle. Some paint systems also let you include video images scanned in with a video digitizing camera or desktop scanner (see Figure 4.6). These digitized images can be altered, combined, or retouched, like any other paint image.

Every paint system has its own bevy of special techniques. Frisketing options let you combine two or more discrete images. Use the airbrush techniques to blend colors. Paint in transparent ink. Probably the most important feature, however, is that your images can be saved to disk at any stage in their development. You can recall the step-by-step creative progression of your image or present the same image with many different color interpretations.

Computer graphics images displayed on a monitor do not look the same as opaque images created on paper. Glowing color phosphors make the images more vibrant when seen on the screen. Like an impressionistic painting, the colors seem to jump out at the viewer. If the picture is used as hard copy or as a slide, special attention must be given to the way the final image will look. Shades of a particular color may not work equally well in all media. For precise conversion to hard copy, the artist must create a customized palette for each output device—inkjet printer, thermal color printer, dot matrix color printer, digital film recorder, or analog film recorder.

Image Processing

The series of 1's and 0's that record the light and dark areas of a digitized photograph can be manipulated by the computer, dramatically altering the way the image is seen on the monitor. Because each pixel light value is recorded as a series of numbers representing the degree of brightness at that point on the screen, these numbers can be systematically altered to produce dramatic effects. For instance, adjacent pixels can be averaged together, creating large blocks of pixels of the same color or light value (this is called pixel averaging). The image becomes a pointillist painting of large abstract patterns based on the original image (see Figure 4.7). Contrast range—the number of gray levels from the very lightest pixel to the very darkest—can be altered so that areas of similar gray level are given the same contrast value, thus creating a high-contrast picture. The contrast range can also be selectively changed so that pictures with too much contrast can be improved. Original artwork that may have too much contrast can be altered by assigning a different contrast value to each extreme. If the original picture went from black to white in 16 levels of contrast, the digitized picture can be improved by using a contrast range that goes from medium black to medium gray in the same 16 levels, thus reducing the contrast.

Image processing is similar to special effects photography, where the camera image is manipulated in the darkroom with distorting lenses and multiexposure printing. In *Beyond Photography: The Digital Darkroom*, author Gerard Holzmann of Bell Telephone Laboratories explains how he manipulates digitized photographs with an interactive image transformation editor called Pico. Using special algorithms (an algorithm is a small program containing a

FIGURE 4.7

(a) The original digitized image and (b) the same image after pixel averaging.

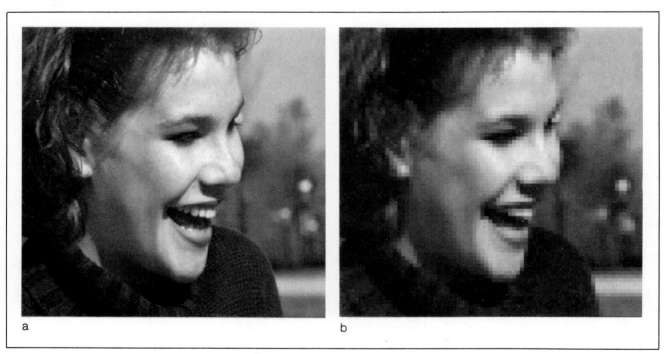

a   b

set of rules for solving a specific problem) that manipulate the matrix of pixels by shrinking, averaging, swirling, expanding, warping, and otherwise distorting the original picture, he created the images shown in Figure 4.8.

Image processing has many applications in the broad field of computer graphics, including pattern recognition and computer vision used in computer-aided manufacturing for quality control and robotics control of the manufacturing process. Image processing is used to analyze CAT scans, X rays, and fingerprints and is also used to enhance the images sent back to us from outer space so that we can see details hidden from the naked eye.

FIGURE 4.8

Examples of image processing. In each case, the original image was an unretouched digitized portrait that was processed with special distorting algorithms developed by Gerard Holzmann of Bell Telephone Laboratories. (Courtesy AT&T Archives, a unit of the AT&T Library Network.)

81

If you must transfer an image to a different graphics card or hardware environment, file conversion programs exist that make this passage possible. A common desire of desktop publishers, for instance, is to use artwork posted on computer bulletin boards. The artwork is sometimes posted in the Compu-Serve Graphics Interchange Format (GIF). CompuServe is a commercial subscription information service that regularly posts hundreds of computer pictures contributed by its subscribers, using the GIF format. GIF images are hardware independent and can be displayed on a variety of computers from Sun minicomputers to IBM PCs and Commodore 64 computers. Hijack, a program from Software Publish-ing, will convert GIF files to many standard file formats, including formats supported by desktop publishing packages. GIF2TGA is a file conversion program available on bulletin boards that will convert GIF files to TARGA file format. If you want to display your scanned-in images or artwork created in the TARGA environment (including Vision Technologies Vision 16 board) on a broader base of computers compatible with the several IBM graphics cards, Videotex Systems sells a program called T-EGA that will convert TARGA files to CGA, EGA, or VGA format. Once converted to the new file format, these files can easily be uploaded to bulletin boards so that others can see and critique your work.

File Conversion

When screen images are saved to disk, they are saved in proprietary formats created for the graphics software being used. Images created on the TARGA card in one program cannot be loaded into another TARGA program unless they use the same file format. Images are also device dependent—that is, they are locked into the pixel and color resolution of the graphics card they were produced on. A picture digitized with the TARGA card cannot be immediately displayed on the Revolution or EGA cards. These problems are more common in the DOS environment, where there is no standard graphics file format and where there are at least a dozen different types of graphics cards. Macintosh and DOS desktop scanners use a standard file format, called TIFF (Tagged Image File Format), so regardless of the software, conversion is not usually necessary between programs. Images digitized with the Apple desktop scanner will load directly into Digital Darkroom (an image-processing software package) or PageMaker (desktop publishing program).

Because artists often have to display images on other graphics cards and in different software environments, techniques have been developed to transfer images between devices and software. The easiest conversion is between software programs running on the same graphics card. If the image remains in the frame buffer when the new program is booted, it will be ready for use by that program, regardless of file format. Even if the file formats are not compatible, the images can be swapped back and forth through the frame buffer. This is a hardware solution. You leave the image on the screen, exit one software program, and boot another. The image will automatically make the transition between applications. Colors will change between programs that use look-up tables, and occasionally the screen will automatically clear when a new program is booted, so this technique may not always work. (See Box 4.1 about file conversion utilities.)

Occasionally, we must use an image created on a Macintosh computer with software running on a DOS computer. In addition to the normal file conversion problems, we must first transfer the image from the Macintosh computer, which uses 3½-inch disks, to the IBM compatible, which uses 5¼-inch or noncompatible 3½-inch disks. Obviously, we cannot take a Macintosh disk and put it in the IBM compatible. Instead, there are network and hardware add-on products that will accomplish this task. Local area networks will connect both types of computer. Then it is a simple matter to send a file to the second computer. An easier solution is to connect a specially designed external DOS-compatible disk drive to a Macintosh computer. The Macintosh screen shows the drive as an additional disk drive, and files can be saved to it in the normal manner. Many programs have their Macintosh and DOS counterparts; that is, the same software is written for both computer systems. For instance, PageMaker on a DOS computer will accept images and text created in PageMaker on the Macintosh without first using a separate file conversion program. Draw and solid-modeling files present a different set of software conversion problems and will be discussed in a later section.

SUMMARY

Computer graphics was born in the early 1950s but has experienced its most accelerated growth since the late 1970s because of both microcomputer-based and minicomputer-based dedicated computer graphics workstations. Computer graphics has become an important tool in animation and the graphic arts.

Paint programs allow you to paint images directly into the screen buffer (a storage place in computer memory where the image is kept). The size of the buffer determines how many colors are available. A buffer with only 1 bit of memory per pixel will display either black or white at that pixel. A buffer with 8 bits of memory per pixel will display any of 256 colors per pixel. If the buffer references a look-up table, a different set of colors can be substituted without redrawing the picture.

Image enhancement allows you to add special effects to your computer drawings and digitized photographs. Using image processing techniques, you can simulate posterization and high-contrast effects, as well as superimpositions and optical distortions. In the next chapter you will see how the computer can create three-dimensional environments where the objects you create can be rotated, lit, and manipulated much like pieces of sculpture.

Exercises

1. What is the smallest unit on the graphics screen? What does the term stand for?

2. Where is information about the graphics screen stored in computer memory? Explain the origin of the term.

3. **a.** Using the grid below to represent a graphics screen, draw a picture by filling in the boxes with solid black or by leaving them open.

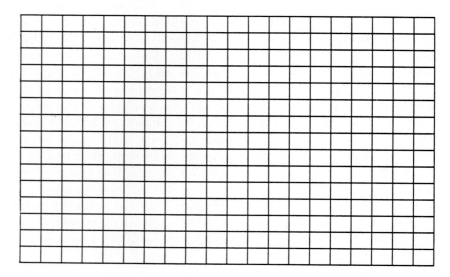

   b. If this grid represents a monochrome screen, how many bits deep is the frame buffer? Explain your answer.

   c. If this were a color screen that could display 16 colors simultaneously, how deep would the frame buffer be?

   d. What is the resolution of the above screen and the x and y axes?

4. How may colors can be displayed at one time at each point on the screen with an 8-bit frame buffer?

5. What is the significance of the color look-up table? Explain the difference between "true-color" systems and look-up table systems.

6. Explain the term *resolution dependent*. Why are pixel images put in this category?

7. Based on your own experience, compare computer paint methods to traditional painting. What are the similarities and differences?

8. **a.** Draw a cartoon-like character with the options in your paint program. Mark off different segments for the shirt, pants, neck, and so on. Fill these segments with different colors or crosshatch patterns.

   b. Try some of the other options in the paint program. Look for the shade command, custom brush, and tint. Capture part of the screen and use it as a brush.

9. Go to the palette editor and customize your available colors. Note how some of the existing colors in your picture will change when you customize the color palette. Why is that?

10. **a.** Create a 24 × 24 box matrix and then create an "Indian Blanket" pattern of colors by filling in the boxes with the fill command. Use a customized palette so that colors change hue in the same row.

    b. If your software has a modify or stretch function, distort portions of the grid by giving it forced perspective.

11. **a.** Use the video digitizing function and digitize a photo or magazine clipping. Colorize the digitized image with colors selected from your customized palette.

    b. If your software has a frisketing option or if it can paint between image buffers, combine two digitized images by selecting portions of each to create a new composite image.

Bibliography

Goodman, Cynthia. *Digital Visions*. New York: Abrams, 1987.

Holzmann, Gerard J. *Beyond Photography: The Digital Darkroom*. Englewood Cliffs, N.J.: Prentice-Hall, 1988.

Hubbard, Stuart. *Computer Graphics Glossary*. New York: Van Nostrand Reinhold, 1984.

Marcus, Aaron. "Color: A Tool for Computer Graphics Communication." In *The Computer Image: Applications of Computer Graphics*, pp. 76–90. Edited by Donald Greenberg. Reading, Mass.: Addison-Wesley, 1982.

Marshall, George R. *Computer Graphics in Application*. Englewood Cliffs, N.J.: Prentice-Hall, 1987.

Rivlin, Robert. *The Algorithmic Image*. Redmond, Wash.: Microsoft Press, 1986.

Truckenbrod, Joan. *Creative Computer Imaging*. Englewood Cliffs, N.J.: Prentice-Hall, 1988.

Vince, John. *Dictionary of Computer Graphics*. White Plains, N.Y.: Knowledge Industry Publications, 1984.

Wilson, Stephen. *Using Computers to Create Art*. Englewood Cliffs, N.J.: Prentice-Hall, 1986.

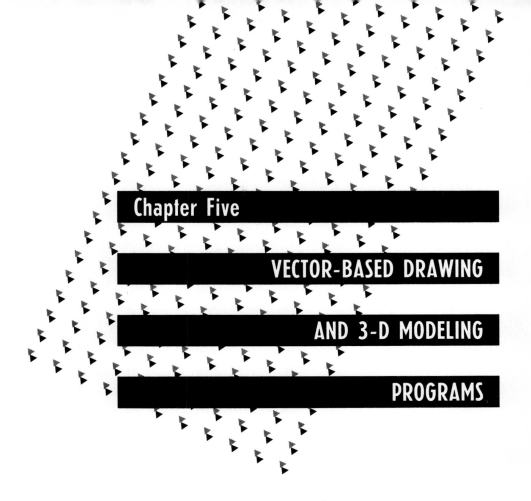

Chapter Five

VECTOR-BASED DRAWING

AND 3-D MODELING

PROGRAMS

I n this chapter you will learn how to create computer-generated solid objects in a true three-dimensional environment. The objects are made up of lines called vectors and begin as two-dimensional shapes called polygons or are created from simple 3-D shapes, which are then combined to form the final object. The objects are given surface properties such as color and texture and are lighted to bring out their three-dimensional character.

DRAWING LINES POINT TO POINT

Computer images fall into two broad categories—pixel based and vector based. In the preceding chapter we discovered that pixel-based images created in the screen buffer are locked into the resolution of the screen. They can only be upgraded to a higher resolution by averaging the values of adjacent pixels.[1] Draw programs, on the other hand, are vector based. They remember the image by keeping track of the end coordinates for each line. The coordinates

---

[1] Many programs let you increase resolution by adding detail to small sections of the screen at a time (zooming them up to full size) and then combining them to form one high-resolution image that can be output on a high-resolution film recorder.

are stored in a database that is independent of the screen buffer and the screen resolution. The database is then displayed on the screen at screen resolution, but images created with a draw program can be any resolution, depending on the output device. On your monitor the vectors are displayed through a matrix of pixels 512×482 (or 1280×1024 on higher-resolution systems), but on a pen plotter the vectors are drawn endpoint to endpoint as continuous lines, so the lines are much sharper.

Because of their higher resolution and precision, vector draw programs are used in engineering and architecture, where they have replaced the pen, compass, and T square. Computer-aided design (CAD) programs automate the design process by providing options not available with traditional means. The programs include such tools as automatic curve fitting between three or more points (known as B-spline curves), mirroring segments to create symmetrical objects, window drag features to change the shape of objects by moving sections of the original drawing, automatic chamferring for rounding corners between adjacent surfaces, automatic crosshatching of surfaces, and snap features that allow you to draw with the aid of an invisible grid. CAD programs also provide automatic dimensioning for drawings drawn to scale, keep track of the time spent on each drawing, and even calculate the cost of the materials used to create the object. Design features found in CAD programs are also found in programs used by artists and animators. Many artists will begin their work in a CAD program, where they create the basic outline of the object, and then transfer the outline to a three-dimensional modeling program for further embellishment.

THREE-DIMENSIONAL WORK ENVIRONMENT

Three-dimensional (3-D) drawing programs create objects with x, y, and z dimensions. These objects are often drawn as enclosed shapes with connecting surfaces and are created with solid modeling programs.[2] As in 2-D drawing and CAD programs, each object is made up of vectors, lines connected to other lines. Three-dimensional programs use a three-dimensional work space, which is like a cube of space in which you construct your objects. The space is oriented in a Cartesian geometric environment, which has an arbitrary number of units on the horizontal x axis, vertical y axis, and depth z axis. Many programs have their x, y, and z origin in the upper left-hand corner of the screen. The x and y axes originate at that position (0) and count across and down respectively. The z axis starts at the origin and travels through the plane of the screen (the surface of the monitor) back into 3-D space and forward toward the eye of the viewer. The plane of the screen is 0 on the z axis (see Figure 5.1).

The origin does not have to be in the upper-left-hand corner but can begin in any corner of the screen or start in the center and count up and down on the y axis and left and right on the x axis. Most 3-D modeling programs assign arbitrary dimensions to this work space. One popular program counts

---

[2] Solid modeling will refer to any program that creates solid objects by means of surface sweeping methods, solids modeling (construction of objects using solid shapes as building blocks), and boundary and voxel methods (not covered in this text).

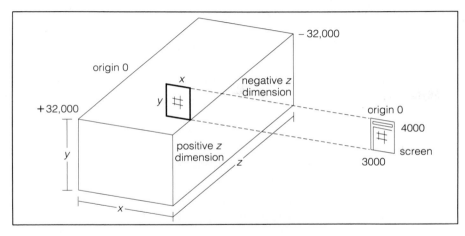

FIGURE 5.1

Three-dimensional work space. The work space is like a cube into which is placed the flat computer graphics screen. The screen is at point 0 on the z axis. This is also called the plane of the screen and is where objects are initially created. Systems that count back from the screen into negative space and out from the screen (toward the viewer) into positive space are called right-handed systems. Systems that count out from the screen in negative units and back in positive units are left-handed systems. The area of the screen may not equal the x and y dimensions of the work space. Often, a small portion of the work space is windowed to the display screen.

12,000 units horizontally along the x axis and 9000 units along the vertical y axis. The z, or depth, axis is 32,000 units back from the plane of the screen into 3-D space and 32,000 units out toward the viewer. Within this work space—ambitiously called the world coordinate space—objects of specific size and x, y, and z orientation are created (see Figure 5.2). Once created, these objects can be manipulated by changing their size, shape, place, or orientation. These manipulations are called transformations. The screen does not usually show the whole work space; however, many programs let you set the resolution of the display window you are working in so that you only see a fraction of the work space on the screen at one time. An object may be full size while you are working on it, but when you show it in the context of the whole work space, it looks much smaller.

Transformations: Translations and Rotations

When you move an object to a different location in the work space, it is said that the object is translated to a new position. You can translate the object along either the x, y, or z axis, or a combination of all three. On a screen that measures 4000 units over and 3000 units down, a translation of 1000 units along the x axis will move the object to the right about 25 percent of the screen. A translation of minus 1000 units on the z axis pushes the object farther away from the viewer. If we translate the back surface of a 3-D object 100 units away from the viewer, the object is now 100 units thicker.

Right-Hand Rule of Rotation Rotations are more complicated, so a quick rule of thumb has been devised. In this Cartesian geometric environment, where the point of origin is the upper left-hand corner of the screen and positive z space is toward the viewer, we use the right-hand rule of rotation. As if you are thumbing a ride, place your right hand in front of the screen along the x axis, with your thumb pointing left. As you rotate the back of your hand toward you on the x axis, the top of the object comes into view. This is called a minus x rotation (see Figure 5.3). Rotating your hand the other way so that your fingers come into view is a positive rotation. The bottom of the object comes into view.

FIGURE 5.2

Views of three-dimensional space. Three-dimensional space can be viewed from any vantage point. Figure (a) shows what is seen from the front view; (b) shows how it looks from the side.

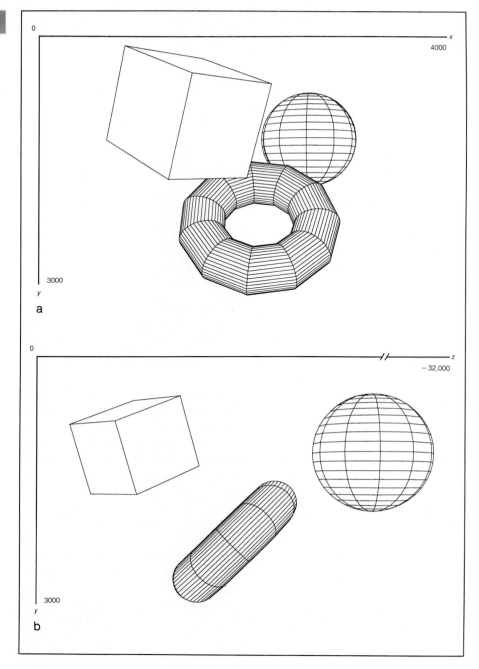

On the *y* axis, a positive rotation moves the face of the object to the right, and a negative rotation turns it to the left (see Figure 5.4). *Z*-axis rotations move like the hands on a clock; objects turn either clockwise or counterclockwise. Point your right thumb toward the center of the screen (origin of the *z* axis). A rotation clockwise, leading with your fingers, is positive; a rotation leading with the back of your hand is negative (see Figure 5.5). To keep track of which part of your hand is negative and which is positive, remember when you went to a dance where they stamped the back of your hand with a black mark. That's the part that's negative!

When rotating an object, most programs will ask you to specify a positive or negative number of degrees, so this quick rule of thumb is handy

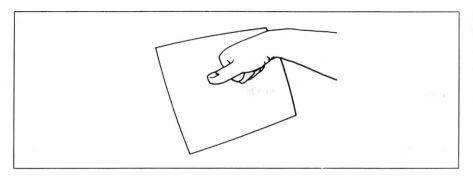

FIGURE 5.3

Example of minus x rotation. As you rotate the back of your hand toward you on the x axis, the top of your hand comes into view. This is called a minus x rotation. Turning your hand the other way so that your fingers (the bottom of the object) come into view is a positive rotation.

FIGURE 5.4

Example of a y-axis rotation. A y-axis rotation brings the left or right side of the object into view. A positive rotation will show more of your fingers. A negative rotation will bring the back of your hand toward you.

FIGURE 5.5

Example of z-axis rotation. Z-axis rotations are like the face of a clock. Positive rotations bring your fingers into view and are clockwise. Negative rotations lead with the back of your hand and are counterclockwise.

to know. Just remember that rotations leading with the back of your hand are negative, and rotations leading with your fingers are positive. If this method does not match the system you are using, then use your left hand. Rotations toward your fingers are always positive, and rotations toward the back of your hand are always negative. Be sure to point your thumb toward the point of origin (0 on the x, y, and z axes).

Transformations: Scaling

A third type of transformation is called scaling. Scaling changes the shape or size of an object. If the upper-right-hand corner of a square is translated 1000 units on the y axis, the square becomes a wedge; the top edge now slants down to the right. If all corners of the original square are moved out from the center of the screen equal units on the x and y axes, the square is said to have been scaled to a larger size (see Figure 5.6).

FIGURE 5.6

Example of scaling. (a) Translating the top right-hand corner of the box a positive 1000 units on the y axis makes the box into a wedge. (b) Moving all the corners out an equal amount from the center of the screen scales the box to a larger size.

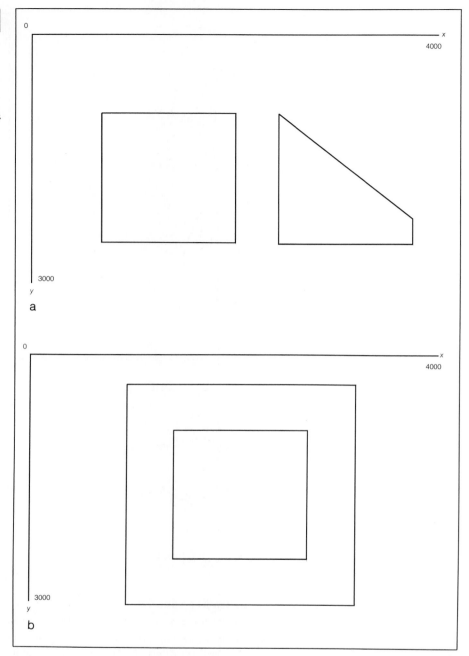

World Transformations

Besides local transformations that act only on individual objects, there are world transformations that act on all objects in the work space. Your whole database can be moved closer to the viewer (on the z axis) or pushed further away. If all of the objects are moved closer to the viewer, the effect is the same as a dolly-in camera movement in a movie. Continue this movement and eventually the object closest to the viewer disappears behind the viewer. As the database moves closer, the perspective relationships among objects change; as in real life, you get a better feeling for the space between objects (see Figure 5.7).

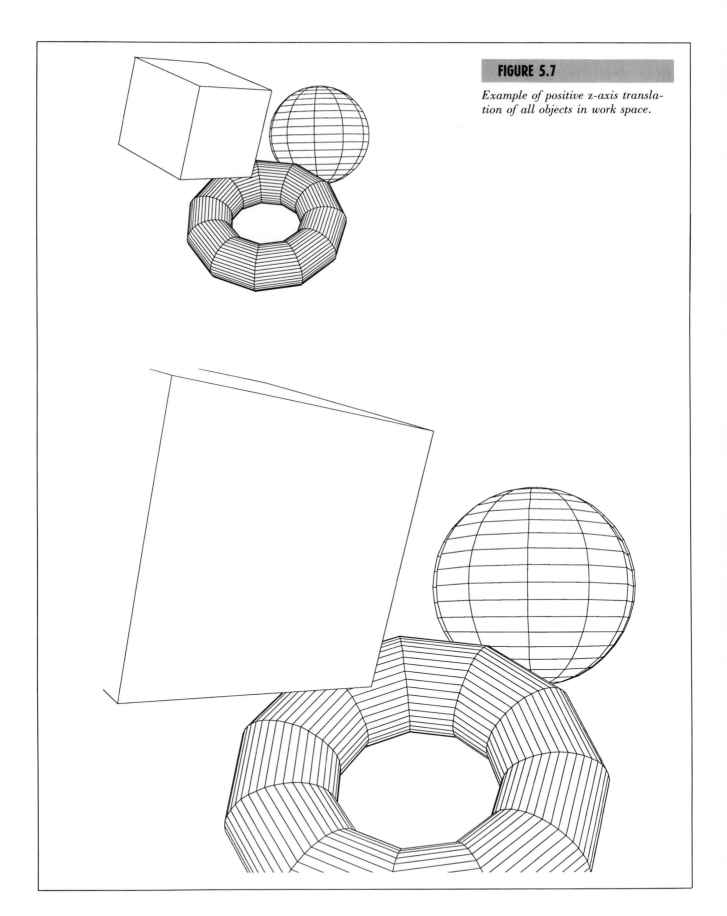

FIGURE 5.7

Example of positive z-axis translation of all objects in work space.

FIGURE 5.8

Example of normal and wide-angle viewing perspective. The objects in (a) are viewed with the equivalent of a normal lens, and objects in (b) with a wide-angle lens. Compare the relative size of objects in the two pictures. Additional perspective makes the background sphere in (b) appear smaller and the torus appear larger. The cube also shows signs of distortion.

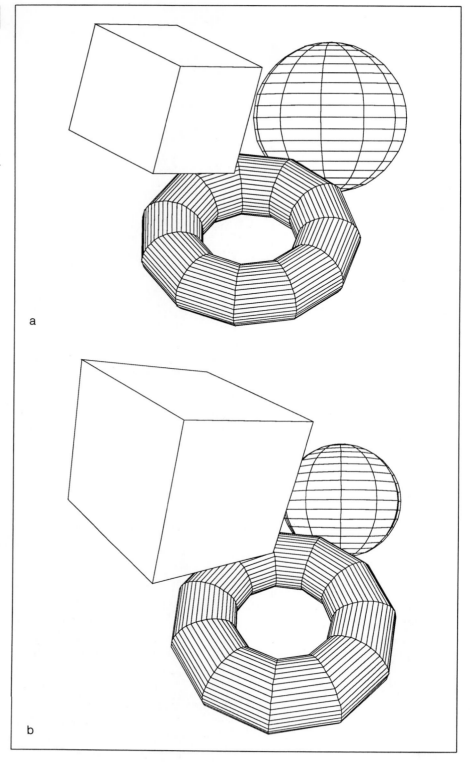

a

b

Camera Perspective and Clipping Planes   Solid modeling programs let you change how objects in the work space are seen on the screen. Just as in normal photography, you can change perspective by calling for a normal, wide-angle, or telephoto lens. A wide-angle lens makes objects in the back-

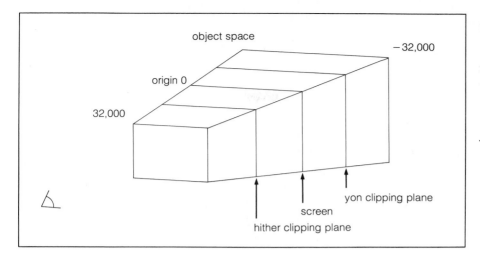

FIGURE 5.9

Example of object space showing position of clipping planes. Clipping planes are arbitrary viewing boundaries placed on the work space. The hither clipping plane is nearest the eye, and the yon clipping plane is farthest away.

ground smaller and distorts objects in the foreground. Space between objects looks greater (see Figure 5.8). Normal perspective is less dramatic because foreground objects are less distorted. Telephoto perspective compresses the images front to back; we sense less space between them. In addition to changing viewing perspectives, you can change the camera position, or viewpoint. Moving the camera position up on the y axis will lower the horizon line. Lowering the camera raises the horizon.

Clipping planes are arbitrary viewing boundaries placed on the work space. They control what is displayed on the monitor. The computer disregards objects beyond the clipping planes so they will not be drawn when displaying the database. When objects are too far away to be seen, or foreground objects are poorly displayed, setting clipping planes to exclude these objects corrects the problem and saves valuable time when a new image is sent to the screen (see Figure 5.9).

CREATING THREE-DIMENSIONAL SHAPES

Where paint systems are similar to traditional two-dimensional media, three-dimensional programs are akin to sculpture. The traditional artist comes to the three-dimensional work environment with a pencil but draws with ideas. Objects are constructed in the work space line by line or are produced from algebraic equations or assembled from elementary three-dimensional shapes. In *constructive modeling*,[3] the artist creates the objects out of points, lines, and polygons. Generating objects from an algebraic equation is called *procedural modeling*. The third approach, assembling objects from elementary three-dimensional shapes, often called graphic primitives, is *solids modeling*. No matter which procedure you use, the first step in the modeling process is previsualizing the object or composition on paper. These sketches save valuable computer time and speed up the design process.

---

[3] This term is not used in the traditional sense of constructive solid geometry where objects are created from solids occupying a volume, but is used in the more general sense describing how we construct objects from lines, points, etc.

Constructive Modeling

Work on the computer usually begins with the construction of a two-dimensional closed shape called a polygon. Polygons can be uniform like a triangle or circle or more complex like the outline of your hand. The polygon can be drawn freehand with a mouse or stylus, or entered from the keyboard. In either case it is drawn point by point one vector at a time. In draw programs vectors are constructed by selecting beginning and ending points, which become coordinates in an object database, not by drawing them into the frame buffer as with a paint program. When creating a polygon, construct it in a clockwise direction and never cross lines as you draw.

In addition to freehand methods, draw software also gives you menu options to interactively create uniform shapes such as circles, arcs, and rectangles. You specify the size, number of degrees, points in the circle, and so on, and the computer automatically constructs the polygon. New shapes can be tweaked from existing shapes by moving points to different locations. For instance, to change a circle into a box with one round corner, eliminate all but one 90-degree arc in a circle, then drag three extreme points out to form the three square corners (see Figure 5.10). Of course, the same object can be drawn segment by segment by instructing the computer to draw an arc and then attaching tangents to the arc. The tangents are then connected with lines drawn at right angles. After the two-dimensional shape is created, it is made three-dimensional by one of several methods.

Extrusions   Depth can be added to a two-dimensional polygon by using extrusion features that make a copy of the original polygon and then translate that copy into three-dimensional space. Lines are then automatically drawn connecting similar points of the two polygons. If the polygon is in the shape of the letter A, for example, then the three-dimensional version will look like a cookie cut in the shape of the letter A (see Figure 5.11). Extrusions create objects with identical front and back surfaces, like cylinders and cubes.

Rotational Sweeps   A half circle or other shape can be rotated around the x or y axis into z space creating a three-dimensional shape based on the initial cross section. The number of sections in the shape, like sections in an orange, depends on the number of duplicates the software creates as the original polygon is rotated in space. Figure 5.12 shows 3-D objects and their original cross sections.

Cross-Sectional Modeling   Asymmetrical shapes are more difficult to create. Rotation cannot be used because it does not allow for deviation in the shape of the final object. Compare the symmetrical goblet to the asymmetrical plastic container in Figure 5.13. The goblet is easily created with rotation, but the container, with its round top and a square bottom, cannot be created with either translation or rotation. However, if key cross-sectional frames from its contour top to bottom are created as separate polygons, a cross-sectional modeling program will connect these templates into the final asymmetrical shape.

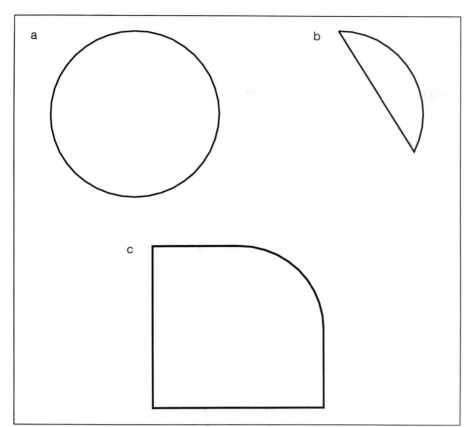

FIGURE 5.10

Example of shape manipulation by point editing. Figure (c) began as (a) a circle from which points were eliminated to form (b) an arc. The extreme points of the arc were then translated to new positions to form lines tangent to the arc. An additional point was added and translated to a new position to form right angles to the tangents.

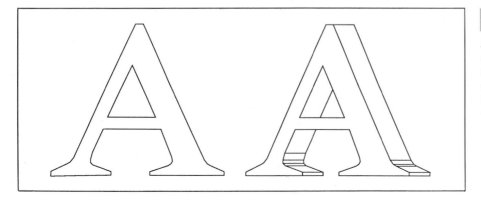

FIGURE 5.11

Example of an extrusion. Polygons can be transformed into three-dimensional shapes using extrusion options in the software. After the letter A was extruded, it was rotated −15 degrees on the y axis.

Procedural Modeling

Models that are created by devising mathematical formulas for their shapes rather than by other methods are called procedural models. Procedural techniques are used quite frequently in draw programs when the artist selects a menu option for a circle, specifies its radius, and the number of points in the circle. (Remember, circles and other polygons are made up of straight lines.)

FIGURE 5.12

Examples of three-dimensional objects created with rotational sweeps. The silhouettes are the original shapes used to create the three-dimensional objects. Note that the torus was created with an off-center rotation of the original polygon. It was then rotated −15 degrees on the x axis to show the inside.

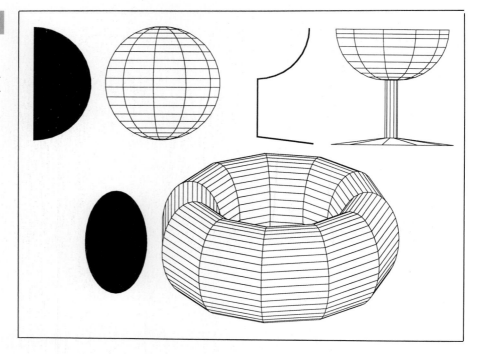

FIGURE 5.13

Comparison of an object created with rotational sweep and an object created with cross-sectional modeling.

The program then draws a uniform circle according to the artist's specifications.[4] Three-dimensional procedural modeling techniques offer the artist a rich and varied selection of computer generated textures and natural forms that would be extremely difficult to create by other means. Fractal generation programs and particle systems are two widely used three-dimensional procedural modeling methods.

---

[4] Issace Kerlow and Judson Rosebush, *Computer Graphics for Designers and Artists* (New York: Van Nostrand Reinhold, 1986), 158.

FIGURE 5.14

Fractals are generated by continually adding detail to the initial pattern. This process can be repeated for as much detail as is needed. (Used with permission of Benoit Mandelbrot.)

Fractals   Until recently, irregular terrains like the craggy surface of a mountain slope or the natural contours of a cloud were difficult and, in many cases, impossible to create. This difficulty was partially overcome by the introduction of fractal geometry. Fractal geometry allows the generation of irregular surfaces and patterns, without having to draw each line. The method of creating these rich and varied patterns was perfected by the mathematician Benoit Mandelbrot, called the "father of fractals." Working at the IBM T. J. Watson Research Center in Yorktown Heights, New York, Mandelbrot was able to create intricate three-dimensional surfaces by devising mathematical formulas that can be applied to the drawing process. Irregular patterns are automatically generated by repeatedly branching each new surface or line into smaller and smaller segments. The process can be continued for as much detail as is needed (see Figure 5.14). Everything from the irregular outline of a snowflake to the intricate texture of a mountainside can be created using fractal geometry (see Color Plate 4).

Particle Systems   Particle systems are used to create clouds, smoke, dust, fire, water, and other natural phenomena. Thousands of tiny computer-generated spheres are dispersed at random to create natural-looking shapes with organic qualities. The spheres can have different densities, colors, and light refraction properties. The process was used to create the wall of fire in the Genesis explosion sequence in the film *Star Trek II*.[5]

Solids Modeling (Additive Modeling)

Models are also created by combining geometric primitives into more complex shapes. The body of a robot, for instance, can be constructed from individually shaped cylinders, prisms, spheres, and cones. These primitives are created using mathematical formulas and become part of a library of geometric shapes that are accessed with a scripting program, or interactively combined from a list of menu options. With a scripting program you type in the shapes to be

---

[5] Robert Rivlin, *The Algorithmic Image* (Redmond, Wash.: Microsoft Press, 1986), 238.

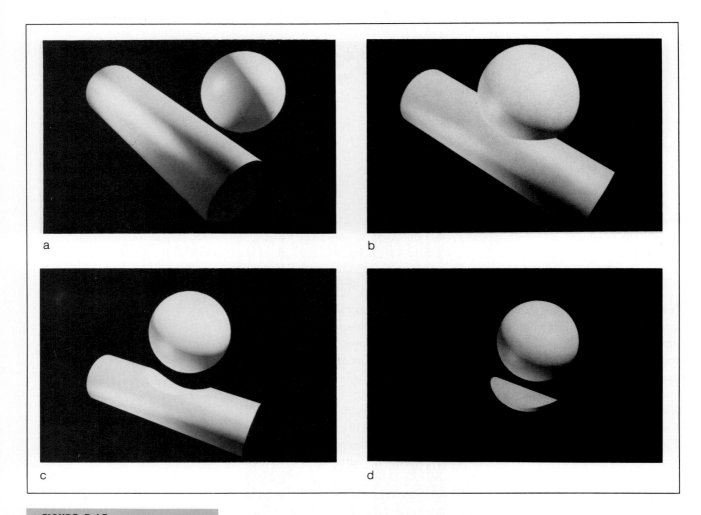

a

b

c

d

FIGURE 5.15

Using Boolean techniques, the two primitive objects in (a) can be (b) united or (c) subtracted, or (d) the intersection can be saved, depending on the modeler's needs. (Courtesy Chris Lasky, Cubicomp Corporation.)

combined, and their orientation in the world coordinate space. Combine large disc + long thin cylinder and the new object, Lollypop, is synthesized from your existing shapes. The objects and their orientation are specified in a list that shows the relationship of all the objects. The additive/subtractive process is a key aspect of this type of model making. A sphere can be combined with a cylinder so that the outline of the sphere is cut into (subtracted from) the cylinder. Or the two primitives can be united—that is, added together. We can also keep the intersection of the two objects and discard the rest, depending on the characteristics of the model we are creating (see Figure 5.15).

Other Three-Dimensional Modeling Techniques

3-D Digitizing   To create a computer model from a real three-dimensional counterpart, computer coordinates can be taken directly from the original object. One method, used for several years, requires that the object be sliced into many thin sections. Each contour is then entered into the computer database, and the program connects the adjacent points to form the computer model.

Another less destructive method is called *photogrammety*. Here a grid is painted on the surface of the 3-D object, and photographs are taken from

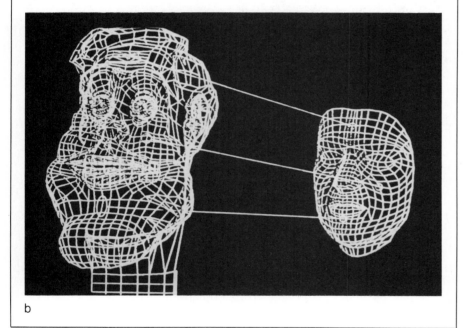

FIGURE 5.16

Example of photogammety. (a) The front and side view of this model was painted with grid lines. (b) Each view was then digitized and merged into a 3-D database, which was later used to provide facial expressions for the character of Tony de Peltrie. Twenty stock expressions were created in this manner. (© 1985 Pierre Lachapelle, Philippe Bergeron, Pierre Robidoux, and Daniel Langlois.)

a

b

the front and side. The photographs are scanned into the computer, and identical grid intersections on the two photographs are identified. By merging the front and side views, the computer creates z coordinates by comparing like x and y intersections and then constructs a 3-D representation of the solid object. This technique is used in computer animation to create natural facial expressions for 3-D puppet figures. The facial expressions in *Tony de Peltrie* were created using this technique (see Figure 5.16 and Color Plate 13c).

Yet another three-dimensional digitizing method uses a stylus and special magnetic transducing technology to input x, y, and z coordinates of nonmetalic objects. The object is placed on a table surface that senses the

FIGURE 5.17

Three-dimensional digitizer.
(Courtesy Polhemus, Inc.)

location of the stylus as it is held against the object. A grid pattern is drawn on the object, the stylus is placed at each grid intersection, and a button is hit to enter the coordinate (see Figure 5.17). The three-dimensional coordinates of the object can then be read by solid modeling programs. The system is not limited to inanimate objects; recently it was used to digitize the facial characteristics of an actress for a three-dimensional animation called *Don't Touch Me.*[6]

Bezier Patches Bezier patches are curved surfaces that are defined by control points not on the patch but exerting influence on it. The surface begins as a group of control points in 3-D space that exerts an influence on the surface, controlling its shape. For example, a tent-like object can be created by anchoring a grid with four control points and placing another control point over the grid. The grid will slope down from the elevated control point. As we move down the tent-like figure from the new position to the outer edges of the grid, the influence of the control point becomes less noticeable as the others take control. As a result, the vertical edges of the tent form sloping curves instead of straight lines. If a second elevated control point is placed near the first and at a different height above the grid, it too will influence the

[6] This animation was created by Kleiser-Walczak Construction Company, Hollywood, California.

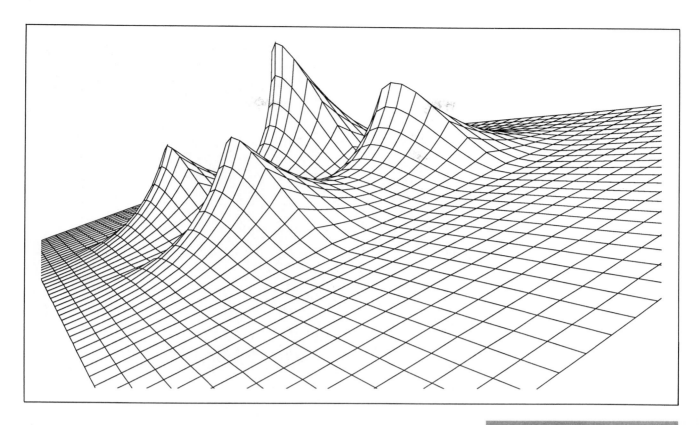

FIGURE 5.18

Contoured grid created with Bezier patch manipulation.

sloping surface, and a gradual transition will be formed between the two peaks (see Figure 5.18). The Bezier patch feature has become an important option in solid modeling programs. For instance, it is useful for modeling the complex surfaces of automobiles and was originally developed for this purpose.[7] Similar shapes can also be created procedurally with quadratic equations. Surfaces created in this way are called quadric surfaces.

Aliasing

Slanting lines sometimes have the "jaggies" when seen on computer monitors. Jaggies are unintentional breaks in diagonal lines caused by the inability of the raster screen to replicate the exact slope of the line. The line jumps to the nearest discrete pixel and creates a break in what is actually a straight line (see Figure 5.19). Jaggies (*aliasing* is the formal term) are more prevalent on low-resolution monitors, which have fewer raster lines. They are much harder to see on high-resolution output devices such as digital film recorders. Since aliasing is the product of the raster interpretation of vector information, it is not seen on devices like pen plotters and vector monitors because these devices do not use raster lines to display the images (see Chapter 2).

Anti-aliasing

Because aliasing can be very noticeable on raster display devices, techniques have been devised to hide the broken lines. Anti-aliasing can be accomplished

---

[7] John Vance, *Dictionary of Computer Graphics* (White Plains, N.Y.: Knowledge Industry Publications, 1984), 5.

FIGURE 5.19

Example of jaggies. (a) Original letter, and (b) letter seen on low resolution monitor.

a

b

FIGURE 5.20

Example of anti-aliasing.

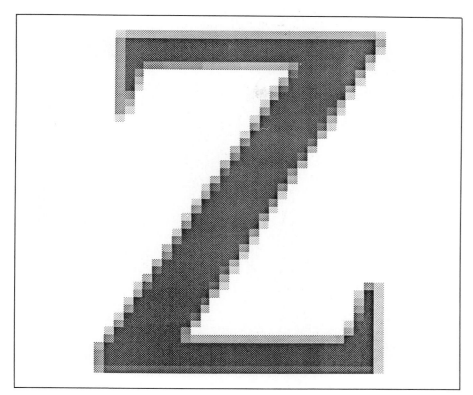

by averaging the pixel color intensity of the broken line with the background color. To the eye, the line looks softer, and the broken portion does not stand out as much. Anti-aliasing is usually built into animation programs so that the animated images do not vibrate along their edges as the objects move across the raster pattern of the screen (see Figure 5.20).

Hidden Line Removal

Three-dimensional objects are first created as wire-frame models with sides open like a birdcage. You can see through them from front to back. But wire frames can be viewed two ways: with or without hidden lines removed. Hidden lines are lines or edges on the back surface of 3-D objects that should normally not be seen from the front. Removing the lines makes it easier to tell the shape and orientation of the object (see Figure 5.21a,b). True hidden line removal also takes into consideration objects that are in front of other objects. Programs for hidden line removal were first developed by Lawrence G. Roberts in 1963 at the Massachusetts Institute of Technology. Before that, all lines in a 3-D object had to be seen at the same time, front and back.[8] With hidden lines removed, it is possible to sense the true volume of an object. However, it looks even better if the object has solid sides and is lit with a strong source of illumination.

---

[8] Cynthia Goodman, *Digital Visions* (New York: Harry N. Abrams, 1987), 101.

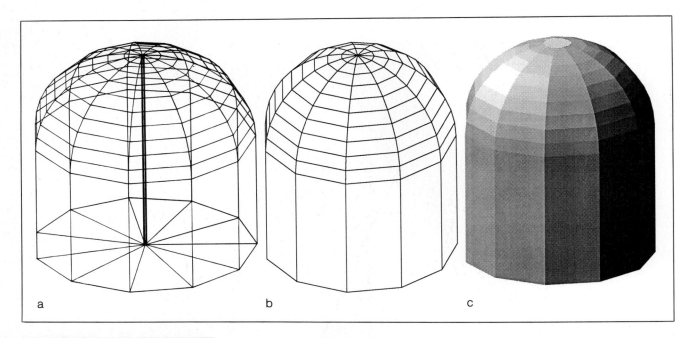

FIGURE 5.21

Example of hidden line removal. In (a) the object appears open like a bird cage; all of the lines are showing. In (b) hidden lines have been removed so that the same object looks solid. (c) is an example of rendering. The wire-frame object in (b) and (c) has been shaded to make it look like a solid object.

Rendering

Rendering is the term used to describe how wire-frame objects are given realistic surfaces and made to look solid rather than open like a birdcage. Rendering takes into account modeling data for both shape (geometric properties) and type of surface (material properties), camera position (choreography data), and lighting data. Rendering programs create (or render) a resultant picture, assigning the appropriate color and intensity value to each pixel on the screen. These programs create solid-looking objects by shading polygons according to lighting from a hypothetical light source (see Figure 5.21c).

Flat Shading When an object is flat shaded, each surface of the object has its own shade. The side facing the light will be the brightest, and the side furthest from the light will be darkest, as if in shadow. The computer decides the brightness of each surface first by computing a line perpendicular to the surface, called the surface normal. The program then checks the surface normal alignment with the light source. If the surface normal points directly at the light source, that polygon is brightly lit. If the surface normal points away from the light source, the polygon is darker. With flat shading, each individual side has one tone (no gradation); so, for example, when a globe is flat shaded, it looks like it is made up of hundreds of separate surface planer polygons, or tiles (see Figure 5.22).

Smooth Shading Smooth shading is a step beyond flat shading. Here the intensity of light on a polygon changes gradually from one side to the other. This smooth shading blends the intensity of adjoining polygons so that pixels

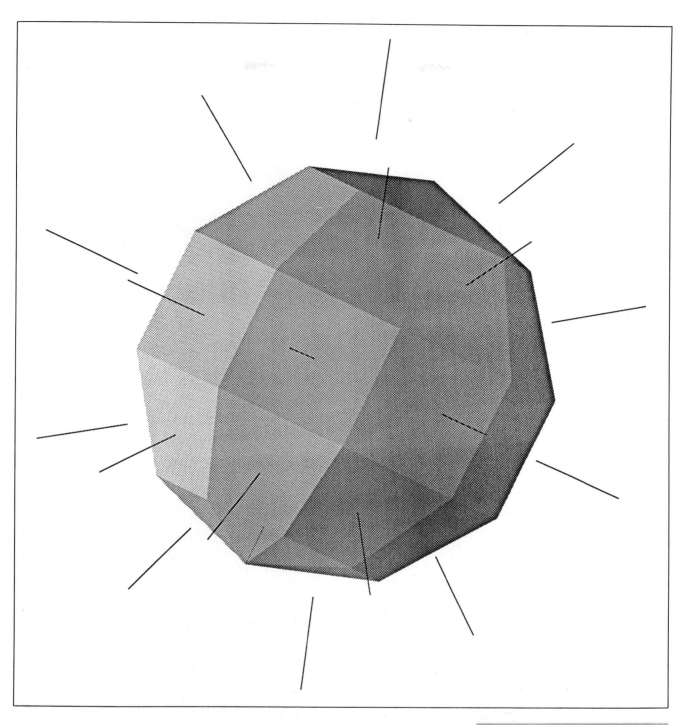

FIGURE 5.22

Example of a flat shaded object with surface normals showing.

nearest the light source are the brightest and pixels furthest away are the darkest. The pixels in between are an average of the two. When a globe is smooth shaded, it looks completely round, like a ball. Beyond smooth shading is Phong shading, a refinement where, instead of averaging midpoints, the surface normal at each pixel is independently computed in relation to the

FIGURE 5.23

Examples of flat, Gouraud (simplest form of smooth shading), and Phong shading. (Courtesy Chris Lasky, Cubicomp Corporation.)

FLAT GOURAUD PHONG

light source so that the edges of each polygon completely disappear and highlights look more realistic. Phong shading is used to produce specular highlights and imitate shiny plastic and chrome surfaces. Because of the sheer volume of calculations, Phong shading on a microcomputer takes considerably longer and is usually done as a final step just before the image is transferred to film or videotape (see Figure 5.23).

Color Map Organization for Solid Modeling For properly shaded objects, the minimum number of shades per color is 16; fewer than 16 shades per color will not produce realistically modeled objects. The more shades you have, the more realistic the object looks. Color maps can be reorganized to allow more shades per color with fewer different colors (hues). An 8-bit system with 256 shades available may normally be organized to allow 16 shades on each of 16 colors. For more realistic looking objects, it can be reorganized to display only 4 different colors, with 64 shades per color ($4 \times 64 = 256$). Where more memory is available per pixel, say 16 bits instead of 8 bits, it may not be necessary to reorganize the color map, since more shades are available per color.

Texture Mapping In addition to appearing solid, surfaces can be textured to look more like real objects. Texture mapping is the technique whereby a pixel file (a paint image), either drawn by the artist or digitized from a photograph, is substituted for the solid color surface of the object. For instance, the digitized picture of a brick wall can be substituted for a flat surface so that the object looks like it is made of brick. When a texture is mapped to the surface of a globe, the individual tiles of the globe can each contain a different picture. Or a single picture can wrap around the entire figure, bent and distorted to fit the contours (Figure 5.24).

FIGURE 5.24

Example of texture mapping.

Bump Mapping   Bump mapping creates a variegated surface texture by assigning predetermined values to the surface normals, thus creating a consistent pattern of light and dark across the surface of the object. By perturbing (agitating) the surface normals in a random way, a more irregular pattern is created. Neither bump mapping nor random perturbing will alter the basic geometry of the object. By using these techniques, surfaces will take on a more complex, natural look, without having to create a specific texture map or make breaks in the surface of the object.

Ray Tracing   Not all surfaces react to light the same way. In the real world, shiny surfaces mirror their surroundings back to the observer. If the reflecting surface is convex (like the surface of a Christmas tree ornament), it will show a distorted view of other objects. Algorithms have been devised to calculate how each ray of light falling on a scene will look after it has bounced off, or traveled through transparent objects. Ray-tracing algorithms follow each ray of light back from the eye of the observer to the objects in the scene and to the light source(s). Rays that pass through or bounce off objects are calculated accordingly. Ray tracing provides a means of adding rich detail without having to texture map or draw by hand each and every additional reflection. Ray tracing is computationally intensive, and for this reason it is not usually found on microcomputer systems (see Color Plate 5).

At a SIGGRAPH convention some years ago, enthusiastic ray tracers formed an ad hoc group called the Ray Tracers' Club. Members were readily identified by a cluster of reflective Christmas tree balls worn on their shirt pockets. When asked about wearing Christmas tree ornaments in the middle of August, one responded, "I'm a member of the Ray Tracers' Club. This is our insignia!"

Reflective texture mapping of pixel images on the surface of objects will duplicate the look of ray tracing, in some instances at a fraction of the computing time. The reflection you see is actually a separate pixel file, however, and not really a reflection of the surrounding objects. Reflective mapping is similar to texture mapping except that the reflection map will appear to move over the surface of the object as you move the object in space.

Lighting

The placement of lights in a three-dimensional computer model is similar to the placement of lights in a photographer's studio. Programs provide you with one or an infinite number of individual light sources. These light sources can be localized—as in the local illumination from a single candle or lamp—or like the sun, they can illuminate the whole scene, hitting every object equally. Highlights and reflections are a special function of the placement of lights, surface attributes, and the particular rendering program in use. All three parameters have an effect on the way the final object will look. In computer modeling, light, like everything else, is a simulation. The computer program calculates the effect the direction and intensity of a particular light will have on an object, given the object's orientation, color, and surface attributes.

In traditional three-point studio lighting, the key light is the principal source of illumination. It is placed in front of the subject at a 45-degree angle, with an imaginary line between the camera and subject. A second light, called the fill light, is also placed in front of the subject but on the other side of the camera. It is closer to the camera and fills in the shadows left by the key light.

Another light, called the back light, is placed high and behind the subject and pointed toward the camera. It is sometimes called the rim light because it separates the subject from the background by highlighting the silhouette outline of the subject. Sometimes side lights are added to accentuate surface textures and to create deep shadows. (See Figure 5.25 for examples of how the placement of a key light affects the object.)

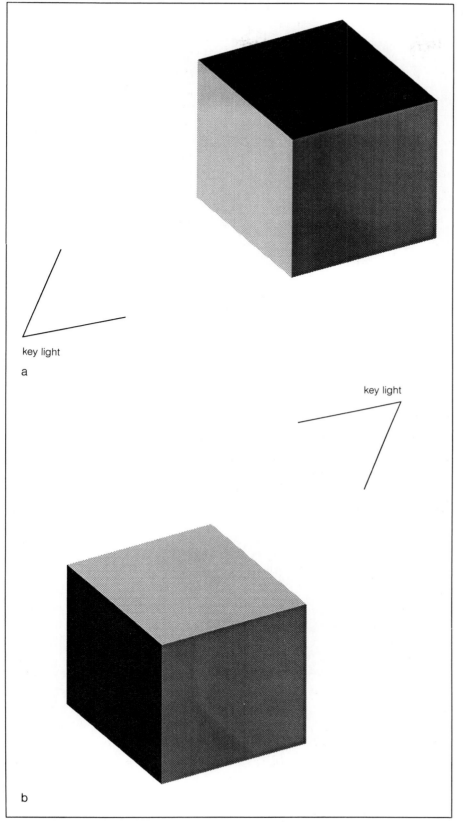

FIGURE 5.25

Examples of key light placement (continues on next page). Figures (a), (b), and (c) show how an object looks with the key light at different angles. Figure (d) shows the effect of a fill light at one-half the brightness of the key light.

key light

a

key light

b

CHAPTER FIVE: VECTOR-BASED DRAWING AND 3-D MODELING PROGRAMS

111

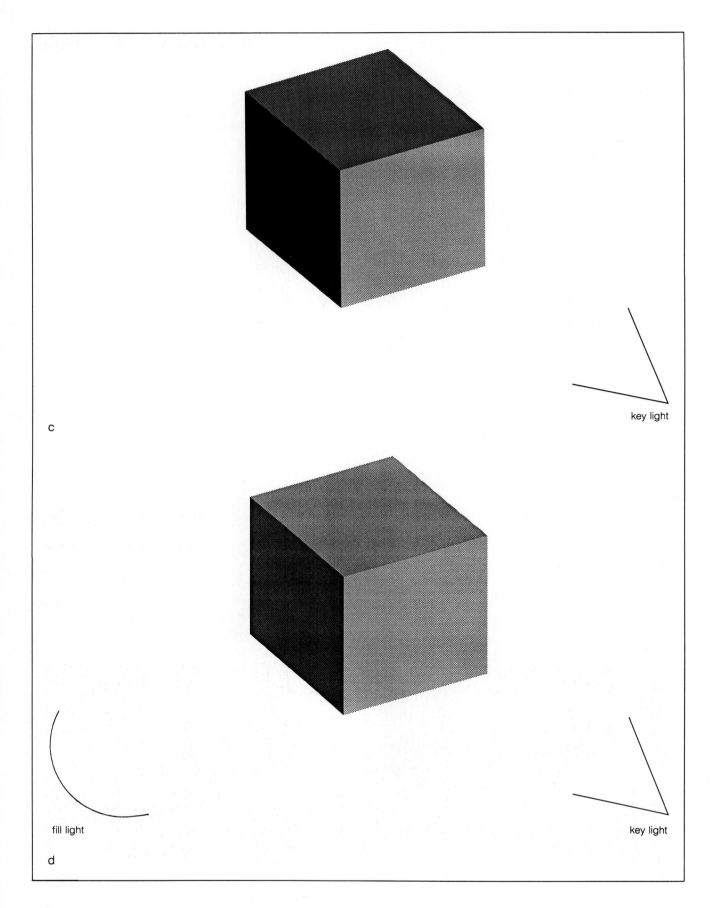

c

key light

fill light

key light

d

Objects created with vector programs are not limited to the resolution of the screen they were created on (that is, they are resolution independent). The better the resolution of the device you use to view them, the better they look. When seen on the graphics screen they are in 512×482 resolution, but when output on a high-resolution film recorder or pen plotter, they will be seen in the resolution of that peripheral, normally 4000×2000 for the typical digital film recorder. Besides x, y, and z coordinates, vector files keep track of the surface attributes of the object. Surface attributes include shading, color, texture, highlights, and direction of light source(s).

What You See Is Not Always What You Get!

Because vector images occupy a three-dimensional environment, it is important to preserve this environment when recording the image on an output device. The relationship between background and foreground objects must be maintained. When rendering three-dimensional objects, the program uses one of two methods to decide which object is in the front and which is in the back.

Painters' Algorithm   The simplest method is called the painters' algorithm. When using this method, objects are added to the screen in sequence, from back to front. Foreground-background relationships are maintained by rendering the background objects first, then painting over them with objects in the foreground. This method does not take into account a true three-dimensional environment, however. Problems arise when objects intersect with each other. In such cases the object rendered first will be partially or completely obscured by the second object, and the objects will not intersect (see Figure 5.26).

Z-Buffer Algorithm   A more precise method for placing objects in true three-dimensional relationship is to use the z-buffer algorithm. When using this method, the rendering program first looks at the placement of objects in z (3-D) space. The algorithm then calculates how much of an object will be

FIGURE 5.26

Example of painters' algorithm and z-buffer algorithm rendering. (a) Figures rendered using the painters' algorithm to sort their position in three-dimensional space. (b) Figures rendered using the z-buffer algorithm.

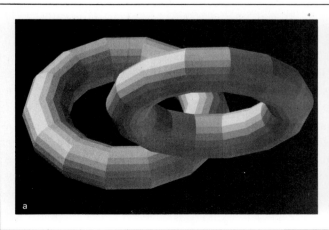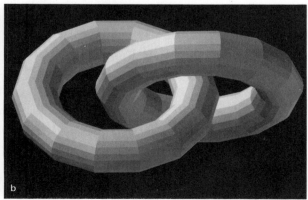

seen from a particular angle, given the objects that are in the foreground. If two objects do intersect each other, their relationship will be maintained. Only that part of the background object still visible will be rendered, so it does not matter which object is rendered first.

Many output devices support only the painters' algorithm method for displaying 3-D environments. To circumvent this limitation, 3-D modeling programs often provide a method for saving screen images at higher than normal screen resolution. While in the 3-D program, you save the z-buffered screen image at greater than normal resolution (1024×964 or 2048×1928). If you select 2048×1928 resolution, your screen image is rendered in 16 parts. Each part is a small window of the full image automatically saved to disk as a 512-$\times$-482-pixel file. When all 16 windows have been rendered, the individual pixel files are merged into a single high-resolution file. However, these high-resolution pixel files are very large. A 2048-$\times$-1928-pixel image will be about 5 megabytes, approximately the equivalent of 14 floppy disks!

File Format Compatibility   Although vector files are device independent and produce high-resolution images, they are saved in proprietary file formats specific to the software package. A vector file created in one program will not automatically load into another. The closest thing to a common file format for vector files is the CGM (Computer Graphics Metafile) format. If your program supports the CGM file format you can bring your file into another program that supports that format. Among the programs that support the CGM standard file format are Artwork, a 2-D and 3-D drawing program from Pansophic; Chartwork, a presentation graphics program from the same company; Mirage, a presentation graphics program from Zenographics; and the desktop publishing programs PageMaker and Ventura Publisher. Some proprietary formats have gained wide use because of the popularity of the software. The DXF file export format from Autocad (CAD software) will allow you to use Autocad files in many other programs. Since many drafting and draw programs support the Hewlett-Packard pen plotter as an output device, their file format called HPGL is often used as a bridge between programs. In the Microsoft Windows environment, WMF (Windows Metafile Format) is used between files that run under Windows.[9]

SUMMARY

Computer graphics techniques are divided into two major specializations: pixel-based paint systems that directly address the screen buffer, and vector-based draw and 3-D modeling programs that generate a database of vector end points. Paint systems are synonymous with two-dimensional art such as painting and watercolor, and 3-D modeling is similar to sculpture. Raster images are resolution dependent—that is, they maintain the look of the image as it is seen on the monitor even when output on high-resolution equipment. Vector images, on the other hand, are resolution independent; they are not

---

[9] Catherine D. Miller, "Graphics File Formats," *PC Magazine*, June 27, 1989, 154–155.

tied to the limitations of lower-resolution output devices such as raster monitors. A vector image can have as many as 8000 lines of resolution depending on the capability of the output device. Paint programs use traditional drawing skills. Three-dimensional modeling programs rely on a more geometric approach, where 3-D objects are constructed from individual polygons or graphics primitives or are created procedurally with mathematical equations. After the objects are created, they are given textures, color, and special lighting and are placed in relationship to each other in a virtual three-dimensional environment.

Exercises

1. Compare paint programs to draw programs. Where are the advantages and disadvantages of each?

2. Define the term *database* and explain how computer databases are used in draw and 3-D programs.

3. Why are draw and 3-D programs also called vector programs?

4. Describe the two most popular rendering options found in solid modeling programs. Discuss advanced rendering methods developed to make computer graphics objects look more like natural objects.

5. Create a box shape with the box option in your draw program. Use the circle or arc option and draw a circle that overlaps the box. Change the box and circle into solids and display the box over the circle.

6. **a.** Transform the box shape into a cube using the extrude function. Turn it 10 degrees toward you and 10 degrees to your right.

   b. Shade the box with solid sides using the render option.

   c. Make a copy of the circle and create a globe using a rotational sweep into *z* space. Note how the globe looks as a wire frame. Now flat shade it with the render option. Smooth shade it and reposition the default light source. Check how the light falls off along the surface of the globe.

7. **a.** Extrude the original circle into a cylinder. Place the box, circle, and cylinder in a three-dimensional composition. Choose contrasting colors for each object. If your program has a rubber stamp feature, duplicate one or more of the objects and place them at different distances from the observer. Change the shape and size of one or all of them using size and scale options.

   b. Allow the objects to intersect and look at the work space from the side or top.

8. Create a "milk crate" by duplicating a grid (16 × 16 squares) and then placing the grids in *z* space to form the bottom and sides of the crate. Put several spheres in the crate and look at them from a different angle.

9. If your program has spline and Bezier functions to transform straight lines into S curves or grids into 3-D shapes, use the Bezier function to create a teepee shape out of a flat grid.

10. Explain the difference between the painters' algorithm and *z* buffering. Why are *z*-buffered images more realistic?

11. Create a letterhead for yourself. Include a 3-D logo that expresses a special interest or hobby you may have.

ADVERTISING DESIGN EXERCISE

This assignment assumes that you have companion paint and solid modeling programs, that is, programs that have file compatibility. Images created in the paint program should be compatible with objects created in the solid modeling program and vice versa.

Create a record album cover, book cover, or poster containing a background picture created in the paint program and foreground 3-D type and design elements (possibly a 3-D logo) created in the solid modeling program. Elements of the 3-D design are created separately and can be addressed as separate objects. For example, the 3-D design elements can be turned and rotated independently of each other. The paint image can contain a scan-in (or scan-ins) of existing artwork or photographs.

1. *Preliminary sketches.* Create on paper several thumbnails (quick matchbook-size sketches) showing how the background and foreground elements will be combined to form a unified composition.

2. *Layout stage.* An important aspect of the layout and comprehensive stages is "technical design," that is, deciding which software options you will use. Before beginning work on the computer, chart a course through the software that will accomplish your goals. If you are going to create a logo, how will it be made? If the shape is going to be three-dimensional, decide which 3-D option will be best for the final object. Will you use the extrude function, rotation, or cross-sectional modeling? If you trace in the shape be sure to always work in a clockwise direction, then use the smooth feature of the program to average out unintentional bends in curved surfaces. Its sides should look uniform, not hand-drawn. Arcs should be round, straight lines look straight. Technical design is an important step and will save many false starts. Carefully plan out the stages of your design. You should know which options you are going to use before you begin work in the solid modeling program.

Using the computer, rough out the background artwork in a paint program, adding detail to the preliminary sketch. Then, in the solid modeling program place the 2-D type where it will be used over the background. Decide where additional text (body copy) will be used if needed. Create a 3-D logo and place it in the composition. Proof your image on a laser or dot matrix printer.

3. *Comprehensive for client approval.* Using the paint program digitize existing artwork or photographs and complete the background composition. Load the paint image into your solid modeling program and place the type and 3-D elements where they will be used. Output the composite image to an ink-jet printer or thermal color printer for client (instructor) approval. Note that the layout and comprehensive stages can sometimes be considered one stage, depending on the complexity of the project. Both stages represent a working out of the design problem on the computer. They may lead to several intermediate variations, which can be saved to disk and developed later if needed.

4. *Final stage.* Make changes suggested by the client and output the final image to a film recorder or high-resolution printer for color separations.

If you are using Artwork from Pansophic, Inc., the final picture containing the foreground design/type and background photograph can be combined by loading the ".IMG" file with the IMG/L option in the Artwork DISK menu. Use DISPLAY to write the object folios over the background image. If you use SHOW, the background image will clear and defeat your intentions. Similar options can be found in the Lumena/Crystal graphics package, in Cubicomp, and in other professional graphics programs.

Most likely you will send the files to a digital film recorder for final output. The background image will be recorded in standard bit mapped resolution (512 × 482). The foreground design and type will be recorded at vector resolution (2000 lines or greater).

Bibliography

Foley, J.D., and A. Van Dam. *Fundamentals of Interactive Computer Graphics.* Reading, Mass.: Addison-Wesley, 1982.

Glassner, Andrew S. *Computer Graphics User's Guide.* Indianapolis: Howard W. Sams, 1984.

Kerlow, Issace, and Judson Rosebush. *Computer Graphics for Designers and Artists.* New York: Van Nostrand Reinhold, 1986.

Unit Three

DESKTOP

PUBLISHING

Potentially the most widely disseminated of all computer graphic applications, desktop publishing will be a common office function in the years to come. Desktop publishing on microcomputers brings the ability to compose professional quality printed material to a wider range of people, people who today are not in the mainstream of publishing and graphic design. For message senders—the person or organization with the need to initiate the publication—the advantages of cost savings and speed frequently become the impetus for establishing a desktop publishing operation. They hope to handle "in house" many of the operations previously sent outside to designers, typographers, illustrators, and graphic artists. You, as the desktop publisher responsible for constructing the publication, will be expected to demonstrate professional expertise in all these areas, only faster. This unit provides a brief introduction to those who want to learn how to produce professional-looking documents and brochures with desktop publishing software. Perhaps also you will glimpse the pulse that drives a designer's heart—the devotion to visualize balance, the wonder of white space, and the loveliness of individual letter forms. Over time your eye will come to recognize how excellence in design is achieved—through education, experience, and meticulous attention to detail. Microcomputer automation of prepress operations now brings the capability of desktop layout and design to thousands of people who are new to the art of publishing. Within the history of prepress operations, desktop publishing is thought by many to be a major revolution, as you'll see from the introductory article by Jonathan Seybold, one of America's foremost authorities on this emerging technology.

From the time of Gutenberg, publishing prepress functions have been performed by specialists using equipment designed specifically for the application and built, sold, serviced, and supported by organizations dedicated to this market. Now, rather suddenly, all of this has changed.

Publishing prepress is becoming a computer application, rooting itself firmly in the mainstream of the computer industry. Consequently, it is benefiting from and contributing to the enormous progress being made by that related industry. Everyone involved in the publishing industry faces a stark choice: either join the mainstream or be left behind in an increasingly irrelevant side eddy.

THE FOURTH WAVE

As we see it, the prepress industry has gone through four revolutionary changes, or "waves," all in less than a century:

▶ The first wave, at the end of the nineteenth century, came with the introduction of hot metal typesetting.
▶ The second had its roots in the 1950s but really made its impact on the industry felt in the 1960s. This "wave" included the introduction of phototypesetters, computers programmed to perform hyphenation and justification as well as the release of the first color separation scanners.
▶ The third came in the 1970s, with the advent of partially proprietary integrated computer systems. This technology has shaped the industry we know today.
▶ The fourth wave is the shift from proprietary integrated systems to solutions that are part of the computer mainstream. This, we believe, will turn out to be at least as important as the previous three waves of change.

Whenever the industry goes through a cycle of change, its entire structure is redefined. New suppliers emerge; some old suppliers fade away. New skills are required; some old skills are no longer relevant. The publishing industry itself opens up—there are fewer barriers to entry. It is easier and less expensive to publish information. Overall, the publishing process is simplified and streamlined. A new cycle of change enables you to do many things that were impossible before.

This is exactly what is happening today. To understand the importance of the current changes, let us review how we got to this point in the first place.

HOT METAL

Beginning at the close of the nineteenth century, a mechanical revolution swept the publishing industry. For most applications, hand setting of text type was replaced by the hot metal line caster, and the industry was in turmoil. But in the end, the hot metal Linotype or Monotype machine was far more efficient, leading the industry into a new era of prosperity.

Machines that would "set" type by exposing characters onto photographic paper or film began to appear in the 1950s, but it wasn't until later in the next decade that they made strong inroads into the industry. The early growth was fueled by the rise of offset printing, which requires a photographic master of the page to be printed, and by the ability to compose complex material directly on the phototypesetter—handy for display advertising.

THE FOURTH WAVE:

PUBLISHING JOINS THE

COMPUTER MAINSTREAM

JONATHAN SEYBOLD

Jonathan Seybold is publisher of the *Seybold Report on Desktop Publishing* and *The Seybold Report on Publishing Systems.* Seybold Seminars sponsor the annual Seybold Computer Publishing Conference. Copyrighted material reproduced from *Seybold Report on Publishing Systems,* vol. 17, no. 9. Reproduction in whole or in part without express permission is prohibited. Please address inquiries to: P.O. Box 644, Media, PA, 19063.

In the late 1960s, phototypesetters were joined by another breed of photomechanical-electronic device: color separation scanners. These devices can scan a color photograph (usually a transparency), size it to the desired dimensions, separate the colors into the proper combination of the four colors (yellow, magenta, cyan, and black) used to print full-color pictures, and expose four film negatives (one for each color).

Starting in the early 1960s, a few crazy, but visionary, pioneers programmed computers to drive the typesetting machines.

INTEGRATED SYSTEMS

The ball game changed dramatically in the 1970s, with the emergence of system vendors. The goal became the complete automation of the process using a single, unified system. The systems took different guises: "front-end" production systems for newspapers, digital color production systems for color trade shops, and combination computer/typesetter systems for small type shops. In almost every case, though, the goal was the same: provide a single turnkey solution to the user's specific needs.

It was at this point that most graphic arts systems moved decisively away from standard, off-the-shelf computers. Part of this movement was undoubtedly caused by the 500-year tradition of building machines specifically for the peculiar requirements of publishing. But there were compelling rational reasons as well.

Put simply, the requirements for integrated publishing systems were beyond the state of the art for the standard computer systems of the day. Publishers wanted highly interactive video terminals; instant computing of hyphenation/justification; versatile, high-quality video screens and keyboards; user interfaces that demanded lots of custom command keys; and on-line interfaces to a wide variety of specialized equipment, such as newspaper wire service lines and OCR scanners. Clearly, they were not an easy lot to please.

THE DOWN SIDE

All of this functionality came at a high cost. System vendors were required to devote most of their resources to developing and supporting proprietary hardware, computer operating systems, and interfaces for a variety of special devices. Weighed down by the need to support an evergrowing base of installed proprietary systems, it became increasingly difficult for vendors to keep up the initial rapid pace of innovation and continued development.

The result of this focus on proprietary systems was an industry that became increasingly stagnant.

THE PARC CHALLENGE

While the graphic arts system vendors were developing their marvelous and sophisticated proprietary integrated solutions, researchers at Xerox Palo Alto (Calif.) Research Center (PARC) were quietly redefining the future of computing. Most of the concepts were not strictly originated at PARC. Some even had parallels in work being done in typesetting systems—the WYSIWYG screens used for display ad composition, for example. But it was at PARC that everything was brought together and a new type of computer system defined.

Although the PARC research did not yield many successful commercial products for Xerox, it would be difficult to overstate the impact it had on the industry in general. Today, PARC alumni are scattered among dozens of cutting-edge hardware and software companies. Even those companies that did not employ "Xeroids" were heavily influenced by visits to PARC, by their products, or by the permeation of PARC methods into the industry.

THE SYSTEM CONCEPT

To be candid, we have to stop and think awhile to remind ourselves how revolutionary the PARC vision was. It always seemed logical, even inevitable, to us. While it certainly has become mainstream now, it was not mainstream at the time.

The basic elements of PARC's agenda were as follows:

▶ A powerful personal computer on every desktop. All interactive computing would be done locally on this desktop machine.
▶ Personal computers linked into systems via networks.
▶ Shared information stored on file servers. This is the one area where we disagreed with Xerox from the very beginning. The PARC researchers understood that people need access to a common, shared pool of information. Our complaint was that they chose the wrong model.

The conceptual model was the office filing cabinet. We argued that a computer system's file handling capabilities should not be bound by the constraints of a paper world. A properly networked system should allow for transparent, distributed access to files; permit multiple users to work concurrently on the same data; and provide extensive tools for organizing, routing, and locating files.
▶ Typographic printers. Xerox was the pioneer in laser xerography. Starting with the earliest experiments, it used these machines to produce modest-resolution typographic output rather than simple office-quality output.

From the beginning, then, typography was part of the PARC system concept. This is critical for understanding what has happened with computer publishing in recent years. Typography was folded into what became the mainstream of computing because the people at Xerox thought that this was the right thing to do. That decision alone ensured that publishing would eventually merge into the computer mainstream. We doubt that the same thing would have happened if this pioneering work had been done at an IBM, Sperry, RCA, or DEC facility.

▶ Integrated text and graphic facilities. The publishing industry had always dealt with text and graphics separately. Even the "integrated" publishing systems were almost always either text or graphic systems. Xerox wanted to be able to combine both text and graphics in the same system.

▶ WYSIWYG screen display. The drive for a graphic user interface led to the use of a "what you see is what you get" screen, displaying black letters on a white background. This, in turn, presumed that the personal computer would have ample computing power to drive the complex screen display.

▶ Mouse/icon user interface. PARC picked up work that had been started at Stanford Research in Palo Alto, California, on using a mouse for a "point-and-click" computer user interface. The PARC concept was to create a user interface that would be natural, easy, and intuitive for people. It was a radical concept at the time. Just remember all of the concern back then about "computer literacy."

▶ Complete page makeup. If you are going to prepare documents that are to be displayed on WYSIWYG screens and printed out on typographic output devices at any time and anywhere in the world, you must be able to perform the entire formatting job on your desktop computer.

Together, all of these ideas represented a powerful vision of what computing should be—a vision that has spread to most of the computing industry. You will certainly note that most of the concepts that characterize what we need to do for

publishing applications, including typography and graphics, were part of the PARC vision.

THE PC REVOLUTION

By the end of the 1970s, virtually everyone in the office automation field was talking about the multi-function workstation that one day would be on everyone's desk. Most did not think in terms of a Xerox-like system because the Xerox work was still under wraps. These, after all, were going to be office systems, and offices, the word-processing people reasoned, only had to cope with typewriter output. Nor did it occur to these office system developers that the multifunction workstation that eventually conquered the office would turn out to be the personal computer. Personal computers, when they appeared, were toys for curious hobbyists, the kind of things that appealed to nerds and other social outcasts.

THE LIMITS OF PCs

Although this view was clearly shortsighted, it is true that the personal computer industry grew up with a view of the world that was not exactly PARC-like.

Personal computers were personal. On the whole, the folks who brought us the PC revolution were iconoclasts. They were concerned with giving each user his own personal computer to "do his own thing."

Personal computers were computers. The objective was simply to bring down to a personal, desktop level the type of computer that had previously been available only as a shared machine.

The one innovation was the introduction of video game graphics. But this was not done in an effort to produce written communications with graphics. It was, rather, a means of supporting computer games.

ENTER THE MAC

It was the advent of the Macintosh in 1984 that began to change all of this. The Mac refined and packaged the PARC vision and brought it to the mass market.

The initial machine was not perfect, but the concept was there, and people who understood the concept began to rally around it. We called the original Mac "almost great" and proclaimed that it was "the closest thing yet to what a personal computer should be."

With the advent of the Laser-Writer the following year, Apple brought to the mass market refined versions of most of the essential Xerox PARC concepts. It set the publishing industry on its ear. Within a year or two, it was apparent that Apple also had changed the course of the computer industry.

DESKTOP PUBLISHING

In essence, the computer systems pioneered at Xerox PARC were invented to serve document preparation and publishing applications. With the advent of the Mac and the LaserWriter, this revolutionary generation of publishing systems was available to virtually anyone who wanted to communicate. Aldus PageMaker and other first-rate software packages soon followed. The result was the explosion we have come to call desktop publishing.

Less than three years after the appearance of the first desktop publishing systems, it is now clear to everyone except perhaps a few die-hards that from now on, publishing is an irrevocable part of the mainstream of the computer industry.

THE NEW REALITIES

The industry today presents a radically different basis for publishing applications than it did five years ago. It is a situation that no one in

Today's graphic designers use the computer in place of, or to augment, traditional paper and pen. The design shown at the left was digitized with a desktop scanner and appears on the computer screen. Now the designer can change the size, position, and picture contrast of the design or even manipulate elements within the composition. The image can be incorporated into a document, reproduced as a slide, or recorded on videotape. (Courtesy Seton Hall University.)

the publishing industry can afford to ignore.

The new realities are:

▶ Mass-produced desktop computers. This is the central fact on which everyone focuses. For a very modest investment, you can now put substantial computing power on every user's desk.
▶ A flood of application software. With the advent of a mass market for computers, the cost of software can be amortized over tens of thousands, hundreds of thousands, or even millions of users.
    The result is not only vastly cheaper software, it is an explosion of software. You can select from an enormous variety of software packages, with new capabilities being offered every month. No proprietary system could hope to keep up with this embarrassment of riches.
▶ Local area networks. It has taken much longer than it should have, but networked

computing is finally coming to the mass market. Apple now provides an effective solution for small work groups. Cabling for the PC market is widely available, and software is improving. Much more sophisticated capabilities are on the way.
▶ Global telecommunications. Global digital communications are now an accepted fact of life for everyone. Any PC user who wants to can link to worldwide messaging and data transfer utilities. It is also convenient to dial into a wide variety of information sources and on-line databases.
▶ Graphic screens. Although the PC has been a holdout, it is absolutely clear that the entire desktop computer market is moving to graphic screens and easy-to-use graphic user interfaces. This permits display of type and graphics on the screen. It also permits simple, consistent user interfaces for complex applications (such as typesetting).

▶ Typography mainstream. Everyone who designs a desktop computer system these days assumes that it needs to cope with typography. WYSIWYG displays, typographic printers, and page description languages are mainstream computer topics. In fact, most of the progress in these areas is being driven not by the needs of professional publishers but by much broader market forces. Typesetting is no longer considered oddball.
▶ Integration of text and graphics. Along with this new mind set has come the assumption that computer systems must be able to cope with graphics in addition to text and must be able to provide an environment that supports close integration of text and graphics.
▶ Consistent graphic user interface. It took the industry a long time to realize that the real power of the Macintosh user interface is not so much its ease of use but the consistency from application to application.

▶ Sophisticated operating environments. Serious publishing applications will ultimately require multitasking computer operating systems and sophisticated network operating environments. UNIX workstation vendors already provide much of this. Microsoft and IBM are jumping from a simple control program to a full-fledged network operating system with OS/2 and its extensions. Apple is evolving in the same direction in a step-by-step fashion.

In every case, the computing environment available even at the desktop computer level is (or will be) much richer than much of what used to be available in minicomputers.

THE FOURTH WAVE

All of this provides a tailormade foundation for publishing applications. With a few exceptions, the mainstream of the computer industry has caught up with and passed proprietary publishing systems. Even where it hasn't, the benefits of being in the mainstream usually outweigh any remaining liabilities. With the energy of an entire computer industry behind it, the mainstream is going to leave proprietary solutions farther and farther behind.

It is very clear, for example, that virtually all of the exciting new developments—computer hardware, operating systems, networking, communications, text and graphics application software packages, input scanners, output devices, add-on processors, and so forth—will take place in and around the mainstream. Users of proprietary systems will not have access to most of these.

It is also clear that future developments in electronic publishing will all be firmly based in the computer mainstream. New and prospective publishing applications include CD-ROMs, hypermedia, interactive video, interactive compound document databases, applications of artificial intelligence, and learning through simulation. The penalties for those who reject the mainstream and the rewards for those who accept it are proportionately high and getting bigger by the day.

Making the shift. Although not everyone would articulate things in the same fashion, we think that most people in the publishing industry, user and vendor alike, have come to see the same reality. There can no longer be any question that the publishing industry is now in the middle of a massive shift from proprietary systems to solutions rooted in the computer industry mainstream.

This is happening (or will happen) across the board, from the smallest publisher right through to the largest color house. Because of the huge amount of data involved, processing of high-quality, full-color picture images will be the last application to move to the computer mainstream. But even here the question is no longer "if" but "when."

For many people, the changes involved will be traumatic. Revolutions are messy. People get hurt. It takes some time for new order to emerge out of chaos. But like it or not, the revolution is taking place. The people who benefit from it will be those who understand what is happening and plan their course accordingly.

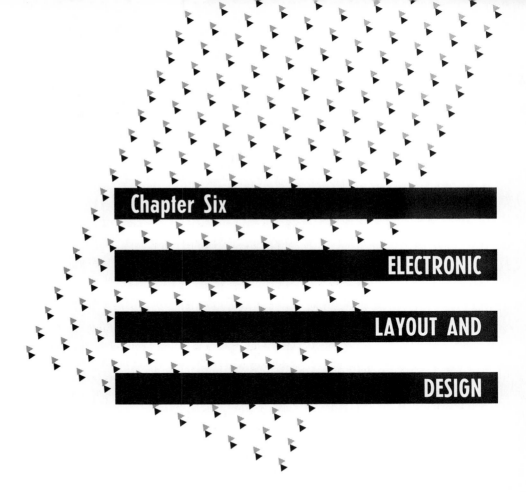

Chapter Six

ELECTRONIC

LAYOUT AND

DESIGN

Desktop publishing uses microcomputers or minicomputer workstations to help you look good in print, with specialized programs that perform electronic layout and design of the printed page. Electronic layout and design are concerned with visual communication that is on par with professionally published material. Instead of looking as though they were created on a typewriter, your documents will have the format and look of a newspaper, magazine, or printed brochure.

When you operate a desktop publishing program, you are primarily formatting: formatting the page the way you want it to look; formatting the pictures and illustrations—making them large or small or cutting off parts you don't want; and formatting text—making headlines large and bold and setting paragraphs in special typefaces. Your desktop computer or workstation helps you quickly implement your ideas. Desktop publishing pages are first printed as hard copy. This hard copy may be printed on plain paper and on an output device such as a laser printer or on photographic paper on a special high-quality printer. In turn, this hard copy is given to a print shop or office duplication department for making multiple copies. Since desktop publishing programs do not provide multiple reproduction (or printing) but rather the material that is given to a commercial print shop, they are often called prepress operations.

In this chapter you will explore the creative means of electronically formatting pages and then assembling both words and graphics into a single visual message. These tools help you present your message with professional or publishing quality. Because electronic layout and design using desktop publishing programs on microcomputers is such a new field, the chapter also compares the computerized process with the manual layout and design process.

PROFESSIONAL PUBLICATION QUALITY

What separates the professional-quality publication from the less-than-professional-quality document? Both types of documents can be printed by a print shop. The most common response to this question is that you can tell by looking at it. Professional-quality documents are visually formatted to please the eye and invite readership. They usually include illustrations, photographs, charts, and graphics. There will be a variety of type styles that visually separate and emphasize headlines, subheadlines, and important text words. The type is letterspaced so that thin characters like i's and l's use less space than wide characters like m's and w's, making the text easier to read and more uniform in appearance. Each letter form has a special style and design that imparts an emotional tone to the text. Hyphenation is used to smooth the right margin, whether justified (straight margin) or unjustified (ragged margin).

There are many individual steps needed to achieve professional-looking documents for reproduction. While discovering each individual step, you will also be introduced to special printing industry and prepress terms as well as computer terms. Some words, such as *pica* (a printer's measurement) and *font* (a typeface design), have meanings that are holdovers from days of hand set type. Other terms, such as *mechanical* (the artwork supplied to a print shop), come from the graphic artist's vocabulary. As the manual prepress process becomes more and more computerized, the traditional printing lexicon takes on new meanings. Finally, there is the terminology associated with microcomputer operations: *WYSIWYG* (What You See Is What You Get), meaning that the document you see on the screen appears exactly the same in hard copy from your printer.

BACKGROUND

Desktop publishing programs are quickly becoming popular with designers, creative services departments in businesses, and others having responsibility to produce attractive professional-quality printed material. As a desktop publishing operator, you will be creating newsletters, flyers, new product updates, proposals, internal and external reports, brochures, catalogs—almost anything that is typeset and uses graphics. Currently, the most widespread use of the desktop publishing process is for publications that are printed with only one or two colors. Nevertheless, high-end systems can be used to produce full-color publications.

The term *desktop publishing* describes the process of computerized typesetting and page composition. The term *desktop* implies convenience, differentiating the process both from the traditional means of creating page artwork by hand on a drafting table and from high-end electronic publishing used in producing newspapers, magazines, and books. The term *publishing* implies quality—the professional typeset look. Summing up, desktop publishing refers to a computer-aided process to facilitate page design; format pages (sometimes called pagination); set type; integrate graphs, charts, and illustrations; and perform hyphenation and justification. With it you can reproduce the pages on an office duplicator or supply camera-ready art to a print shop—all with professional quality. The nice part is that desktop publishing programs can accomplish all this with relative ease, convenience, and speed.

The advantages to users of electronic layout and design programs are improved speed, closer control, faster revisions, and lower cost as compared with the former manual cut-and-paste process. Improved speed for the graphic designer means faster layout creation and quick resizing of graphic elements in order to explore different visual ideas. Instead of felt-tip marker sketches, hard-copy laser printouts provide more visually accurate communication of designs. Creating a revision or alternative version can be as simple as changing the software's page formatting instructions and running another printout. All of these steps can be accomplished at a much lower relative cost. On the other hand, the disadvantages can be lower visual quality and a diminishment of professionalism if layout functions are assumed by people without a good design background.

Understanding desktop publishing first requires knowing what is physically needed for a print shop or office duplication department to use for reproduction. Three interchangeable terms are used to describe the physical pages: *camera-ready artwork*, *pasteup*, or *mechanical*. These are all the pages of the publication with black type and graphics pasted on white illustration board exactly as they will appear when printed. Exactly means in precise position and with high-quality resolution. Resolution refers to dots per square inch (DPI), a measure of visual detail.

Many desktop publishing programs are available in the marketplace, notably Aldus PageMaker and Xerox Ventura Publisher. These programs are essentially page layout software; additional software, such as word-processing and drawing programs, and hardware, such as laser printers and desktop scanners, are still required to perform desktop publishing on a microcomputer or workstation. The additional requirements vary with the type of system being used (Apple, MS-DOS, UNIX) and the quality of output desired.

ELEMENTARY OPERATIONS

The desktop publishing process first can be separated into its three most elementary operations: text creation, graphics creation, and page assembly. Text creation means writing the words. Eventually set in type, the copy or manuscript is generally created and edited on a computer using word-processing software. Graphics creation means developing the photographs,

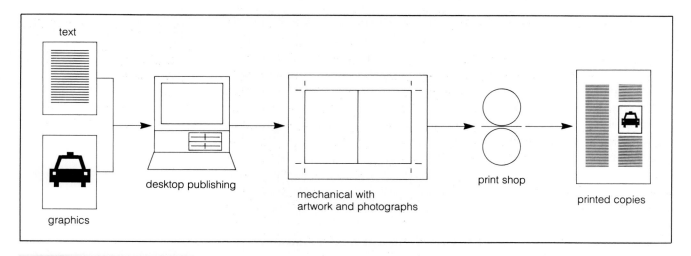

text

graphics

desktop publishing

mechanical with
artwork and photographs

print shop

printed copies

FIGURE 6.1

*A desktop publishing, or prepress,
program uses a microcomputer to
format text and graphics. The hard-
copy printout is called a mechanical, or page artwork, and is sent to
a print shop for reproduction.*

charts, and illustrations that are to be part of the publication. Photographs
are supplied by a photographer. Charts and illustrations are hand drawn by
an artist or created on a computer using painting or drawing software. Finally,
page assembly brings together the text and graphics in a page format and
generates a hard-copy printout (the mechanical). The layout or overall look
of a page typically has been created by a graphic designer, while the mechanical is usually prepared by a pasteup artist. Separate programs for word
processing, illustration, and page assembly generally allow more power, flexibility, and ease of use for each separate task. Some desktop publishing
programs can perform all three functions—some more easily than others (see
Figure 6.1).

With text creation, graphics creation, and page assembly forming the
three basic segments of desktop publishing, a full range of enhancements is
available to make the whole process even easier and more efficient. A normal
computer screen shows only part of the page being formatted; special full-
page or even double-page (facing page) monitors are available to enhance your
system. Scanners copy photographs and hand-drawn illustrations and convert
them into computer files. Special computer output devices, such as laser
printers, let you finish the page as a camera-ready mechanical or simply
supply a paper proof. And as with most everything else, the more money you
want to invest in the system, the greater its capability—which in desktop
publishing means more software options, greater visual resolution (monitor or
printer output), additional color (monitor or printer output), greater memory
capacity for handling larger files (for larger and more complex graphics), and
faster processing speed.

WHAT DESKTOP PUBLISHING PROGRAMS DO

Desktop publishing software imports text files from word-processing programs
and graphics from scanners or paint programs. Most desktop publishing programs perform electronic layout and design in four basic steps: page design,
graphic placement, text style and placement, and fine-tuning.

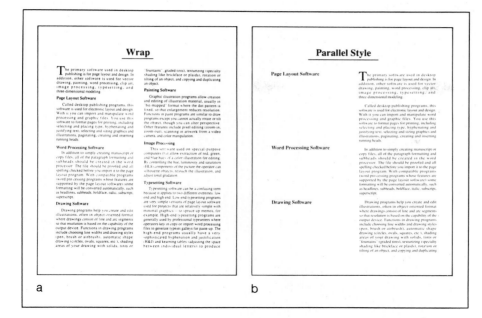

FIGURE 6.2

Example of grid formats—(a) wrap style and (b) parallel style.

Step 1: Page Design

In page design, you begin by determining the number of pages you will want for your publication and the grid format that you want to use. The grid format, a tool for visual consistency throughout your publication, is a matrix of non-printing guides you set up on the screen: vertical guides to define side margins and column widths; horizontal guides to define top and bottom margins and graphic alignment positions. You may decide you want newspaper style columns, where your story or article "wraps" from the bottom of one column to the top of the next. This style is good for continuous reading applications such as brochures and newsletters. Or you may decide you want parallel columns, where a short description or heading appears in one column and the associated text of the article appears parallel in the adjacent column. The parallel column format is used to visually reinforce equally weighted topics for discontinuous reading applications (text charts and manuals) (see Figure 6.2). Next you determine if there will be a masthead—that is, the area at the top of a newsletter showing the name of the newsletter, volume number, and date. You determine where page numbers will appear and how they will look. You insert the rules (lines) that you want to have on each page.

Step 2: Graphic Placement

Your next step is to import the graphic files you have chosen. One by one, you size and place your illustrations in position on the appropriate pages. Here the desktop publishing program allows you to resize the graphics to fit them where you want, crop them (cut off the parts you feel are not important or that distract attention) (see Figure 6.3), enclose them in box rules (draw a line around them), or float them (no rule). You may wish to bleed a photograph, which means when printed it will run off the edge of the paper. Through the use of snap-to functions, the artwork automatically aligns itself to the columns you have set up.

FIGURE 6.3

*Example of a photo (a) before and
(b) after cropping.*

Step 3: Text Style and Placement

Now you format the text, essentially performing the typesetting function. You
tell the program the overall typeface format you want to use for each headline,
subhead, text section, caption, chart, and footnote. You choose the paragraph
alignment style you want. Do you want each line centered or flush (justified)

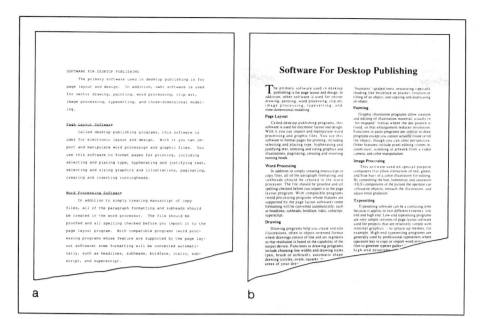

FIGURE 6.4

(a) Manuscript output from a word processor and dot matrix printer compared to (b) typeset copy from a desktop publishing program.

against the left or right margins (or both)? Do you want the paragraphs indented, with no indents, or hanging (outdent), where only the first line extends to the margin and subsequent lines are indented? How much space do you want between paragraphs? Do you want long words to break at the end of a line (hyphenation)?

Next you import the copy (text) from the word-processing program. Here you begin to recognize the power of the desktop publishing program as it takes a file that appears as if it came from a typewriter and performs the many functions that gives it the professional typeset quality you are familiar with in magazines, brochures, and books (see Figure 6.4). If your publication is several pages long, the copy will often flow from one page to the next, around graphics, filling the pages column by column. If properly integrated with style formats from the word processor, headlines and subheads will appear as you specified, and the paragraphs will appear to format themselves. If you are doing a newsletter, you will often have separate copy files to import. Here you may want to start a story on page 1 and have it continue on an inside page.

Step 4: Fine-Tuning

Finally, you fine-tune the document. You format or adjust major headlines. You adjust the letterspacing: try letting the letters touch each other, or become tight not touching (TNT), or spread out evenly across the column or page. Then you add captions to photographs and charts. Within sections of text, you specify words you want to underscore, set in italic or bold type, or in small caps. Then you check for widows (the last word of a paragraph appearing in a line by itself) and orphans (the first line of a paragraph appearing by itself at the bottom of a column). You explore copyfitting, adjusting how the text will "run around" an illustration. Fine-tuning your publication is where you apply the craftsmanship that gives it a true professional-quality appearance.

In using a desktop publishing program, many traditional prepress disciplines come together—editing, proofing, design, composition, and typesetting. In many cases, desktop publishing will be an iterative process—you try an idea, print out hard copy to look at, then try a different idea. Desktop publishing programs are ideal for making revisions and changes both quickly and inexpensively.

DESKTOP PUBLISHING HARDWARE

Hardware for desktop publishing varies with the complexity of the job and the software you intend to run on the system. All systems start with a microcomputer or workstation. To this you add a variety of peripheral equipment to improve speed, function, and capacity. Figure 6.5 shows a typical desktop publishing equipment configuration. In this example, the equipment configuration makes use of a variety of input and output functions. Input devices digitize hard-copy information or facilitate transfer of computer files. In this case, prepress processing is accomplished in two stages: the preliminary stage is performed on a Macintosh SE. (Typically, a design department will have a number of these lower-cost computers, one at each designer's workstation.) Hard copy is produced on a LaserWriter for intermediate checking. Output is then produced on a Mac II equipped with a faster processor and more memory to efficiently handle proper processing of the large graphics files. Final output (digital or hard copy) is produced on a high-resolution printer or color separator, which provides professional-quality reproduction on photographic paper.

Computers

The basic computer for desktop publishing is a microcomputer or workstation equipped with 2 MB or more of random access memory (RAM). Some will incorporate a coprocessor to speed up operations with large graphics files.

Mass Storage Devices

These devices provide permanent memory for your document, graphics, and text files. The devices include hard disk drives, floppy disks, removable hard disk storage devices (such as Bernouli drives), and optical disks (laser CDs).

Monitors

Many types of monitors are available, depending on your needs and budget. The simplest and least expensive are monochrome monitors. As you go up in expense, you add color and larger size screens. At the most expensive end, you work with two monitors: one shows a full spread (facing pages) in page white (black type on a white background) or color, while the second shows your program menu choices.

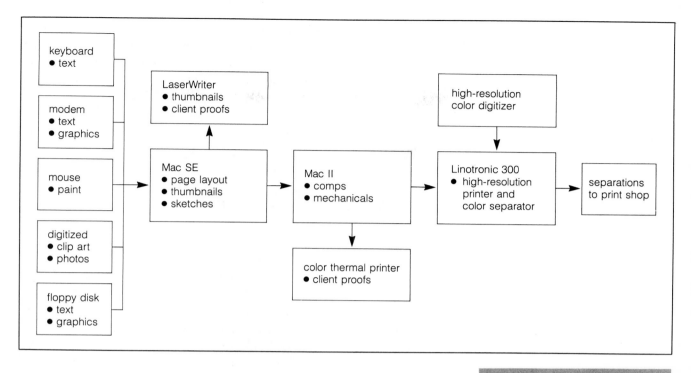

FIGURE 6.5

Example of typical desktop publishing equipment configuration.

Printers

Computer printers use one of three basic methods of generating hard copy: dot matrix and inkjet printers for low-to-medium resolution (300 DPI or less), laser printers for medium-to-high resolution (300 to 600 DPI), and photographic printers for typeset-quality resolution (over 1100 DPI).

With dot matrix printers, you can choose an extremely low-resolution 9-pin model where you can easily see the individual dots with your eye. A 24-pin dot matrix printer has a lot more dots, so the letters begin to closely approach typewriter type, although specialized fonts for professional typeset output still appear ragged. Individual dots are quite evident in graphics output. Dot matrix printers are good for printing and proofing text generated with a word-processing program.

The second method of printing uses laser printers that can print combined text and graphics at medium-to-high resolution. Higher-cost laser printers incorporate extra circuit boards that provide the ability to handle PostScript files—computer output encoded with a special page description language. Laser printers are often used to make proof copies before sending the job to a computer typesetter or to produce the final mechanical for reproduction copying on an office duplicator.

The highest-quality printer generates what is called typeset-quality output. The hard copy is produced on photographic paper or film negatives to maintain a high level of resolution, and type and graphics appear as they would in a magazine (see Figure 6.6).

Additionally, there are color thermal printers that produce proof copies of color pages. In this case, the color usually will not exactly match the

FIGURE 6.6

Three levels of resolution. (a) Low-resolution hard copy from the dot matrix printer is used for word processing mauscript text and rough page proofs. (b) Medium-resolution hard copy from a laser printer at 300 dots per inch (DPI) allows a wider choice of fonts and is used for office photocopy reproduction and client proofs. (c) High-resolution hard copy is produced on photographic paper at 1100 DPI or more and is sent to a print shop for professional-quality publication.

a

b

c

final printing ink colors, but the basic differentiation of red, blue, yellow, and black helps in visualizing how the final page will look.

Desktop Scanners

Desktop scanners generally come in three basic configurations: hand-held, sheet-fed, and flatbed. With a hand-held scanner, you pass a device slightly larger than a mouse across the document. With a sheet-fed scanner, you insert the paper with the illustration you want copied into a slot and the scanner reads the graphic and generates a digital computer file. Flatbed scanners work the same way, but they scan through a piece of glass and allow reproduction from art mounted on illustration board or books that won't run through a sheet-fed scanner. Low-end scanners generate files with fewer gray scale levels, while higher-end scanners have increased gray scale levels for improved tonality. Working in tandem with scanners are special software programs that let you edit gray scales. Other software can read typewritten text, or equivalent-sized typeset fonts, for use with word processors.

Retouchers

These are expensive ($50,000 and up) graphic computer stations that allow very precise graphic editing (sometimes called dot etching) and creation of color separations using a computer instead of a print shop camera.

Other Input Devices

Other graphics input devices include digitizing pads and tablets, mice, and video cameras (see Chapter 3).

DESKTOP PUBLISHING SOFTWARE

The primary software used in desktop publishing is for page layout and design. In addition, other software is used for vector drawing, painting, word processing, clip art, image processing, typesetting, and three-dimensional modeling.

Page Layout Software

Called desktop publishing programs, this software is used for electronic layout and design. With it you can import and manipulate word-processing and graphic files. You use this software to format pages for printing, including selecting and placing type, hyphenating and justifying text, selecting and sizing graphics and illustrations, paginating, and creating and inserting running heads.

Word-Processing Software

In addition to simply creating manuscript or copy files, all of the paragraph formatting and subheads should be created in the word processor. The file should be proofed and all spelling checked before you import it to the page layout program. With compatible programs (word-processing programs whose features are supported by the page layout software), some formatting will be converted automatically, such as headlines, subheads, boldface, italic, subscript, superscript.

Painting Software

Graphic illustration programs allow creation and editing of illustration material, usually in bit-mapped format, where the dot pattern is fixed so that enlargement reduces resolution. Functions in paint programs are similar to draw programs except you cannot actually rotate or tilt the object, though you can alter perspective. Other features include pixel editing (zoom in, zoom out), scanning in artwork from a video camera, and color manipulation (see Chapter 4).

Drawing Software

Drawing programs help you create and edit illustrations, often in object-oriented format where drawings consist of line and arc segments so that resolution is based on the capability of the output device. Functions in drawing programs include choosing line widths and drawing styles (pen, brush, or airbrush), automatic shape drawing (circles, ovals, squares, and so on), shading areas of the drawing with solids, tints, or fountains (graded tints), texturizing (specialty shading like brickface or plaids), rotating or tilting an object, and copying and duplicating an object (see Chapter 5).

Clip Art Disks

Clip art is a term from the graphic artist's vocabulary describing books full of illustrations that artists can clip out and paste on the mechanical. Computer clip art is similar to the printed clip art, except the artwork is supplied on a floppy disk in a file format that can be imported into page layout programs. Clip art is usually sold by category, such as holidays, business illustrations, people, animals, and so forth. With purchase of the disk comes the right to use the artwork without violation of copyright laws.

Image-Processing Software

This special purpose software allows extraction of red, green, and blue hues of a color illustration for editing. By controlling the hue, luminosity, and saturation (HLS) components of the picture, the operator can silhouette objects, retouch the illustration, and adjust tonal gradation (see Chapter 4).

Typesetting Software

Typesetting software can be a confusing term because it applies to two different extremes: low end and high end. Low-end typesetting programs are very simple versions of page layout software used for projects that are relatively simple,

COLOR PLATE 1

Color additive process. Like spotlights on a stage, additive colors produce new colors when they overlap. If all three colors overlap, the result is white. Because the elements of each CRT triad are so close together, the perceived effect is the same when seen at a distance even though the elements do not overlap. When pigments are used (associated with painting and printing), a subtractive color process produces black when all three color primaries (yellow, magenta, and cyan) overlap. (Courtesy Seton Hall University.)

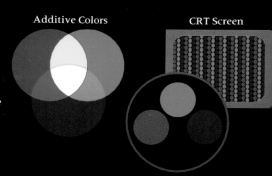

Additive Colors

CRT Screen

COLOR PLATE 2

Hue, lightness (luminosity), and saturation model. In this three-dimensional color model, different hues (colors) can be found around the circumference. Saturation (the amount of color) is shown on the horizontal axis. As colors move toward the center they become gray in appearance. Lightness (luminosity) is shown on the vertical axis. As colors approach the top of the model they become progressively lighter; they become darker as they approach the bottom. (Courtesy Zenographics, Inc., Irvine, Calif.)

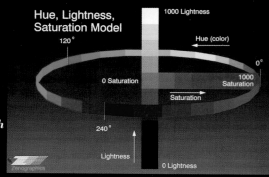

Hue, Lightness, Saturation Model

1000 Lightness

Hue (color)

120°

0°

0 Saturation

1000 Saturation

Saturation

240°

Lightness

0 Lightness

COLOR PLATE 3

Two different color maps for the same image. (Courtesy Paul Murtha, Seton Hall University.)

COLOR PLATE 4

Example of a fractal scene showing fractal-generated mountains, color, and clouds. (Courtesy R/Greenberg Associates, Inc., New York.)

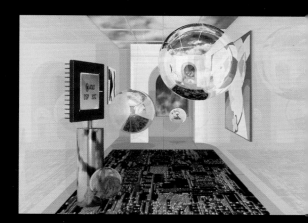

COLOR PLATE 5

Example of photorealistic ray tracing. (Rendered on the AT&T Pixel Machine. Courtesy R/Greenberg Associates, Inc., New York.)

Here's the proof.

Macintosh Plus or SE screen

ImageWriter proof

LaserWriter proof

Macintosh II or other screen

Thermal proof

Pre-film high resolution proof

Separated matched print proof

This brochure was first conceived on an Apple Macintosh Plus, developed on an Apple Macintosh SE, and finally designed and created in color using a Macintosh II and the Lightspeed Color Layout System. For page layout we also used Ready, Set, Go! 4.0 software from Letraset and Aldus Pagemaker 2.0; for retouching - ImageStudio software from Letraset and PixelPaint from SuperMac; for scanning - Datacopy and Howtek; for printouts - ImageWriter, LaserWriter, Linotronic, Mitsubishi and IRIS. The 37" monitor is manufactured by Mitsubishi. The shoe illustration is by Barbara Nessim. Networking was via TOPS and all word processing done on Microsoft Word. Typography was Bitstream ITC Garamond Light and ITC Garamond Light Italic. Original images were scanned on a Crosfield scanner and combined with the digital information from Lightspeed on a SCITEX system with final, high resolution film made by Wy'east Color of Portland, Oregon. Original photography was done by White Light of Bethel, Connecticut. This brochure was printed by Dynagraphics of Portland, Oregon.

Mac proof?

Prove it.

PLATE 6

(a) The front cover (right) uses several color bars that progress from black and white to final printing in color. The back cover (left) identifies the graphic used to capture attention on the front cover.

Prove it every day.

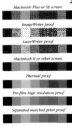

Macintosh SE screen

At Weisz+Yang, we have incorporated technology into our every day working life. We decided to do this brochure as an illustration of the process, and so it was initiated at a Macintosh Plus and developed on an SE. While we set out to do it during regular working hours, being the over-worked people we are, we worked on it when we could – at odd hours whether it be at home or in the office, during lunch or in the late evening. Using our established network, we were able to exchange ideas no matter where, no matter when.

ImageWriter proof

If we must work overtime, at least these days we can do it in the comfort of our own homes. But make no mistake, while the comforts are there, it is still work, and for any number of reasons we must be able to output our ideas. An ImageWriter produces the most cost effective, quick output for roughing out concepts.

LaserWriter proof

Monday mornings can be a confusion of staff meetings, clients and production. While we are tangled in telephone lines, there is great satisfaction in being able to quickly output the past weekend's work on the LaserWriter for a more detailed look at the project. The layouts are also input to our network so that key people can access the progress of the ideas and help them along.

of brochure

Prove it anywhere.

37" monitor in conference room

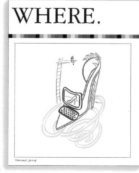

Thermal proof

Designer's screen

Whether it is at the office, in the home, at the designer's desk or in the corporate conference room, Weisz+Yang is using technology to visualize the creative concept. With a remote large screen Macintosh II monitor placed in a client's office, we can send over work-in-progress in "soft" proof form and get the immediate feedback necessary to meet intricate schedules.

Thermal proof

With a color thermal print, we can give clients a "hard" presentation document that replaces the comprehensive traditionally done with markers, color transfers and C-prints. Extra large monitors, (up to 37 inches) give us the scope and the impact to present and exhibit designs. If need be, changes can be effected via the Mac network back in the studio.

c) Moving to color proofs, the "soft-copy" proofs are shown full size on a 37-inch monitor and on a Macintosh II. A color thermal printer supplies hard-copy color proofs.

Prove it with anyone.

FINI!

Thermal proof, concept revision

The creative process is a constant shifting of gears, scanning and thermal proofing give us the chance to visualize changes quickly. That brings us to a juncture, to execute the creative work and begin the production process. Digital information can now produce Linotronic output on paper or film that replicates traditional, black and white, camera-ready mechanicals with all the familiar crop marks, windows for photographs, and type, or, as in the case of this brochure, send our designs directly to pre-press.

Pre-film high resolution proof

Something to look forward to in the immediate future is pre-film, high-resolution, color-separated proofs. In other words, the color information has been separated digitally on disk and the output, your layout, is produced on a single surface color proof.

Separated matched print proof

The next to the last step of the production process is the post-film color match print. This shows original artwork separated and stripped, as well as exact color and placement.

Simple? Yes and no. Yes, the process becomes simpler as insight is gained. But the creation of information, the communication, transportation and translation of that information requires talent, expertise, organization and vision – never easy, nor simple. Rather than the end, we at Weisz+Yang believe we are at the beginning. We've proved that we have all the qualities and resources to go from start to finish. Let us prove it to you!

concept and t
re-film high-res
esy Weisz + 1

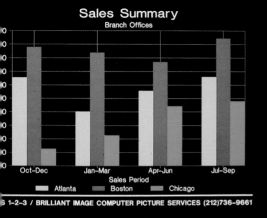

(b)

e created with an off-the-shelf charting program and output on a
lm recorder. (b) The same slide but with a trend line and improved
ound added at the service bureau. (Courtesy Brilliant Image, Inc.,
rk.)

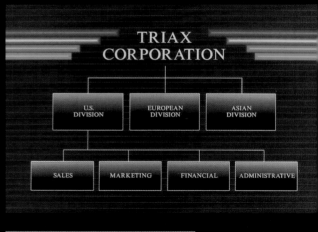

COLOR PLATE 8

Note the continuity of color, background, and design
elements in slides from the same presentation.
(Courtesy Brilliant Image, Inc., New York.)

with minimal graphics—layouts for sprucing up memos, for example. High-end typesetting programs are generally used by professional typesetters where operators key in copy or import word-processing files to generate typeset galleys for pasteup. The high-end programs usually have a very sophisticated hyphenation and justification (H&J) and kerning tables (adjusting the space between individual letters) to produce professional-looking typeset columns.

Three-Dimensional Modeling Programs

Most often used by engineers, artists, and animators, this special software allows creation of three-dimensional shapes, often used for technical illustrations such as cars and equipment parts. Files are imported to page-formatting programs to use as illustrations (see Chapter 5).

SUMMARY

Now you should be familiar with the objective of desktop publishing programs: the formatting of text and graphics for a professional-quality publication. You have learned that one measure of quality is dots-per-inch resolution. You have seen that the major advantage of desktop publishing over other types of prepress operations is its comparative economy, especially in making revisions. The three basic parts of desktop publishing are text creation, graphics creation, and page assembly. You have been introduced to the hardware and software elements that are used in this process. In the next chapter you will see how to operate a desktop publishing program step by step and how this new electronic method of layout and design compares with the manual method of composition.

Exercises

1. Go to your school desktop publishing laboratory or electronic newsroom and make a list of all the hardware, designating it as an input, processing, or output device.

2. Read the documentation for the desktop publishing program.

3. Contact a local design studio and ask for a tour.

4. Review the graphics files available for use in your laboratory. What programs are they compatible with? What conversion programs are available for incompatible formats?

5. Download a graphics file from a local bulletin board, and use it to illustrate text in a desktop publishing.

Bibliography

Desktop Publishing. "On Becoming a Desktop Publisher," *Product Demonstration and Tutorial Videotapes.* San Jose, Calif.: The Computer Show Network, 1988.

GA MacWEEK's Graphic Arts Supplement. San Francisco: MacWeek, Inc., 1988.

Lem, Dean Phillip. *Graphics Master.* Los Angeles: Dean Lem Associates, 1974.

Chapter Seven

THE

PREPRESS

PROCESS

To best understand the prepress process, it is helpful to know something about traditional print production. The term *traditional print production* is used to describe the essentially manual process of preparing mechanicals for brochures, newsletters, flyers, and annual reports. By understanding manual prepress and computerized prepress, you will be in a better position to evaluate, judge, and use each desktop publishing enhancement as it comes along. To begin reviewing this process, let's look at the various disciplines and talents involved in prepress operations.

TRADITIONAL PREPRESS CRAFTS

As a publication goes through the prepress process, there are various disciplines involved that contribute to the project, each requiring special skills. An individual using a desktop publishing program should have a good idea not only of the separate skills involved but also of how those skills are used to produce the final document, as discussed below.

Designers Create the Format

The designer is responsible for the creative concept, strategy, and overall look of the piece and is usually a graduate of a design school with many years of experience. The designer's continuing challenge is to supply an exciting and different solution to the design problem—within the client's budget.

Copywriters Create the Text

The copywriter's job starts with the client's input, which can include an outline, previous versions of the piece, competitive literature, draft copy, and account executive's notes. This information is sometimes supplemented with special research. The copywriter will usually participate in the creative strategy and is then responsible for creating copy in user terminology that effectively communicates the benefits and features of the product or service. The copywriter's continuing challenge is to coherently organize the material and make the text lively, interesting, and readable.

Art Directors Implement the Format Concept

The art director is responsible for implementing, if not originating, the design concept by creating a comp (comprehensive layout). The comp will show—page by page—the size, cropping, and position of photographs and illustrations; size and position of headlines; amount and placement of text; and location of any design elements such as rules and blocks of colors. The art director is also responsible for specifying the type on the copy sent to the typographer and contracting and directing outside talent such as photographers, artists, and retouchers. For the art director, the continuing challenge is maintaining the graphic look throughout the publication, in spite of too much or too little copy for a section, too few or too many illustrations, or disparate art, photographs, and illustrations.

Typesetters Produce Camera-Ready Text

The typesetter is responsible for operating the typesetting equipment that produces the type. The typesetter is given spec'd (pronounced "specked") copy—that is, copy with notes specifying the font style, justification, and leading (line spacing) for each paragraph, headline, and subhead. The typesetter's continuing challenge is accuracy. Good typesetters will also proof for spelling, raise questions regarding grammar and punctuation, and read through material for general sense.

Pasteup Artists Assemble the Graphics and Type

The pasteup artist is responsible for production of the page artwork, or mechanical, that will be sent to the print shop. After collecting the type from the typesetter, photographs from the photographer, and artwork from the illustrator, the pasteup artist will physically cut and paste every piece in proper position on ⅛-inch-thick white cardboard called illustration board. Physical accuracy to hundredths of an inch is the pasteup artist's continuing challenge.

Illustrators Create Artwork

The illustrator is responsible for producing artwork in a certain style to be used as illustrations in the publication. The artwork can be graphs, special art treatment of headlines or logos, product illustrations, industrial process illustrations, or simple illustrations of houses, landscapes, and people. Illustrators, sometimes called commercial artists, face the continuing challenge of creating a quality illustration within a narrow time frame. Since the illustrator is usually selected for a particular style, ability is usually not the question. More often it's the deadline for the job that puts significant pressure on the illustrator.

Photographers Take Pictures

The photographer is responsible for producing a high-quality photograph, usually with the composition, lighting, and background ideas already specified by the art director. For photographers, working under pressure is the continuing challenge. Often there is only a single opportunity to take the photograph—owing to the model's schedule, location limitations, or timing—so there is only one chance to get the shot and to get it right.

Photo Retouchers Fine-Tune Photographs

The photo retoucher is responsible for enhancing, sometimes fixing, or changing the tonality of sections of the photograph. The work is usually performed using an airbrush or by painting on an enlargement of the photograph. Typical assignments include eliminating background clutter, adding highlights to products, softening shadows, and toning down highlights that are too bright. In retouching, the continuing challenge is knowing when enough is enough and producing the retouched photograph within a limited time frame. Often retouchers are called in when the photograph is not up to standard, an extra step not usually accounted for in the original production schedule.

Account Executives Manage the Project

The account executive (AE) is the project manager who oversees the complete job. This person is from the creative services department or design agency and supervises the job, interfaces with the client, assigns tasks, and tracks production. The AE usually has strong experience in the graphics industry (advertising, creative services, or publishing) and a background in either design or copywriting. For the account executive, the continuing challenge in the beginning is helping the client clarify thinking about the purpose of the piece and gathering sufficient information so the copywriter and art director can do an effective job. After the job is underway, the continuing challenge for the AE is to maintain the client's goodwill in spite of any obstacles that may occur during the production process.

PAPER AND INK: WORKING WITH LITHOGRAPHERS

The mechanicals and artwork that you give to a lithographer or print shop are black and white, even if your publication is to be printed in a different color; the lithographer's ink provides the color. It is important to understand how your black-and-white mechanicals are made into printing plates, because the process will change depending on whether you have line art, flat-tone images, or continuous-tone images to reproduce.

Line art is everything that appears in a solid color in your publication. It usually includes the type, headlines, rules, and sometimes the illustrations. In a two-color publication, the line art that is to appear in the second color is noted on a tissue paper overlay to the mechanical. At the print shop, two duplicate negatives are made from your mechanical, one for each color. On each negative, any part that is not to appear in that color is cut away or opaqued. Starting with exact duplicate negatives helps assure proper *registration* (that is, precise color alignment) when your job is on the press. Often with desktop publishing programs, you can provide separations (that is, a printout for each color) that include special registration marks for proper press alignment.

A flat tone, sometimes called a tint or Ben Day, is a shade of the solid ink—either black or a color. The lithographer creates a flat tone by photographing the image with a special lens that breaks the solid area into tiny dots. Light blue, for example, can be derived from dark blue ink to add visual variety to your publication. On your mechanical, the area to be shaded appears as solid black, but a note on a tissue overlay specifies the percent tint you want: a 20 percent tint is very light, a 50 percent tint is medium, and an 80 percent tint is dark. 100 percent is the solid ink color. Often with the shading menu option in desktop publishing programs, you can specify flat-tone tints, as well as several shading patterns, thus saving this step at the print shop.

A halftone is used to reproduce a photograph on a printed page and is different from a photograph from your local camera store. A black-and-white photographic print contains a continuous range of tonality, from very light (white) to very dark (black). However, a printing press cannot produce a continuous range of tonality; it can only apply or not apply ink to certain areas to create an image. Just as a light is either on or off, a spot on the paper either has ink or it doesn't; there is no gray in between. With only one color to work with, a lithographer creates an optical illusion of gray tones by rephotographing the original image through a halftone screen that converts the image to thousands of tiny dots. Smaller dots produce lighter tones; larger dots produce darker tones; mixing small and large dots results in a photograph. You can see these individual dots in a newspaper comic strip; to see the dots in a magazine, look at a shaded area with a magnifying glass (the printer's term is *loupe*). Some desktop publishing programs can supply halftone screens, thus allowing your printout to be processed by the print shop as line art, saving both time and money. Reproduction of color photographs is achieved the same way, except that four plates are made in a subtractive color process, one each for yellow, magenta, cyan, and black (as is done in four-color process printing).

If you are using continuous-tone scanned images in your document, two factors must be considered: the gray-scale level and the dots per inch (DPI) specified when scanning the image. Like a lithographer's halftone, your scanner segments the continuous-tone image into tiny dots. But where the lithographer's halftone registers the varying shades of gray with varying size dots, your scanner creates a digital halftone that registers varying levels of gray within uniform size dots. The number of gray levels available to you depends on your hardware and software configuration, but essentially the more levels of gray the better the image quality. In addition to levels of gray, you can specify the scanning rate in DPI, usually based on the DPI capability of your output printing device (300 DPI for laser printers). Remember that the DPI measure-ment from your computer's printing device is not equivalent to the lines-per-inch (LPI) measurement at your lithographer.

To simplify production and to assure the best possible reproduc-tion quality of halftone images, many desktop publishers send the original photograph with the mechanical to the print shop to be screened and stripped in on the negative. Where the halftone is to be supplied in position, a general rule is to use a 50 LPI screen for 300 DPI output and a 90 LPI to 150 LPI screen for higher resolu-tion 1270 DPI output.*

---

* For a more detailed discussion on the rela-tionship between traditional and digital half-tones, see "Amazing Grays," by Richard Jantz, *Publish Magazine* 3, no. 8 (August 1988), and Aldus Pagemaker (Version 3.0) Technical Manual (Seattle, Wash.: Aldus), 2–15.

Resolution of halftone images is defined in lines per inch (LPI), which refers to the number of rows of dots imposed by the halftone screen. News-papers generally use a relatively coarse 85 LPI screen because the ink tends to spread slightly when it hits the newsprint. Magazines, printed on glossy paper, can take advantage of a higher 133 LPI to 150 LPI screen (see box 7.1).

STEPS IN PRINT PRODUCTION

Let's look at the prepress process and identify where savings can be made through the use of desktop publishing techniques. This example will track the prepress development of an advertising brochure. Imagine that the pres-ident of Travelong, Inc., a regional corporate travel agency, wishes to have a brochure to use for mailing to prospective clients. It is envisioned that this brochure will cover several of the following topics:

- ▸ The extensive travel experience of the staff in managing travel and accommodations plus on-the-road experience.
- ▸ Verification by outside auditors that the fees charged for tickets are the lowest possible.
- ▸ The experience and assistance Travelong can provide corporations in developing their travel policies.

- ▸ Seminars and training assistance that Travelong provides the corporate travel arrangers at client organizations.
- ▸ Fully computerized operations that provide complete, detailed management reports for clients.

For this sales brochure, the president is initially thinking of an 8½ × 11-inch document of eight pages. It would be printed on two sides of two 11 × 17- inch sheets of paper, folded in the middle, then saddle stitched (stapled in the fold to make a booklet). The production process will be described as though the company had a creative services department, although the functions would be similar if an outside design shop or advertising agency were used.

The development of this solicitation brochure goes through three stages: concept development, prepress, and printing. Desktop publishing is most directly involved in the second stage of prepress: streamlining the process, improving opportunities for visual review, and allowing for any changes to be made along the way on a more cost-effective basis.

Stage 1: Concept Development

Concept development is the planning process for the publication and is important equally in manual and computerized methods of prepress. In this stage there are no significant savings in using a desktop publishing program. Clear and careful planning is an often-overlooked area in publication development, yet planning significantly impacts the final content and cost.

1. *Client assembles information.* The president, whom we will call the client, has determined that the organization needs a sales brochure. The president gathers appropriate information, including Travelong, Inc., background; a description of the facility; ideas and suggestions from the sales staff; original photographs that are available; and brochures from competitive companies. At this point, the more information gathered, the better. Time involved: 3 days.

2. *Client meets with creative services manager.* After all the information is assembled, the president arranges to meet with the creative services manager to initiate the project and explain the type of brochure desired and the target audience. To develop the most effective piece, a key question to be answered is: What is the brochure expected to accomplish? Should the reader be expected to take action by phoning for more information? Should the reader simply come away with a good feeling about the company? The more focused and single-minded the objective, the more effective the publication will be. In this case the president has decided that in order to get the most mileage from the brochure, the basic intent will be to provide a good feeling about the company.

   The creative services manager, who usually is responsible for many jobs for various departments throughout the company, first wants to make sure the assignment from the president is clearly understood. The discussion will probably include purpose and intent of the brochure, quantity required, ball-park costs, timing, number of pages, quality of printing, type of paper stock, number and type of illustra-

FIGURE 7.1

Sketchpad with thumbnail sketches. (Courtesy Calibre Five, Inc., Landing, N.J.)

tions, photographs (whether they exist or whether a photographer must be scheduled), information about the target audience, and so forth. Time involved: 1 day.

3. *Creative strategy is established with the designer and copywriter.* The creative services manager returns to the creative services department and meets with the designer and copywriter to explore alternatives and decide on a creative strategy for the job. The design ideas are first considered using thumbnail sketches, matchbook-size sketches where headlines, graphics positions, and text can be quickly blocked out (see Figure 7.1). The discussion starts with the mechanical basics: number of pages, illustrations desired, and style format. Next, the discussion moves to strategic considerations: headline concepts, basic copy points, and subjects to be covered per page. Finally, the aesthetic characteristics are delineated: typeface alternatives, illustration treatment (for example, line art, mezzotint, pen-and-ink sketch, wash drawings).

For this project, the creative team has devised four general concepts: "Travelong, for the Compleat Traveler," which emphasizes full-service capabilities; "Comprehensive Travel Management," which emphasizes complete control of ticketing, budget, and reports; "Travelong, the Way to Go," which focuses service and amenities, and "Travelong, the Professionals," which supports the trust relationship. These four general concepts provide four different directions for the style and content of the brochure. In this case, the second concept is selected as the creative strategy because it most nearly meets the intent of the brochure: to give the reader a good feeling about the company's philosophy. Time involved: 1 day.

Stage 2: Prepress Operations

So far there has been no difference between the manual and electronic prepress process, although thumbnails could have been produced with a desktop publishing program. During this next stage of development, you will begin to see a variation between the manual and electronic prepress process (as identified by **a** and **b** parts to the function; part **a** describes the manual process, and part **b** describes the electronic process).

1. *Copy and layout are developed.* All the information supplied by the client and the basic creative strategy are given to the copywriter and designer. The copywriter reviews the information and highlights everything significant to the creative strategy. Next the information is organized, and the copywriter drafts text for the brochure. This is the copy and includes full text, headlines, subheadlines, and parenthetical notes describing illustrations and photographs. Working from the creative strategy, the copy developed by the copywriter and the photographs supplied by the president, the designer develops a comp, a comprehensive layout or rendering of what the brochure or page will look like. The designer will often use a grid pattern, an underlying general format of the brochure. The first difference between the manual process and the desktop publishing process occurs at this step, as we can see when we compare manual and computer layout development in 1a and 1b.

   a. *Layout and design are done manually.* The designer uses felt-tip markers to render a full-color comprehensive layout of what the brochure will look like. Headlines are hand drawn in the recommended typeface, text is rendered with parallel lines indicating size and leading, and sketches show how the illustrations and photographs will look (see Figure 7.2). Time involved: 4 days (copy, 2 days; comp, 2 days).

   b. *Layout and design are done on the computer.* Using a desktop publishing program, the designer creates a page format and tells the program how many pages will be needed. The general page format (called style or style sheet in some programs) defines the columns, running heads that appear on each page, page numbers—all the elements that give overall visual continuity and personality to the publication. The master pages normally set up the typestyle codes for text, headlines, and subheadlines, which are selected in conjunction with the type of printer being used. With many desktop publishing programs, the designer will perform most of these operations from point-and-click menus using a mouse (see Figure 7.3).

   With the overall page format in place, the designer next retrieves and formats the graphics and illustrations (see Figure 7.4). With a scanner, photographs and artwork are digitized and saved as individual computer files. Once imported into the electronic layout and design program, these illustrations are cropped, sized, and positioned within the pages of the brochure. If commissioned photographs or artwork are to be used, surrogates are substituted at this point, pending final approval of the document before additional expense is incurred.

   Now the designer retrieves the text files. The text files created by the copywriter on a word-processing program are now imported

FIGURE 7.2

Hand-drawn comps showing what the Travelong brochure might look like.

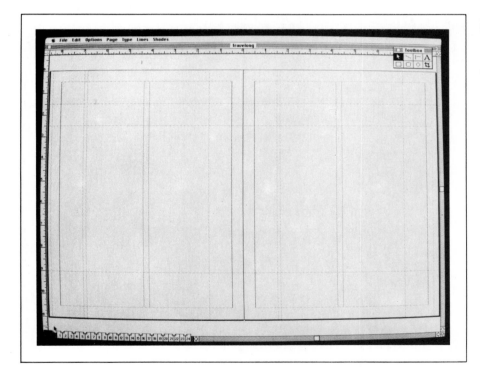

FIGURE 7.3

Grid pattern. The initial grid pattern, or style sheet, establishes the vertical margins and column widths. The horizontal lines establish the top and bottom margins and positions for consistent placement of graphics and text paragraphs.

to the desktop publishing program. If the page format instructions do not specify the typesize and style, these instructions are selected from menu options, or typesetting codes are added to the text. In many programs, the text will flow into the document column by column, page by page (see Figure 7.5).

The designer now previews the document on the screen and makes any adjustments required—starting new articles on a new page, adjusting hyphenation, and resizing photographs or illus-

FIGURE 7.4

Basic graphic elements, photographs, headlines, illustrations, and graphs are positioned on the page using the grid. At least two sides of each graphic element are positioned on a grid line. Other sides are cropped or allowed to bleed, adding variation while conforming to the overall layout style.

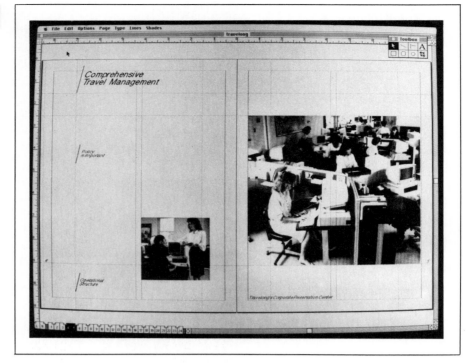

FIGURE 7.5

Text is added to the page. Note the flush-right position of the caption for the lower left photograph; the short text is now graphically associated with the photograph it describes, providing a visual signpost for following the designer-intended reading pattern.

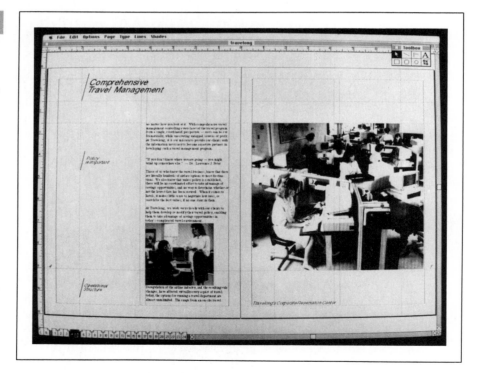

trations. Text and typeface adjustments are made for headlines, subheads, photo captions, index, and footnotes. Time involved: 4 days (copy, 2 days; comp, 2 days)—about the same as the manual process.

FIGURE 7.6

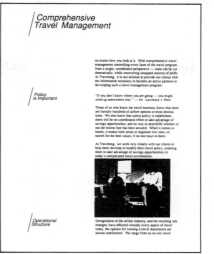

a   b

Comparison of (a) a hand-drawn comp with (b) a computer comp.

Figure 7.6 compares hand-drawn and computer comps. Note the differences between the hand-drawn comp and the output from the desktop publishing program. In the hand-drawn comp, the graphic elements of the layout are sketched: headlines are finely rendered, text is shown with lines, and photos and illustrations are symbolized with vignettes. In this case, the desktop publishing comp was printed on a laser printer with a resolution of 300 DPI. Here the headlines not only appear typeset, but the copy is in position, the photographs are in place, and the type is close to reproduction quality. Preparing a computer or hand-drawn comp may take equally long, but revisions of a computer comp can be done in minutes, which is not true for the hand-drawn comp.

2. *Creative services manager reviews the full copy and the comp with the president.* The creative services manager presents the copy and comp to the client to show what the brochure will say and how it will look. This is the president's last opportunity to make any changes on a cost-effective basis—that is, before any significant expenditures for art, typography, and photography are incurred.

In this example, the president has some suggestions that require a revision of the copy and layout. It is decided to expand the brochure to 12 pages to incorporate information on the company's new corporate meetings division. Time involved: 1 day.

3. *Copy and comp are revised.* With this additional information from the president, the creative services manager again meets with the copywriter and designer to review the necessary revisions. The copywriter adds the copy sections on the new corporate meetings services and then edits the other sections to provide continuity of thought. Time involved: 1 day (for copy revision).

It is in the updating of the comp that a major difference occurs between the manual process and the desktop publishing process. In 3a and 3b manual and computer revision processes are compared.

    a. *Comp is revised manually.* Since the brochure is on a rush schedule and the revisions were not provided for in the original production schedule, instead of spending two days for a new hand-drawn comp, the designer opts for a tissue instead. (A tissue is a brief sketch on tracing or tissue paper showing the revised position of the graphic elements.) Time involved: less than 1 day.

    b. *Comp is revised on the computer.* Since the page format is in place, all that is needed is to scan in any new graphic elements, retrieve the revised copy, and make a new, complete printout of the layout on the laser printer. Here the real advantages of desktop publishing begin to take effect. Time involved: A few hours.

4. *Revision is approved by the president.* Again, the creative services manager meets with the president to review the updates to the copy and layout, and agreement is reached to proceed. Thus far in the production process, the creative services department has incurred no outside costs, unless a photograph or commissioned artwork is needed. All prepress work to date has been performed in house.

5. *Creative services proceeds with the mechanical.* It is now the responsibility of the creative services department to produce camera-ready art to give to a print shop. Camera-ready art, or a mechanical, is photoreproduction-quality artwork, usually provided on illustration board (white ⅛-inch cardboard). The print shop uses the mechanical to make the printing plates.

Any outside services are now retained if needed. If commissioned illustrations are called for, the illustrator is given the data that will appear in any charts, along with pencil sketches of the overall design of the illustrations. The illustrator then creates each illustration on a separate piece of illustration board. The photographer is given a pencil sketch of the photographs to be taken and a shoot is scheduled, models lined up, and props arranged. The designer will normally plan to attend and supervise the shoot. The photographs produced will usually be 8 × 10-inch prints for black-and-white pictures and 35mm format slides, or larger, for color. In 5a and 5b we'll compare manual and computer layout development at this stage, excluding, for this example, any time required for outside services.

    a. *The mechanical is prepared manually.* This portion of the manual process is called cut-and-paste, because a pasteup artist will physically paste the elements in position on the illustration board. For the manual process, respective tasks are assigned to the typesetter, illustrator, and art director. Type from the typesetter, supplied in the form of galleys (long strips of text on photographic paper), is proofed by the copywriter and then given to the pasteup artist. The pasteup artist cuts the galleys into appropriate sections and pastes the sections on illustration board in print position. Photostats (high-contrast black-and-white photographic copies of illustrations) are made to the proper size and pasted in position.

FIGURE 7.7

Paste-up artist at work at a drafting table, using a printer's pica ruler, T square, dividers, and triangles for accurate alignment. (Photo courtesy Calibre Five, Inc., Landing, N.J.)

Screened veloxes (black-and-white photographic copies of photographs) are also made and pasted in position. Every piece of type, every photograph, and every illustration must now be positioned exactly as it will appear in final print (see Figure 7.7). Time involved: 4 days (typesetting and proofing, 2 days; pasteup, 2 days).

b. *The mechanical is prepared on the computer.* With the desktop publishing program, all or most of this work has already been done. Rather than send out for commissioned artwork, some or all of it can be done on the desktop computer. If photographs are taken, they are scanned in. For medium resolution quality (300 DPI), laser printer output is sufficient for a print shop. For higher-quality publications, photographs may be sent with the mechanical to be stripped in by the print shop. Or, if a high-resolution scanner and printer are available, the output from the printer, incorporating both text and photographs, can be sent to the print shop. Time involved: 1 day.

Now the mechanical is complete (see Figure 7.8). The full brochure is set in type with illustrations in place, all arranged with each two-page spread on a separate board. The mechanical is then sent to the printer to be used to make negatives for printing.

FIGURE 7.8

Completed mechanical (two-page spread).

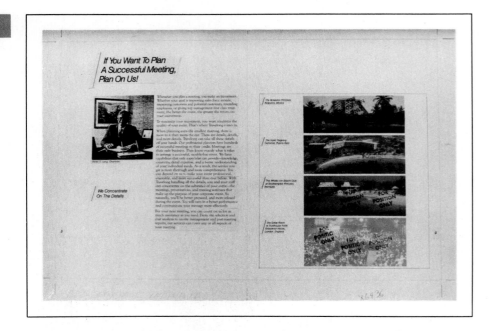

Notice that with the desktop publishing program, three days have been saved in production. In manual production, there are typesetting costs and costs for photostats and veloxes. If errors are found in the galleys, paragraphs will need to be reset, requiring an additional trip back and forth to the typesetter (usually a rush). With desktop publishing, the copy is not rekeyed, so the likelihood of error is minimal. Since a digital typesetter produces the illustrations and photographs in place, there is a cost savings in photostats and veloxes. Desktop publishing has advantages in time and cost savings.

6. *Final approval is obtained from the president.* All the completed elements of the job—mechanicals with type in place, separate boards with illustrations and photographs—are reviewed with the president. The complete job is also proofed again, and every detail is double-checked, since this is the last opportunity to make changes before the brochure goes to the print shop.

Stage 3: Printing

While a complete discussion of print shop reproduction of the mechanicals is beyond the intended scope of this text, an understanding of this process is essential to effective prepress operations. You should know what is involved in printing, particularly with regard to timetables.

1. *The creative services manager and designer meet with the printing sales representative.* The completed artwork (see Figure 7.9) and the comp are given to the printer, along with full written or verbal instructions on the production of the brochure, and a production timetable is determined.

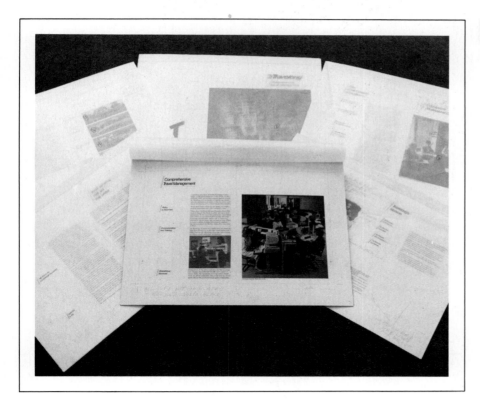

FIGURE 7.9

Mechanical for 12-page booklet. The mechanical is developed in page pairs: 12 and 1, 2 and 3, 4 and 5, 6 and 7, 8 and 9, and 10 and 11. In the final assembled booklet, pages 6 and 7 are called the center spread—one continuous sheet of paper.

2. *The brochure is put into production.* The sales representative puts the brochure into production at the print shop. Paper is ordered from the paper supplier. The mechanicals and artwork are sent to the camera room for stripping. This is another cut-and-paste function; the mechanicals and line illustrations are photographed in line format, simple black-and-white (even if it is to appear in color in the brochure). Black-and-white photographs are sized and screened using a special lens that breaks photographs into tiny dots to allow printing. The result are halftones. Color separations in cyan, yellow, magenta, and black (hence the term *four-color process*) are made for any color photographs or illustrations. Now all the negatives, each the correct size with appropriate screen, are combined in a stripping process to produce the plate negative (see Figure 7.10). A separate negative and printing plate are required for each color ink to be printed. Some printers use sophisticated scanning equipment to make their plate negatives.

3. *The printer supplies a blueline.* A copy of the printer's plate negative is made on special photosensitive paper that produces a blue image. Called a blueline, or blue, this proof copy is an assembled version of the brochure, with all photographs and illustrations shown exactly as they will appear in the final printed version. The blue is reviewed by the designer and the client for final checking to ensure that the printed brochure matches the specifications and artwork. It is the final step before printing.

4. *The brochure is printed.* With the sign off (final approval) from the client and designer, the plate negatives are used to make the printing

FIGURE 7.10

Stripping in artwork at a print shop. (Courtesy Compton Press, Morristown, N.J.)

plates, and the brochure is put on the press. Sometimes the client and designer will review a press proof, several of the first sheets that come off the press. This is normally done at the print shop, because the printer will hold up the press run until sign off (see Figure 7.11). The brochure is then printed.

5. *The brochure is bound.* The large press sheets are sent to the "guillotine" (paper cutter) to be cut to size. The cut pages are run through a folding machine and then saddle stitched (stapled in the fold). Finally, the finished brochures are bundled, boxed, and shipped to the client, and the job is complete.

YOUR JOB AS A GRAPHIC DESIGNER

As a graphic designer, your responsibilities in the area of desktop publishing could fall in several areas: illustration, drawing, presentation graphics, or page formatting with a desktop publishing program (see Figure 7.12).

If you work with painting and drawing programs, you will most likely have a designers workstation and will work from thumbnails created with a page layout program. You will receive instructions from the art director as to subject matter and execution style, as developed during the conceptualization process for the document. You might need to refine scanned-in photographs or illustrations. Illustrations created with a CAD program, such as architectural renderings, may need tints added, lines or text removed, or borders emphasized. You might develop illustrations using three-dimensional modeling programs. Imported graphics from clip art programs need to be tailored to the

Checking the press proof at the printer. (Courtesy Compton Press, Morristown, N.J.)

Graphic designer operating an Autoprep 5000, a high-end vector system for creating rules and solids. (Courtesy Compton Press, Morristown, N.J.)

design style of your publication. However, instead of using felt-tip markers, you use a mouse and computer screen. Instead of pens, rulers, brushes, and press-on type, you use their electronic equivalents. Instead of a large, cluttered design table, you work at a much smaller computer workstation. And instead of producing finished art, your output, in most cases, is data sent to the page layout program.

Or you may work directly with the page layout program and have responsibility for layout and design of the publication as well as the illustrations that go in it. Here you will generate the conceptual thumbnails, format pages on screen, import the text and graphics files, and probably work with clients.

THE CHALLENGE OF DESKTOP PUBLISHING

Desktop publishing with microcomputers presents a new and different challenge for the prepress industry. In developing programs for spreadsheets and word processing, designers of software have relatively simple parameters to take into consideration: a single user or discipline to computerize and simple output consideration (such as text printers). The first challenge in desktop publishing, however, is to integrate as well as computerize multiuser or multidiscipline operations (such as copywriting, page design, typesetting, illustration, retouching, and so on). Early software (1.0-type versions) addressed these disciplines individually, relying on the desktop publishing program to allow for convenient integration. Later desktop publishing programs (2.0- and 3.0-type versions) have begun to integrate these functions into one program.

The second challenge in desktop publishing is to address the various output choices. This problem is further compounded by the difference in screen display and printed output. The codes used to control print output are different from the codes used to represent type and graphics on the screen. Thus, to develop a good WYSIWYG program, two completely different text and graphic codes are required; one for the monitor and the other for the printer. Further, different printers require different codes. The output sent to a dot matrix printer is different from the codes sent to a laser printer. These codes will also vary between printer manufacturers. The result is that users are asked to specify the printer model before beginning a desktop publishing program job. In many cases, this can limit typeface choices, page design alternatives, graphics style, and resolution. Thus, the output of the desktop publishing program is often dependent on your printer.

For the near future, the challenge for the desktop publishing program operator or designer is learning computer skills. Trading in the felt-tip marker for a mouse is not simply a matter of changing tools; it means learning new skills to accomplish many of the same tasks. But the benefits in speed, accuracy, and flexibility make the effort worthwhile.

SUMMARY

In this chapter you have been introduced to the prepress crafts—design, copy, layout, illustration, photography, management—and the challenges involved in producing a professional-quality publication. You have also seen how a publication evolves through three stages: (1) concept development, in which a strategy is devised to solve the client's communication problem within budget; (2) prepress operations, in which the concept is implemented: the publication is written and designed and camera-ready copy is produced; and (3) printing operations at a commercial print shop, in which the camera copy is printed and bound. Finally, you have seen how desktop publishing programs have combined all the prepress crafts into a single, convenient system, in which software and hardware are integrated to supply accurate, attractive output quickly.

Exercises

1. Conduct a 15-minute telephone interview with each of the following about the challenges and opportunities arising from computerization for that particular craft: copywriter, graphic designer, photographer, typesetter, illustrator. (Check your local yellow pages or industrial directory under the appropriate heading.)

2. Arrange for a tour of a local color separations shop that provides services to printers. Ask to see the computerized photo digitizer and retoucher in operation.

3. Draw a picture using your lab's paint program and another using the draw program. Import each picture to your desktop publishing program and resize each print. Explain the difference in operation and output.

4. Go through recent issues of computer and desktop publishing magazines for reviews on paint, drawing, and desktop publishing software, then write a one-page summary about where you think the leading edge of technology is today. What do you think will be the next breakthrough?

Bibliography

Desktop Publishing. "On Becoming a Desktop Publisher," *Product Demonstration and Tutorial Videotapes.* San Jose, Calif.: The Computer Show Network, 1988.

GA MacWEEK's Graphic Arts Supplement. San Francisco: MacWeek, Inc., 1988.

Lem, Dean Phillip. *Graphics Master.* Los Angeles: Dean Lem Associates, 1974.

Parker, Roger. *The Aldus Guide to Basic Design.* Seattle, Wash.: Aldus.

Simone, Luisa. "Power Publishing," *PC Magazine* 7 (December 27, 1988): 89.

Stockford, James, ed. *Desktop Publishing Bible.* Indianapolis, Ind.: Howard W. Sams, 1987.

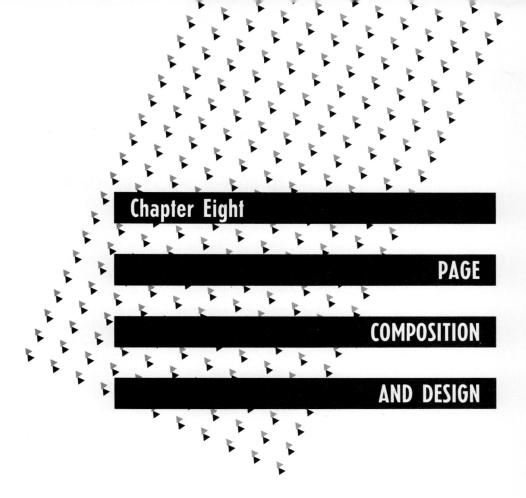

Chapter Eight

PAGE

COMPOSITION

AND DESIGN

During the past 50 years, the dominant philosophy regarding communication design is that its purpose is to facilitate and enhance the communication of information: to emphasize the song, not the singer. This may seem self-evident, but one of the resulting corollaries is that any design that calls attention to itself as opposed to the message is in violation of this philosophy. Thus the highly decorative illuminated manuscripts of the middle ages would not fit this definition, as beautiful as they are.

Following this definition, there are certain concepts covered in design theory that have proven successful in advertising, magazines, manuals, and newsletters. While different visual ideas are pleasing to the eye, good design teaches that what separates the exceptional from the mundane is energy of communication—the power of the design to make the message touch our minds or hearts.

Your layout and design will either complement or impede delivery of the message. Good design not only leads the reader's eye through the message in a logical progression, but it supports and reinforces the content by its style and graphic tone. As Allen Hurlburt, former president of the American Institute of Graphic Arts and well-known author and lecturer on design, notes:

It would be a major error to assume that gaining the attention of the reader represents the end of the exercise. Unless the visual response induces an intellectual or emotional reaction, no true communication has taken place. This is true whether the objective is information or persuasion, and the degree of reaction to the content of the layout will be intensified or reduced by the form and, finally, by the style of its presentation.[1]

TO INFORM, PERSUADE, OR INSTRUCT

There are generally three reasons to publish a document: to inform, to persuade, or to instruct. Newsletters, magazine or newspaper editorials, and analytical reports are used to inform the reader—so the form and style of each page should help the reader easily follow the continuity of the information. Advertising, flyers, posters, and recommendation reports are used to persuade—so the form and style often contrast with the visual environment and are emotionally charged to demand the reader's attention and dramatically present the message. Manuals, some memorandums, and notices are used to instruct—so the form and style should visually reinforce the step-by-step methodology.

To create the appropriate form and style for your publication, you need to effectively straddle both sides of the visual communication problem: what the sender (writer, advertiser, publisher) wants to communicate and what the reader wants to receive (the reader's frame of mind). For example, a reader who picks up a paperback expects, and perhaps relishes, the idea of spending several hours focusing on following the plot. The form and style of paperbacks (except for the cover, which is designed to persuade) continues without interrupting the reader's concentration.

Sometimes the sender's and the reader's intentions are in conflict. In a second example, a magazine advertisement addresses a reader who is either involved in an editorial article or skimming the publication. Here the form and style of the layout uses photographs, dramatic scale of headlines, and color to arrest attention and divert the reader to the advertiser's message.

Senders who do not keep the reader's attitude in mind may never have their message read. Direct mail letters and memos are usually scanned quickly by the reader, who is searching for a reason to take time to read the communication thoroughly. In this case, the form and style often make use of short, hanging paragraphs; highlighted words; and bulleted sentences to help the reader quickly find points of interest. Finally, if you are involved in the design of a corporate magazine, you may employ a different form and style in different sections, depending on whether the purpose of the section is to inform, persuade, or instruct. Also, you would also be concerned with the overall graphic personality and visual continuity of the publication.

All communication design involves problem solving. The challenge in each job is to determine the content of the message to be communicated and the form and style most ideally suited to the reader's frame of mind. This normally involves defining a basic creative concept, which is achieved by reducing the volume of information to a single idea, then searching for a

---

[1] Allen Hurlburt, *Layout: The Design of the Printed Page* (New York: Watson-Guptill Publications, 1977), p. 146.

visual presentation concept to dramatize that idea. The form of the concept supports the specific emotion the designer wants the reader to feel.

The tools available to the designer in achieving this response are first the basic layout form: symmetry conveys a sense of order; asymmetry conveys a sense of tension. Within the layout, the designer can control the balance of basic shapes. Headlines, whose combined letter forms become a unified whole, take on a specific shape and density. Text copy forms gray blocks, rigid squares (in the case of justified copy), or intriguing designs (in the case of unjustified copy). Each photograph and illustration has its own focal point and visual weight. These elements must be combined to achieve visual balance and power on the two-dimensional plane of the page. Elements of the design that call attention to themselves, rather than enhancing the unified message of the piece, detract from the value and energy of the communication. Given visual unity as the objective, there are certain guidelines to be followed.

GENERAL GUIDELINES

Page layouts should be clean, consistent, and welcoming. Hence, use grid patterns to develop consistency in page design. Don't design single pages; instead, design spreads—the two facing pages the reader opens to and initially sees as a unit. Use white space to balance the text and graphics; it lets the reader pause for breath. Be concerned with flow of elements so that the reader's attention is carefully guided through the message. Don't interrupt the reader's concentration by placing graphics within text or decorating the page with blobs of color tints. Use rules (lines) sparingly and only as guides, not as obstacles that impede natural eye movement.

Graphics and illustrations should support the message. Communications design is not art for art's sake. Hence, select or design the illustrations to match the mood of the text. Crop photographs to focus the reader's attention on the salient feature (don't make the reader have to work to understand the message). Size and position the graphics to gently guide the reader through the design. Pictures of people should face or be looking into the page, not out toward the edge of the paper (readers will tend to follow the eyes). Do not use odd polygon-shaped photographs; don't overlap one part of a photograph over another.

Text typography should be easy to read. Keep the number of fonts used to three or fewer. Keep line length under two alphabets, or 50 characters. The longer the line length, the larger the typesize needed. Use upper- and lowercase letters. Keep text type between 8 and 12 points. Don't set text in decorative type; it's too hard to read. The overall feel of the text should look like a smooth 40 to 60 percent gray if you were to squint at the page.

DESIGNING TO INFORM

Use magazine articles for ideas. Note how the lead page of an article uses a large photograph, illustration, or special headline typeface to help the reader quickly understand the benefit of reading the entire article. Usually, benefits fall in one of two major categories: ways to improve an area of life or ways to prevent problems.

Graphic Guidelines

1. Wherever possible, use the full two-page spread to introduce the article.

2. Compose your graphics for the strongest possible dramatic effect. Make use of scale for drama. Use a full-page, or larger, bleed photograph. Leave plenty of white space around the headline and give the headline a graphic treatment.

3. Consider an oversize initial to begin the first paragraph so the reader's eye quickly focuses on the place to start reading.

4. Start the article with only two or three paragraphs, continuing on to another page once you have the reader's attention.

5. Illustrations, graphs, and photographs that illustrate the text can be smaller but should be located on the same page as their reference. Captions should summarize the information (for example, "This chart shows a 50 percent increase in growth over 10 years," not simply "Growth Chart").

Copy Points

1. Write the opening paragraph using word pictures for dramatic effect, thereby reinforcing the advantages to the reader for reading the article.

2. Summarize as you go, pausing every so often to restate the premise and support the logic developed thus far.

3. Provide pointers where the article is continued (for example, "Continued on page 12"), and on page 12, key the follow-up with the headline from the article.

DESIGNING TO PERSUADE

Use magazine advertising and billboards for ideas. Note how a dramatic photograph, illustration, or special headline typeface captures attention. Here again, the initial concept usually focuses on a help or avoidance benefit.

Graphic Guidelines

1. Compose your graphics for the strongest possible dramatic effect. Make use of scale for drama. Use exaggeration—overstatement or understatement—to dramatize your message.

2. Use color to add impact to your message. Reverse (make white) your headline out of a strong color or black. Leave plenty of white space around the headline. Give the headline a graphic treatment. Make

the photograph or art element and the headline a single graphic unit that can be understood as one idea. Often the content of the illustration and the meaning of the headline are in direct conflict, which helps create tension and interest.

3. Be sure the name of the advertiser or sender is prominent. Readers know they are trying to be persuaded, but if they cannot quickly discern the name of the advertiser, they have misgivings and a feeling of distrust.

Copy Points

1. Keep the paragraphs short; even one word is okay. The copy style should be conversational rather than academic, and the layout should reinforce this tonality.

2. Use the second person (you) form of address rather than the third person (they).

3. Provide a call to action and specifically ask the reader to make the decision.

DESIGNING TO INSTRUCT

Use the instruction manuals from top software publishers for ideas. Follow the traditional three steps for effective communication:

Step 1: Tell them what you're going to tell them (introduction and table of contents).

Step 2: Tell them (step-by-step procedures).

Step 3: Tell them what you told them (provide a final checklist and operating test).

Start your publication with a photograph or illustration of the completed project. Text and graphics should work to continually build the self-confidence of the reader. Paginate to coincide with natural pauses in the instructions.

Graphic Guidelines

1. Clarity takes precedence over drama, even over accuracy (feel free to make certain visual relationships larger than actual size to focus on the essential detail).

2. Use color to highlight critical points of your message. Put key messages and reminders in an alternate color or reverse type. Use headline type and white space to provide a clear visual logic to the document.

3. Illustrations, graphs, and photographs that illustrate the text should be located on the same page as their reference. As with messages to inform, captions should summarize the information (for example,

"Attach part A to part B with three round-head #5 screws," not simply "Attaching Part A").

4. Conclude with a photograph or illustration of the completed project.

Copy Points

1. Keep the paragraphs short. The copy style should be businesslike, and the layout should reinforce this tonality.

2. Use the demand form of sentence structure. Rather than being politely asked to do something, the reader wants to be told.

HOW TO IMPROVE YOUR LAYOUTS

To provide an opportunity for you to visualize how these guidelines can improve your layouts, a version of the Travelong brochure has been intentionally designed without following the design guidelines described above (see Figure 8.1). Step by step, we will apply the guidelines to subsequent versions of the brochure so you can see their effects on improving the communication value and power of the layout.

The layout in Figure 8.1 crams text and graphics, with no consideration for the reader. Take a minute to consciously consider how your eye moves in this layout and the feelings you have while trying to understand the message. Your eye bounces around the page, trying to make sense of the design and to find the message. The harder you have to work, the more likely you will be to move on to something else.

Page Layout

By installing a grid pattern, the layout already becomes more organized (see Figure 8.2). Notice how the grid has given the layout a more pleasing unity and how the use of white space makes the piece easier to read.

Graphics

By cropping the photographs to emphasize the central idea and eliminating extraneous areas, pictures become more powerful communicators (see Figure 8.3). By squaring off and eliminating overlaps, photographs become stronger individual visual units. It is also important that the subject's eyes in the photographs don't lead the reader's attention off the page.

Typography

Now we make adjustments to the typefaces. By reducing the number of typefaces to three, the reader has less work adjusting to the changes. Eliminating the decorative text font makes reading easier, so the reader concentrates on the message, not the type. By reducing the line length, we ensure that the reader's eye doesn't accidentally jump lines as it moves across the page. Just

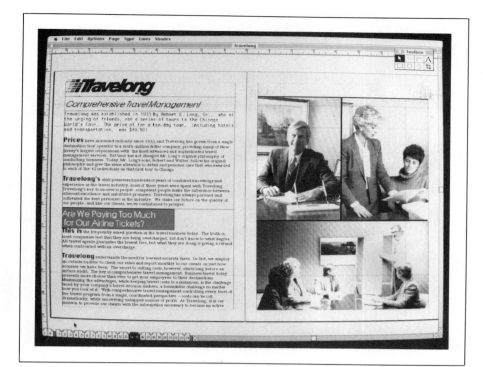

FIGURE 8.1

Travelong brochure page that ignores design guidelines.

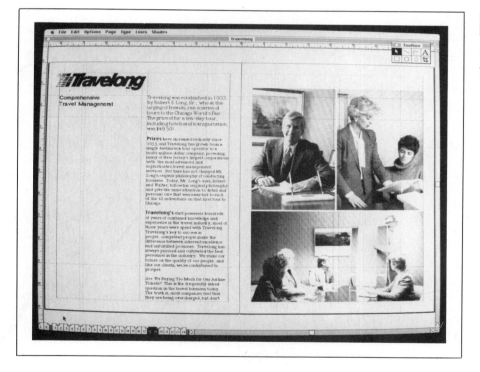

these few changes have improved the communications effectiveness of the page (see Figure 8.4). Keep in mind that the simple guidelines presented here do not constitute all the factors considered by a designer, but they can help you begin to understand the factors of good design.

FIGURE 8.3

Cropping and visually organizing the photographs add to the professional design of the page.

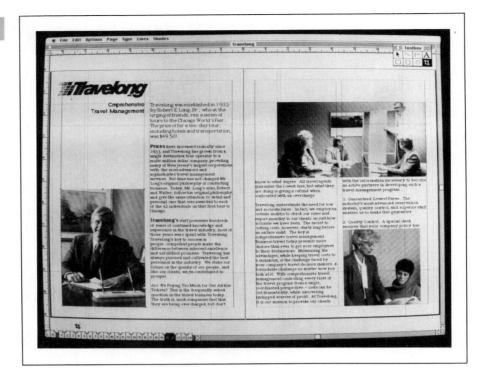

FIGURE 8.4

Fine-tuning for consistent typography completes the makeover.

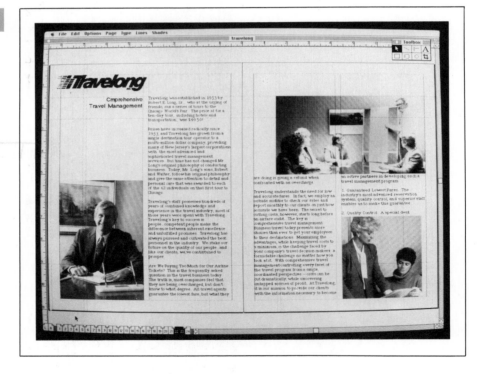

Compare this final revision with the original version. Note how much easier it is to read and especially how the message now seems to "come off the page" at you. Here we have applied only a few basic guidelines but nonetheless have achieved a significant improvement. A top-flight designer would go much further, particularly in the area of emotional tonality, in the use of white space, typeface selection, appropriate color, and graphic rhythm.

CASE STUDY: TOMORROW'S EDGE

To understand how computer graphics are integrated in a business environment, what follows is a case study of Weisz Yang Dinkleberger (WYD) Graphic Designers, a firm located in Westport, Connecticut. The studio is located on Wilton Road overlooking the Saugatuck River near where it flows into Long Island Sound. The studio has 12 employees: four principals, four board artists, a bookkeeper, a secretary, and a receptionist. Their client list includes IBM, GTE, Olivetti, Champion International, ITC Corporation, Seybold Publications, Letraset USA, and Lefkoe & Associates.

WYD has been in the forefront of computer-aided graphic design for a number of years. Tom Weisz, who created design work for IBM for over 16 years, tried to interest them in developing PC input for a Dicomed film recorder in 1981 while working for the ad agency BBDO. He also recommended a program linking all the BBDO offices across the country using this technology and a Scitex printer. It wasn't until 1983, however, three years before Aldus PageMaker came on the market, that an opportunity to really explore desktop publishing was brought about by one of WYD's clients, Champion Paper Company. Although the Champion piece was never printed because of budgetary constraints, this first led WYD to purchase their first desktop publishing system, a PC-based configuration. Because this system was difficult to use, it gathered dust for two years until one of the designers suggested upgrading it. At this point (1986), desktop publishing had moved out of the imagination of early dreamers into the first commercially available versions. Weisz felt it was time to reevaluate the market rather than just add on to the PC-based system. As a result, the firm purchased an Apple Mac Plus system, primarily because it is more designer friendly.

ELECTRONIC LAYOUT AND DESIGN EXAMPLE

WYD has created an eight-page brochure, which is an excellent example of electronic layout and design. It is called "Mac proof? Prove it." and it describes its own development. Since it provides such valuable insight in the process, we'll review it page by page (see Color Plate 6).

Mac Proof? Prove It

This publication is intended to show designers the full capability of desktop publishing programs. The initial problem for a designer is creating an overall concept. Here WYD has developed a concept that is both visually appealing and introduces the basic message to be communicated. They have chosen to illustrate the cover with color bars a designer would recognize from a press proof. The color bar sequence represents the steps in development, starting with the screen, then moving through black-and-white proofs to color proofs and finally to the press proof. Note the increase in resolution and the changes in color tones. Also note the use of white space, which gives the overall graphic size and a sense of dignity and quality. Any larger and the brochure would be too demanding; any smaller, and it would seem an understatement (see Color Plate 6a).

Prove It Every Day

Here the brochure describes its own conceptualization, beginning with a Macintosh SE, next showing an early proof from an ImageWriter, then thumbnails created with the electronic layout and design program. The shoe art, drawn by Barbara Nession, serves as a surrogate for final art in these layouts. Notice the headline reinforces the overall "prove it" theme of the brochure while adding a "daily" aspect to the message. This daily aspect is reinforced by the selection of visuals, which are things designers use every day. The color bars conform to the grid pattern, help the reader differentiate the illustration area from the text area, and establish continuity with the color theme from the cover (see Color Plate 6b).

Prove It Anywhere

With the design in digital form, it can be electronically—even simultaneously—viewed in a number of places. This is the message of the headline and is reinforced with the illustrations displaying the brochure on a 37-inch color monitor in a conference room and on a SuperMac monitor on a designer's desk. Notice the difference between the conference room photograph on the left and the conference room photograph on the monitor at the right. The one on the right, used for layout, is a composite consisting of scanned-in art from a magazine (shown for style and color) plus the screen image drawn in. This composite served as a guide for taking the final photograph you see on the left. Finally, the illustration on the far right represents a thermal proof that allows a hard-copy look at the colors (see Color Plate 6c).

Prove It with Anyone

The left-hand page shows a color thermal proof, while the right-hand page shows the true press proof. (Note the color guide across the top and the crop marks that serve as guides for trimming the page.) Examining the finer points in the design, note that each illustration has a light gray shaded area on the left and bottom edges, which gives the illusion of "lifting" the graphic off the page (see Color Plate 6d).

Here's the Proof

Paying off the promise of the front cover headline, the back cover recaps the process described inside the brochure and identifies each step of the process, with its appropriate color bar. The paragraph describing the details of the design and topography is called a colophon, which means finishing touch (see Color Plate 6a).

Today, WYD has a full Apple Macintosh system that includes Mac IIs, Mac Pluses and Mac SEs. Projects are initiated on individual workstations and transferred by a local area network (LAN) between stations, or with a modem, to other sites. Scanning devices include Datacopy and Howtek scanners. Designs are developed on the Mac SE, then finalized (adding color) on a Mac II. Display output for client presentations can be sent to the 37-inch Mitsubishi color monitor in the studio conference room. Hard-copy output equipment includes ImageWriter and LaserWriter laser printers for proof copy output and Linotronic 300 and QMS color printers for comprehensives and reproduction quality output (see Figure 6.5).

Software includes Ready, Set, Go! (Version 4.0 from Letraset), Aldus PageMaker, Quark XPress, and Lightspeed (for page layout). Retouching software includes ImageStudio (from Letraset) and PixelPaint from SuperMac. Word-processing input is done on Microsoft Word. Also available are some proprietary programs under beta test from developers.

CONCLUSION

Microcomputer automation of prepress operations now brings desktop layout and design to thousands of people who are new to the art of printing. Within the printing industry, the tradition of craftsmanship runs deep. From the early days of the printer's apprentice to today's advertising and design industry (where you generally need a good portfolio and experience before being hired), the field has been relatively closed to the uninitiated. Those who chose to enter the profession almost always had a senior colleague available to consult for questions of quality, design, composition, or style. Through this process, the newcomer could develop the trained eye, attention to detail, and pride in craftsmanship that pervades the printing trade. Some in the design and printing industries are concerned that there will be a severe loss in the quality of design and craftsmanship with the proliferation of publications so easily produced with desktop publishing programs. The burden of excellence falls on the desktop publisher, who must learn how to apply the readily accessible technology to the prepress craft.

The impetus for purchasing desktop publishing systems often comes from corporate management looking at the cost-benefit—a practical standpoint. Actual use of the program involves art and design functions—a creative standpoint that is difficult to quantify. This means that there is a learning curve to consider when implementing desktop publishing procedures within organizations. Management may have to adjust its expectations in terms of speed. While electronic layout and design can be faster, it is not instantaneous. Good design, like good food preparation, takes time.

Procedures and lines of authority used in the past may have to be changed to take full advantage of this new technology. For example, where many separate departments acquire desktop publishing programs and are able to generate their own publications, the individual operator may not be equipped with the design skills to meet the organization's graphic standards. Hence some organizations have a publications director, someone who will supervise the design standards throughout the organization. Establishment of company-wide design guidelines inevitably leads to the question of individual creativity versus compliance with proscribed procedures. The more the individual tries to be creative to make the specific job new and different, the more the piece can vary from corporate standards. However, the more the organization selects people to comply with corporate guidelines in operating desktop publishing programs, the more mundane the output. Finding the right balance will be a major challenge for organizations wishing to take advantage of today's desktop publishing technology.

THE NEXT STEPS IN DESKTOP PUBLISHING

Desktop publishing is a field that remains in flux. Within the area of software development, changes occur almost daily. Yet the potential for using microcomputers for prepress operations has only begun to be realized. Desktop publishing efficiency is now measured against precomputer manual processes, which are usually just the first step in software development. Currently, enhancements are being based on computer interface (handshake file importing from other software publishers), higher-resolution software, and the beginning of packaged graphics on disks. An important next step will come when automation will make advancements—such as bundled operations (word processing, drawing, transparent file integration), smooth hardware interface, and leveraging of hardware enhancements—that will streamline the automation of the computerized process.

We are still in the early stages of applying computer technology to the prepress process. In the foreseeable future, improvements will be based on the process of desktop publishing rather than on manual procedures. Parameters of good design will be built into electronic layout and design programs. Context-sensitive help screens will answer design questions, not just operational questions, on how the program works.

Drawing programs will offer a menu of art styles so that drawings can be made to reflect the special touch of well-known artists. Clip art selections will grow to include various art styles. Just as there is graphics clip art today, clip text—that is, boilerplate copy that can be quickly tailored to a specific use thorough the search and replace and paragraph insertion functions of word-processing programs—will become available.

New issues will come to the fore, particularly with regard to copyright protection. For instance, if an operator of a paint or draw program takes a piece of art, owned by someone else, and makes changes in it, how many changes can be made before the original becomes a new piece of art? With scanners, it is easy to copy an illustration or photograph from a magazine. But everything in a magazine is owned by the magazine and is copyrighted. In the past, when publishing was done by publishers, extraordinary care was taken to conform with copyright laws. In the future, people who perhaps have no knowledge of copyright laws may inadvertently use the work of another. How can artists and publishers protect themselves from people who, either inadvertently or purposefully, take their art?

Looking to the future of hardware, it is evident that costs will continue to come down. New, more powerful computers with vast amounts of memory will open doors to faster and more detailed art editing capabilities. The kind of dot etching currently done on expensive machines like the Scitex will be done on relatively inexpensive machines. The resolution capability of scanners, screen displays, and laser printers will improve. In all, the entire desktop publishing process will become faster, better, and cheaper.

All this will begin to lead to a change in expectations in the business world. With the ease and cost savings of electronic layout and design, there will be more professional-quality brochures, house organs, flyers, reports, and printed matter of all kinds. Each one will be attractively produced. With improved computer-to-computer communication (faster modems, more use of office networks, and electronic mail), documents will be "published," but not on paper. As this occurs, the challenge will be to make electronic documents as attractive as printed documents. All of this foretells a bright future for those who are involved in computer graphics and design.

SUMMARY

This chapter has introduced you to many of the basic elements of design, perhaps starting you on a lifelong quest to understand and explore the process of visual communication. All the areas that have been touched on—communication styles, grid patterns, use of white space, rules, and reverse type—are fascinating worlds in which to venture. As you gain in knowledge and apply your talent, you will hear comments from the uninitiated that your work looks professional. Give yourself a pat on the back. Eventually you will come to understand that how your publications look is only the beginning; you will become more interested in how they work, how efficiently and dramatically they communicate the message. As you progress along the learning curve, you will push your software and hardware to their limits. You will surmount technical problems to implement creative solutions to communication problems. You will be called on to communicate a message when the sender is not completely clear what that message is (with your communication expertise you can help clarify the message for the sender). In this chapter you have seen examples where copy doesn't measure up to design and where design hurts exquisitely tight copy. In your own work you will have to make trade offs between quality and practicality, accuracy and speed, excellence and "good enough." But you will also have gained a deep respect for craftsmanship. Each new communication challenge will present new opportunities, and improved technology will offer not only speed and efficiency but also new creative possibilities. Desktop publishing technology provides the opportunity to do yourself what it once took many different specialists to accomplish, and the graphic design art form provides you with the opportunity to link the minds and hearts of many people in many places through visual communication.

Exercises

1. Start a personal resource file showing examples of the three basic purposes of printed communication: to inform, to persuade, to instruct.

2. Find one example from each of these kinds of communication that you think can be improved and prepare a set of thumbnails showing your revised concepts.

3. Read the instruction manual and install the desktop publishing program for your computer (check with your instructor). You will need to know how the hard disk and local area network are set up, the type of peripherals you will be using (printer, scanner, word processor, paint and draw programs, and so on).

4. Review the style sheets available with your desktop publishing program and identify them by communication category.

5. Find an information article in a magazine that parallels one of the style sheets in your desktop publishing program. Prepare a one-page spread by typing in the text in a word processor, scanning in the graphics, and making adjustments using the style sheet.

6. Make a list of the kinds of graphic and word-processing files that can be imported by your desktop publishing program. Set up a practice document and import each of these types of files. Print the results to check compatibility. Change some of the parameters in your program—such as printer selection, base fonts, paragraph description, and so on—and print the output.

7. Find an advertisement in a magazine and load the text and graphics into your desktop publisher with a word processor and scanner. Recrop the photograph or illustration several different ways to add drama. Reset the text in alternative type styles. Print and compare your output.

8. Write and illustrate an instruction manual on how to install your desktop publishing program on your computer or workstation. Start by generating a set of thumbnails and review your concepts with your instructor or a classmate acting as a client. Then proceed with the final version.

9. Create a newsletter (text and graphics) about your graphics class. Each person in the class can contribute the text for one article (be sure to include at least one article on each of the three categories of communication). Ideas for articles can include class update (inform), student profiles (inform), why PageMaker (or other program) is the best (persuade), how to ace the final (instruct). All students in the class can use the same articles in preparing their own newsletter.

10. Compare your newsletter with others in your class for visual interest graphic continuity. Note the different approaches to a similar problem.

Bibliography

GA MacWeek's Graphic Arts Supplement. San Francisco: MacWeek, Inc., 1988.

Hurlburt, Allen. *Layout: The Design of the Printed Page.* New York: Watson-Guptill Publications, 1977.

Lem, Dean Phillip. *Graphics Master.* Los Angeles: Dean Lem Associates, 1974.

Newcomb, John. *The Book of Graphic Problem Solving.* New York: Bowker, 1984.

Simone, Luisa. "Power Publishing," *PC Magazine* 7 (December 27, 1988): 89.

Stockford, James, ed. *Desktop Publishing Bible.* Indianapolis: Howard W. Sams, 1987.

Turnbull, Arthur T., and Russell N. Baird. *The Graphics of Communication.* 3rd ed. New York: Holt, Rinehart & Winston, 1975.

Words into Type (based on studies by Marjorie E. Skillin, Robert M. Gay, and other authorities). 3rd ed. Engelwood Cliffs, N.J.: Prentice-Hall, 1974.

ADDITIONAL DESKTOP PUBLISHING INFORMATION

For additional information on desktop publishing, you may wish to look to the following sources. (Price information is not included, since prices will change. Those publications that are free are indicated by "no fee.")

Periodicals

Font & Function. The Adobe Type Catalog. Adobe Systems, Inc., P.O. Box 7900, Mountain View, CA 94039.

Graphics Design: USA. Kaye Publishing Corporation, 120 East 56th Street, New York, NY 10022, (212) 759-8813.

Macintosh Business Review. VNU Business Publications, P.O. Box 1714, Riverton, NJ 08077.

Macintosh Today. Subscription Department, P.O. Box 5456, Pasadena, CA 91107, (800) 351-1700. (no fee)

PC Publishing. Subscription Department, P.O. Box 5050, Des Plains, IL 60019. (Provides hands-on tutorials, case studies, and product reviews for beginners through professionals, especially for the PC DOS environment.)

Publish! The How-To Magazine of Desktop Publishing. Subscriber Services, P.O. Box 55400, Boulder, CO 80322, (800) 222-2990. (Provides user information for Apple and DOS applications for page makeup programs, product updates, layout ideas, and reader questions and answers.)

U&lc. International Typeface Corporation, 2 Hammarskjold Plaza, New York, NY 10017.

National User Groups

Bulletin board systems (BBS) are accessed with a modem. Users are asked to sign on (register with your name, address, and a select password). Some systems require a fee to join. Once on, the user can download files, which can include downloadable fonts, artwork and illustrations, graphics, page format templates, and macros. Additionally, these systems usually provide a forum where you can join in discussions and ask questions. Set your communications software for either 1200 or 2400 baud, (speed at which your modem communicates), *8* data bits—parity none—1 stop bit (8-N-1) unless noted. Some systems are listed below.

BBS-Buena Park, (714) 821-5014 (modem).
Compuserve, (800) 848-8199 (voice).
The Desktop Publisher, (415) 856-2771 (modem) or (415) 856-4080 (voice). (no fee)
The Well (415) 332-7190 (modem 7-E-1) or (415) 332-4335 (voice).

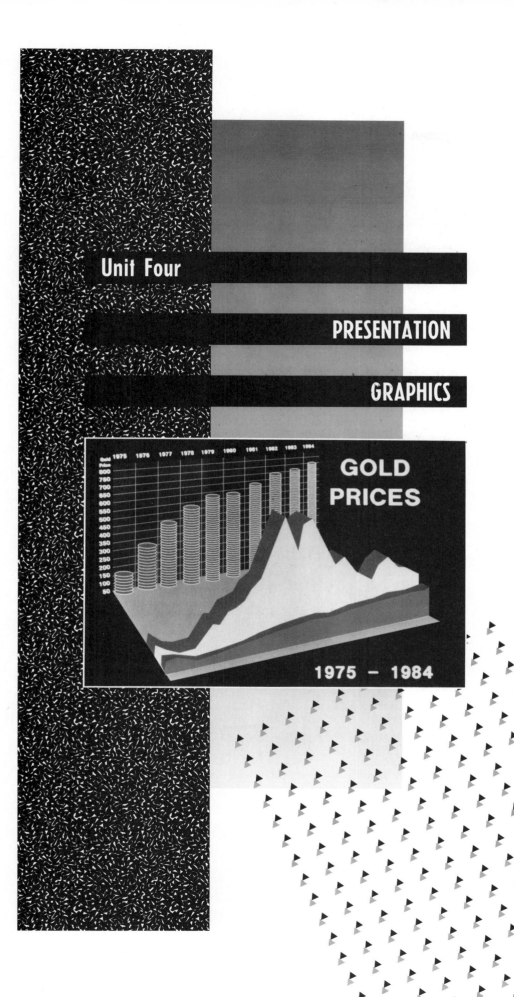

Unit Four

PRESENTATION

GRAPHICS

Presentation graphics—the creation of visual materials to illustrate sales presentations, lectures, and reports—is a rapidly expanding field for computer graphics artists. Presentation graphics opportunities exist in corporate art departments, computer slide service bureaus, and instructional media departments at colleges and universities. Many artists work with clients to interpret their presentations graphically, using original art and scanned-in photographs when time and money permit. The artist who understands the total production process, from client input to finished presentation, is more likely to find a rewarding career, perhaps as a client service manager or corporate graphics coordinator.

Susan Bickford's article examines some of the popular features of presentation graphics software. She makes a distinction between unadorned analytical graphics, used by individuals or small groups, and presentation-quality graphics, enhanced for larger groups or upper management. Her article provides a glimpse into the future, where she forecasts that almost every desktop computer used in business will be equipped with some form of business graphics software.

ithin the next few years, business graphics programs for personal computers will become as popular as word processors, spreadsheets, and databases are today. What are the latest software availabilities, and what criteria should you use to evaluate them?

Industry analysts are particularly fond of giving out market research statistics on the size and direction of the personal-computer-based business graphics market. According to the Hope Reports, for example, by 1990 business and industry will be producing some 1 billion presentation slides annually, with almost a quarter of them produced by computer. Frost & Sullivan's latest figures project the total market for management presentation graphics to reach $605 million by 1989; the figure includes all management presentation graphics from PCs to mainframes, but since the market is moving sharply in the direction of PC-based products, it is assumed they form the lion's share of the total projection.

Behind all the facts and figures and projections there lies a simple truth: within the next decade, it's likely that virtually every desk top computer in use in corporate America, whether at a large or a small company, is going to be equipped with some form of business graphics capability as today they are equipped with word processors, spreadsheets, and databases. And that's a massive market no matter how the pie (chart) is sliced.

KEEN COMPETITION

Exactly what the nature of those graphics programs will be is causing a great deal of competitiveness among the various software companies these days. As Kleinman of Pacific Technology points out, "there are some currently 120 programs for creating business graphics with personal computers, and some 20 criteria people use to evaluate PC-based business graphics packages; the best programs only satisfy 17 or 18 of them." But who decides which criteria are the most important? "Ultimately it comes down to a question of how close to WYSIWYG (what you see is what you get) a package comes," says Kleinman, "and how long it takes to get there. But there's a lot of gray area surrounding the ideal state."

First, not everyone agrees on exactly what constitutes business and/or presentation graphics. The term "business graphics" is the older of the two, and refers generally to all types of computer-generated images used in the business context. According to an analysis of Management Graphics (Toronto), this breaks down into some 55 percent word and text images, some 30 percent charts and graphs, and the remainder devoted to photographs and other forms of artwork and illustration.

Business graphics encompasses all forms of graphics output, starting with a display of chart and graph data on the video screen at the manager's desk. Frequently part of an MIS (management information services) or corporate accounting/financial system, and often tied into a large, company-wide mainframe database, these displays need only be for the user's own reference. They're quick, visual, easy-to-understand replacements for the mounds of green-lined computer paper that used to spill forth from printers continuously and provide an analysis of large amounts of data.

When the manager wants to share some of this material with peers and place the charts and

PUTTING YOUR DESK TOP TO WORK: PC BUSINESS GRAPHICS

SUSAN BICKFORD

Susan Bickford is special assignments editor for *Computer Pictures Magazine*, where this excerpted article originally appeared. From Susan Bickford, "Putting Your Desk Top to Work: PC Business Graphics—Part 1," *Computer Pictures Magazine* 5 (March/April 1987): 37–41. Used with permission.

graphs in a report, he turns to a hardcopy device—more and more often a laser printer—or, in some cases, a color hardcopier such as those from Calcomp, Seiko, and Mitsubishi (Shinko). Recently the term "peer graphics" has been coined to describe this form of distribution.

PRESENTATION QUALITY

It's not until the material goes public, however, that we enter the realm of "presentation graphics"— i.e., those graphics, either in the form of overhead transparencies, or most often 35mm slides, and now occasionally a high-resolution video display such as that offered by VideoShow, used to illustrate lectures, talks, and presentations being given to the company's upper management, stockholders, public meetings, and the like.

To generate the slides and overheads and carefully-laid-out video screens, presenters have several choices. They can do it themselves—creating the graphics on their own PCs and using a desk top slide camera such as those from General Parametrics and the Polaroid Palette (soon to be available as the PalettePlus, offering support of EGA card-based computers with 4096 colors). Or they can ship the data representing the graphic off to a slide-making company such as MAGICorp, Management Graphics, or the new Koala CompuFilm (more later).

More often, especially in large companies whose volume of presentation graphics can justify a price tag ranging as high as $250,000, the company will have one or more presentation graphics workstations such as those from Dicomed and Genigraphics.

CHARTING AND GRAPHING CAPABILITIES

All the systems offer the ability to transform sets of data into charts and graphs of various types, falling into four main categories: bar, pie,

line, and area. Within each of these, of course, there are many variations. Bars can be laid out horizontally or vertically. If two or more data sets are being laid out on the same chart, the bars representing each can either be placed side by side or stacked. In a pie chart, one or more pieces can be "exploded"—moved away from the body of the pie for emphasis; the area below an area chart can be filled with color or not.

In the more sophisticated packages, different types of charts can be combined into the same plot. Harvard Presentation Graphics' list of graph types includes, for example: pie charts; pie/bar combinations; horizontal and vertical bars; clustered, overlapped, and stacked bars; area charts; lines, curves, and trend lines; bar/line combinations; scatter graphs; and high-low/close charts.

In general, analytical graphics packages are quite similar in what they will accomplish, given either a set of data brought in from a spreadsheet program such as 1-2-3 or with a data table entered directly into the graphics program. One difference that should be noted among systems, however, is the number of data points that can be accommodated with a single chart—usually not a limiting factor for most applications, but something to consider when high volumes of data have to be charted.

INTERACTIVITY

Although all systems offer basic charting and graphing capabilities, there are several features that distinguish one from another. Most important among these is probably the level of interactivity between the user and the computer system.

FONTS

Another area in which systems differ considerably is in how many different styles of lettering they

offer. Since word charts form over 50 percent of the slides created for presentation graphics, this can be an important factor. But having a wide range of fonts is also important for graphics and charts as well. Some systems, for example, force you to use lettering of a certain height placed in virtually the same location on each chart. Others are more free-form, allowing the lettering to be placed almost anywhere on the chart.

ARTWORK CAPABILITY

When looking at cost/performance ratios of different systems, one of the features that drives price up is the availability of more or less sophisticated artwork capabilities. Artwork is considered anything that is not part of the graph itself and ranges in complexity from libraries of symbols that can be called up in the same way as lettering to actual freehand drawing capability—particularly useful when a program is driven with a mouse that can also be used as a graphics input device.

One of the most basic "graphics" functions is the ability to edit and manipulate chart data once it has been created—moving charts from one position on the screen/page, for example, or placing multiple graphs on the same page, or changing color palettes for emphasis, and so forth.

CONNECTIVITY

Still another important distinguishing characteristic from one system to another has to do with how data to create charts and graphs is input. All the programs offer the ability to create data files directly through the PC's keyboard, entering a small spreadsheet-like data table on the spot; the program then automatically takes row and column headings and treats them as bar or pie segment labels and uses the data values to construct the chart.

Where the systems differ is how they handle data sets created by other programs. The most common are the almost ubiquitous files produced by Lotus 1-2-3 and Symphony. This means that a file created with the spreadsheet program can be directly imported into another business graphics program other than the rather limited graphics offered by 1-2-3 and can be treated as if the data were entered into the business graphics program directly through the keyboard.

OUTPUT CAPABILITY

Perhaps the most important feature to be evaluated when choosing a PC-based business graphics package is its output driver support, for unless the application is only for the user's own information, presented at the desk top terminal, then it will have to be output to some form of hardcopy device—whether a dot matrix printer, film recorder, or high-resolution slide service.

EMERGING TRENDS

It has been said that analytical graphics reached their peak during the "VisiCalc[1] era," when the ability to display spreadsheets on the graphics screen was "the greatest thing since sliced bread." Today, integrated packages offering all manner of business graphics functions are taking over the market. Will this trend continue? Certainly for the foreseeable future. By 1990 it is estimated that some 5 million corporate personal computer users will have access to some form of slide-making capability—either with one of the new desk top slide-making systems or else through a centralized resource. And as this capability grows, so will the demand for more sophisticated graphics.

But the future seen by some in the industry is even more far-reaching: the use of the personal computer, even a lap-top with monochrome display, as a management tool to specify graphics without necessarily needing to create them on the spot. "The typical business graphics user isn't an artist—he or she is a corporate executive," explains Philippe Girouard, prod-

---

[1] Early spreadsheet program that predates Lotus 1-2-3, an extremely popular program that was used on the Apple II computer.

uct marketing manager for Pansophic Graphics Products. "And it just isn't fair to expect them to be able to create their own slides. The executive knows what the data should say, perhaps where it should appear on the screen, whether it should be a pie or a bar chart, and so forth. But the actual aesthetics of the final image will ultimately be left up to the corporate art department. So the executive needs to only have a tool that can produce a sketch of the final image."

David Solomont, president of BPS (a presentation graphics software supplier), sees a future in which the corporate executive will need to make fewer and fewer choices about the aesthetic qualities of the final image. "The key is in the attention to graphics provided by the software," he says. "We're coming to the point where all you need do is tell the computer what kind of data you want to present and make some very basic choices about its format. Then it's the software's job to make it look good—to give the executive the image he wants quickly and clearly—that's the ultimate direction we've got to head in."

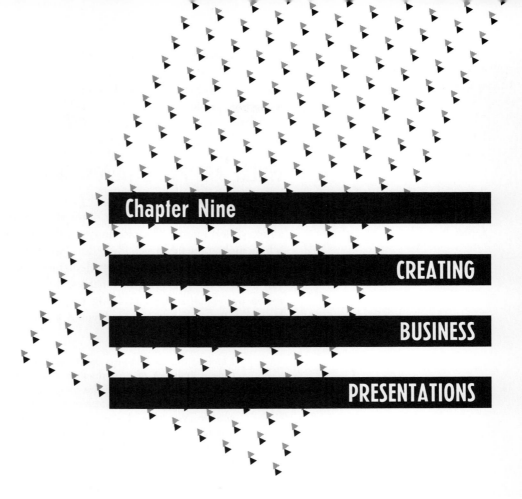

Chapter Nine

CREATING

BUSINESS

PRESENTATIONS

P resentation graphics are used in industry, education, and government to illustrate lectures, anchor sales meetings, and provide graphics for newsletters and annual reports. These graphics enhance communication by helping the audience quickly to visualize the meaning of statistical information—showing trends, comparisons, correlations, parts of the whole, summaries, and projections rather than just listing the numbers themselves. Basic analytical graphics produced by spreadsheet programs are enhanced with color, attractive typefaces, and simplified design (see Figure 9.1).

The production of presentation graphics is a multimillion dollar industry and will continue to grow. As Susan Bickford notes in her article, the *Hope Reports*, an audiovisual market newsletter, forecasts that by 1990 business and industry will produce 1 billion presentation slides annually, with almost a quarter of them produced by computer. In 1983 only 3 percent of the slides used by corporations were created by computer. In 1985 that figure was 14 percent. Hope forecasts that in 1988, 22 percent of all slides used by corporations will be produced by computer.[1] Backing up this projection, *Computer Pictures* magazine states, "U.S. demand for computer-generated

---

[1] Thomas Hope, editor of *Hope Reports Newsletter*, Rochester, N.Y. Interview with author, Apr. 8, 1988.

Relevant Terminology

Analytical graphics

Business graphics

Graphics coordinator

In house

Presentation graphics

Presenter

Service bureau

35 mm slides will burgeon from 104 million pieces created (in 1987) to 214 million in 1992, a compounded annual growth rate of over 15%."[2] Presentation graphics is certainly one of the largest commercial applications of computer graphics.

WHERE ARE PRESENTATION GRAPHICS USED?

Presentation graphics are not limited to boardroom presentations held in smoke-filled rooms. The old image of the chairman of the board glaring down a long mahogany table as a lower-level manager makes a fumbling presentation is being replaced with succinct, decision-making discussions focused around full-color strategic trend summaries. Increasingly, business communication relies on visualizations to bring the point home. Jerry Cahn, president of Brilliant Image, a company devoted to creating presentation graphics, describes their uses in industry:

> I look at this as business communications, not business presentations. Anytime a manager of a product, a department, or division has information to convey, as long as there are more than a few people in the group, you are going to need a more professional means of communicating. And the minute you do, you should start thinking graphically. Not just using words. By graphically I mean: (1) using charts to convey trends and key points and (2) using symbols and icons—not just to make it look pretty, but to dramatize your point.[3]

In small groups of two or three, visualization may mean using an easel stand, paper, and felt-tip marker. In larger groups, however, visualization means hitting the major points quickly with graphics—diagrams, charts, and key terms—making visual the points you want the audience to remember.[4] A presentation can be part of one speaker's remarks before a medium-sized group or it can be a multiprojector audiovisual production before an audience of hundreds. When there is more than one speaker addressing the audience, presentation graphics can help unify many individual presentations.

Presentation graphics are used for a variety of purposes in industry, but the principal purpose is for selling products and ideas. Your marketing department may have a new product that needs promotion. A presentation might describe its special features, benefits, and market projections. The presentation could be shown to management and then again to the sales force. If the company is in the pharmaceutical industry, the same presentation may be used at a medical convention to inform doctors who will prescribe the medication. Individual sales representatives may take the presentation on the road (on self-contained slide projection screens or on portable computers),

---

[2] Suzan Prince, "PC, Video, and Print Presentations: The Power Is in Your Hands," *Computer Pictures* 6 (May/June, 1988): 11.

[3] Jerry Cahn, Ph.D., president of Brilliant Image, Inc., New York. Interview with the author, Mar. 14, 1988.

[4] If in the course of a conversation you tell someone that you live at 162 Main Street, people only think of the words, but if you say "I live on Main Street across from the library," they have a visual picture of where you live.

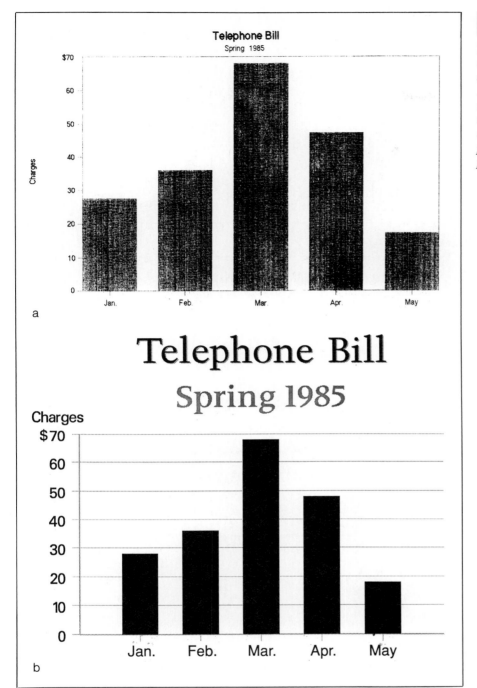

a

b

FIGURE 9.1

Two charts containing the same information. The first chart is an analytical chart produced in Lotus 1-2-3, version 1A, printed on a dot matrix printer. It is for limited distribution. The second chart was produced in a presentation graphics program and output on a laser printer.

showing it to prospective customers in their offices. As the retail level, presentation graphics are also used in do-it-yourself home centers and in other retail point-of-sale displays (see Figure 9.2).

Corporate management uses presentation graphics to illustrate progress reports (for example, division sales for the last quarter), status reports for specific capital projects, strategy meetings, peer presentations, and reports on how decisions are made at other management levels. Presentation graphics often serve as a summary device to illustrate trends on a variety of subjects

FIGURE 9.2

New product presentation. The same presentation is often made before several audiences.

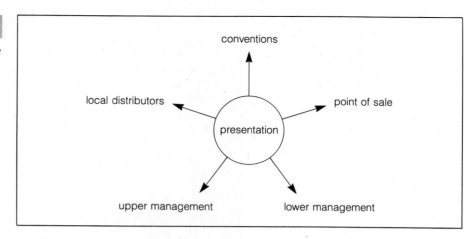

FIGURE 9.3

Charts can be quickly updated from mainframe data. (Used with permission of General Motors Corporation.)

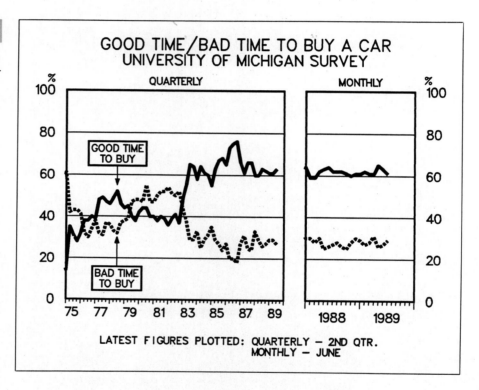

contained in corporate databases. For instance, General Motors regularly creates summary slides from mainframe financial information to brief management in its Treasurer's Office.[5] (See Figure 9.3.) This summary information is automatically collected from the mainframe database and organized according to a predetermined slide format. Since the presentation format doesn't change from presentation to presentation, the slide-making process is done automatically by the graphics software. Slides are created on a weekly, monthly, and daily basis, or as needed.

---

[5] Suzan Prince, "How the Fortune 100 Use Computer Graphics," *Computer Pictures* 5 (Nov./Dec. 1987): 14.

UNIT FOUR: PRESENTATION GRAPHICS

FIGURE 9.4

Documents created with desktop publisher software often include presentation graphics.

WHERE ARE PRESENTATION GRAPHICS PRODUCED?

Presentation graphics production is traditionally found in advertising, corporate design, audiovisual, or public relations departments. These graphics centers often use minicomputer turnkey workstations to produce slides and overhead transparencies. Leading manufacturers of these workstations include Genigraphics Corporation and Dicomed Corporation. Both companies produce highly efficient, high-speed workstations that sell for about $250,000 or more. Increasingly, however, graphics departments are purchasing PC-based software such as Mirage from Zenographics, Inc., or AVL Starburst from Pansophic Systems. PC software has much of the same charting capability of software found on larger systems at a fraction of the cost.

In this rapidly changing environment, turnkey manufacturers such as Genigraphics and Dicomed are now promoting inexpensive PC systems that are software-compatible with their high-end units. These satellite systems can be added to provide more capacity when needed. Image files created on the smaller desktop systems are then taken to the turnkey workstations for conversion to slides, or they can be embellished with special effects not available at the PC level. Not to be outdone, PC-based software suppliers are now selling scaled-down versions of their art department software. Zenographics has a charting package called Pixie for nonartists that runs under Microsoft Windows. This software is friendlier than the art department version and can be operated by business managers who begin the charting process in their own offices.

As companies bring graphic capability closer to the end user, the process becomes more streamlined, saving time and money while improving accuracy. Ideally, the

Presentation Graphics Systems

Mainframe or Mini workstation	Micro - high end	Micro - midrange
Access large database	Special graphics hardware	CGA/EGA/VGA or Mac
Boardroom-level graphics	Boardroom-level graphics	Pre-formatted styles
		Off-the-shelf software
D-Pict	Chartwork	Chart-Master
SAS/Graph	Lumena	Freelance Plus
Tell-A-Graph	Mirage/Autumn	Harvard Graphics
Dicomed	Starburst	Microsoft Chart
Genigraphics	Autographix	Show Partner
	Videoshow	Power Point*
		Aldus Persuasion*
		Cricket Presents..*
		VBS No. 6*
		*For the Macintosh.

data should be typed only once at the presenter level, rather than having the data typed in memo form for the art department and then given to an artist, who must rekey the data into a charting package. The process of thinking into a desktop charting package has the same advantage for the presenter as thinking into a word-processing program. The user takes full advantage of the charting program by crafting the chart personally. Chart variations can be tried immediately, and improvements are made by the user before the end result goes to the art department.

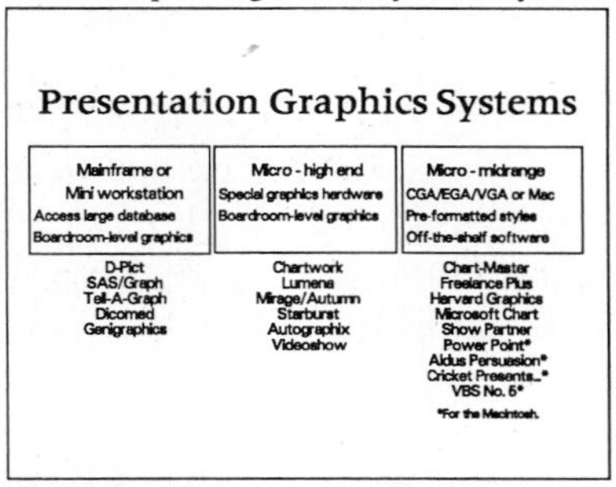

After the data is typed into the desktop

Other uses include advertising agency reports to clients on media buying (radio, television, newspaper, magazine, outdoor, and direct-response advertising), illustrative slides and word slides for employee training, and technical reports for scientific conventions.

Outside the corporation, presentation graphics are used at public hearings—both judicial and political—and in education. Increasingly, presentation graphics are finding their way into newspapers, magazines, annual reports, and newsletters. Charting software is often compatible with desktop publishing software, so that charts created in charting programs can be printed with reports on laser printers (see Figure 9.4).

WHERE ARE PRESENTATION GRAPHICS PRODUCED?

Corporations

Presentation graphics production is traditionally found in advertising, corporate design, audiovisual, or public relations departments. These graphics centers often use minicomputer turnkey workstations to produce slides and overhead transparencies. Leading manufacturers of these workstations include Genigraphics Corporation and Dicomed Corporation. Both companies produce highly efficient, high-speed workstations that sell for about $250,000 or more. Increasingly, however, graphics departments are purchasing PC-based software, such as Mirage from Zenographics Inc., or AVL Starburst from Pansophic Systems (see Figure 9.5 later in this chapter for additional systems). PC software has much of the same charting capability of software found on larger systems at a fraction of the cost.

In this rapidly changing environment, turnkey manufacturers such as Genigraphics and Dicomed are now promoting inexpensive PC systems that are software-compatible with their high-end units. These satellite systems can be added to provide more capacity when needed. Image files created on the smaller desktop systems are then taken to the turnkey workstations for conversion to slides, or they can be embellished with special effects not available at the PC level. Not to be outdone, PC-based software suppliers are now selling scaled-down versions of their art department software. Zenographics has a charting package called Pixie for nonartists that runs under Microsoft Windows. The software is friendlier than the art department version and can be operated by business managers who begin the charting process in their own offices.

As companies bring graphics capabilities closer to the end user, the process becomes more streamlined, saving time and money while improving accuracy. Ideally, the data should be typed only once at the presenter level, rather than having the data typed in memo form for the art department and then given to an artist, who must rekey the data into a charting package. The process of thinking into a desktop charting package has the same advantage for the presenter as thinking into a word-processing program. The user takes full advantage of the charting program by crafting the chart personally. Chart variations can be tried immediately, and improvements are made by the user before the end result goes to the art department.

After the data is typed into the desktop software, the files are sent via floppy disk, modem, or local area network to the art department. Artists load the bare-bones graphics into their more sophisticated software and add graphics, icons, and other visual detail. In some cases, style templates automatically standardize the style of slides created throughout the company. Style may reflect a standard look for the company or represent a special look for a specific conference or presentation. Many art departments would like to have desktop charting packages be as common a tool for corporate executives and other presenters as word-processing and spreadsheet packages are today.

If a company does not have an art department, or if it is too small to warrant a specialist in presentation graphics, easy-to-use off-the-shelf charting packages are often purchased. Packages like Harvard Graphics, Freelance Plus, Aldus Persuasion, and Microsoft Chart, costing only $200 to $300, can

Presentation Graphics Systems

Mainframe or Mini workstation	Micro - high end	Micro - midrange
Access large database Boardroom-level graphics	Special graphics hardware Boardroom-level graphics	CGA/EGA/VGA or Mac Pre-formatted styles Off-the-shelf software
D-Pict SAS/Graph Tell-A-Graph Dicomed Genigraphics	Chartwork Lumena Mirage/Autumn Starburst Autographix Videoshow	Chart-Master Freelance Plus Harvard Graphics Microsoft Chart Show Partner Power Point* Aldus Persuasion* Cricket Presents...* VBS No. 5* *For the Macintosh.

FIGURE 9.5

Three types of presentation graphics software.

quickly create charts and word slides with a uniform, though perhaps uninspired, look (see Color Plate 7). Chart files created with these packages can be sent by modem or by mail to slide service bureaus that convert them into high-resolution slides. Turnaround time can be as little as 24 hours (see Figure 9.5). (See Appendix A for further information.)

Service Bureaus

Computer graphics service bureaus are outside service companies that prepare slides and other visuals for presenters. These companies grew up several years ago when presentation graphics workstations were very expensive. On a cost-per-slide basis, the services of these companies are about the same as those for traditional typesetting. Economies accrue significantly, however, when slides are updated, revised, or when you can make use of artwork created for previous slides. Service bureaus provide design, storyboarding, layout, and production services. They will also add music and narration if a project requires more elaborate production. Some bureaus are set up to receive data by modem from their customers. Overnight express return mail returns completed slides within 24 hours anywhere in the continental United States.

Changes in the economics of presentation graphics have begun to bring changes in the services provided by bureaus. Technology is changing the rules. Companies are now doing more of their own low-level slides on PC software and going outside only for elaborate presentations. In-house departments produce most of the simple word charts and bar charts. More elaborate visuals that encompass flow charts, configuration diagrams, and original art are created by bureaus. It's like having a free-lance artist who comes in for special jobs. Service bureaus can supply custom-designed logos, icons, and identifications (IDs) for special jobs and can design opening and closing graphics and special visuals that break up the tedium of long presentations (called relief slides).

Increasingly, service bureaus are used for high-quality backup of corporate capability. A company might have 80 slides due on Monday. It's now Friday noon, and there are still 40 slides left to go. You call the service bureau and send them the copy and format for the remaining slides. The bureau creates them over the weekend and has them ready by Monday. Often, service bureau software provides greater complexity for special cases. Stand-alone programs that are compatible with files created by commercial charting packages and software overlays for existing packages meet special needs not met by the off-the-shelf software.

Probably the largest potential market for slide bureaus is the very small company or individual with limited or no graphics resources. Traditionally, this market has not used slide bureaus because of the high cost—usually $40 and up—of creating individual custom-made slides. However, if individuals buy off-the-shelf charting packages and create their own charts and diagrams, the cost of converting these charts into slides at a service bureau can be as little as $10 per slide. The file is sent by modem to the bureau, and slides arrive back at the company the next day. The use of PC-charting packages and electronic file transfer are bringing more potential users into the presentation graphics market.

One service bureau in New York regularly does work for a free-lance marketing director in the state of Washington. The marketing director has an off-the-shelf charting package and does all his own charting on a lap-top computer. Since he is frequently in airports, he does his graphics while waiting for planes to arrive. He then sends his files to New York, usually with a modem and public telephone, and receives the slides the next day by overnight express mail. If he needs artwork or special designs, the service bureau does that as well. He is a prototype of the graphics user of the future; not someone who spends time sitting at a desk but someone on the move, carrying his office with him in his lap-top computer. He knows that by using the telephone and overnight mail services, his presentations created while on the go will benefit from the use of graphics. More people can make visually supported presentations because, through advances in technology, they can create all but the most elaborate slides themselves.

Education and Government Agencies

Besides the corporate market, there is a specialized market for presentation graphics in education and government. Educational material is produced in media centers found at most educational facilities or purchased from textbook and educational media suppliers. Educators can regularly update their presentations with charting software. Media centers also supply traditional slide services, such as slide duplicating, photo copying, and slide-strip production.

As in industry, the emphasis is on letting the presenter do as much of the production work as possible. Media centers or art departments supply enhanced services that are more difficult for the individual to do.

ESSENTIAL SKILLS FOR GRAPHICS COORDINATORS AND GRAPHIC ARTISTS

In the structured environment of the corporation and in the large service bureau, the tasks of creating presentation graphics can be divided into at least two job categories: (1) The graphics coordinator (sometimes called the customer rep or client manager), who supervises the production of graphics within a department or corporation, and (2) the graphic artist, who plans and creates the presentations. Both individuals must be familiar with the uses and capabilities of computer graphics and usually have a design background or related training in visual media. They understand the specific capabilities of PC graphics and are aware of hardware and software options, peripherals, and related equipment.

Graphics Coordinators

Business communication skills are an important asset for a graphics coordinator. Because the presentation graphics department is a support facility and not considered a profit center within the corporation, the graphics coordinator must use business communication skills to improve the service capability of the graphics department and advance department responsibilities within the corporation.

Establish Companywide Graphics Policy   The graphics coordinator initiates companywide policy on presentation graphics. A primary function is to educate presenters on the value and components of visual communication, to promote early planning, and to encourage presenters to type chart data directly into desktop charting packages rather than trying to communicate verbally or by memo.

Manage Graphics Department   In addition to setting companywide presentation graphics policy, the graphics coordinator manages the presentation graphics department. The coordinator makes sure presenters have provided accurate and complete information on a timely basis, supervises staff artists who input data and create original art, negotiates turnaround time and delivery dates with presenters, balances work flow within the department (allocates work to graphic artists), and coordinates production with outside service bureaus. Working with the presenter, the graphics coordinator also sets the graphics standards: how much text should be on the screen, how large the type should be, and how often a graphic icon should appear in a long presentation. The graphics coordinator determines the style for individual presentations and for company presentations as a whole (see Color Plate 8).

Plan Presentations   An important aspect of the graphics coordinator's job is working directly with individual presenters on planning presentations. Presenters are often word oriented, thinking in terms of words rather than pictures, and assume that slides will be phrase summaries of their presentation. The message, however, may be more clearly stated using charts and diagrams. Graphics quickly summarize what the presenter is saying and provide visual variety for lengthy presentations.

Determine Goal of Presenter   Charts can show spatial relationships between quantitative data that are not easily understood unless visualized—for example, this year's sales versus last year's. Charts show trends over time—such as projected sales based on population growth—and can make comparisons quickly and effectively. Graphics direct the viewer's attention to the goals of the presenter. Goals are not always clear, however. One of the graphics coordinator's jobs is to listen to presenters and help them determine the goals of the presentation.

Presenters are usually process oriented. They see a presentation as a series of steps:

What do I want to say?

How much time do I have?

What are my subtopics?

How many slides do I need?

Which topics will need charts or diagrams?

They go to the graphics coordinator with a list of word slides and suggestions for a few graphics and expect the process of visualization to end there. The graphics coordinator listens to the presenter, looks at the suggested slides, and plays the role of the audience. An outcome, or goal-oriented, approach will first concentrate on what the audience should learn from a presentation. Discussion with the presenter begins with questions related to the ultimate objective of the presentation. Is it to sell? To educate? To convince? Does past performance warrant future business? The coordinator brainstorms with the presenter and establishes the project's goals. The ultimate goal may not be clear from the presenter's list of word slides, but after discussion, a visual motif based on the overall goal will make the presentation much sharper for the audience. A single image might sum up the whole presentation and give the audience something to take away with them, something to remember.

For example, if a client is selling pension planning (IRAs and tax-deferred investments) to workers in various companies, the graphics coordinator might sit in on an actual presentation prior to designing a slide program. Jerry Cahn, president of Brilliant Image, relates such a story:

> I have a client that does pension planning [e.g., pensions and IRAs] for various companies. They did a major presentation for very large law firms where the audience included hundreds of people ranging from CEOs to secretaries. Law firms have learned investment jargon, but they're not number oriented. When you present pension plans, you are necessarily dealing with lots of numbers. Well, we watched their presentation in terms of the numbers and I learned a lot; 401K's advantages over certain IRAs; this fund over

that fund. But after the whole presentation, which lasted about a half hour, I said, "You know, I'll sleep through this, and I'm interested! I can imagine employees getting lost before slide 14."

I started asking the critical questions, "What's the bottom line?" The bottom line is to get 60 percent of the people to agree to join the plan. You never said that. You gave me all my options but you never convinced me this is the best thing since sliced bread. I said, "Visually let's come up with an image that makes that point." So we eventually came up with a picture of a guy and his wife, two people sitting on a boat sipping champagne. It's their yacht, you know, the "Retirement One" we called it. Basically lifting their cups with champagne—"Thank you (name of company)." That was the bottom line. They could retire on their own yacht. Here's their retirement plan.

Then we reduced to a minimum the number of slides describing the details of each option and tried to demonstrate the "power of compounding" by showing how money bags grow over time, with the eventual result being different sized yachts. In sum, from beginning to end the audience understood why they should consider a retirement plan, and how much better their retirement would be depending on their choice.[6]

There is no reason presentations have to be 55 percent word slides (the industry norm). Slides that use graphics have more impact, break up the stream of words from both the screen and the presenter, and subtly reinforce the message of the presentation. The presentation is a reflection of both the professional reputation of the company and the presenter and should look right and should use the full potential of the visual medium. Presenters will never have the time or inclination to be trained to think graphically, and this makes the graphics coordinator's job that much more vital.

While "a picture is worth a thousand words," beware of the presenter who wants to enliven the presentation with too many pictures, irrelevant pictures, or trite sayings. A presenter may suggest showing a girl in a bikini or may want to put the word *sex* on the screen so he can say, "Now that I have your attention" before proceeding with the real content of the presentation. The graphics coordinator monitors good taste and may suggest more refined means for getting (and keeping) audience attention.

You may find presenters with two hours of information and only 15 minutes to make the presentation. Since presenters "own" the information, they often feel that all of it is important, and you may end up with too many words on a slide or slides that move too fast. The graphics coordinator has to help presenters clarify their thinking by asking "Tell me in one sentence what you want the audience to remember."

Graphic Artists

The graphic artist is the person who creates the actual slides. Much of what is said about the presentation graphics coordinator can also be applied to the graphic artist. Many artists work directly with presenters, especially if the work is complicated or if the presenters are regular users of presentation graphics.

---

[6] Jerry Cahn, Ph.D., president Brilliant Image, Inc., New York. Interview with the author, Mar. 14, 1988.

FIGURE 9.6

Graphic artist using microcomputer and presentation graphics software. (Photo courtesy of Brilliant Image Company, New York.)

The best artwork comes from artists who understand that the computer is a tool they are in control of, not something that limits them. Default settings and preconceived limitations of the software can be surmounted when you feel comfortable with the computer system and understand its capabilities. The graphic artist is expert at using charting packages and freehand graphics software to create dynamic visuals. Training and experience in traditional media play an important role. But above all, the graphic artist can visualize how the image will eventually look when recorded on film or seen on videotape. Knowledge of color, composition, and how to select the proper chart type are important attributes, especially as they are related to the special environment of computer graphics (see Figure 9.6).

SUMMARY

Business graphics is an important sector of computer graphics production. It can be broken down into analytical graphics—automatically produced in spreadsheet programs with limited distribution, sometimes to only one individual—and presentation graphics, which are more attractively designed and which are shown to a wider audience.

Presentation graphics is a multimillion dollar industry that will more than double by the year 1992. Graphics highlight key points in lectures and visually quantify numeric data. They are useful in sales, training, management, and marketing presentations. Companies either produce their own presentation graphics or have them created by outside service bureaus. The presentation graphics coordinator and graphic artist are specialists at visualizing the written word. They are part artist, part communicator, and part educator. In the following chapter we will discuss the steps to creating computer graphics slide presentations.

Exercises

1. Go to your school media center and report on its slide-making capability. Questions to ask the staff might include:

   ▸ Which department uses the most slides per month?
   ▸ What kinds of slides do they produce and which do they produce most often?
   ▸ What brand of charting software do they use?
   ▸ Do they use a service bureau or do they output their own slides in house?
   ▸ What is the training and background of the graphic artists creating the slides?

2. What are the differences between business graphics made for analytical purposes and graphics created for presentations before larger audiences outside the immediate department or group?

3. What is the role of the graphics coordinator in a large corporation?

Bibliography

Bishop, Ann. *Slides: Planning and Producing Slide Programs*. Rochester, NY: Eastman Kodak, 1984.
Holmes, Nigel. *Designer's Guide to Creating Charts and Diagrams*. New York: Watson-Guptill Publications, 1984.

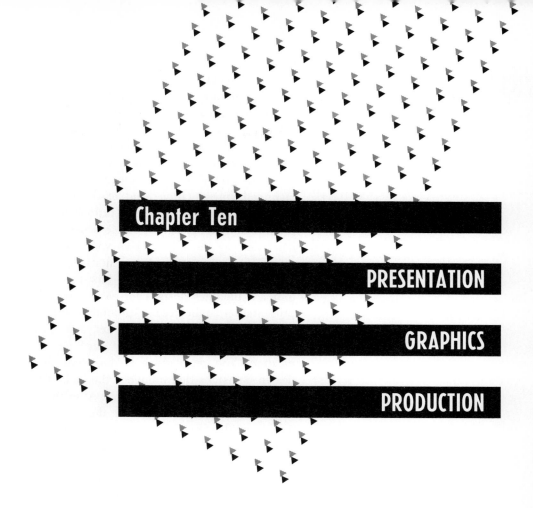

Chapter Ten

PRESENTATION

GRAPHICS

PRODUCTION

G ood presentations require careful planning. At a minimum, thumbnail sketches are made. Longer presentations use color sketches and sometimes storyboards. An important consideration when creating a chart is selecting the appropriate chart type. Chart visualization should be consistent with the original data. There are at least a dozen different chart types to choose from, the most common being word, pie, bar, line, and area (or mountain) charts. Some presentations use a combination of two or more types. The graphic artist must choose the most complete and unambiguous means to visualize the data. In larger presentations, the client approves your treatment at various stages in the production.

COMPUTER GRAPHICS WORK FLOW

Larger presentations go through a series of steps, beginning with the initial client consultation. The graphics coordinator discusses the client's needs and the capabilities of the graphics department. The client may also be shown examples of other slides produced by the department or service. At this point, either the graphics coordinator or the graphic artist brainstorms with the presenter about the presentation, making suggestions about goals, interpretation, structure, and general design. For example, a department manager who is doing a simple presentation may arrive with 20 sheets of paper and ask you to turn them into slides. You might ask, "How much time do you have, and what do you want the audience to remember?" You might also make some suggestions: "Why don't we have an introductory slide with your name on it? And today's date and a logo signifying that you're the company or person making the presentation? And let's have one or two break slides and conclusion slides, because it's getting a little heavy here." Based on discussions on preliminary sketches, you create a list of specific slides. Depending on how much leeway the client gives you, storyboards and sometimes scripts are written for more involved presentations.

The storyboard shows how the presentation will flow from topic to topic. It includes designs for each subheading (or presenter if it is a larger presentation); indicates background treatment (style, color, artwork); and specifies slides for openings, breathers, and closings. The advantage to planning your presentation using a storyboard can be summed up in one word: *organization*. You get a sense of the whole project, and you are able to make design decisions that influence the look of the whole presentation instead of just one part (see Color Plate 9). After the storyboard has been approved, it is used as a guide for speccing the job—that is, defining specific treatment for each slide. Speccing includes specifying chart type, picking fonts for main title and text type, and choosing color specifications and line widths. Finally, the artist selects icons from clip art files or creates original art if needed.

When slides are shown before a large audience or at a sales presentation, they contain a number of design elements to improve their appearance. The artist selects from a wide variety of graphics, including digitized backgrounds, electronic clip art, 3-D titles and other illustrations from draw and solid modeling programs. The basic data for the chart can come from information supplied by the presenter on typed sheets of paper or on computer disk, mainframe data downloaded to the graphics workstation, or from spreadsheet information that is automatically loaded into the presentation graphics program. All of these elements are carefully combined to create an appealing chart that attractively presents the information and advances the image of the organization (see Figure 10.1).

Design Considerations for Presentation Graphics

Choosing the Format   Format refers to the display medium. Presentations can use 35mm color slides, 8 × 10 overhead transparencies, paper (hard copy) handouts, or videotape. The format depends on the type of presentation and the number of people in the audience. If it is a sales meeting or presentation before a large audience, the presenter may use 35mm slides. Slide presentations are easily controlled from the podium and convey a strong corporate image. There are disadvantages, however. The presenter may not have control over the amount of light in the room from windows and nearby lighting fixtures. Also, presenters sometimes read their scripts verbatim as the slides click off in the background, making the presentation dull.

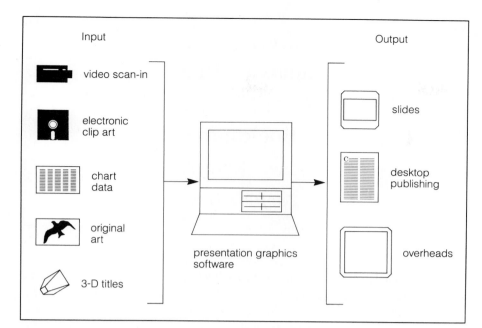

FIGURE 10.1

Input sources for presentation graphics, with types of output.

Peer presentations and briefings before smaller groups are usually more interactive and use a less formal presentation medium. Overhead transparencies—8 × 10 slides used in overhead projectors—are a good medium for brainstorming sessions in smaller groups. Paper handouts are ideal if the presentation is technical or if detailed notes are important.

The number of illustrations depends on the type of presentation. Scientific presentations usually require more illustrations—diagrams, schematics, and charts. Motivational talks require fewer illustrations but may contain more artwork—icons, scanned-in photos, or cartoons. When in doubt follow a simple rule: KISS (Keep it simple, stupid). Don't let the presentation overpower the personality of the speaker. The best presentations let the speaker's personality come through. The speaker should talk to the audience rather than read the material verbatim.

As a general rule, the slide segment of the presentation should balance with the personality of the speaker. With a dynamic speaker, keep the slides simple and the presentation slow. Spotlight the podium. With a less dynamic speaker, use more graphics and a faster presentation. Each key point should have its own slide, which should be as visually interesting as possible. The last slide must be upbeat and memorable.

Try to get the speakers to use the remote switch for the projector (called the pickle) so they can advance their own slides. Speakers should have a script that describes each slide in case they lose their place. When speakers are not able to advance slides themselves, the audiovisual technician should have a full script and rehearse with the presenter before the presentation.

Type Style   Select a medium-weight, clean-looking font with minimal or no decoration. Helvetica is an ideal font. If more style is desired, you can choose

FIGURE 10.2

Examples of typefonts.

Helvetica

Helvetica Bold

AvantGarde

Bookman

Times Roman

ZapfChancery

a font with moderate stylization, such as Bookman or Times Roman. Avoid fonts with ornate serifs and extreme changes in weight (see Figure 10.2). To promote a unified look, avoid using more than two fonts on the same visual. Bold and italic variations from the same font can be used for the headline and for emphasis. The size of the typeface should be consistent with legibility. One rule of thumb is to hold the slide at arms' length; if you can still read the text, the slide will be legible in the back row of a medium-sized room.

Color Color selection is based on legibility. Always plan the color scheme for the whole presentation before picking colors for individual segments. For slides, television, and overhead transparencies, use bright colors (that is, colors high in saturation or luminance) for foreground information (see Color Plate 2). Darker colors, which are low in saturation and luminance, should be used for the background. They draw less attention to themselves and provide a good contrast for the brighter foreground colors. The brightest colors should be used for the most important information. Use the dominant color for the message not the graphics. Never select a bright color for a footnote or secondary data; it will distract from the primary foreground information.

When picking colors to represent diverse information select colors that are as different as possible from each other. Choose colors that are appropriate to the subject. For example, use red for deficits; never use green to mean danger. The total number of colors should be kept to a minimum. Too many colors will make the chart look busy; try to limit the number to five or six. If you are using a digitized background, limit color to a single hue. Avoid placing red and green next to each other. They tend to vibrate visually and most digital film recorders will introduce a pale yellow borderline between the two colors. Some people feel this combination produces greater eyestrain.

Colors on a color monitor will differ considerably from colors produced on a film recorder or thermal color printer, so always check your color selection on the output device to be used to produce the final form of the presentation.[1] When creating hard copy for handouts or publications, use dark type on a white background. Shades of gray should have strong contrast if used next to each other in graphics such as pie charts and bar charts.

---

[1] Aaron Marcus, "Color: A Tool for Computer Graphics Communication," in *The Computer Image: Applications of Computer Graphics*, ed. Donald Greenberg (Reading, Mass.: Addison-Wesley, 1982), 86–90.

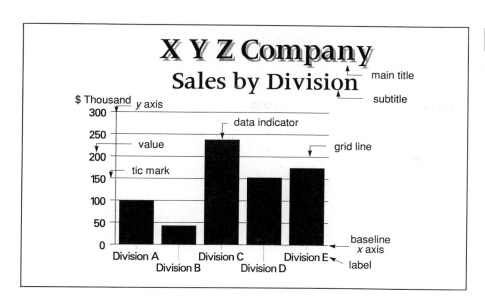

FIGURE 10.3

Parts of a chart.

Picking the Right Chart for the Data

Most presentation graphics fall into one of four major chart categories: word charts and tabular tables, bar and column charts, line charts, and pie charts. Word and tabular charts display information in text form; sometimes called laundry lists, these are the most popular form of chart. Bar and column charts use bars to depict numeric information and are useful for making quick comparisons. Line charts use lines as data indicators and show trends over time. Pie charts show the relationship of individual elements to the whole. In addition, there are bubble charts, Gantt charts, map charts, and scatter diagrams. Each chart type will be discussed in greater detail later. Individual charts are composed of several key elements, including the title, subtitle, x and y axes, labels, and data indicators (see Figure 10.3).

Isolating the Data to Be Summarized   Before selecting a specific chart, isolate the data to be compared and decide what is significant and what is not. What is the goal of the presentation? The same data can be used to make different charts, depending on the goal. For instance, a presenter may use a tabular chart summarizing data in three areas:

▸ The increase in carbon monoxide in the air per year over a ten-year period.

▸ The increase in temperature on a year-by-year basis for that same period.

▸ The yearly increase in yields for tobacco crops.

Jumping to conclusions, you might easily create a bar chart that shows the one-to-one relationship between rising carbon monoxide and temperature. This would be a socially relevant and interesting scientific comparison but may be only a minor factor that has little to do with the actual thrust of the presentation. Emphasizing this point may be counterproductive, since it could sidetrack the audience. The real objective of the slide might be to show how carbon monoxide in the atmosphere is good for certain agricultural crops because it

TABLE 10.1

MOTION PICTURE REVENUE (20 Top-Grossing Pictures)

	1980	1981	1982	1983	1984
First-run theaters	$450	$500	$ 560	$ 475	$ 475
Cable TV	150	195	210	200	190
Cassettes	50	75	125	180	240
Broadcast TV	215	200	235	227	205
Total (in millions)	$865	$970	$1130	$1082	$1110

Note: Data for illustration only.

extends the growing season. The interim data about rising temperature could be brought out later, after the audience has seen the most important relationship—that a slight rise in carbon monoxide produces a greater yield in tobacco crops. Data from the same report can be made into different charts, depending on what is emphasized. After you decide what to emphasize, use the chart title to direct the audience to your message.

Table 10.1 is a tabular chart summarizing the data but not indicating a specific comparison. It does not have a specific point of view; even the table title is generic. The first step in choosing a chart type is to decide how to use the data. What do you want to say? Based on the above data, we could create a bar chart comparing yearly sales in each category (see Figure 10.4). Or we could create a line chart to compare trends in each category over the full period (see Figure 10.5). The bar chart would emphasize the year-by-year comparison, and the line chart would emphasize a leveling in theater box office while cable revenue was on the increase. The presenter will have to tell you what to emphasize before you select the chart format.

Slides are meant to summarize. When possible, eliminate a string of zeros by using a legend to signify millions, billions, and so on. Don't get caught in the minutiae that can obstruct the point of the visual. A client may call you at the last minute to update a chart figure from 9.87 to 9.88, but the last two digits may not really matter, much less the very last digit. Tactfully remind the client that the purpose of the chart is to show trends, not convey precise information. Save minute detail for handouts and articles in technical journals.

Word Charts Word charts are like billboards along the highway. They convey a simple but pointed message to an audience with limited viewing time.[2] Word charts are meant to summarize the presenter's comments. Keep them simple and eliminate anything that isn't essential. When creating word charts, try to break up the information into concepts and be as brief as possible. Use phrases instead of full sentences. If more than one phrase is put on a slide, the phrases should be logically related. Limit the number of lines on a slide to six to eight, depending on how much of the slide is taken up with artwork.

Bullets are a good way to add variety to the screen and to delineate topics. They are placed at the beginning of each topic line and come in a

---

[2] David Benchley, "Presentation Pointers," *PC World* 4 (Feb. 1986): 133.

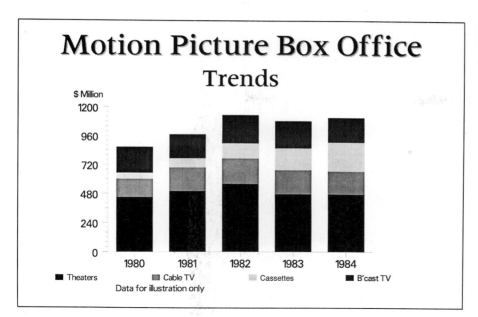

FIGURE 10.4

Bar chart.

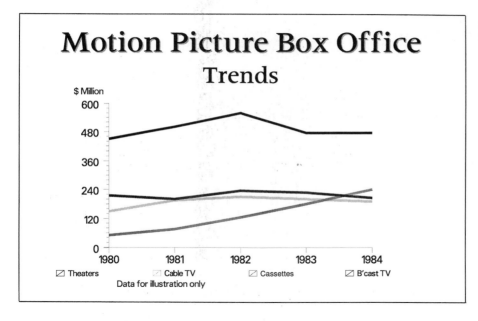

FIGURE 10.5

Line chart.

variety of shapes and sizes (see Figure 10.6). They can be round, square, outline, or filled in. You can use check marks or dashes. Some programs even let you use a small picture or original art as a bullet. Bullets can be made a shade or two darker than the text so the text will stand out.

The fewer words on a slide, the better. Sometimes a single word or short phrase will summarize lengthy comments. Phrases that begin with bullets should be declarative and state the conclusion, not the subject. For example:

This	**Not this**
▸ Use san serif type.	▸ San serif type
▸ Make foreground colors bright.	▸ Foreground colors
▸ Make background colors dark.	▸ Background colors

FIGURE 10.6

Types of bullets used to set off each line.

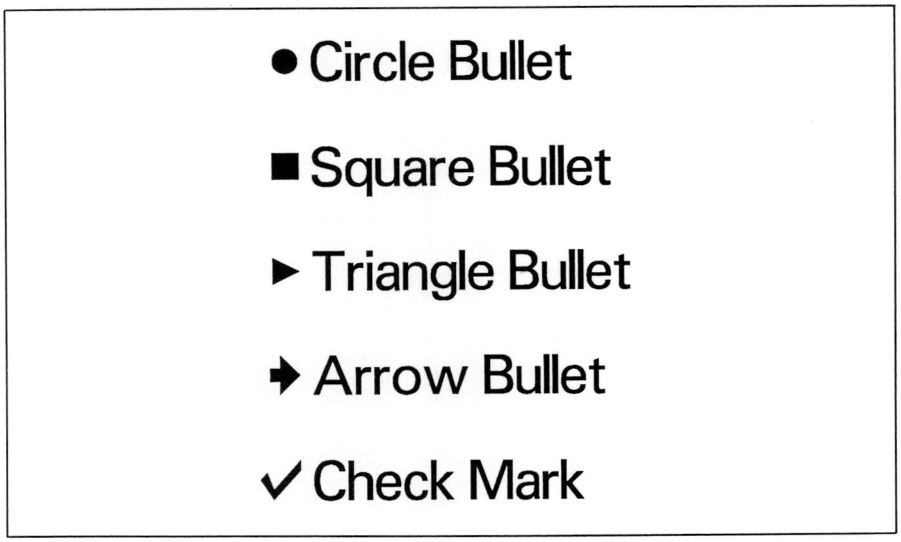

- ● Circle Bullet

- ■ Square Bullet

- ▶ Triangle Bullet

- ➜ Arrow Bullet

- ✔ Check Mark

Use a series of progressive disclosure slides (a series of slides that adds additional items to a list as the speaker talks, also called build slides) to give visual variety (see Figure 10.7). This will keep the audience in step with the speaker, reveal new items one at a time, and build a list of points to be used in a summary at the end.[3] The last word or phrase added to the list should be brighter or of a different color than the others. Use adequate margins and don't crowd too much text on the screen. Type style, headlines, and margins should be uniform throughout the presentation. Be sure to provide strong tonal contrast between text and background so people in the last row will not have trouble reading the text. Use dark rather than light backgrounds.

Tabulars   Tabulars are structured word charts delineating tables of information in columnar form, usually with key data highlighted. The name comes from using the tab key on a standard typewriter to move the carriage to the next column. Tabulars make up about 15 percent of all charts (see Figure 10.8).

Pie Charts   Use pie charts to compare one or more items to the whole—for instance, factors that contribute to death among teenagers, national debt broken down into its components, or number of illiterate people in the United States as a percentage of the whole (see Figure 10.9). Be sure the total adds up to 100 percent. Avoid using more than five to seven sections. If the client gives you a sheet with 12 items, reduce the number by combining the smaller values into an "others" category. If all the elements are important to the presentation and you cannot eliminate any of them, break out the others category with a tabular chart listing the elements in descending order by percentage (see Figure 10.10). Presentation graphics are visual tools that summarize. Slides with too much information look cluttered and will not be legible from the back of the auditorium.

---

[3] "The View from the Back Row—How to Make Legible Slides (. . . and Video Graphics, Too)," *Audiovisual Notes from Kodak* (Rochester, N.Y.: Eastman Kodak).

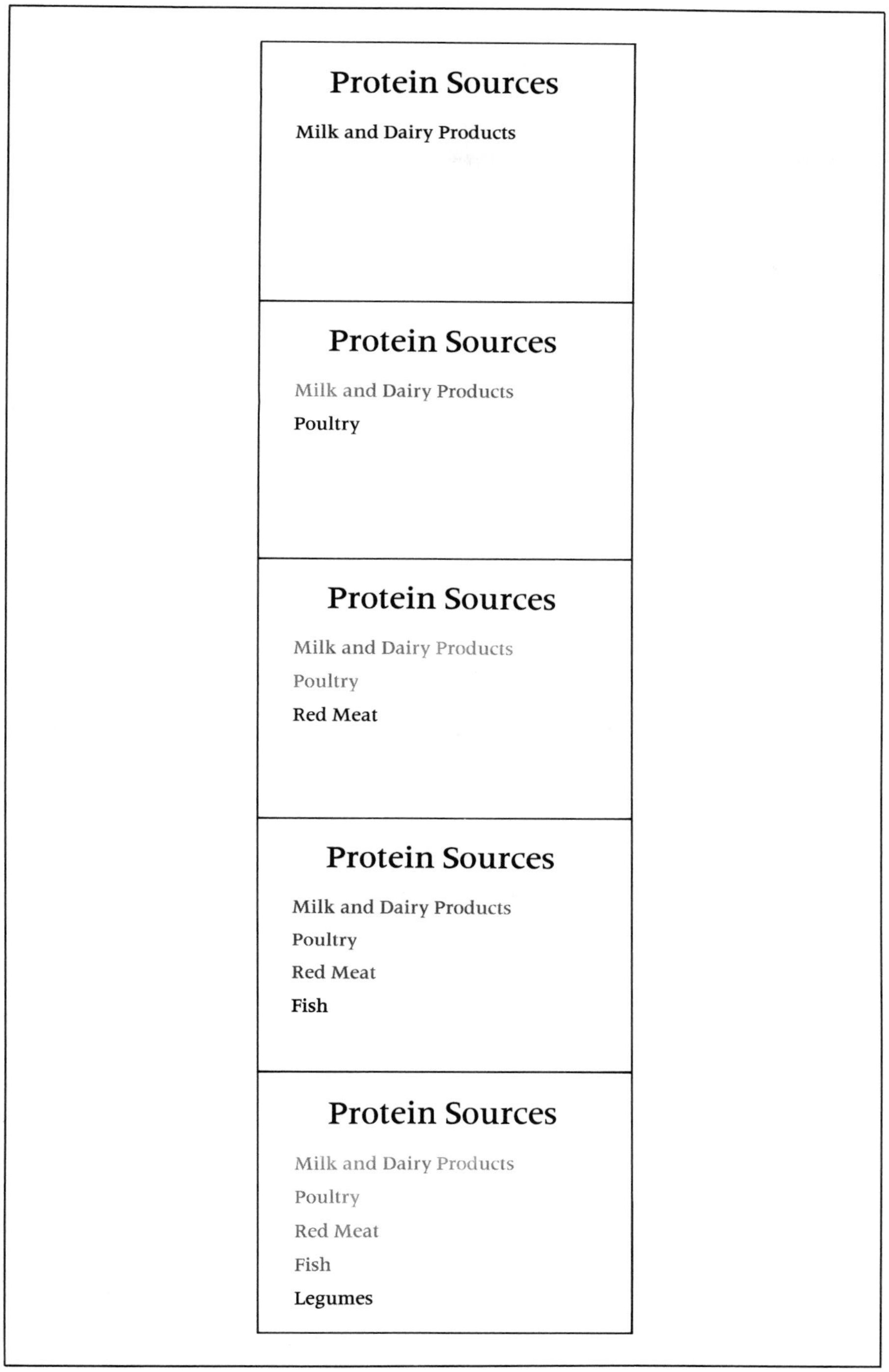

FIGURE 10.7

Series of progressive-disclosure slides.

Protein Sources

Milk and Dairy Products

Protein Sources

Milk and Dairy Products

Poultry

Protein Sources

Milk and Dairy Products

Poultry

Red Meat

Protein Sources

Milk and Dairy Products

Poultry

Red Meat

Fish

Protein Sources

Milk and Dairy Products

Poultry

Red Meat

Fish

Legumes

Occasionally, a segment or segments of a pie can be "exploded" away from other segments to emphasize your point. Try not to explode more than two segments; it splits the viewers' attention. Individual segments should be in contrasting colors. In addition, you can outline all the segments in a contrasting color for greater separation from the background. Labels for each

FIGURE 10.8

Tabular chart.

Career Types

PROFESSIONAL	58.8%
MANUFACTURING	10
GOVERNMENT/PUBLIC ADMINISTRATION	8
FINANCIAL/INSURANCE/REAL ESTATE	5
BUSINESS SERVICES	5
WHOLESALE/RETAIL	4
AGRICULTURAL/FARMING	3
CONSTRUCTION	1
ENTERTAINMENT/RECREATION	1
OTHER EMPLOYMENT	2

FIGURE 10.9

3-D exploded pie chart.

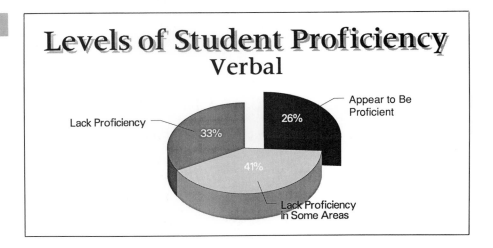

FIGURE 10.10

Pie chart showing break out of "others." (Adapted from chart provided by Brilliant Image, Inc.)

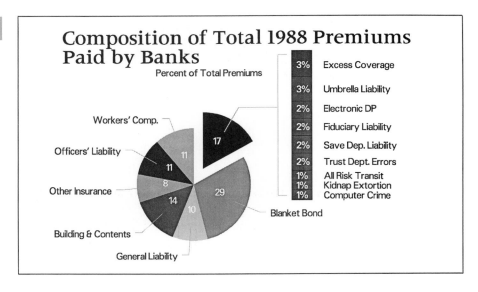

segment must be brief. Lines pointing to the segments should be drawn uniformly. Use color code boxes to identify segments when there are too many indicator lines. This will make the chart look less complicated. Three-dimensional pie charts can be used, providing that they do not confuse the viewer.

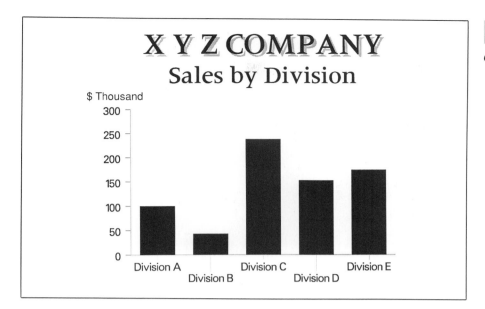

FIGURE 10.11

Column chart.

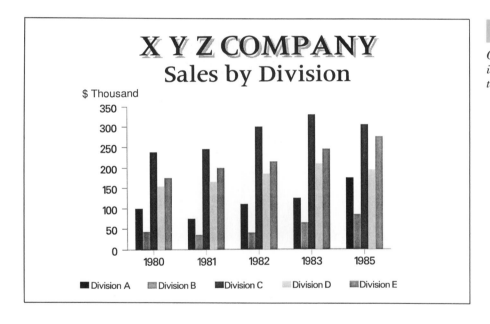

Column and Bar Charts   Vertical bar charts are sometimes called column charts. Both types are used for a variety of applications. Such charts can be used to compare one value to another (such as profits to sales), to show changes over time (profits over a five-year period), and, when values are stacked on top of each other, to show parts of the whole (balance of payments deficit broken into contributing factors).

The most elementary use of a column chart is for simple comparisons (for example, profits to sales or sales by division) (see Figure 10.11). Use the y axis for the quantity (values) and the x axis to anchor the columns and labels. Cluster column charts are an excellent way to show and compare discrete changes within a group of variables by year (see Figure 10.12).

FIGURE 10.13

(a) Stacked bar chart and (b) multiple pie chart. Both charts use the same data. The stacked bar chart is more compact and easier to read.

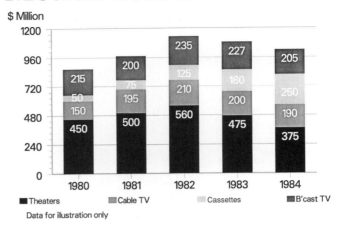

Motion Picture Box Office

a

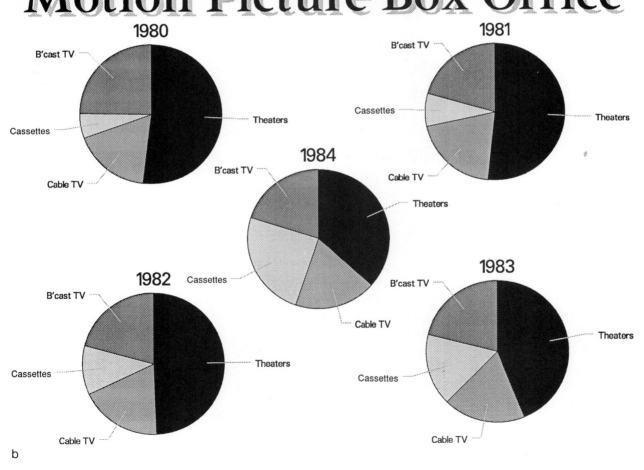

Motion Picture Box Office

b

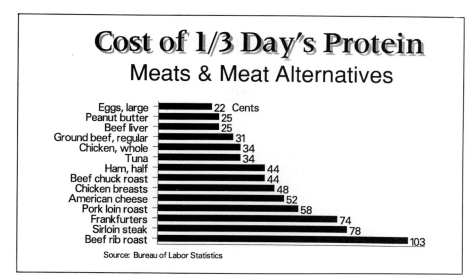

FIGURE 10.14

Horizontal bar chart.

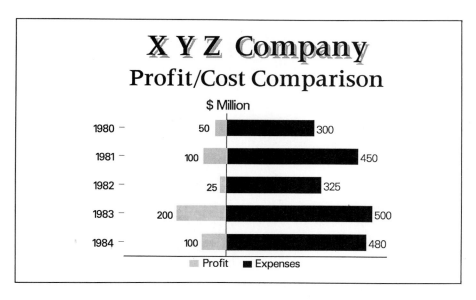

FIGURE 10.15

Floating bar chart. This chart shows the relationship of expenses to profits. Expenses are on the left, and profits are on the right.

Stacked column charts are used to show parts of the whole and are similar to pie charts. Unlike pie charts, stacked column charts will also show comparisons over time (see Figure 10.13). In each column in Figure 10.13a, the amounts near the bottom are in darker shades. This method is useful for showing relative changes in the proportional distribution of expenses among divisions over time. However, the exact amounts for each segment are hard to gauge, and you should label them if necessary.

Use horizontal indicators (bars) when labels will not fit easily under the baseline and when time series is not required (see Figure 10.14). You can use horizontal bar charts for comparisons between two closely associated variables (see Figure 10.15).

A variation of the column chart is the step chart, which has a solid shaded portion instead of individual bars. This chart is useful when you want to show discrete changes over time but have too many variables to leave space between each column (see Figure 10.16).

FIGURE 10.16

Step bar chart. The space between the indicators has been eliminated to make the chart less cluttered.

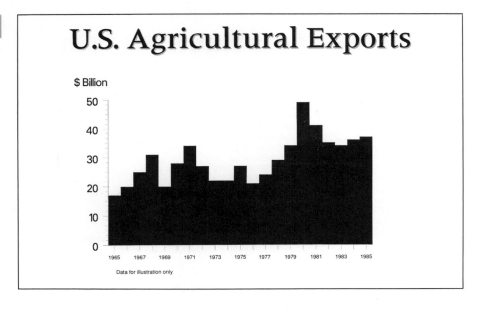

FIGURE 10.17

Line chart. The dollar amount is shown on the y axis, and time (days, months) is shown on the x axis.

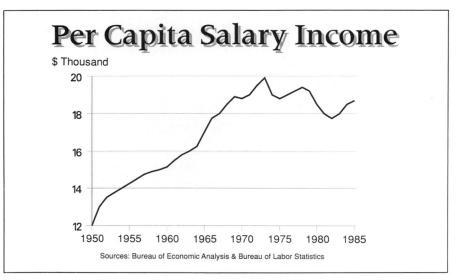

Line Charts   Use line charts to communicate a sense of continuity over time. These charts are often used for stock prices, cost-of-living index, or inflation. Trend analysis is an important use for presentation graphics. The dollar amount is shown on the y axis, and the years, days, months, and so on are shown on the x axis (see Figure 10.17). This chart is sometimes called a fever chart because the line looks like fever charts used in hospitals. Be sure to make the fever line heavier than the background grid.

Constructing Line Charts   For clarity, always start the chart at 0. If this is not possible, use a line under the baseline with 0 next to it (see Figure 10.18). If you must, emphasize small changes in variables at the top of the columns by using a different scale; make it clear that you did not start at 0.

Poverty Rates by Age

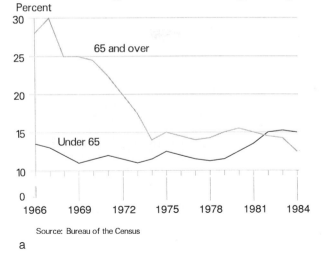

Percent

30 ─────

65 and over

25 ─────

20 ─────

15 ─────

Under 65

10 ─────

0

1966   1969   1972   1975   1978   1981   1984

Source: Bureau of the Census

a

Poverty Rates by Age

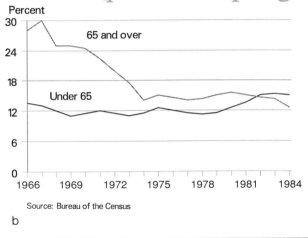

Percent

30 ─────

65 and over

24 ─────

18 ─────

Under 65

12 ─────

6 ─────

0

1966   1969   1972   1975   1978   1981   1984

Source: Bureau of the Census

b

FIGURE 10.18

Comparison of line charts. Both line charts include a 0 for clarity. In (a) differences in data between years are more pronounced because the 0 is below the baseline.

Always make the numbers along each axis as large as possible. Eliminate in-between numbers and count in 5s or 10s—whatever number you can divide evenly into the maximum amount for that axis. To improve readability, limit the number of tic marks (indicator lines next to each value on the x or y axis) to five.

Always check the maximum data amount you are plotting and customize your x axis accordingly, so that the highest amount will fit comfortably on the scale. Break this rule when you want to dramatize rapid growth in sales or earnings. In such cases, let the data line surge above the top of the x axis so the increase will be obvious (see Figure 10.19).

Never let the grid lines go through your data indicators (bars or columns). Grid lines are for visual reference and should appear to go behind

FIGURE 10.19

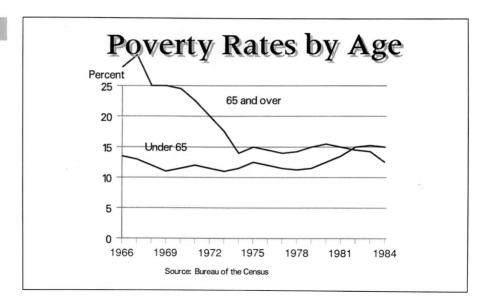

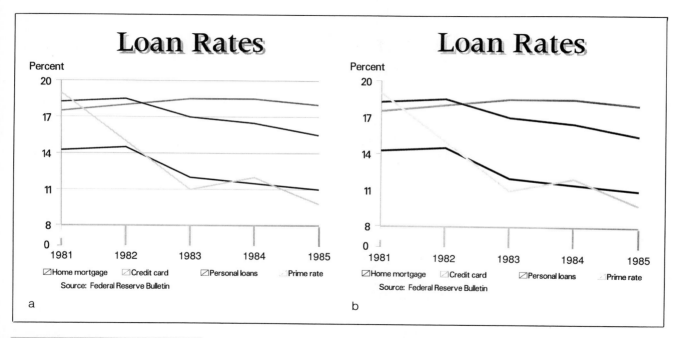

a

b

FIGURE 10.20

*Line chart comparison. Chart (b) is
more readable because the grid lines
do not interfere with the data
indicators.*

each indicator. Sometimes grid lines will make the chart look too busy and
shouldn't be used at all (see Figure 10.20).

Mountain Charts   A variation of the line chart is the mountain, or area,
chart. The mountain chart is similar to a line chart except that you will fill
in the area under the line. These charts emphasize volume and are useful for
plotting something big or bulky—such as changes in national debt or cubic
tons of coal.

Mountain charts can also be used to compare changes in several
variables over time. Stacked mountain charts can be used when plotting the
relationship of two or more variables or to emphasize the intersection of two
variables (such as cost to gross sales) (see Figure 10.21). The area between

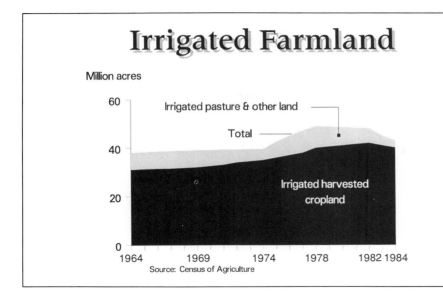

FIGURE 10.21

Stacked mountain chart.

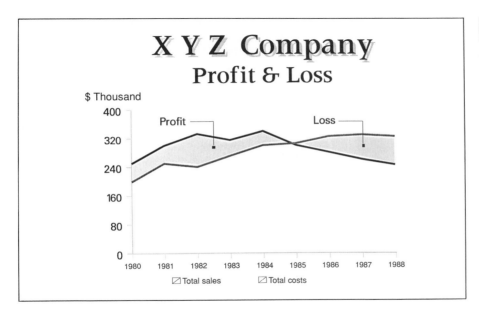

FIGURE 10.22

Line chart with inside area marked off.

the two lines can be colored green to represent profits. If the costs line rises above gross sales color, the area between the lines can be colored red for losses (see Figure 10.22). When creating mountain charts, always place data with a more irregular shape on top so that it does not distort the shape of less irregular data (see Figure 10.23).

Gantt Charts Gantt charts use double-ended floating bars that mark the starting and ending points of specific steps in the completion of a project. These charts show the relationship between several steps in a complex project, such as the building of an office building or the assembling of an automobile. Gantt charts are useful when planning a project because they reveal bottlenecks that might otherwise slow a project if not planned for in advance (see Figure 10.24).

FIGURE 10.23

Comparison of mountain charts. Chart (a) is easier to read because the irregular data is on top.

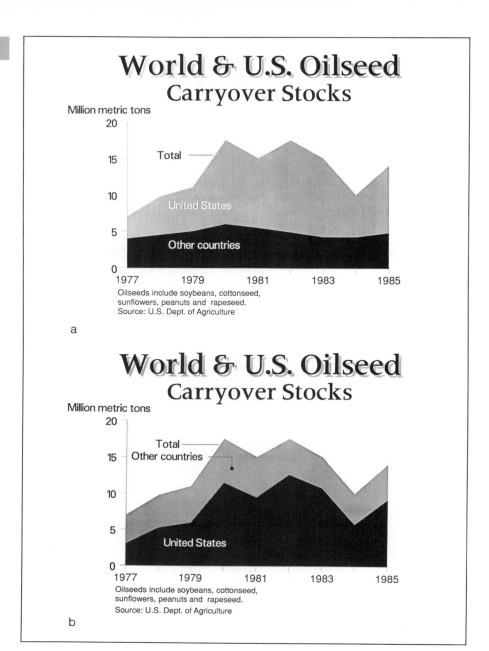

High-Low Charts   Closely related to the Gantt chart is the high-low chart, used to follow fluctuations within a given range of values over a discrete period of time. This chart is most commonly found in newspapers, where it is used to chart daily stock trends. The range is marked by the high and low trading prices for the day. The tic mark through the center of the range indicates the closing price for that day (see Figure 10.25).

Scatter Charts   Scatter charts are made up of a grouping of individual points, resembling the grouping of bullet holes in a target. A tight grouping indicates a relationship between data, and a loose grouping shows less of a relationship. Scatter charts are used to plot irregular data that may or may

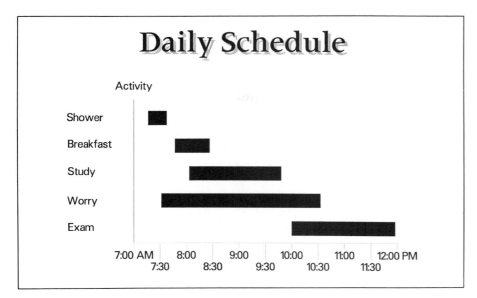

FIGURE 10.24

Gantt charts.

FIGURE 10.25

High-low chart. (Used with permission of Standard & Poor's, Inc.)

not have a significant correlation. A significant correlation, or trend, will reveal itself if the dots follow a pattern. If the grouping of dots slopes up to the right, there is a positive correlation: the value of x increases as y increases.

FIGURE 10.26

Scatter chart, with positive correlation.

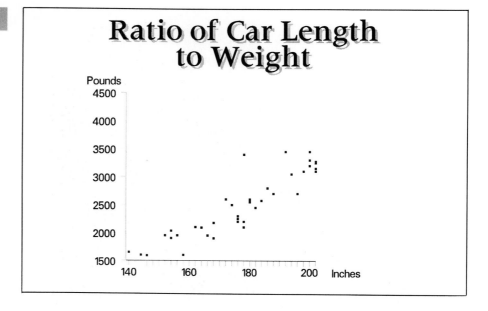

FIGURE 10.27

Co-axal chart.

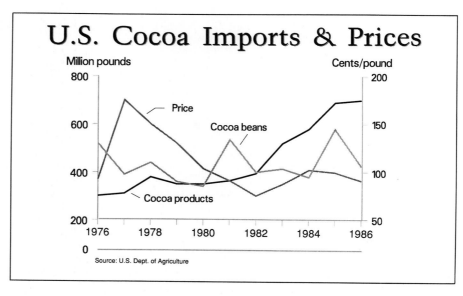

If the grouping slopes up to the left, there is a negative correlation: as *x* increases, *y* decreases. In Figure 10.26 the weight of each automobile is charted on the *y* axis, and the length on the *x* axis. The chart shows that as cars get heavier, they tend to get longer. Sophisticated statistical software will fit a curve line to the average value at each point on the chart, making it easier to see positive or negative correlation.

Co-Axal Charts   Co-axal charts plot dissimilar but related data on the same chart and are useful when comparing the relationship of the cost of one item to the availability of another, for instance, or the profits of a company to the number of sick days taken by employees. In Figure 10.27, the cost of cocoa

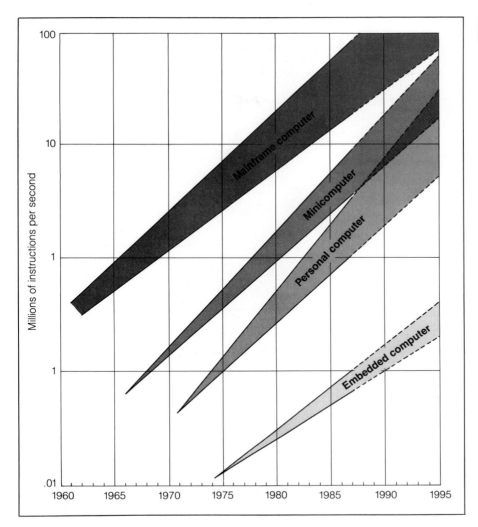

imports is plotted on the same chart with the amount of cocoa products imported. Note that the price drops as the amount imported increases, illustrating a negative correlation between cost and availability.

Logarithmic Charts Logarithmic charts differ from regular charts because the scale changes as the numbers increase in value. A chart might begin with equal increments from .01 to 1 and then go from 1 to 10 in the same amount of space. This sliding scale is useful when showing rate of change between two or more variables or when the extremes on the scale are so large that it would be impossible to chart the data without gradually changing the scale. In Figure 10.28, the dramatic increase in computer power can easily be seen. Look carefully at the *y*-axis scale. Note that it begins at .01 and rises to 100. Such scales should be used with extreme caution and only when the audience knows how to read such information. If the chart is clearly labeled and the audience is familiar with this technique, these charts can be useful. Otherwise, find another way to chart the data.

FIGURE 10.29

Bubble chart. The third variable, market share, is represented by the size of the bubble.

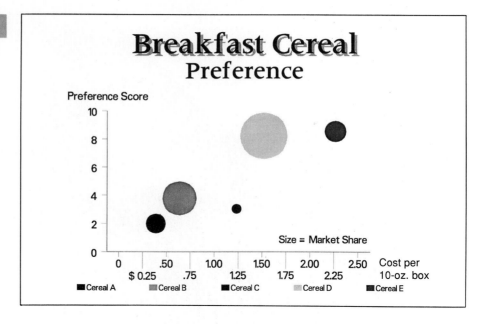

FIGURE 10.30

3-D scattergram. Variables are measured on the x, y, and z axes.

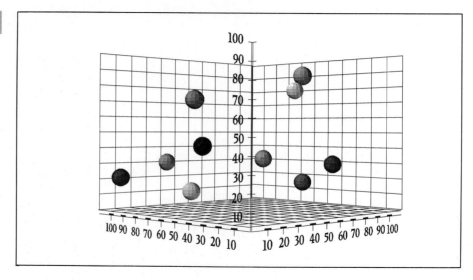

Multivariable Charts   It is sometimes necessary to plot the progression of more than two variables on the same chart. This can be done using multivariable charts, as follows.

1. *Bubble charts.* Bubble charts present three variables while still using a two-dimensional plane. Besides the x and y variables, the third variable is represented by the size of each bubble. In the bubble chart in Figure 10.29, the x axis represents price, the y axis is performance (taste), and the diameter of each bubble shows market share.

2. *3-D scattergrams.* Three-dimensional scattergrams can be created with variables running along the x, y, and z axes. The z axis is plotted back into three-dimensional space from the intersection of the x and

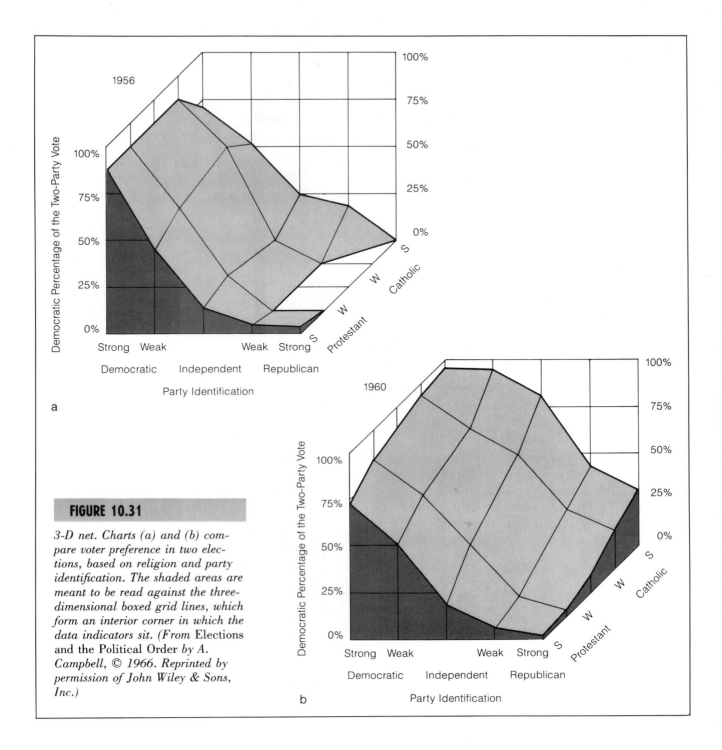

FIGURE 10.31

3-D net. Charts (a) and (b) compare voter preference in two elections, based on religion and party identification. The shaded areas are meant to be read against the three-dimensional boxed grid lines, which form an interior corner in which the data indicators sit. (From Elections and the Political Order by A. Campbell, © 1966. Reprinted by permission of John Wiley & Sons, Inc.)

y axes. Special-purpose computer-graphic charting software makes this operation fairly easy (see Figure 10.30).

3. *3-D nets.* Three-dimensional nets are similar to 3-D scattergrams except grid lines are used to connect the points into a matrix that looks like the perspective view of a mountain (see Figure 10.31).

Map Charts Map charts are a convenient way of presenting information dependent on geographic data (such as altitude, time zone, zip code, country,

FIGURE 10.32

Map chart. (Adapted from chart provided by Brilliant Image, Inc.)

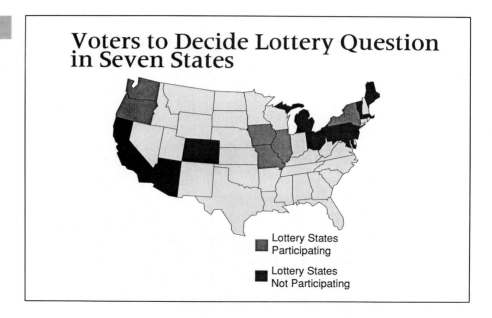

FIGURE 10.33

Line graph, with related picture used as a background.

state, or county) (see Figure 10.32). Because of their unique nature, most map charts are created using traditional graphic arts methods. However, several companies provide computer mapping services and software.

Illustrations   Besides text and statistical representations, there are several other visual aids used in presentations, including flowcharts, chains of command, photographs, cartoons, and original art. Special computer graphics software will create flowcharts and chains of command, which also can be created using standard draw and paint software. Photographs and original art can be added to chart slides with scan-in devices that digitize the original flat art. The digitized image is then used as background behind the chart or

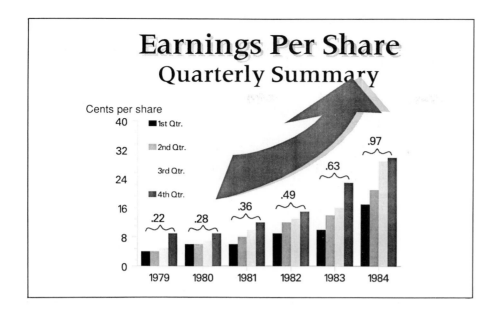

FIGURE 10.34

Example of a visual metaphor. The arrow emphasizes upward growth of earnings. (Adapted from chart provided by Brilliant Image, Inc.)

diagram. Charting software makes it easy to incorporate digitized backgrounds into presentation graphics (see Figure 10.33). The image file format must be compatible with the charting program, however.

INFORMATION GRAPHICS

The best slides are those that dramatize the presenter's comments by finding a visual metaphor for what is being said. If the presenter wants to show that earnings are shooting upward, then dramatize that point by showing earnings "breaking through" the top of the chart (see Figure 10.34). Remember that presentation graphics is part show business. Graphic art (icons, original art) is an important element in presentation graphics. Check out presentations on the evening news shows or in *Time* or *Newsweek* magazines and see how graphic art is used to add impact to charts and diagrams. Don't overuse graphics. In business presentations the most important element is always the information.

Artful interpretation can sometimes distort the truth. Look carefully at your charts to make sure that visual representation is proportional to numerical representation. Perspective will sometimes unintentionally distort the truth (see Figure 10.35). Visual distortion of quantitative data is a potential problem whenever the artist tries to dramatize a point. Be careful when using three-dimensional data indicators. The three-dimensional view of an exploded portion of a pie, for instance, may look larger than its nearest neighbor. If the 3-D portion of the pie is in the foreground and you are using perspective, the pie segment will look bigger than it is.

Be careful when illustrating relative increase in size. In Figure 10.36a, the coffee cup on the right is 20 times larger in volume than the one on the far left, even though it is only 4 times as high. In such cases, use stacked icons rather than creating one larger one.

FIGURE 10.35

Importance of appropriate perspective. Chart (a) uses normal perspective. Chart (b) uses exaggerated perspective and could be misread: the 19 percent section appears larger than the 23 percent section.

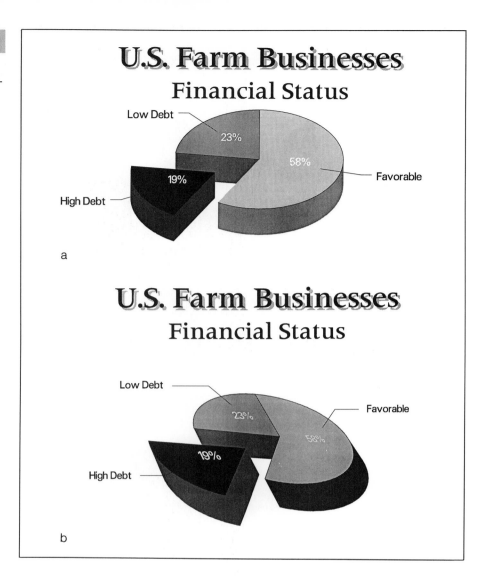

SUMMARY

Presentation graphics is the artful depiction of quantitative information. The graphic artist and graphics coordinator improve presentations by objectively listening to the presenter and advising how and where graphics (charts, icons, photographs, and original art) will enhance the message. Sound graphic practices should be followed. Use colors sparingly, keep typefaces simple, and minimize the number of chart elements. Be aware of how the graphics will eventually look when output on a film recorder, pen plotter, or videotape recorder.

Presentation graphics combine skills in art, education, showmanship, and business with specific expertise on the subject. The number of presentations that must be prepared every week, the short deadlines, and the importance of each presentation to the reputation of the presenter make presentation graphics a special challenge for the graphics department.

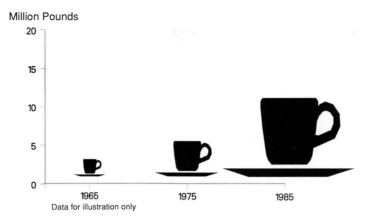

a

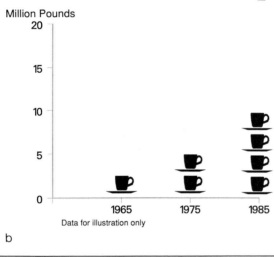

b

FIGURE 10.36

Illustrating relative increase in size. Both charts are meant to convey the same information. Chart (a) is misleading because the icon at the right has a larger mass than the difference in data justifies.

Exercises

1. Become familiar with the options in your presentation graphics software. Complete the exercises that come with the software tutorial if one is included.

2. Practice making computer-generated charts from printed charts in newspapers and magazines. You may want to purchase the U.S. Department of Agriculture Chartbook, which contains over 500 different charts of all varieties. (See the Bibliography for further information.)

Bibliography

Chambers, John, William S. Cleveland, Bert Kleiner, and Paul A. Turkey. *Graphical Methods for Data Analysis*. Belmont, Calif.: Wadsworth, 1983.

Huff, Darrell. *How to Lie with Statistics*. New York: Norton, 1954.

"Legibility—Artwork to Screen." *Eastman Kodak Company pamphlet no. S-24*. Rochester, N.Y.: Eastman Kodak Company.

Marcus, Aaron. "Color: A Tool for Computer Graphics Communication." In *The Computer Image: Applications of Computer Graphics*, pp. 76–90. Edited by Donald Greenberg. Reading, Mass.: Addison-Wesley, 1982.

Paller, Alan, Kathryn Szoka, and Nan Nelson. *Choosing the Right Chart: A Comprehensive Guide for Computer Graphics Users*. San Diego, Calif.: Integrated Software Systems Corporation, 1981.

Sunier, John. *Slide/Sound and Filmstrip Production*. New York: Focal Press, 1981.

Tufte, Edward R. *The Visual Display of Quantitative Information*. Cheshire, Conn.: Graphics Press, 1983.

U.S. Department of Agriculture. *1988 Agricultural Chartbook*. Washington, D.C.: U.S. Government Printing Office, 1988.

UNIT FOUR: PRESENTATION GRAPHICS

Unit Five

COMPUTER

GRAPHICS

ANIMATION

Computer animation, a distinct and highly specialized application of computer graphics, is known for spectacular visuals that have appeared in movies, television commercials, videos, and station IDs. But in spite of millions of dollars and hundreds of thousands of work hours that have gone into computer animation research and development, it is an industry that has barely scratched the surface of its true potential.

The recent history of computer animation has been characterized by upheaval in the animation service industry. For most of us, our first contact with computer animation was in television advertisements prominent in the mid 1980s. These advertisements dazzled the eye with colorful special effects and simulated futuristic environments. Unfortunately, most of the early companies responsible for these productions have gone out of business or have been acquired by larger companies that, in turn, have also gone out of business as the animation service industry became a victim of rapidly advancing computer technology. The high cost of starting a computer animation company was difficult to recoup because rapid advances in technology made later arrivals more productive at lower cost. Beth Anderson, West Coast editor of Videography *magazine, documents the recent history of computer animation service companies in her article, "Animation's New Generation." She shows how animation for commercial applications has moved from mainframe to mini and microcomputer. As you continue through the chapter, you will see how important an understanding of filmmaking is to understanding the animation process. Finally, in the case study featuring a short animation for station KSDK, St. Louis, you will see that computer animation today is not completely computerized but instead is a creative blend of live photography, computer-generated imagery, and television special effects.*

Computer animation facilities are arising from the ashes of their predecessors to fly on newer, better wings.

The first generation in the age of computer animation is no more; the next generation has only just been born. The evolution of technology was what created that first generation; it caused its downfall as well. Out of that upheaval was born the second generation, which is only now in its infancy.

Even with all that has been done during the first generation of computer animation, efficient application of the technology is still fairly recent. The makers of these revolutionary images are still laboring to convince potential clients that computer animation is a practical tool. Delivering on that promise will be the key to survival of this new generation.

If practicality was not foremost in the minds of the early computer animation pioneers, then magnificence surely was. The sense of wonder that swept over audiences at the sight of the first movie images made using a computer—such as the stargate sequence in *2001: A Space Odyssey* (1968)—further inspired those early innovators to create striking new visuals in the entertainment market. Computer science and Hollywood—two previously separate worlds—realized that they had something to offer each other. Motion-control special effects eventually became a big business and was used extensively in such movies as *Star Wars* (1977) and *Close Encounters of the Third Kind* (1977).

Other movies benefiting from computer-generated imagery (CGI) followed, including *Westworld* (1973), *Tron* (1982), and *The Last Starfighter* (1984). *Starfighter* marked the first time that viewers saw full-screen high-resolution computer-generated animation presented as live action for extended periods of screen time. A realistic, 3-D spaceship was created and animated for the film, using the $12.6 million Cray X-MP supercomputer. The Cray rendered the ship and its outer space background at between 750,000 and 1.5 million average detail elements per frame.

A few years before that landmark movie, broadcast television had gradually been showing mass audiences more and more computer animation. These came in the form of promos, commercials, and music videos and elaborately choreographed logos and 3-D objects. Originally, the technology to create these images was super high-end, and expensive mainframes were borrowed from other applications to do the job. A handful of major companies were supplying all of the CGIs seen on TV. Clients who could afford it bought it; those who couldn't, didn't.

On January 20, 1985, during Super Bowl XVIII, a commercial by Robert Abel & Associates aired on network television, marking another milestone in computer animation. The spot was titled *Brilliance*, and it featured a totally computer-generated, lifelike, gleaming chrome female android that the Abel team affectionately called Sexy Robot. Abel produced the spot for a Ketchum Advertising campaign for the Canned Food Information Council. In it, Sexy Robot spoke on the brilliance of food in cans in the year 3000.

Not to be outdone, Digital Productions soon countered with *Hard Woman*, a Mick Jagger music video that began a trend toward combining live action with computer animation. Digital Productions executed the project on a Cray, which made it possible to film the four-minute animation in only 12 weeks.

ANIMATION'S NEW GENERATION

BETH ANDERSON

Beth Anderson is the West Coast editor of *Videography*. She regularly covers computer animation and computer special effects for the magazine.

Without using rotoscoping or cell animation, Digital applied digital scene simulation (DSS)—its Oscar-winning proprietary animation technique—to simulate graceful human motion in the wire-frame figures in *Hard Woman*. With DSS, each computer-generated performer was made up of more than 400 moving parts. Thousands of lines of new software were created to accomplish the task, over 5500 animation frames were generated, and yet another new level of expression in computer animation was achieved.

As prominent players prepared to address the next phase of the ever-evolving computer animation technology, the industry began to shift. Innovative software emulating advanced techniques became available for smaller engineering workstations, minicomputers, and microcomputers. Clients who previously could not afford high-end technology suddenly found it accessible at the mid-range and low-end levels. Systems that were smaller and cheaper brought the technology home, not only to more clients, but to more users as well. The resolution limitations of television—as opposed to wide-screen film—permitted the use of lower-resolution systems as capable design tools. Some of the high-end production houses began to experience the pressures associated with excessive overhead. Acquisitions and mergers began making the news.

Filmmaker George Lucas sold Pixar, the computer graphics division of Lucasfilm Ltd. Time and cost constraints had finally dissuaded him from continuing R&D efforts in computer graphics and special effects. In February 1986, he opted to relinquish the division, which then was acquired by the former chairman of Apple Computer, Steve Jobs, and the employees of Pixar.

A few months later, the Canadian firm Omnibus Computer Graphics acquired Digital Productions in a hostile takeover, followed by a merger with Robert Abel & Associates. Key talent behind this award-winning work began scattering. Digital founders John Whitney, Jr., and Gary Demos started Whitney/Demos Productions in Culver City, California, to continue their pioneering efforts in computer-generated animation and simulation. The word leaked out that Omnibus/Abel was experiencing financial turmoil and dissension within its ranks. During this commotion, Wavefront Technologies—a Santa Barbara–based developer of high-level computer graphics software and integrator of state-of-the-art computer hardware and media recording equipment—acquired what was left of the Abel company, the software R&D arm Abel Image Research. Just weeks later, Omnibus/Abel closed its doors, unable to make payroll.

Although rumors indicated that the shutdown resulted from flagrant mismanagement, talk continued that these events marked the "passing of an era," the end of the "first generation." While certain clients remained unaffected, some became gun shy, questioning the stability of an industry whose star players could meet such a fate. To make matters worse, MAGI/Synthevision, the New York–based firm heralded for its innovative work in the computer animation field, had recently met a similar fate.

If this wasn't enough, Columbus, Ohio–based Cranston/Csuri Productions—one of the premier first-generation computer animation companies—shut down when its president, Jim Kristoff, was unable to convince the board of directors that the company needed additional financing to open a much-needed Los Angeles office. When the shareholders refused, Kristoff resigned and relocated to Los Angeles to start the new company himself. Suddenly, Pacific Data Images (PDI), Sunnyvale, California, temporarily found itself the only first-generation company operating. By the close of 1987, after rethinking their strategies, many of the key, first-generation players resurfaced in new companies with different technology. 1988 arrived just in time to unofficially mark the beginning of the second generation.

The term *second generation* seems amusing when you consider that the average time frame, from start-up to shutdown, for most of the first generation companies was about five years. This alone is testimony that the industry has not passed its infancy and that second-generation pioneers dare not be complacent.

"The marketplace, as we've learned from the pitfalls of the past, is never wrong," says John Whitney, Jr., head of Optomystic Productions, a recent second-generation start-up in Los Angeles. "Over the 14 years that Gary [Demos] and I have been in this industry, we've observed some fundamental equations about the relationship between the marketplace, the hardware/software technology, and the creative and financial elements. In the current business climate, the problems that face this industry are multidisciplinary. They call for solutions that balance all these elements."

Computer graphics, he stressed, has had the reputation of being so expensive that advertising agencies remain skeptical, and TV cartoon programmers think that computer animation is out of their ballpark altogether. Motion graphics, once a bread-and-butter marketplace that helped sustain first-generation computer image producers, is no longer a viable business because there are enough stand-alone workstations available now to allow clients the luxury of producing jobs in house. Buying those services from a production company is essentially a thing of the past. Clients now are unlikely to opt for computer graphics unless they can have—on time—high production value at a competitive price. Without that reality, magnificent, complex images are strictly academic.

"One of the distinguishing characteristics of second-generation CGI companies will be workstations that allow a designer the easiest possible contact with the computer. Interaction with any machine, whether it's a camera or a computer, should not be a barrier to creative manipulation," says Whitney.

Jim Kristoff, a former Cranston/Csuri president and currently president of . . . MetroLight Studios in Los Angeles, clearly remembers the days of deciding on equipment. "You take your best shot with what's known about technology at the time," he offers, "but it seemed like we went through a change from '81 to '87 where the changes in technology started coming more quickly. The plateaus weren't as long, so rather than a new generation of computers coming every few years, they were coming every nine months. As soon as you'd make a decision and take delivery of the equipment, that same company would announce something new that was smaller, better, faster, and cheaper. You'd then sit there, wringing your hands, wishing you'd waited just a few more months."

"The first systems, which had such extensive software and hardware requirements—with costs being extended into the $3,000 to $5,000-per-second range—created the market and did a beautiful job of it. As computers became faster and the software more integrated, as it became more of a software industry instead of a hardware industry, the prices of the technology, the simplicity of use, the turnaround—all of which dropped dramatically and continues to drop—the people locked into expensive technology were doomed. These are the pioneers who got the arrows shot in their backs. They should be respected by the industry and held, not as poor business people, but as what they were and are—pioneers who have charted a new path. Unfortunately, they were unable to respond to the market's changing needs in a manner that would have guaranteed their suc-

cess," states video pioneer Steve Michelson, president of Steve Michelson Productions in San Francisco.

While the post houses [videotape post production] have other work to balance their computer graphics overhead, companies doing 3-D computer graphics exclusively do not have that luxury. What happens next is something that even industry professionals cannot agree upon. Some believe that a few more companies will suffer hardship before too much more time passes; others believe things will remain status quo for a while. The various applications that different companies pursue will also weigh heavily in their destinies. Computer-generated special effects for television are one thing; computer-generated motion pictures are another.

No one knows this quite as acutely as MAGI founder Phillip Mittelman, who also worked on the Disney release *Tron*. In spite of the fact that *Tron* was a technical triumph, the film did not take the world by storm. "We were so enthusiastic about that film," remembers Mittelman. "We had the feeling that once *Tron* hit the streets, all the other major production companies would jump on the bandwagon of using computer animation for creating sets and even whole action scenes. Everybody thought it would be the start of a whole new world, but like most things, it wasn't. And there we were, spending a million dollars a year on a fantastic facility in Los Angeles, entertaining producers, and so on. You see how long that lasted.

"Of course while *Tron* was being made there was a tremendous amount of publicity on this fantastic, computer-generated film. A number of people approached us, saying that they had films they

wanted us to do also. So it seemed clear at that point that there were probably three to four other films just waiting for us. It looked like the feature film business was going to open up to us. The commercial business was always there—a limited number of very high-value productions that were worth nice money, maybe $100,000 to $200,000 per commercial.

"But the real kick was feature films, where you could get a million dollars, and that's what we were gearing up for and that's what created all the excitement. It's a market that is going to open up. It's just going to take longer than anybody ever thought," notes Mittelman.

Undaunted, several of the second-generation companies have their eye on this market. Computer-generated character animation is struggling to become a practical application. "There are some interesting trends going on now in the business," says Mittelman. "If you see what people are doing now on the leading edge of research, we've redeveloped all kinds of realism in a particular image, and now people are adding realism to motion. Simulating realistic movement, but automatically simulating it. Having the computer figure out how to move things so that they look realistic. Anybody can make a frame that looks great, but to make a whole sequence that looks like it's really happening is the next big step people are taking now."

"What everybody has to understand," insists Carl Rosendahl of Pacific Data Images, "is that this industry is still an infant. There is still so much to learn and to experiment with, so many directions to go, that to try and predict with any degree of accuracy what's going to happen in the future is impossible."

Chapter Eleven

ROOTS

IN

THE PAST

n this introduction to computer animation, you will see the early attempts at computer animation in science and the arts. To enhance your background you will learn about film theory as it applies to animation. Finally, a description of traditional animation techniques will round out your understanding of the roots of computer animation.

COMPUTER ANIMATION OVERVIEW

You are among the first generation of computer animation artists who will interact directly with the computer without having studied computer programming or engineering or having found a friendly computer programmer to carry out your commands. This is a big step from the distant 1960s and 1970s when mainframe computer graphics were carried out in the climate-controlled impersonal environment of the computer laboratory. During the early days of computer animation, instructions were given to the computer via punched cards (see Figure 11.1). These cards had to be prepared using keypunch machines such as those used for data processing. Most animations were created with command-oriented programs, in which the artist or programmer gave the computer a series of commands and then waited for the computer to execute the commands in batch mode. Interactive control of animation programs in a user-friendly environment, where the artist selects options with a stylus from an on-screen list, was not widely available until the 1980s.

Like many art forms based on complex technology, computer animation evolved gradually from attempts by many artists and engineers over the course of many years. John Whitney, Sr., is probably the best known of the early computer animators. With his brother James and son John Whitney, Jr., he began making analog computer animations in the late 1950s, using a mechanical analog computer salvaged from a World War II antiaircraft fire control director. The device was retooled by the Whitneys to hold a motion picture camera and could independently control the movement of the camera and artwork. The artwork took the form of a template with a moiré pattern or hand-painted design. The template was secured to an animation table, and light was then passed through from behind. Using motors and cam systems, the animation table could move up or down, turn in a complete circle, or move horizontally. The camera could also move on its own axes and was synchronized with the art work.[1] (See Figure 11.2.) Their films were composed of intricate, colorful patterns of moving light that were synchronized with music. In 1961 Whitney released *Catalog 1961*, a collection of experiments done using the analog computer (see Figure 11.3). The analog computer was also used for commercial production. In 1966 Whitney received a grant from IBM to investigate the creative capabilities of the IBM model 360 digital computer and graphics display console. Several animations were produced with this equipment, including *Experiments in Motion Graphics* and *Permutations*.

In 1963 Edward E. Zajac, a scientist at Bell Telephone Laboratories, created a wire frame animation of an earth satellite traveling through space. This is generally believed to be the first digital computer animation and was part of a scientific experiment to determine if a satellite could be stabilized so that a surface was always facing toward earth.[2] Judson Rosebush notes that "this was one of the first instances where an animated graphic visualization

---

[1] Gene Youngblood, *Expanded Cinema* (New York: Dutton), 210.

[2] Cynthia Goodman, *Digital Visions* (New York: Abrams), 153.

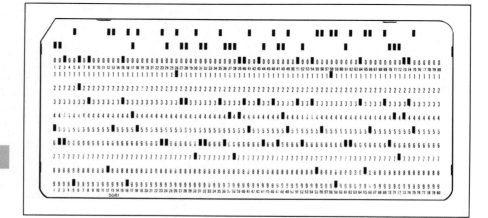

FIGURE 11.1

Punched cards were used for the input of computer data and/or instructions.

was instrumental in deriving a solution to an experiment."[3] Other computer graphics experiments at Bell Telephone Laboratories dealt with visual perception and image processing.

During the 1960s and early 1970s, Bell Telephone Laboratories encouraged artists and independent filmmakers to use Bell's computer graphics facilities (computers and software) free of charge. Experimental filmmaker Stan VanDerBeek used the facilities extensively. Bell Laboratories programmer Ken Knowlton worked closely with VanDerBeek and other artists, developing an animation language called BEFLIX that permitted the creation and modification of gray scale pixel images. Between 1965 and 1968, Knowlton and VanDerBeek created several experimental films titled *Poemfield 1 Through 8*. They also collaborated on the one-minute computer animation called *Man and His World*, which was shown at Expo '67 in Montreal.[4]

Knowlton had hoped that artists would learn the computer language so they could program their own films, but he came to realize that artists wanted to

---

[3] Judson Rosebush, *Computer Animation: An Historical Survey* (Syracuse, N.Y.: School of Public Communications, 1979), 17.
[4] Ibid.

FIGURE 11.2

Modified antiaircraft fire control director used by John Whitney, Sr., to create Catalog 1961.

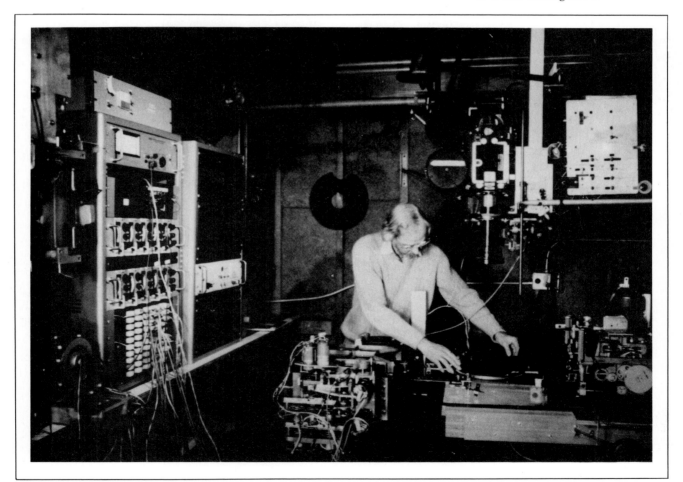

FIGURE 11.3

Still frames from John Whitney's
Catalog 1961.

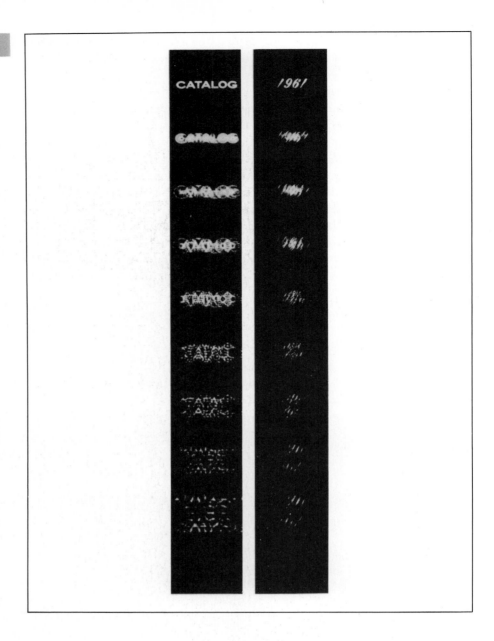

create images the language could not accommodate. He also found that some artists were reluctant to learn programming skills. As a result, he wrote a special extension to BEFLIX for VanDerBeek and in 1970 created a completely new language called EXPLOR (*EX*plicitly *P*rovided 2-D patterns, *L*ocal neighborhood *O*perations, and *R*andomness[5]) with artist Lillian Schwartz.

EXPLOR allowed artists to specify the x and y coordinates for a particular shape, usually a polygon. The program would then draw the shape at that location and loop through a subroutine (a small portion of the program set aside for a specific task), drawing the shape again and again, slightly smaller or larger, in many different places. Lillian Schwartz states that the program

---

[5] Nadia Magnenat-Thalmann and Daniel Thalmann, *Computer Animation: Theory and Practice* (New York: Springer-Verlag, 1985), 20.

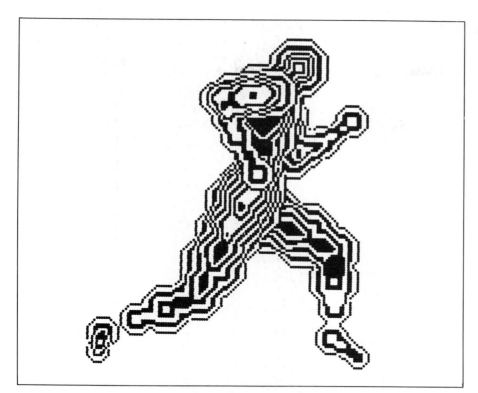

was based on probability. "There were a lot probabilities of what would happen: where the shapes would appear, how many, and if they would overlap."[6] These rules were controlled by a certain amount of built-in randomness. Since each was slightly different from the last, the images could be saved as individual frames of animation. Schwartz made several films using EXPLOR, one of the most well known being a three-minute film called *OLYMPIAD* (1971) (see Figure 11.4). The lightning pace of her earlier film *U.F.O.s* (1970) inspired one reviewer to liken it to "drumbeats on the eyeballs." Schwartz maintains that these early animations were meant to be fast so that you couldn't see all the glitches. "People have said that my work is getting slower [today], but in truth it is because computers are getting better. Sometimes the glitches were delightful. They would give you a whole new idea for going in another direction, which is what I love. I love the idea that back then you interacted with the machine and the machine became a collaborator. And because of a mistype some wonderful new thing would happen. I miss that."[7]

After Schwartz's animations were generated on the computer, the images were saved in digital form on magnetic tape—the same type of tape used for data processing. The digital images were sent to a Stromberg Carlson high-resolution microfilm recorder where they were recorded on black-and-white motion picture film. Color and special effects (freeze frames, dissolves, superimpositions, and so on) were added in the motion picture laboratory.

Computer generated 3-D color animations, with hidden surfaces removed so that objects look solid, were created in the mid-1970s and used

---

[6] Lillian Schwartz. Conversation with the author, July 21, 1988.
[7] Ibid.

in military applications such as in flight simulators. The Evans and Sutherland flight simulator helped train aircraft pilots by allowing them to land and take off from aircraft carriers without ever leaving the ground. The deck of the aircraft carrier, the horizon, and other airplanes were represented by realistic-looking solid objects that moved in real time as the pilot "flew" the simulator. In 1981, James Blinn, working for the Jet Propulsion Laboratory, showed us the spacecraft *Voyager* approaching the planet Saturn. The computer-generated simulated pictures were quite realistic, even to the surface texture and colors of the planet. The animation was broadcast to millions of viewers who could appreciate for the first time what the *Voyager* space program was all about. Blinn's contributions to the art of computer graphics include algorithms for bump mapping to create realistic computer-generated surfaces.

John Whitney, Jr., feels that one of the distinguishing features of computer animation is its ability to realistically depict environments we can only imagine. He has stated that "there are, in the spectrum of human experience, moments that are known but not necessarily caught on film. As techniques of film production mature, it may be possible to bring to the screen, utilizing computers, for instance, experience that relates to dramatic context but that has never been seen before."[8] For instance, computer effects created for the film *The Abyss* show a wormlike, translucent three-dimensional form that shapes itself into the likeness of one of the film's live characters. Computer models can be freely altered to suit the needs of the story and are not limited by the physical restraints of clay or plaster.

A SHORT COURSE IN FILM THEORY

Computer animation is a form of filmmaking. It requires the same intuitive talents and sensitivity to visual storytelling and is subject to the same rules of organization and laws of visual perception. The only difference is that computer animators use the computer instead of a sheet of paper or acetate.

The Laws of Visual Perception

As you probably know, motion pictures are made up of a series of still images. Each image captures and holds a moment in time, slightly different from the one before. When projected on the screen, the staccato of still images creates the illusion of movement. Like pictures from a slide projector, each individual image is still. The succession of still images are projected fast enough so that the human eye interprets them as one continuously moving image. Physiologists explain that the illusion of movement is due to three attributes of the eye and vision system.[9]

---

[8] John Whitney, Jr. Conversation with the author, April 4, 1981.

[9] The following discussion of the illusion of movement in the cinema is summarized from David Bordwell and Kristin Thompson, *Film Art: An Introduction* (Reading, Mass.: Addison-Wesley), 19–21.

The Phi Phenomenon This theory explains why we think we see movement when none exists. Experimenters have shown that when two small lights are placed a few feet apart at the end of a darkened room and intermittently flashed on and off at intervals of 25 to 400 milliseconds, the viewer sees a single moving light jump the distance between the two, rather than two independent lights. The phi phenomenon refers to the ability of the eye to see a single moving light instead of two lights flashing independently.

Masking Closely related to the phi phenomenon is the idea of masking. Later images "mask" prior images, displacing them in our minds and convincing us that we are seeing a single moving image.

Flicker Fusion Flicker fusion explains why, when images are projected on a screen, we do not notice that the projected light is flickering. What we think we see is a continuous beam of light, even though it is interrupted by an opaque shutter in the projector 24 times a second. The faster the beam of light is interrupted, the more continuous it will appear. Motion pictures are projected at a rate of 24 frames per second. The shutter on some projectors, however, interrupts each projected image three times, for a total of 72 flickers per second ($3 \times 24 = 72$). Because of these interruptions, the movie screen is dark for a good portion of the time. For every hour we are in a movie theater, we are sitting in total darkness for about half that time. Our eyes retain the last image projected so we do not notice that the screen is totally dark! A flicker rate of only 24 flickers per second will cause a noticeable flicker, hence the nickname flicks for old-time movies.

Flicker fusion can be explained by the theory of persistence of vision, what some people call a visual hangover. Simply put, a bright image tends to remain on the retina of the eye for a brief period of time after the image has been viewed. The combination of flicker fusion and the masking and phi phenomena gives the illusion of moving pictures. But remember: the images never move. Motion pictures and television images are a succession of still images.

Television images are transmitted at a rate of 30 frames per second. To reduce flicker, the images are interlaced—that is, every image is scanned twice for each frame. First the even lines of the image are painted on the television screen, and then the odd lines are painted. Thus, two scans (fields) make up each video frame. The interlace scanning technique does for video what the faster shutter rate does for film projection—it reduces flicker.

Visual Storytelling

Every medium, whether visual or oral, has its syntax, grammar, and way of organizing reality and presenting ideas. Oral and written communications (known as discursive media) make freer use of metaphors. Visual media like film and television (called nondiscursive media) can make fewer abstract visual comparisons. For example, consider the following passage from the short story "An Occurrence at Owl Creek Bridge" by Ambrose Bierce describing a man under water trying to free himself from ropes tied about his feet: "He gave the struggle his attention, as an idler might observe the feat of a juggler, without interest in the outcome."[10] This description plays well in the short story, but would not transfer well to film. People might laugh when the film cuts from a man struggling to free himself under water to a street juggler standing in front of a crowd of people. They would not understand the transition. Nondiscursive media such as film and television must make comparisons in the context of the physical environment and cannot use abstract literary metaphors.

If you have seen Robert Enrico's film version of "An Occurrence at Owl Creek Bridge," you will remember the following passage taken directly from the short story:

> He looked at the forest on the bank of the stream, saw the individual trees, the leaves and the veining of each leaf—saw the very insects upon them: the locusts, the brilliant-bodied flies, the gray spiders stretching their webs from twig to twig.[11]

Descriptive references to trees, leaves, and insects, and so forth were easily adopted by the film, helping the viewer share the protagonist's exhilaration on reaching the surface of the water. The language and syntax of visual storytelling should always be used when adapting works originally created for another medium. The scriptwriter translates the discursive text of the original novel into its visual counterpart.

Elements of Effective Visual Storytelling

Camera Composition   Computer graphics animators use the same terminology filmmakers use to describe individual shots and compositions. If the camera frames just the person's head, it is called a close-up (CU). If the camera frames just the person's face, excluding the area around the face, it is said to be an extreme close-up (ECU). A medium close-up (MCU) is from the shoulders up. A medium shot (MS) is a shot from the waist up. A medium long shot (MLS) is from the knees up, and a long shot (LS) includes the entire person with a little space in front. A full shot (FS) shows the person from head to toe. An extreme long shot (ELS) includes a significant amount of space in front of the person. Panoramas (PAN) are vistas, as seen from a mountain top or high building. If two people are in the same medium shot together, it is called a medium two shot.

Camera angle plays an important role in film composition. If you photograph a person at eye level with the camera, this is a normal angle shot. If the camera is below eye level, it is a low-angle shot. A high-angle shot is one in which the camera is above the subject (see Figure 11.5). Low-angle shots tend to make people look more important. Tilting the camera lens up at the subject—a person or building, for instance—makes the object look larger than life. High camera angles have the opposite effect. People tend to look less significant, less tall, and less important. Using this terminology, which describes specific camera angle and composition, can help you when you're discussing composition of shots with others.

---

[10]Ambrose Bierce, "An Occurrence at Owl Creek Bridge," in *Ghost and Horror Stories of Ambrose Bierce,* ed. E. F. Bleiler (New York: Dover, 1964), 54.
[11]Ibid., 55.

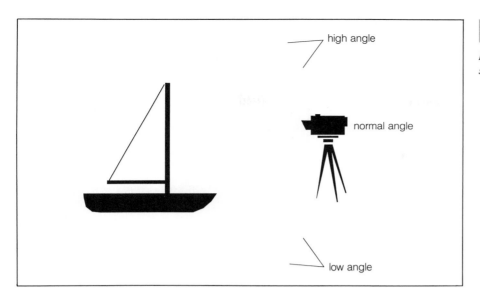

FIGURE 11.5

Example of high- and low-angle shots.

Shot   Films have a logical structure based on a division of material into shots, scenes, and sequences. The smallest unit in a film is the shot, which is defined as when the camera is turned on to when it is turned off. A shot can be as short as one frame, or it can be as long as hundreds or even thousands of frames.

Scene   A group of related shots make up a scene. A scene is usually defined by locale (all the shots taken in a given location), but it can also be defined by an idea you are trying to communicate. When you have fully explored that idea, the scene is concluded. Much like a paragraph in a novel, the scene is a small unit of related ideas that defines a single concept.

Sequence   A group of related scenes make up a sequence. A travel film, for instance, may have several scenes shot in New York, which together make up the New York sequence. Within the New York sequence may be a scene at Washington Square Park. This scene will have several related shots about the people and activities in the park. A sequence is akin to a chapter in a book.

If we ignore the concept of shots, scenes, and sequences, the result is an illustrated lecture—a slide show, not a motion picture. Motion pictures need detail. If you want the audience to think a character is repulsive, use a medium shot or a close-up showing the character belching; a long shot will not have the same impact. Each idea must be explored in depth. Cover the action in a scene from more than one camera angle. The action may be first covered in a long shot: The camera sees all the people and things related to the action. The camera is then moved closer to the characters: the same action is repeated but the camera now sees one of the actors, possibly from the waist up. Finally, close-ups of the characters are photographed as they repeat the same action. Later the editor picks the best angles and matches the action with the same action in other shots so that it seems to flow smoothly from one shot to the next, without breaks in continuity.

Movement   There are three types of movement in film: subject movement, camera movement, and edited movement. Subject movement is when a person or thing moves while it is photographed. Subject movement adds a dynamic quality to a film. We enjoy slapstick comedy because the characters' acrobatics bring us into the action. Movement should be choreographed with the camera in mind. Exits toward or away from the camera are more dynamic than exits to the right or left.

Camera movement, or frame movement, refers to movement introduced by the camera. The camera can pan left or right, as though it is pivoting on the tripod. It can truck left or right, moving parallel to the action, or it can dolly in or out. Most animation software will allow you to place the camera on any plane or position relative to the subject. You can then move the camera point of view similar to the way you would move a traditional camera. The camera can also be raised or lowered relative to the action—elevator up or elevator down. Broad swooping movements can be made with simulated crane shots.

Edited movement is created by quickly cutting between shots so that the object photographed appears to jump from one position to the next. If you photograph a stone statue of a lion lying down and cut to another statue of a lion standing up, it looks like the first lion jumped from the prone to the standing position. This was done by Sergei Eisenstein in his 1925 film *Potemkin*. It is easy to think of instances in computer graphics where static objects can be given "movement" by using the same technique. Editing is an important tool in filmmaking and should not be overlooked in computer animation.

Besides the three types of movement mentioned above, the simulated world of computer animation allows the movement of light sources. One or more light sources can be rotated around a stationary or moving object. Reflections and highlights on the surface of objects will change as you move the light source. If the object has an irregular surface texture, highlights will undulate as the light crosses the object.

Lens Perspective   In photography, perspective refers to the relative size and foreshortening of objects within the frame. Perspective gives your composition a sense of depth. If the camera is brought close to the subject, for instance, the subject will look much larger than it actually is. A greater sense of depth will be created because the foreground object will appear much larger than objects in the background. You can see the effect of close camera placement by holding an object close to your eye while closing the other eye. The object will look very large in comparison to objects farther away because it is taking up a disproportionate amount of space on the retina (see Figure 11.6). Similarly, if we photograph a person lying on a couch with his or her feet facing the camera, the feet will look enormous when compared with the rest of the body. By using a wide-angle lens (one that covers a wider angle of view by squeezing more into the frame), we can exaggerate this effect. The background now appears even further away, thus increasing our sense of depth. A telephoto lens has the opposite effect; it compresses distance between objects. A long line of telephone poles will look like they are stacked on top of each other when seen through a telephoto lens.

FIGURE 11.6

Example of lens perspective. The hand looks very large compared to objects farther away because it is taking up a disproportionate amount of space on the retina.

Computer animation software gives the artist a variety of lens perspectives from which to view the work space. By substituting a wide-angle view, foreground objects will appear much larger and background objects will appear farther away. Because actual distance between objects remains the same, subject movement toward and away from the lens seems faster when using an exaggerated wide-angle perspective.

Screen Space Screen space is the area of view in front of the camera. It can be as wide as the universe (as in the opening scene to *Star Wars*) or as intimate as the smallest detail in the time-lapse opening of a flower bud. Think of screen space as a cube. The sides of the cube are defined by the camera frame. The back of the cube is defined by objects that block the view of the horizon. The front is defined by the camera lens. Beyond the walls of the cube is off-screen space, but it is space that may also be used by the director (animator). If a car drives out of view frame right, we hear it turning around off screen, and then it returns into view and drives through the frame (exiting frame left), the director is using off-screen space. This space is part of the playing area, even though the car is not seen. Off-screen space is any area beyond the boundary of the frame or behind the scenery that becomes part of the playing area. If two characters are playing a scene in a small

FIGURE 11.7

Example of vanishing lines. The tracks leading away from the lens appear to meet at the horizon.

bedroom where there is a closet door and the audience knows that there is a body in the closet, the director is using off-screen space.

Cues to Depth Perception   The two-dimensional screen has no inherent depth. Like a piece of paper, it is flat. But as in everyday life, there are many cues to depth perception that do not rely on stereoscopic viewing. These 2-D cues give the compositions in your animation a sense of depth. By using cues to depth perception, the two-dimensional frame can take on the dynamics of the three-dimensional world. Composing for depth is an important consideration for the filmmaker and animator.[12]

Vanishing Lines   Probably the most universal cue to depth perception is the use of forced perspective. We have all seen pictures with train tracks going off into the distance, the tracks meeting at the horizon (see Figure 11.7). We associate such images with a greater sense of depth because of our learned responses: we know from experience that the parallel tracks remain parallel, even at the horizon, and seem to meet only because they are farther away.

Gradation   Simply put, gradation means that a pattern of objects, such as the cobblestones of a roadway, will look smaller at greater distances from the

[12]R. L. Gregory, *Eye and Brain: The Psychology of Seeing* (New York: McGraw-Hill, 1966).

FIGURE 11.8

Example of gradation. The picture has greater depth because the stones appear smaller at greater distances from the camera.

camera. Like the railroad tracks, we know that the stones don't get smaller, so we assume they must be farther away (see Figure 11.8).

Overlapping A greater sense of depth is created when objects can be shown to overlap. We assume objects that are partially blocked by foreground objects are farther away. Foreground objects are understood to be closer because nothing is blocking them (see Figure 11.9). Similarly, the frame may be partially blocked by a wall or a large object. The rest of the frame is left open all the way to the horizon. The contrast between the two areas gives a greater sense of depth.

Scale Scale is similar to gradation. If you position two characters so that one looks much smaller, we assume that the smaller one is farther away and not diminished in size. The contrast of scale adds depth to the frame (see Figure 11.10).

Atmospheric Perspective Atmospheric perspective is also part of our natural way of interpreting reality. Hazy objects are assumed to be farther away, the atmosphere supplying a cue to distance (see Figure 11.9). Many computer

FIGURE 11.9

An example of frame depth achieved
with overlapping (building shapes)
and atmospheric perspective (haze).

animation programs will render objects at farther distances with less clarity.
We call this process depth cueing, and it is used to add a greater sense of
depth to computer-generated images.

Editing   The actual process of editing animated films is carried out in the
planning phase. Each shot is then photographed to length and in proper order.
The theory of editing is still very important, but in animation, editing is done
before the shooting.

When planning your animation, keep the camera on the same side of
the action. We call this the 180-degree rule (see Figure 11.11). If the camera
is kept on the same side of the action, you will be able to cut to any of the
shots within that scene and not have a mismatch—that is, a shot that doesn't
fit in with the other shots. If you cut to a shot that ignores the 180-degree
rule, movement will look as though it is going the other way (see Figure
11.12).

When planning a scene that continues in another location, be sure to
have the subject exit on the opposite side of the screen from where they will
enter the next shot. For instance, if your subject exits left, then have that

FIGURE 11.10

Example of contrast of scale.

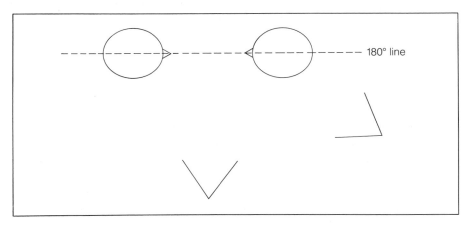

180° line

person enter right (see Figure 11.13). When the use of two shots back-to-back will cause a jump in the action (a break in continuity), cut away from the action to a related shot and then back to the action. For instance, if a batter has just hit the ball, cut to the crowd standing up. The cutaway will allow you to condense time by letting you resume coverage on the runner as he rounds second base. Cutaways are shots related to the main action but not part of that action. A person looks off camera, and the editor cuts to a clock on the wall or to a traffic accident. The cutaway is motivated by the actor looking off camera.

FIGURE 11.12

Three storyboard frames showing a runner from both sides of the imaginary line.

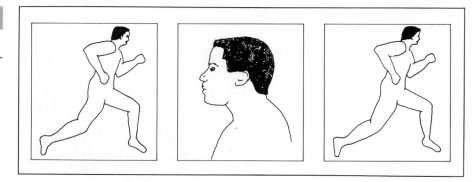

FIGURE 11.13

Two storyboard frames showing a person exiting right and entering left.

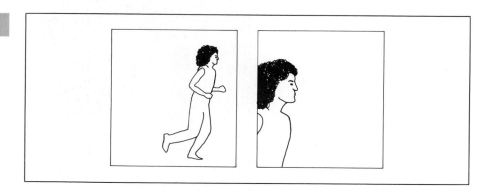

TYPES OF TRADITIONAL ANIMATION

The animator can use a wide variety of animation techniques, the simplest of which doesn't even require a camera: individual stick figures can be created by scratching them directly on opaque film. Norman McLaren popularized this technique with the film *Blinkety Blank*. Each frame in his classic animation was created by scratching figures directly on the blank film emulsion. He added color to the clear etchings by painting them with transparent ink. Scratch-leader films are a useful way to learn the basics of animation. You learn the relationship between individual still frames and the moving patterns they produce when projected. The process is somewhat tedious but inexpensive. No lens or motion picture cameras are needed, and no processing is required (see Figure 11.14).

Two-Dimensional Animation

Two-dimensional animation includes traditional cell animation. The artist draws opaque figures on sheets of clear acetate, although drawings on paper can be substituted for acetate. The principle is the same, but the paper drawings cannot be layered, as they can with clear acetate, to create multiple planes of movement (see Figure 11.15). Two-dimensional animation also includes collages of paper cutouts, which are then repositioned for each new frame.

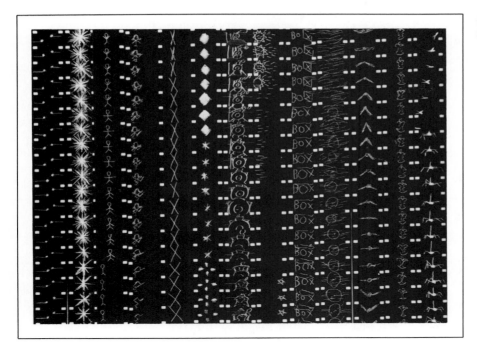

FIGURE 11.14

Still frames from scratch leader films.

FIGURE 11.15

Person working with acetate cell. (Courtesy R/Greenberg Associates, Inc.)

Three-Dimensional Animation

Several methods of animation use three-dimensional figures instead of flat drawings. This popular form of animation has been around for many years and can be found in special effects animation scenes in *King Kong* and in the four-legged imperial walker scenes in *Return of the Jedi*. The lifelike

FIGURE 11.16

Mindscape *by Jacques Drouin. A pin screen was used to create each frame of the film. (Used with permission of the National Film Board of Canada.)*

three-dimensional characters are photographed a frame at a time using stop-motion techniques. Each time a frame is recorded, the jointed models can be repositioned and photographed again. This technique is popular with special effects animators because the 3-D models are lifelike and can be lit so that they are indistinguishable from live action scenes used as backgrounds.

Other forms of three-dimensional animation include animating with clay figures, called claymation (which was recently made popular by the television ads for California raisins), and pixilation (in which actors move slightly between one or two frame exposures, as in the film *Neighbors* by Norman McLaren, in which actors move about like cars without moving their legs).

Pin Screen Animation   A precursor to today's computer pixel animation is the technique of animating pin screen drawings, which was invented by the team of Alexander Alexeieff and Claire Parker in the early 1930s.[13] Their technique involves the repositioning of thousands of small pins held in a frame as a matrix of tiny shafts that when lit with extreme side lighting cast realistic shadows. The pins are used to create landscapes and lifelike figures. A popular recent film done in this technique is *Mindscape* by Jacques Drouin. The animation looks very much like a 2-D pixel animation done on a computer, except that the film is in black-and-white. The film traces a man's journey into his art and psyche and back to the relative security of reality (see Figure 11.16).

---

[13]Charles Solomon and Ron Stark, *The Complete Kodak Animation Book* (Rochester, N.Y.: Eastman Kodak, 1983), 54.

SUMMARY

Computer animation originated in commercial and academic research laboratories in the early 1960s. Later in that decade, Bell Telephone Laboratories invited artists and filmmakers to its facilities. Working with staff programmers and engineers, who developed software tools for the artists, the artist–programmer teams demonstrated the creative potential of the new medium. As equipment became more accessible, artists learned programming skills and created their own programs.

The field of computer animation is more accessible today and has rightfully gained its place alongside other forms of traditional animation. Advances in hardware technology and interactive software capabilities have de-emphasized the role played by the programmer–artist. Programming experience is an important asset, however, if you want to add additional options to existing software or explore new areas of computer graphics.

In addition to understanding computer graphics procedures, the computer animator should be familiar with the elements of film theory and visual storytelling. Study animation classics, both narrative and abstract. Pay special attention to the films of Disney, Zagreb Studios, the National Film Board of Canada, and Faith and John Hubley, to name a few. Regional film and video libraries and college media departments are important resources for the study of animation. There are several anthologies of animated films; one very good anthology is *Masters of Animation*, available on video cassette (four volumes) and produced in 1986 by John Halas. It can be purchased from Home Vision, P.O. Box 800, Concord MA, 01742, or (800) 262-8600. The ACM:SIGGRAPH series of videotapes on computer animation is also an excellent resource; they can be purchased from ACM, Inc., 428 East Preston Street, Baltimore MD, 21202, or (301) 528-4261. The bibliography has additional information on film production and traditional animation.

Exercises

1. Ask your campus media center or local library if they have any films or video cassettes on animation or computer graphics. Make a list of titles and view as many as you can. Write a paragraph about each film summarizing the plot and suggesting the intended audience. Include the name of the animator/director, the year it was made, and the company distributing it.

2. If you have access to a super-8mm camera, make a film or animation that uses the long shot, medium shot, and close-up techniques. Overlap the action so that the same action is covered in each shot. Include cutaways from the main action, such as bystanders at a parade or a person listening while another is talking. Edit the film after it is shot rather than in the camera.

3. Take several still shots with a 35mm camera that illustrate the concepts described in the section on cues to depth perception (vanishing lines,

gradation, overlapping, scale, and atmospheric perspective). The subjects should interest you, and you may want to use the pictures as backgrounds for other projects in computer graphics assignments.

Bibliography

Arnheim, Rudolph. *Art and Visual Perception*. Berkeley: University of California Press, 1971.

Arnheim, Rudolph. *Film as Art*. Berkeley: University of California Press, 1957.

Goodman, Cynthia. *Digital Visions: Computers and Art*. New York: Abrams, 1987.

Gregory, Richard L. *The Intelligent Eye*. New York: McGraw-Hill, 1970.

Markowski, Gene. *The Art of Photography: Image and Illusion*. Englewood Cliffs, N.J.: Prentice-Hall, 1984.

Munsterberg, Hugo. *The Film: A Psychological Study*. New York: Dover, 1970.

Perisic, Zoran. *The Animation Stand*. New York: Hastings House, 1976.

Pincus, Edward. *Guide to Filmmaking*. New York: New American Library, 1969.

Rivlin, Robert. *The Algorithmic Image*. Redmond, Wash.: Microsoft Press, 1986.

Youngblood, Gene. *Expanded Cinema*. New York: Dutton, 1970.

Zettl, Herbert. *Sight, Sound, Motion: Applied Media Aesthetics*. 2nd ed. Belmont, Calif.: Wadsworth, 1990.

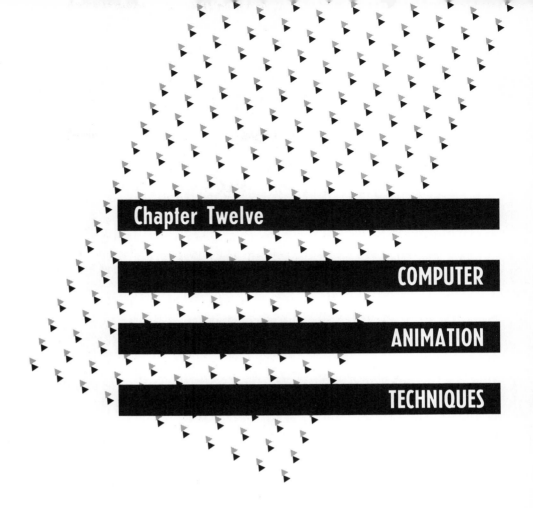

Chapter Twelve

COMPUTER

ANIMATION

TECHNIQUES

I n this chapter you will learn about computer-assisted animation—
including marquee animation and computer-assisted cell animation—
and three-dimensional computer-generated animation. Near the end of
the chapter you will learn about the equipment and procedures for
recording computer animation on film and videotape.

COMPUTER-ASSISTED ANIMATION

Computer-assisted animation puts the computer in control of traditional animation equipment—animation stands and optical special effects equipment.
The equipment operates as before except computers control adjustments for
pans, tilts, zooms, and other movements (see *camera movements* in Glossary).
The billboard-type pixel animation we see at Times Square or on home computer screens are other examples of computer-assisted animations.

Marquee Animation

Marquee animation is pixel-based animation, where individual pixels are
quickly turned on and off or changed in color, like the lights on a Times

Square billboard. This is low-tech computer animation and is found at point-of-sale computer displays—which are often selling home computers. By systematically altering the colors in the color look-up table (see Chapter 4), we can cycle through all of the colors for each object on the screen. A rainbow will appear to vibrate as it cycles through colors in the look-up table.

In another form of marquee animation the artist assigns colors to discrete areas of the screen. The software cycles through the colors and the objects appear to switch places. You have probably seen illustrations in television news stories showing helicopter rotor blades turning as the helicopter falls from the sky. The effect is created by alternating the colors for each rotor blade from the color of the blade to the background color. As the blades cycle through the two colors, they appear to rotate. This is a quick way to animate simple drawings because it requires very little computing time. You can record the animation on videotape as it is seen on the screen in real time.

A related form of 2-D animation is sprite animation. Sprites are small user-defined figures that you can move quickly around the screen. They are implemented in hardware by a special chip devoted to displaying them on the screen. Most systems allow several sprites on the screen at once, and the hardware has special checks so that sprites are automatically kept from bumping into each other. You can find sprite hardware implementation on Amiga, Atari, and Texas Instruments computers. An effect similar to sprite animation can be achieved by programming the computer to swap sections of screen memory. The object looks as though it is moving, but you are only changing its location in the screen buffer. A car can appear to move across the screen or a plane to fly through the air. Software sprites are possible on any computer, but they are considerably slower than hardware sprites.

Computer-Assisted Cell Animation

Much of the repetitive work associated with traditional cell animation can now be accomplished using computer techniques. At Hanna-Barbera Studios, where "The Flintstones," "The Jetsons," and other Saturday morning animations are produced, a computer-assisted scan-and-paint animation system has automated the animation process. Individual drawings are scanned into the computer and then painted with colors chosen by the cell painter. The painting process is done much the way computer artists fill-in pixel-based paint images. By selecting a color and then selecting the area to be filled in, the color automatically fills to the boundaries of the area. Once the individual cells are completed, they are combined with digitized backgrounds and recorded on videotape according to a plan specified by the animation exposure sheet. This computer process is at least five times faster than the manual process. Individual computer images (called soft cells) can also be sent to a film recorder or computer disk.

In addition to coloring and frame assembly, computer techniques are also used to create atmospheric effects, which are very difficult to create by traditional means. If, for instance, it is raining and a character moves further away from the audience, we expect to see him disappear in the rain. Computers have made this effect less difficult by providing a three-dimensional environment into which the two-dimensional drawing is placed; characters move through a rain field or snow field and disappear just as they would in real life. Rain, snow, fog, and other atmospheric effects are now much more realistic.[1] In contrast to scan-and-paint systems, which are raster-based, 2-D draw systems create animations by drawing directly on the data tablet. The drawings become vector representations in a computer database much like other draw images. Draw animations can be output to a pen plotter or vector microfilm recorder. Often they are manipulated with key-frame metamorphosis software, which transforms one shape into another. Technically this form of animation falls under the category of computer-generated animation because the computer generates the images from a database of vertices (see "Metamorphosis" under "Computer-Generated Animation" later in this chapter).

Two-dimensional cell animation has limitations. For example, in-betweening (the process of creating individual frames between key frames of action) presents a set of difficult problems for two-dimensional scan-and-paint and draw systems. Computers cannot achieve the subtleties and refinement of movement that human animators can. Animators can be very expressive with just a pencil or paintbrush. Line width and intensity can be changed, and characterization can be emphasized or exaggerated. Computers have difficulty creating natural looking in-between drawings of 2-D characters that overlap themselves or turn in space. If a character is walking, and one foot goes behind the other, it is difficult for the computer to detect which foot is in the foreground.[2] For these reasons, most in-betweening is done by hand. Often, the repetitive work of creating individual drawings is exported to "tween factories" in Taiwan or other Asian countries, where it is done for a fraction of what it would cost in this country.

Motion Control Animation

Since the mid 1970s, computers have been used to automatically control mechanical animation equipment, thereby eliminating the drudgery associated with manually adjusting camera position and table controls between frames. The animator types in the instructions for each scene, including the beginning and end positions for each degree of freedom (camera height, x and y axes table orientation) and shutter position for fades and dissolves. The computer is then given the number of frames for each of these moves. The software automatically calculates the increments of camera movement per frame and begins the animation process. After every exposure, table orientation and camera position are set for the next frame. Of course the animator still has to replace the artwork when the computer calls for the next cell.

We call such animation systems motion control systems because the computer controls the motion of the mechanical device. The device can be an animation stand, studio camera, or optical effects printer (see Figure 12.1). Motors are connected to the cranks that adjust camera height; shutter opening; x, y, and z axes table positioning; and other adjustments. When given a signal from the computer, the motors adjust the position of the artwork and camera for the next frame. Often computers are used to define the original moves for

---

[1] Chris Odgers, Director of Computer Animation Systems, Hanna-Barbera Studios. Conversation with the author, August 18, 1989.

[2] John Lewell, "Behind the Screen at Hanna-Barbera," *Computer Pictures* 3 (March/April 1985): 18.

FIGURE 12.1

Optical printers (a), animation stands (not shown), and studio cameras (b) are connected to motion control computers, which automatically adjust camera and table positioning, shutter openings, and other settings. (Courtesy R/Greenberg Associates, Inc.)

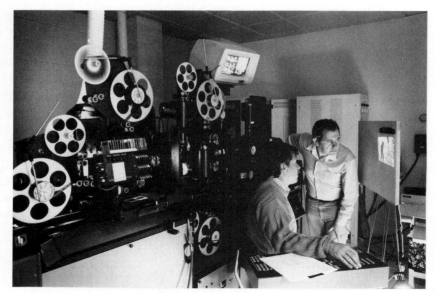

a

b

the camera equipment. If the moves are planned using a computer, they will have classical, mathematically perfect curves, slow moves in and out, and so on. They will appear more graceful, and the viewer will not be reminded that the camera is under the control of a person.[3]

Motion control computers play an important role in the creation of special effects for motion pictures. Many special effects are created by rephotographing objects, using the identical camera movements but with different

[3] Richard Edulund and Jerry Jeffress, "Motion Control Cinematography," in *American Cinematographer Manual*, ed. Fred H. Detmers (Hollywood, Calif.: ASC Press), 281.

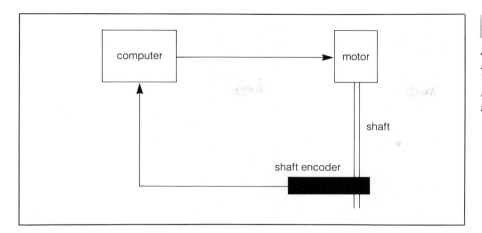

FIGURE 12.2

Shaft encoder system. The computer starts the motion control motor. When it has turned a specific number of revolutions, the computer turns it off.

lighting. The first time the object is photographed, it is front lit and looks normal. The second time it is back lit against a white background, and the object is in silhouette. The two pieces of film are then used to "marry" the subject to a different background. The silhouette (*matte* is the film term) blocks out an area on the new background identical in size to where the object will fit. If the object is a spaceship, the final shot may show the spaceship in the foreground married to a background of stars and planets.[4]

The problem for the motion control special effects artist is to repeat each camera movement as it was in the first shot. Tilts, pans, dollies, and zooms must be repeated exactly. To accomplish this, shaft encoders (devices that transmit camera movements to the computer) monitor all camera movements. There is a shaft encoder for each degree of freedom, sometimes as many as 16, including tilts, pans, dollies, zooms, and other movements. Shaft encoders send exceedingly precise information back to the computer—sometimes measuring movement to 10 thousandths of an inch.[5] When the shot is repeated, the computer starts the motors connected to each degree of freedom. The motors turn the same number of revolutions as in the original camera movement, moving the camera just as in the original shot. In this way, camera movements can be repeated exactly. The velocity is also controlled by the computer. The camera operator's original movements are repeated exactly, and a second piece of film, this time a silhouette, is photographed (see Figure 12.2).

Blue Screen Photography   People cannot be photographed using motion control equipment because of inherent movement. For this reason, chromakey electronic matting (used in television production) and blue screen photography (used in film production) are used to create composite scenes. In each case, the actors perform in front of a solid color background (usually blue) that is later replaced with the second image. In television production, the blue area

---

[4] Motion control technology dates back to the late 1940s. According to Alison Johns ("Life in the Dollhouse," *Millimeter* 14, Nov. 1986), analog motion control equipment was assembled at MGM studios. "Camera moves were recorded as a series of tones on either a phonograph record or wax cylinder. When replayed, the frequencies would cue a pan/tilt head to move to the same positions that had been encoded either in wax or on vinyl" (p. 56).

[5] Jim Linder, "The Animation Stand and Computer Control," *Millimeter* 8 (July 1980): 131.

is electronically replaced with a second video source. In film production, after the film containing the blue background is processed, a special black-and-white high-contrast silhouette, called a traveling matte, is made, in which the blue background becomes clear and the area containing the person becomes opaque. This opaque area is called the black core because the black area is surrounded by clear film. It is printed with the background, leaving a clear hole in the background of the print where the foreground action will fit. The foreground is then printed to the same piece of film using the reverse of the black core traveling matte, called the clear core (a clear area surrounded by black), to block out the background. The result shows the foreground action in front of a new background. In some instances, blue screen photography is also used in conjunction with scenes shot with motion control equipment. A blue background is substituted for the white background behind the physical model and the scene does not have to be photographed twice (see Color Plate 11).

Motion Graphics   Motion graphics are the animated designs and logos used for television identifications and commercial announcements. They can either be created using traditional cameras under control of motion control equipment, or they can be computer generated. When they are created using motion control equipment, the tasks of repositioning the camera and deciding length of exposure time for each frame are controlled by the computer. The streak effects seen in logo animations are created with motion control equipment. Each frame of the film is a time exposure. The lens is held open while the camera is moved toward the subject. The next frame is given the same treatment, but the movement is shorter. The result is a streak of movement, which takes the viewer from position A to position B. (See Color Plate 10 for examples of streak and strobe effects.) Strobe effects do not require that the camera move while the shutter is open. If these effects were done manually, it would be very time consuming. The camera would have to be moved a set distance for each exposure and returned to the original position. Motion control computers automate this process. The desired effect is preprogrammed. The computer advances the film to the next frame and moves the camera to the new position. Retakes exactly like the original can be shot if needed, without introducing additional errors. For this reason, computer-controlled systems are less problematic for the animator. Often, the animation stand, motion control cameras, optical effects equipment, and computer-generated graphics are controlled by the same computer program. The movement of all the equipment is synchronized so that live photography, computer-generated images, and animation can be combined in the same shot.

COMPUTER-GENERATED ANIMATION

In this form of computer animation, the individual frames are created from numerically defined databases inside the computer—much like the objects we create in 2-D and 3-D drawing programs, except instead of creating one image, the program creates a series of images. These images later become the individual frames of the animation.

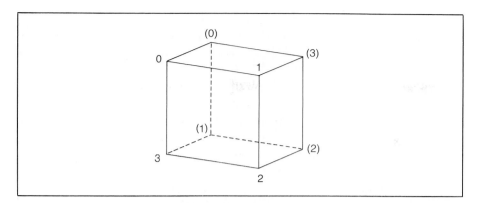

FIGURE 12.3

Numbering of a cube for encoding by computer. Vertices are numbered clockwise for front facing polygons and counterclockwise for back facing polygons.

Computer-Generated 3-D Animation

The unique capability of the computer to generate three-dimensional cartoon characters and control their movement in a synthetic environment offers almost limitless possibilities for the animator. Computer-generated 3-D animation combines the realism of puppet animation with the plasticity and control of traditional cell animation. Understanding the concept of a database is the key to understanding computer-generated animation. All the individual characters and objects on the screen (both 2-D and 3-D) are represented in memory as a coherent collection of endpoints, or vertices, where lines meet (see Figure 12.3). Unlike color table animation, where the description of objects is found only in the frame buffer, computer-generated objects have a database of vertices that is used to build (generate) the objects to be animated. The database also holds additional information about the object, such as surface attributes that describe the object's color and whether it is flat-shaded, smooth, or so forth. The objects are oriented in what is called the "world" coordinate space, which can be thought of as a 3-D cube into which objects are placed. Each vertex has an x and y coordinate for its horizontal and vertical orientation and a z coordinate for its depth placement within the 3-D environment. The modeling program reads the coordinates of each object, assigns them surface attributes, and then projects them on the two-dimensional viewing plane. Special algorithms are used to interpret perspective based on the hypothetical lens and subject distance so that the objects appear in proper relationship to each other. This projected information is then sent to the frame buffer where a pixel map of the 3-D image is generated. The pixel map looks like any other 2-D pixel image that could have been created by a skilled artist with a paint program. It is, however, the 2-D projection of a 3-D database.

Once the database is created, objects can be reoriented, scaled, or deformed and then reprojected to form a new pixel image. Often the artist will combine computer-generated vector images with pixel images. Digitized backgrounds captured with a video camera can be used behind computer-generated objects. Digitized images can also be used as texture maps on the surface of 3-D objects (see Figure 5.25).

Three-dimensional computer animation is computationally intensive. The size of the database is dependent on the amount of detail in the image. The database for a cube floating in space may contain as few as eight lines

FIGURE 12.4

Still from the film The Last Starfighter. *(Courtesy of Museum of
Modern Art.)*

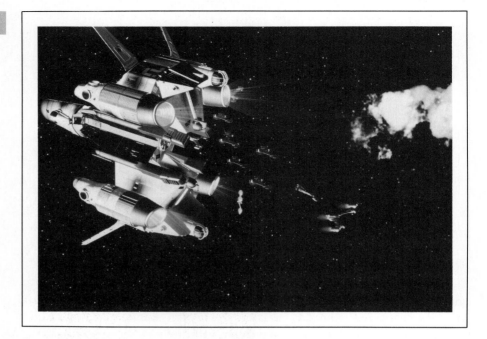

of information. The database for a complex 3-D image, however, may contain enough information to fill 200 or 300 typewritten pages. For example, the average frame in computer-generated scenes from *The Last Starfighter* contains 250,000 polygons and took 25 minutes to render using a Cray supercomputer (see Figure 12.4). Because the objects are continually moving, the database must be rerendered for each new frame of animation. Computing time on even the fastest computers can take anywhere from a few seconds to 30 minutes or more per frame. At a screen resolution of 3000 × 4000 pixels with 10 bits of color per pixel, it will take 8.64 billion calculations to produce one second of film animation.[6] Fully rendered detailed computer-generated animation is never seen in real time on the computer. The animation can be seen only after the frames have been recorded on film or videotape.

Animation artists have just begun to explore the narrative possibilities of three-dimensional computer animation. The works of John Lasseter (*The Adventures of Andre and Wally B, Luxo Jr., Red's Dream, Tin Toy,* and *Knickknack*), Philippe Bergeron (*Tony de Peltrie* and *Breaking the Ice*), Yoichiro Kawaguchi (*Ocean, Flora,* and other films), the Advanced Technology Group at Apple Computer (*Pencil Test,* and *Her Majesty's Secret Serpent*), Dave Inglish and his colleagues in the Late Night Group at Disney Productions (*Oilspot and Lipstick*), and animators at Ohio State University and New York Institute of Technology, to name a few, have led the way for others to follow (see Color Plate 13). As computers become more powerful and programs more adept at synthesizing real objects and movement, three-dimensional computer-generated animations will become more prevalent in films and television. This form of animation combines the special features of puppet animation—realistic models, lighting, and movement—with the free and unbounded fantasies we associate with 2-D cell animation. The creation of lifelike, computer-generated

---

[6] Mike Tyler, "3-D Images for the Film Industry," *Computer Graphics World* 7 (July 1984): 64.

© 1988 Kroyer Films, Inc.

FIGURE 12.5

Still from Technological Threat. *(Courtesy Kroyer Films Inc.)*

"human" characters in everyday settings may soon transform the art of animation into a special class of movie making—the art of creating synthetic reality!

Some animators use a combination of computer-generated and traditional cell animation. Bill Kroyer routinely uses the computer to create the mechanical-looking characters and objects in his films and then has artists draw the more difficult human forms. His short animation titled *Technological Threat*, released in 1988, uses a combination of computer-generated 3-D figures and hand-drawn artwork.[7] (See Figure 12.5.)

THE PROCESS OF 3-D ANIMATION

The process of creating three-dimensional computer animation can be broken down into several logical steps. As with all animation techniques, the idea for the animation and the design elements must be worked out in advance. Preparation for a narrative may begin with a short treatment describing the characters, conflicts, and story. Sketches are then drawn of individual figures in various poses and situations.

Storyboard

A storyboard is created from the treatment and preliminary sketches. The storyboard illustrates each shot or significant change in camera angle and

---

[7] Bill Kroyer, "Integrating 2-D and 3-D Character Animation," in *3-D Character Animation by Computer* (Chicago: SIGGRAPH, 1988), 9–16.

positioning, providing a visual thread for checking continuity (mismatches, compatibility of camera angles, and so on) and for previewing how the animation narrative will flow when finished. If the project is a television commercial, preparation begins with a short script that describes the action for each shot. The script may take the form of a storyboard, with the dialog written below each picture. Detailed sketches are then created for each of the graphic elements—logos, products, characters, and sets—and are then used as prototypes for the computer models.

Model Construction

Model construction, sometimes called object definition, can be done in several ways: Models can be created constructively, a line or polygon at a time; they can be created procedurally from formulas; or they can be created from primitive graphic shapes using solids modeling (see Chapter 5). The artist may begin the modeling process by tracing a sketch of the object into a 3-D modeling program. The sketch (or possibly an engineering drawing) is placed on a digitizing tablet, and the artist traces it into the database, noting each endpoint or line intersection. If a tablet isn't available, the object (possibly a logo) can be traced onto a piece of graph paper. Each line on the graph paper then corresponds to the x and y coordinates in the modeling program. Where the object intersects with lines on the graph paper, coordinates are noted and typed into the database.

The coordinates are entered by using one of two methods. They can either be entered as absolute x, y, and z locations, where each coordinate is the actual position in the coordinate space. Or the data points can be entered in relative terms–that is, each new position can be entered as an off-set from the last position. Relative position notation is sometimes easier for the animation artist to comprehend, because the new position can be related to the old position. Most programs will accept either form of notation (see Figure 12.6).

After the object has been digitized (entered into the computer database), it can be further modified by using a shape editor. Shape editors modify existing shapes by selectively changing their dimensions. Shape editors contain scale and size options that perform uniform transformations on existing shapes and also contain spline editors that smooth out curves drawn by hand. Spline editors will fit a smooth curve between three or more specified points or change a straight line into a uniform S curve.

When you have finished editing the 2-D shape, it can be three-dimensionalized using one of several methods. In Chapter 5, the subsection "Creating Three-Dimensional Shapes" explains several common 3-D modeling methods, including extrusion, rotation, and cross-sectional modeling. Each method is unique and is used for specific applications. Extrusion creates block shapes like 3-D letters and cylinders. Rotation is used for creating symmetrical shapes like globes and goblets. Cross-sectional modeling can be used in place of the above methods, but it is most often used for creating asymmetrical shapes—a bottle with a square footprint (four flat sides) and a round cap on top, for example. You should be familiar with all the modeling methods and understand their individual applications and advantages.

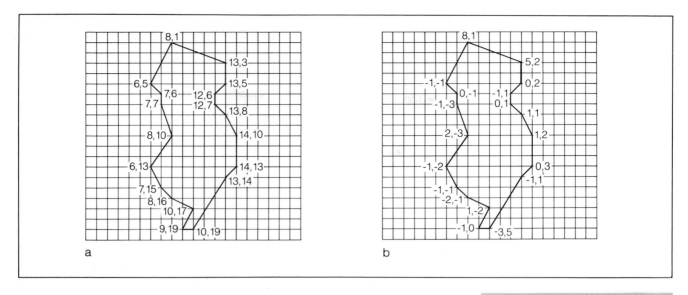

FIGURE 12.6

Absolute and relative notation. In (a) the outline is marked with absolute coordinate notation. In (b) the outline uses relative notation.

Intricate 3-D shapes create special problems for the modeler. Traditional modeling methods can be used, but they are time consuming and do not adapt well to objects with complicated shapes. Three-dimensional photo digitizing is one method of capturing a complicated 3-D shape directly and automatically. It is normally a three-step process. First, key features of the physical object—a person's head, for example—are marked as control points. The object is then photographed from two distinct angles, and the two images are scanned into the computer. Last, 3-D interpolation software compares the two views at each control point, and a 3-D representation is created in the computer database.[8] Three-dimensional digitizers can also be used to enter the coordinates of a 3-D object (see Figure 5.17).

Modeling Strategies The first consideration in model building is to use the most suitable digitizing method and modeling procedure for the particular object. Time, money, and accuracy are usually deciding factors. For instance, an animation with three-dimensional characters ideally would use realistic models like the character in *Tony de Peltrie* (see Color Plate 13c), but if there isn't time to create characters with skinlike texture and realistic detail, then other modeling styles have to be considered. For instance, when Digital Productions created the characters in Mick Jagger's *Hard Woman* video, it was decided to construct them out of neonlike vector shapes rather than create solid-jointed wire frame objects with shaded surfaces. The wire frame approach would have required considerably more time and money to model and render. Since the project had budget and time constraints, it was decided to go with vector representations. Each character was constructed from multicolored vector segments that looked like bent neon tubes. Probably the most memorable aspect of the video is the colorful three-dimensional vector characters.

---

[8] Philippe Bergeron, "Controlling Facial Expressions and Body Movements in the Computer-Generated Animated Short *Tony De Peltrie*," in *Advanced Computer Graphics Animation* (Chicago: SIGGRAPH, 1985), 61ff.

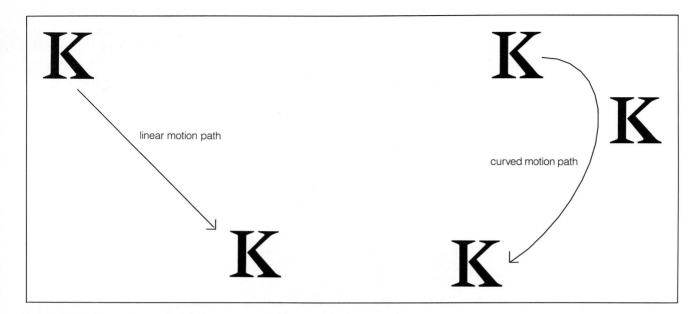

linear motion path

curved motion path

FIGURE 12.7

Linear and curved motion paths.

Had the animator used a more realistic approach, the characters might not have had the same impact.[9]

When creating computer models, always use the minimum number of data points for each figure. A globe having 25 sections may look no different to the audience than one having only 15 sections. The fewer the sections, the quicker the animation will be recorded on videotape. Background objects don't need the same amount of detail as foreground objects. In videotape animation, objects that remain static for a good part of the animation can be represented by stand-in pixel images. These images do not have to be calculated each time a new frame is generated and are read to the screen as part of the background directly from the frame buffer or disk storage. When the static object must move, the original 3-D model can be substituted for the pixel representation.

Establishing the Motion Path

Motion path is a general term used to describe the trajectory of an object during the course of an animation. The motion path is assigned in an animation editing program compatible with the program used to create the models. The motion path of a television logo may begin at the horizon and finish at a point close to the camera, or the object may spin on its own axis, changing into another object (metamorphosis) but never moving from a set position in space.

If the path of the object is a straight line, there will be only two key frames in the motion path: a beginning and ending position. If the object is to travel in an arclike path, however, an intermediate key frame is needed. The object then travels along a spline curve that fits smoothly between the three points. Most programs have tension control, which allows the motion path between the midposition and the ends to be sharply curved or made

---

[9] Bill Kroyer, "Preface to the Course Notes," in *3-D Character Animation by Computer* (Chicago: SIGGRAPH, 1987), 9.

BOX 12.1

MOTION SCRIPT

The figure below shows a page from a motion script as it appears on the monitor. In this software, each object gets a different page, with the frame numbers written across the bottom. Boxes at the left show which option you are working with. The tapered horizontal lines show the length of the move, tapers indicating the length of the acceleration or deceleration. POSIT controls positioning of the object; SCALE controls size changes; X, Y, & Z ROT enable you to spin the object; CENTR allows you to specify an off-center rotation; EYE controls perspective; METAM enables the changing one object into another; VISIB controls whether the object is visible at that point in the animation; UNCUP uncouples the object from the Scene page that controls the movement of all of the objects as a group; VIDEO brings individual video frames into the animation from a prerecorded videotape; TRANS controls the transparency of the object.

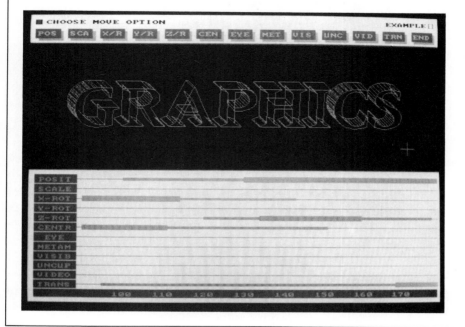

Screen page from an animation motion script, which is similar to an exposure sheet used in traditional animation. (Pansophic Inc.)

closer to a symmetrical arc (see Figure 12.7). Programs vary in the methods used to create the motion path. Some programs allow you to place the object where you want it to begin its move, and you then add additional positions as interim key frames. The program creates a curve through the key frames, which becomes the motion path. Other programs use a scripting approach where you type in the opening and ending coordinates as well as additional information on rotation and size.

Control Features of Animation Editors   Animation editors provide control options for various types of movement: x, y, and z rotation; scaling (sizing); translation (placement in the world coordinate space); and perspective. In addition, animation software controls the placement and movement of light sources, which can be animated so that they move around the object.

Animation software also provides a means of controlling the velocity of an object. Beginning and ending velocity are controlled by the length of

FIGURE 12.8

Still from Hunger. *(Courtesy the National Film Board of Canada.)*

the taper—what is called a faring, or ease—the gradual acceleration or deceleration of an object. Tapers ensure that an object will start gradually and decelerate smoothly. The artist specifies the length of the taper, which can be as short as one frame for instant acceleration or as many as 40 to 80 frames for a gradual acceleration. Full velocity is reached at the end of the taper.

Metamorphosis Another feature of animation editors is metamorphosis—the ability to change one shape into another. This technique was used by Peter Foldes in a series of films, the most famous being *Hunger* (1974) (see Figure 12.8). Foldes digitized a series of pen sketches and then used them as key frames. He metamorphosed one frame into the next: A belly dancer in the arms of a grotesque man transforms into a pillar of pots, which crumbles to the floor from under his arms. He kicks the pots and they become the walls of a kitchen. His physique transforms to reveal rolls of fat bulging from his midsection. The film won the Prix du Jury award at the Cannes Film Festival in 1974 and was nominated for an Academy Award.

Hierarchical Control The movement of objects encountered in everyday life is considerably more complex than logos spinning in space. To accurately control the movement of complex models, like the segmented body of a three-dimensional cartoon character, hierarchies of dependent objects are created so that when you move the upper arm, the lower arm and hand move as well. This kind of control makes creating realistic movement much easier for the animator because he or she does not have to worry about hand movement until it is time to move the hand independently of the arm. A more complex model may even have independently moving fingers, which will automatically

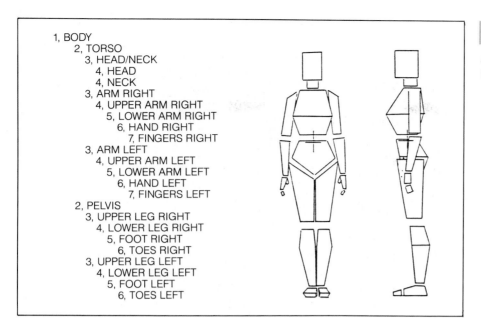

FIGURE 12.9

*Basic hierarchy of "Block Woman."
(Courtesy Kroyer Films Inc.)*

```
1, BODY
    2, TORSO
        3, HEAD/NECK
            4, HEAD
            4, NECK
        3, ARM RIGHT
            4, UPPER ARM RIGHT
                5, LOWER ARM RIGHT
                    6, HAND RIGHT
                        7, FINGERS RIGHT
        3, ARM LEFT
            4, UPPER ARM LEFT
                5, LOWER ARM LEFT
                    6, HAND LEFT
                        7, FINGERS LEFT
    2, PELVIS
        3, UPPER LEG RIGHT
            4, LOWER LEG RIGHT
                5, FOOT RIGHT
                    6, TOES RIGHT
        3, UPPER LEG LEFT
            4, LOWER LEG LEFT
                5, FOOT LEFT
                    6, TOES LEFT
```

turn as the hand turns but which will move separately when needed. To understand how the various parts of the body relate to one another, animators create hierarchy outlines depicting body movement subgroups. In the hierarchy outline in Figure 12.9, when you move the body, all the other subgroups move with it. If you move the torso, the head and neck and arm sections will move but the pelvis will remain stationary. The primary movement of the character walking down the street is controlled by the body structure. However, secondary movements, such as leg placement and arm swing, are controlled separately. Often hierarchies will work from the extremities up; if the model has one foot on a skateboard, the hierarchy will list the skateboard first, then the foot, the lower leg, and so on.[10] In this case, the skateboard controls the movement of the whole body; as we move the skateboard, we move the rest of the body as well.

Rule-Based Systems Control The laborious positioning of objects, groups of objects, and subgroups in motion paths makes the orchestration of complex movement extremely time consuming. Movements that depend on complex laws of physics, such as the fall of a chair down a staircase, may be almost impossible to duplicate.[11] Even a hierarchical system does not make the complex movement of a body walking over rough terrain or the gentle lapping of waves against a beach easy for the artist to duplicate. However, rule-based systems that use physical, biological, and behavioral laws to control the movement and behavior of objects may eventually make such tasks routine. Judson Rosebush and Gail Goldstein report that with rule-based systems, "a

---

[10]Bill Kroyer, "Animating with a Hierarchy," in *3-D Character Animation by Computer Course Notes* (Chicago: SIGGRAPH, 1987).

[11]Judson Rosebush and Gail Goldstein, "Complex Motion Automation: A Further Step Toward Realism in Animation," *Computer Graphics Review* (Mar./Apr. 1988): 34.

FIGURE 12.10

Still from Skirt Research. *The dancer's skirt consists of a springy polygon mesh that responds to the forces of gravity and the momentum of the dancer. (Courtesy Richard Lunden and Susan Van Baerle, NYIT Computer Graphics Laboratory.)*

user need only define the object's physical characteristics, its initial position, the forces acting on it, and the duration of the action. The system then automatically calculates the object's motion through space."[12] Such systems are still in the experimental stage but will eventually use software that can calculate how objects behave, given specific perimeters. For example, the draping and swirling of a dancer's gown as she turns or stops momentarily will depend on how fast the dancer is moving, the weight of the garment, and other natural forces (see Figure 12.10).

Motion Preview Pencil Tests   Quality of movement must be checked occasionally by running pencil tests of the animation. This term is a holdover from traditional cell animation, where pages of preliminary pencil outlines were flipped back and forth to check the smoothness and character of the movement. A computer graphics pencil test serves the same purpose. A small section of the animation (one or two sequences, depending on the amount of computer memory) is computed in wire frame mode and saved in the frame buffer at low resolution (one-quarter or less normal screen resolution). The pixel images are flashed on the screen in rapid succession. Since the test runs for only a few seconds, it is repeated over and over in a loop. Pencil tests can be sped up or slowed down to check the quality of movement for that short section of the animation. They are not normally shown to clients because of the low resolution of the images and limited length of the tests. The advantage of a pencil test is that the movement can be quickly checked. Computations take only a few minutes, whereas full renderings take hours. If the animation contains many complex models, bounding boxes are substituted for the actual models in the animation. Bounding boxes occupy the area normally taken by the model. Because they contain only a few polygons, rendering time for bounding boxes is considerably shorter.

---

[12]Ibid.

UNIT FIVE: COMPUTER GRAPHICS ANIMATION

COLOR PLATE 9

(a) Sample partial storyboard, (b) comprehensive, (c and d) color specs, and (e) computer-generated slide from a major slide presentation. The storyboard contains a sketch for each slide in the presentation and shows how the presentation will flow from topic to topic. The artist must consider how each slide will work with the accompanying narration. Key images and backgrounds are taken to the comprehensives stage and colored in by hand so that the client can see how they will look. Once the project is approved by the client, preset computer colors are selected and noted on the color specification sheet. The spec sheet also notes special software tools for creating the desired effects. (Courtesy Brilliant Image, Inc., New York.)

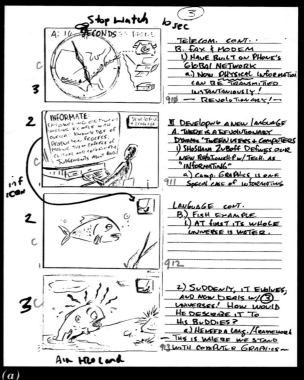

(a)

(b)

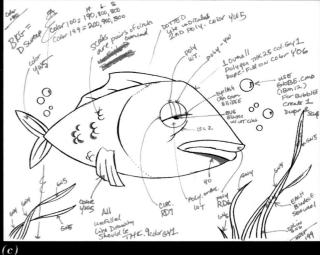

(c)

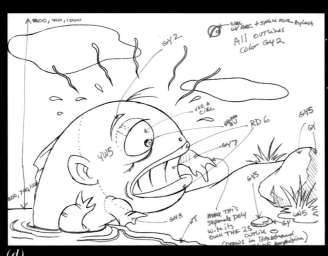

(d)

(e)

OXBERRY

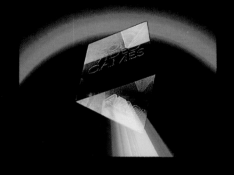

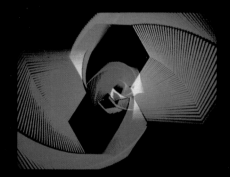
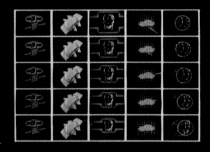
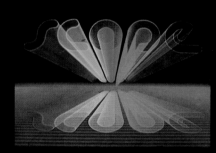

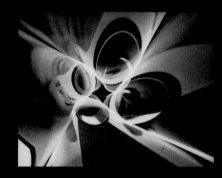

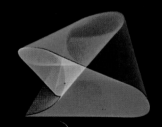
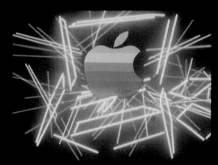

The technology behind the images.

COLOR PLATE 10

Motion graphics created with a traditional animation camera under the control of a motion control computer (see Figure 12.1). (Courtesy Oxberry, Carlstadt, N.J.)

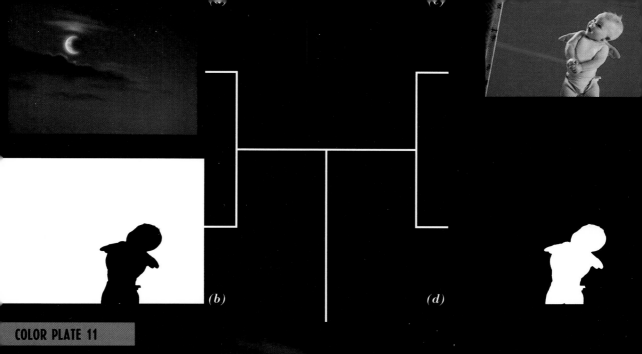

(b)

(d)

Blue screen matte
process for creating
composite scenes.
(a) Background and
(b) a black core
matte are printed (bi-
packed) to a new piece
of film. After being
exposed, the film is re-
wound to the beginning
and (c) the foreground
and (d) clear core matte
are printed, creating
(e) the composite scene.
(Courtesy R/Greenberg
Associates, Inc.,
New York.)

(e)

(a) Still from the KSDK station ID, showing the
station logo, NBC peacock, right and left side of
the arch with metallic tiled surfaces, and soft
shadow matte behind the letters. (b) Wire frame
rendering of the St. Louis arch. (Courtesy David
Gieselmann, Station KSDK, St. Louis, and Post
Perfect, New York.)

(a)

(b)

COLOR PLATE 13

Examples of three-dimensional computer animation. (a) Luxo Jr. by John Lasseter (© 1986 Pixar, San Rafael, Calif.); (b) Tin Toy by John Lasseter (© 1988 Pixar, San Rafael, Calif.); (c) Tony de Peltrie (© 1985 Pierre Lachapelle, Philippe Bergeron, Pierre Robidoux, and Daniel Langlois); (d) Stanley and Stella: Breaking the Ice (© 1987 Symbolics Graphics Division and Whitney/Demos Productions); (e) Flora (© 1989 Yoichiro Kawaguchi, Nippon Electronics College, Tokyo); (f) Pencil Test, created by Apple Computer Advanced Technology Group (Courtesy Apple Computer, Inc., Cupertino, Calif.); (g) Snoot and Muttly by Susan Van Baerle and Douglas Kingsbury.

(c)

(d)

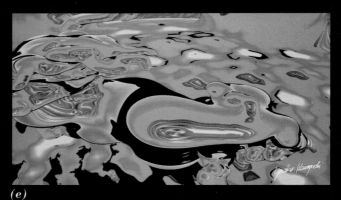

(e)

(f)

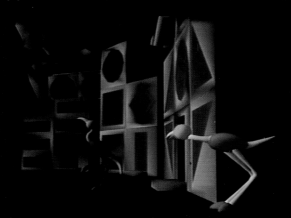

(g)

Wire Frame Tests After a sequence or short animation is completed, a full wire frame test is recorded on videotape or film. This test runs longer than a pencil test and usually is in higher resolution. Besides checking spatial movement, it verifies pace and rhythm. Wire frame objects travel the same paths and are the same size and dimension as the objects in the final film.

Adding Detail

After the wire frame test is approved, the animator focuses on set details— chairs, lamps, potted palms, and so on—and surface detail—color, texture, reflectance, and transparency. Background props and set decoration not associated directly with moving objects are added to the environmental space. Walls, windows, wallpaper design, tables, and patterns of light on the floor are added. Texture maps are created for objects that need more surface detail than solid shading can provide. Lighting highlights are tried on various surfaces. Surfaces meant to look like chrome, for instance, are given smooth, metallic highlights. In short, the scene is decorated, and objects are given surface attributes that will be used in the final version of the animation.

Lighting

As in a traditional filmmaking or theatrical production, lighting is an essential component, being a powerful indicator of mood. Motivated lighting (low key) is selected for scenes lit by a single source of illumination, such as a candle. High-key lighting is assigned to brighter scenes where emphasis is on highlights and bright colors. Most programs give the animator at least 10 hypothetical light sources to work with. Options for lighting are extensive. Object-specific local lighting can be used to highlight individual objects, such as table lamps, and infinite or global lighting can be used for lighting the whole scene. Besides fixed-position lighting, lights can be made to move around the object if necessary.

Closely related to lighting effects are those special effects where swirls and streaks are added to moving objects and logos are embellished with glows and tints. Special effects can be part of the original animation, can be added in the editing phase, or can be created with paint programs and added after the animation is completed.

Render Tests

Render tests are conducted at various stages in the production to check surface highlights, texture maps, lighting, and special effects. These tests are conducted at less than full resolution to save time and money. Instead of full broadcast resolution of 640×480 pixels, the images may be rendered at half resolution. Individual still frames can be output to a film recorder at full resolution if better detail is required. Spatial resolution—the number of frames rendered in a second of animation—is normally 30 but this can also be reduced. Instead of rendering every frame, only every other frame can be rendered. Overall timing is maintained by printing every frame twice. The animation is the same length but lacks nuance in some movements.

Render to Motion Picture Film

When you have completed all the render tests and your client has approved the animation, it is ready to be recorded on film or videotape. Computer-generated images are recorded out of real time, frame by frame, in a fashion similar to time-lapse photography. An inexpensive way to record animation on film is to place a 16mm camera with single-frame capability in front of the color monitor. Every time a frame of animation is rendered to the screen, a single frame is clicked off in the camera. A special light shielding camera cone can be placed between the camera and the monitor to prevent reflections from hitting the screen. Use an exposure time of ⅓₀ second or less to allow a full video frame (two scan fields) to be recorded. A reflective light meter will help in determining the proper exposure. Run exposure tests at various exposure settings before recording the full animation.

The film camera can be controlled manually, or an automatic shutter control mechanism can be used. A motor control device fires the camera shutter automatically, thereby recording one frame of animation when the signal is received from the computer. While images can be photographed directly off the screen for pencil tests and informal screenings, this method is not suited for high-quality recording. One problem is that the film image is locked into the screen resolution of the monitor, and video scan lines are very noticeable when projected on a large screen. Another problem is that the curvature of the monitor surface will sometimes distort the image. Be sure that the camera is directly in front of the screen (at right angles, vertically and horizontally).

The best quality (that is, the highest resolution) film animation is produced using digital film recorders, which are the same recorders used for creating presentation graphics slides except that the recorders are equipped with a motion picture camera (cine back) instead of a still camera (see Figure 12.11). The vector images that make up the individual animation frames are first rendered to a hard disk as high-resolution pixel files. These files are then sent to the digital recorder operating in batch mode. As each image file is recorded on film, the camera advances to the next frame and a new image is recorded. This is a time-consuming process. Digital film recorder resolution for motion pictures is typically 4000 pixels per line. Render time to disk for high-resolution images takes several minutes to an hour per frame, and each frame takes several minutes to record on film. Such systems are generally found on mainframe and minicomputer systems.

Because of the higher resolution, it will take many times longer to render an image to a digital film recorder than to record it on videotape. For this reason, most animation used on television is recorded on videotape rather than on film. When rendering to videotape, there is no need for frame rate conversion between film (24 frames per second) and video (30 frames per second); video images are steadier and not subject to frame jitter, there are no negative scratches or dust to worry about, and color values are more easily maintained between successive generations. Of course, video images are locked into a lower resolution and are not suitable for theatrical screenings.

FIGURE 12.11

Oxberry motion picture camera connected to a digital film recorder manufactured by Solitaire, Inc.

Render to Videotape

Whether you are working in the minicomputer workstation environment or at the personal computer level, the videotape recording process is basically the same. A typical animation hardware configuration includes the graphics workstation, color encoder, frame controller, and videotape recorder. High-resolution minicomputer workstation systems (1280 × 1024 and greater) also require a scan line converter to drop the screen resolution down to broadcast television standards. Facilities that do a great deal of frame-by-frame recording have high-capacity disk drives or tape drives and frame buffers to store the completed frames prior to recording on videotape (see Figure 12.12).

Rendering to videotape is similar to direct film recording off the monitor. The graphics system generates each new frame, loads it into the frame buffer, and displays it on the color monitor. Where the process differs, however, is in the electronics. The RGB (red, green, blue) signal coming from the computer is not compatible with normal videotape recorders and must be converted from RGB to composite video before being recorded. The

FIGURE 12.12

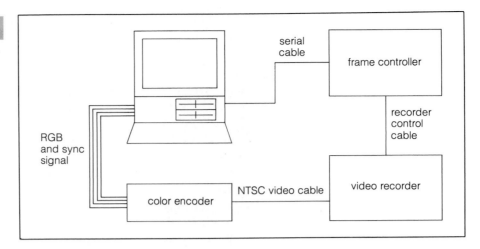

RGB signal is sent to a color encoder, where the red, green, and blue components are combined into a single composite NTSC signal.[13] The color components are converted from four separate signals (three color plus one sync), traveling on three or four separate wires down to one wire, which carries the composite signal to the video recorder.

The frame controller is a special piece of equipment that governs the operation of the videotape recorder (see Figure 3.15) and transforms a videotape recorder capable of insert editing into a single frame recorder. The frame controller also can be used as an interface for traditional cell animation. The cells are placed on a copy stand and photographed individually on videotape, a frame at a time. The procedure is the same as recording frames from a computer, except that the video source is a camera instead of a color graphics card.

The key to frame-by-frame recording on videotape is an electronic address code identification that gives each frame on the videotape a sequential number. The code can either be generated by the frame controller or created separately by an SMPTE (Society of Motion Picture and Television Engineers) time-code generator. Either way, each frame of video is labeled, and the controller knows exactly where to find each frame on the videotape. SMPTE time code consists of a series of numbers marking off the hours, minutes, seconds, and frames. Time code is recorded on the cue track or in the address code area of the videotape. If SMPTE time code isn't used, the frame controller records its own address code on the tape. Without an address code of some type, it is not possible to make frame-accurate edits. Frame accuracy is very important when you are recording a sequence consisting of only one-frame or one-field edits (two fields make up one video frame).[14] Using the address code, the controller can also find and replace bad frames, which are poorly rendered or recorded frames that must be redone.

---

[13]NTSC stands for National Television Standards Committee and is the standard used in the United States for television signal compatibility.

[14]Single field edits are sometimes used instead of single frame (two field edits) when the recorder is only recording wire frame or render tests.

Frame-by-Frame Video Recording   Before any animation is recorded on tape, a signal containing no image at all is recorded. This is called a black burst and prepares the tape for single-frame insert edits by supplying a sync pulse control track for the whole tape. The frame-by-frame recording process begins when a frame of animation is displayed on the computer screen. An image-ready control signal is sent via a serial port connection to the frame controller. The controller starts the videotape recorder, which records one frame or one field of animation. The recorder then sends a frame-recorded signal back to the computer, and a new frame of animation is rendered to the screen. This process is repeated 30 times for every second of animation recorded on videotape.

It is not surprising that constant recycling of the record and playback process, 30 times for every second of animation, takes its toll on the mechanical parts of the videotape recorder and the videotape itself. Recent improvements in videotape recorders now make it possible to record a single frame of animation without jockeying the tape back and forth. The tape remains stationary while the record head adds a new frame to the tape. This feature is available on one-inch videotape recorders specifically made for recording animation. Because frame-by-frame recording is tedious, it is usually done automatically at night when the graphics workstation is not being used for other purposes. The next morning you view the animation at normal speed by playing back the videotape.

Professional animation facilities will save completed animations on high-capacity digital disk drives before recording on videotapes. The advantage is that the videotape recorder is not kept waiting for each new frame to be rendered, which sometimes takes 20 to 30 minutes. When the full animation has been rendered to disk, the images are read from the disk to a display buffer and recorded, frame by frame, on videotape. If the images are loaded from the disk to a large frame buffer called a DVE (digital video effects) unit, frame-by-frame tape recording is not necessary. The DVE can read images to the screen in less than $\frac{1}{30}$ second—quickly enough so that short two- to three-second sections of animation can be recorded without stopping the tape recorder.

Single-frame video recording is the weakest link in the animation process. Even with state-of-the-art video equipment, this crucial frame-by-frame step can be nerve-racking for the graphic artist. Advances in solid state memory technology will make this operation more tolerable, even for small operations. As the cost of solid state memory decreases, it will be possible to store a second or more (30 frames plus) of animation in a separate frame buffer for the tape recorder. The contents of the buffer will then be dumped to the tape recorder as a single block of animation, in a process similar to the DVE operation. The videotape recorder will be used only once instead of 30 times per second of animation, saving wear and tear on the tape recorder's mechanical parts. Currently, large DVE animation buffers of this type are expensive and are found only at animation facilities that can justify their considerable expense. The buffers must hold over 15 MB of information, roughly 500 K per frame. They must also be able to read a full frame of information to the graphics screen in less than a thirtieth of a second. In the future, such devices will become more affordable and may eventually eliminate the need for a frame controller.

Besides other video equipment, a sync generator is needed to keep all the various pieces of electronic equipment—graphics card, color converter, frame controller, and videotape recorder—in electronic step. Many graphics cards generate their own sync and NTSC signals, but these signals are not broadcast quality. Broadcast-quality recording requires a separate sync generator and video encoder.

Postproduction   The postproduction phase includes steps in the production process after the animation is recorded on film or videotape. Sound effects or music may be added, or the animation may be synchronized with dialogue— a process not covered in this text but similar to traditional methods where the words are recorded first and the lip movements timed to fit the dialog.[15] Animation images may be composited (combined) with live action footage and the main title and credits added at this time.

EQUIPMENT AND FACILITIES COSTS

In computer graphics production, better image quality is a function of additional expense. The lowest quality level is direct recording from the computer graphics card's own composite video output. Although these signals are only good enough for ½-inch VHS recording, the costs are still very high. If your graphics card can produce composite video signals, you must purchase a single-frame tape recorder and frame controller. These items will total about $5000 at the low end.

If you are aiming for broadcast quality (that is, signals that meet the FCC standards for resolution and color fidelity), the sync generator/color converter combination must be purchased. These items add at least another $4000 to the cost. In addition you need a ¾-inch video recorder. These recorders start at about $6000 for a recorder that is audiovisual production quality but not broadcast quality. Total cost for the second quality level— which includes a sync generator/color converter, a frame controller, and a ¾-inch videotape recorder—is about $17,000. A marginally broadcast quality recorder adds another $5000.

The third level marks true broadcast-quality recording. Add $7000 for a better animation recorder, capable of running a greater variety of recorders, and from $20,000 to $85,000 extra for the video recorder. Most of the video animation seen on television is recorded with equipment of this level.

Costs will vary, but you can calculate that total costs for an initial animation system (solid modeling and animation software, personal computer, graphics add-on products, and frame controller) will be about $20,000 at the first level. Most schools already have an AT-level personal computer and single-frame VHS recorder, so the costs can be somewhat less. A recent trend among animators is the use of animation recording services; there are regional facilities that will produce the final videotape from data files (model files and

---

[15]Philippe Bergeron, "Controlling Facial Expressions and Body Movements."

motion-path files). These animation services use minicomputers instead of microcomputers to render the frames, so the rendering time is much faster. They also record at broadcast quality, so the animations can be shown at festivals and on television. Many animators find this to be a cost-effective way to create animation, one that does not tie up resources in interface equipment, frame controllers, and high-end videotape recorders. Renderman from Pixar Corporation, a minicomputer-based high-speed rendering system, is compatible with animation programs running on microcomputers. Of course, you will want to see preliminary wire frame tests before sending the files out to the animation service, so a VHS recorder and controller or a 16mm frame-by-frame motion picture camera may still be needed.

SUMMARY

Computer animation is a separate and distinct field of computer graphics production, including both computer-assisted and computer-generated animation. Computer-assisted animation places the computer in control of traditional animation equipment—such as optical printers, studio cameras, and animation equipment—and also includes color-table and sprite animation. Computer-generated animation refers to animation that uses a computer database to create the images. The database is a collection of points in a Cartesian coordinate system that defines the objects to be animated. The objects can be animated by assigning motion paths using animation editing software. Individual frames of animation are then generated from the database and displayed on the computer screen one at a time. They are automatically recorded on videotape or motion picture film.

As in traditional animation, there are several steps in the animation process. The process can be divided into preproduction, production, and postproduction. Preproduction includes scripting, storyboarding, and budgeting. Production begins with the creation of the objects in a draw or solid modeling program and includes motion scripting, pencil tests, wire frame tests, render tests, and recording of the individual frames on film or videotape. Postproduction includes videotape editing, sound recording and mixing, and additional effects work such as titling and compositing with live action footage. In the following chapter, we will look at how computer animation is combined with video production to create animated television logos.

Exercises

1. Sketch a free-form design on graph paper. It can be a logo, letter of the alphabet from a custom font, or an element from a proposed magazine illustration.
    a. Determine the coordinates of the object with the graph paper.
    b. Enter the x and y coordinates used for each line segment into your modeling program.
    c. Add additional points with the smooth function.

2. Create a box with one round corner by point editing a circle (see Figure 5.10).
   a. Be sure the three other corners are 90-degree angles.
   b. Extrude the box a minus 400 units.

3. Create a three-dimensional shape with a drill hole in the center. Two facing sides should be flat so that you can drill from one side to the other. Shade and then rotate the object so that you can see the hole through the center.

4. Using either a rotational sweep or extrusion, three-dimensionalize the shape created in exercise 1. Letters should be extruded; other shapes can be rotated or extruded depending on how you want them to look. Experiment with off-center rotational sweeps.

5. Create a cross-sectional model of a beverage bottle. The bottle should have a round top and angular bottom corners. There should be an indent for the label on one side. Design a label for the bottle. Create the cross sections for the bottle (minimum three).
   a. Using the cross-sectional modeling option, create the shape.
   b. Render and light it with the "translucency" option.
   c. Place it in front of a digitized video background.

6. Animation Exercise 1
   a. Load the object file containing the cube with one round edge into the animation editor.
   b. Assign a 360-degree rotation to the object for a total of 48 frames. Always start your tapers at frame 1 instead of 0 so you can check the original position and size of the object.
   c. Save the move.
   d. Run a pencil test on your animation, selecting every third frame.
   e. Add additional moves to the animation; make the object bigger or smaller.
   f. Repeat steps c and d.
   g. Delete the object from the animation page and save the motion path under a different name (Zmtrn + your initials).

7. Animation Exercise 2
   a. Using the cube with one rounded edge, start a move toward the camera by first positioning the object at the horizon. Then bring it up close to the camera using a z axis translation. Turn the object on the x, y, or z axis as it moves toward the camera.
   b. Save the move and run a pencil test.
   c. Delete the object from the animation page and save the motion path under a different name (Dolly + your initials).

8. Animation Exercise 3
   a. Substitute a logo or 3-D font for the cube used in 6 or 7 above. Load the command (Zmtrn or Dolly).
   b. Run a pencil test and make changes if needed.

    c. Save your new animation to disk with a new name.

    d. Record on a VCR.

9. Animation Exercise 4

    a. Substitute a Metamorphosis object file (one that will transform one shape or letter into another) for the logo cell. Use the same motion path and command file.

    b. Specify the number of frames for the metamorphosis.

    c. Save the motion path and run a pencil test.

    d. Record on a VCR.

10. Load a globelike object into the animation editor and using the "squash" option in your software, create a motion path for the object so that it appears to bounce several times. It should squash slightly as it hits the ground and then regain its shape as it goes up again.

11. Create a 15- to 20-second animation that either explores a fantasy, demonstrates a procedure, or illustrates a business concept. The animation should contain:

    a. three-dimensionalized shapes and fonts

    b. texture map and/or reflection map

    c. Independently articulated movement (objects should move independently of each other)

Bibliography

Adams, Lee. *High-Speed Animation and Simulation for Micrcomputers.* Blue Ridge Summit, Pa.: Tab Books, 1987.

Baldwin, Huntley. *Creating Effective TV Commercials.* Chicago: Crain Books, 1982.

Canemaker, John. *The Animated Raggedy Ann and Andy. An Intimate Look at the Art of Animation: Its History, Techniques, and Artists.* Indianapolis, Ind.: Bobbs-Merrill, 1977.

Detmers, Fred H., ed. *American Cinematographer Manual.* Hollywood, Calif.: ASC Press, 1986.

Fox, David, and Mitchell Waite. *Computer Animation Primer.* New York: McGraw-Hill, 1984.

Glassner, Andrew S., ed. *An Introduction to Ray Tracing.* Chicago: SIGGRAPH, 1988.

Halas, John, ed. *Computer Animation.* New York: Hastings House, 1974.

Halas, John, and Roger Manvell. *The Technique of Film Animation.* New York: Hastings House, 1959.

Hayward, Stan. *Computers for Animation.* Boston: Focal Press, 1984.

Kroyer, Bill, ed. *3-D Character Animation by Computer.* Chicago: SIGGRAPH, 1987, 1988.

Laybourne, Kit. *The Animation Book.* New York: Crown, 1979.

MacNicol, Gregory. "Animating Motion." *Computer Graphics World* 11 (Sept. 1988): 44–50.

Magnenat-Thalmann, Nadia, and Daniel Thalmann. *Computer Animation: Theory and Practice.* New York: Springer-Verlag, 1985.

Mathias, Harry, and Richard Patterson. *Electronic Cinematography: Achieving Photographic Control over the Video Image.* Belmont, Calif.: Wadsworth, 1985.

Merritt, Douglas. *Television Graphics: From Pencil to Pixel.* New York: Van Nostrand Reinhold, 1987.

Perisic, Zoran. *The Animation Stand.* New York: Hastings House, 1976.

Rosebush, Judson, ed. *Advanced Computer Graphics Animation.* Chicago: SIGGRAPH, 1985.

Rosebush, Judson, and Gail Goldstein. "Complex Motion Automation: A Further Step Toward Realism in Animation." *Computer Graphics Review* 3 (Mar./Apr. 1988): 33–39.

Solomon, Charles, and Ron Stark. *The Computer Kodak Animation Book.* Rochester, N.Y.: Eastman Kodak, 1983.

Thalmann, Daniel, ed. *Synthetic Actors: The Impact of Artificial Intelligence and Robotics on Animation.* Chicago: SIGGRAPH, 1988.

Weinstock, Neal. *Computer Animation.* Reading, Mass.: Addison-Wesley, 1986.

Zettl, Herbert. *Television Production Handbook.* 4th ed. Belmont, Calif.: Wadsworth, 1984.

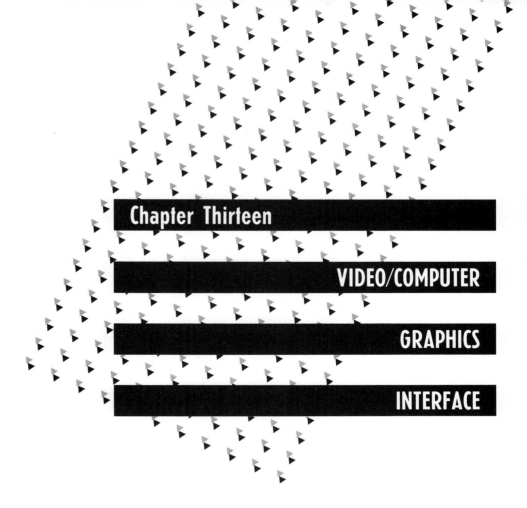

Chapter Thirteen

VIDEO/COMPUTER

GRAPHICS

INTERFACE

I n this chapter you will learn about a professional video postproduction facility that specializes in computer animation. You will see how computer graphics are combined with traditional video effects to create complex television commercials, station IDs, and other video productions.

While computer graphics have been used to create high-resolution special-effects sequences in motion pictures, the primary outlet for computer graphics animation is television. Computer graphics are used in advertising and in the making of music videos and station identifications. For this reason, computer animation equipment is increasingly used by video postproduction facilities for sophisticated editing and for productions that need three-dimensional animation.

THE FULL-FUNCTION, ALL-IN-ONE POSTPRODUCTION FACILITY

Postproduction is the term used to describe the final stage in the making of a film or videotape. This stage includes film and videotape editing, optical or electronic special effects, and sound mixing (or sound sweetening, in video terminology). More and more postproduction facilities provide computer animation services for their clients, whereas formerly the producer would have to carry the unfinished footage from shop to shop. A full-function postproduction facility puts all these services under one roof: electronic special effects, 2-D and 3-D computer graphics, rotoscoping, motion control, digital video layering, and on-line and off-line video editing.

With a wide variety of services available, the producer is not locked into one technique to solve a particular production problem. There are things that 3-D graphics do better than traditional video effects, and there are things that 3-D graphics are less than ideal for. Writing in *Millimeter* magazine, Alison Johns notes that "motion-control shots of models and miniatures are often more time-effective and convincing than computer-generated imitations and that raster imaging is better employed to solve other problems, like quick changes in color or texture. While a galaxy-worn spaceship might play better as a model, the glittering starfield it blasts through is more efficiently created as a computer graphic."[1]

Many special effects require the integration of several techniques—animation, video layering, and 2-D titling. If the services are at the same location, the chances of more consistent and integrated postproduction are increased. Simply put, the producer has only one company to work with, not several companies that might each pass the buck to the other. A disadvantage of using a single facility is that you may sacrifice flexibility in choosing production personnel for each stage of the project.

Services in an All-in-One Facility

The following discussion highlights the postproduction services of Post Perfect, an all-in-one postproduction facility in New York City. Projects are brought to Post Perfect for videotape editing, titling, and special effects. Because of the complex nature of many projects, experienced producers usually plan the shooting after talking with people who will supervise the postproduction phase. Postproduction services at Post Perfect include technical as well as creative services.

Film Transfer to Videotape and Color Correction   Many television commercials are still photographed on motion picture film because film offers the best image quality and film equipment is more portable. They are then edited on videotape. When the film footage arrives at a video postproduction house for editing and special effects, it is transferred to videotape. During this transfer process, the overall color balance of each scene is checked and compared with other scenes. For example, an outdoor scene begun early in the day when warm rays from the sun give images an orange cast may need color correction to match footage shot at midday when the sun's rays are much cooler. Corrections are made where necessary.

In some cases, color correction means dropping out colors—making the footage black and white and then adding back color in specific areas. Music videos and commercials often appear to be shot in black and white,

---

[1] Alison Johns, "Life in the Dollhouse," *Millimeter* 14 (Nov. 1986): 58.

with only the lips of the singer or the product itself being shown in color. Color manipulation is an important function of a video postproduction facility.

Videotape Editing   Videotape editing can be divided into off-line and on-line editing. The term *off-line editing* means that preliminary editing is done on less expensive ¾-inch or ½-inch editing equipment. The original broadcast-quality tapes are transferred to work copies for editing. Creative editing decisions are made on the off-line editing equipment, and the final off-line cut is approved by the client. An edit decision list containing all the editing information—scene number and exact scene length—is then generated by the off-line editing computer. This list is then used to automatically edit the original broadcast-quality tape on the more expensive on-line editing equipment. Off-line editing saves money because the more expensive equipment is not used until the end, after all the editing decisions have been made. For smaller jobs, or when a tape needs only minor changes, on-line editing is used immediately. With on-line editing, you work with the original master tapes; duplicates are not made for the purpose of editing. The client walks out the door with the actual videotape ready for broadcast or other exhibition.

Digital Video Layering   Video layering is one step beyond videotape editing. Layering enables you to combine many different pieces of videotape into one composite image. By manipulating the perspective of separate video images on the x, y, and z axes, the flat images can be made to flip and tumble, zoom through space, and take on a pseudo-three-dimensional look. Hundreds of different pieces of video can be digitally combined so that they seem to be interacting in 3-D space. Digital video layering equipment (Ampex ADO and Kaleidoscope are two systems commonly used) allows you to take a frame of moving video and combine it with other pieces of video. An object in midground can be combined with another object in the foreground. For instance, you can put a television station logo in the foreground and TV call letters in midground and then "travel" in between them. The foreground logo passes out of view as we get closer to the call letters. These elements are combined in real time, and their motion paths can be adjusted, or tweaked, as the client watches.

Two-Dimensional Computer Graphics and Animation   Postproduction facilities use 2-D computer graphics in a variety of ways. At the very basic level, character generators create opening titles, lower-third identifications for interviews (in which the interviewee's name appears near the bottom of the screen), and closing credits. Two-dimensional computer graphics packages, such as the Quantel Paintbox system, are used to create illustrations for news and training programs, supply special artwork for station identifications, and provide a means of image touch-up and manipulation in a variety of applications.

Two-dimensional computer animation is similar to traditional cell animation. Any effect that can be created with an airbrush, water colors, or other traditional methods can be done with a paint/2-D animation system. Combination paint/animation systems, such as the Quantel Harry system, create traveling mattes (opaque silhouettes of foreground objects used to separate them from the background) to add lighting effects—streaks and laser beams—and to retouch existing footage. A scratch of dirt across the narrator's face can be cleaned up, eliminating the need for reshooting. Anything from medical illustrations to character animation can be created with 2-D computer animation. You still need an artist to draw the individual pictures, because most systems do not create in-between frames. One popular practice is to trace artwork over existing video, adding artwork to individual video frames as you would to transparent cell overlays. Using this technique, a picture of a horse galloping across the screen can dissolve into a sepia-toned charcoal animation of the same scene.

Three-Dimensional Computer Graphics and Animation   Three-dimensional modeling and animation are used for station IDs and commercials. Because it is more elaborate, three-dimensional animation is usually more expensive. It is the current top-of-the-line television effect and is used to simulate environments that cannot otherwise be created. When a client wants a high-tech look or elaborate 3-D fantasy environment, three-dimensional animation is called for. Occasionally, however, a client will insist on a 3-D approach when one may not be needed. For example, Dean Winkler, video artist and creative services director at Post Perfect, notes that the goal of 3-D computer animation is to do the special things that you can't do with normal photography. Sometimes it is easier to go out and find the object rather than create it with a computer. He cites the following example:

> We had a client who had a product shot that included a telephone on a table. The storyboard called for us to do a camera move and zoom in on the phone. And they wanted us to do that with computer graphics. And we asked—
> "What does the phone do?"
> "It sits there; it's a phone."
> "It doesn't do anything?"
> "No."
> "Well, do you have the phone? Does it exist?"
> "Yes."
> "Why don't we shoot it?" The scene was photographed by traditional means.
>
> On the other hand, let's say when we got up to the phone we wanted to dive into it and see an electronic network inside. Or let's say you wanted the phone to fly apart into a thousand pieces that were precisely choreographed. Or let's say you wanted to start up in outer space and do a move from outer space down to the table. Now those are things that you can't do in reality. And that's where computer graphics is great. But believe me, if you can shoot it, you are better off shooting it.[2]

A limited production budget and time constraints will often govern what you can create on the computer. Natural phenomena—for instance, plants, dirt, shrubbery, and people—are much harder to create than flat metallic surfaces or simple geometric shapes. Other effects—such as soft shadows left by extruded letters or live video panels flying in space—are more easily created with ADO and Kaleidoscope digital video effects equipment. For this reason, 3-D animation is often used in conjunction with less expensive video effects to solve a particular problem.

---

[2] Dean Winkler, creative services director at Post Perfect, New York. Conversation with the author, May 31, 1988.

MAKING A COMPUTER-ANIMATED STATION IDENTIFICATION

The animated station identification is an often-used television visual. It is used by television networks and local stations to tell viewers about special programming and upcoming features. The style of the animation creates a special identification or look for the broadcaster. Because of their importance, station identifications are usually created by animation and graphics specialists working for animation or postproduction service companies. Animation services create the animation and then use postproduction services for editing and special effects compositing. Many postproduction services are now offering creative services such as animation, paint, and video special effects. Let's look at the development of a 20-second news opening used by station KSDK in St. Louis. It was created at Post Perfect in conjunction with David Gieselmann of KSDK. Note how the various production stages relate to the hypothetical stages discussed earlier.

1. Review of client's storyboard
2. Budgeting
3. Design
   a. Revise storyboard, adding detail where needed
   b. Time the music track
   c. Do technical design
4. Model building
   a. Trace in artwork
   b. Extrude artwork
   c. Assign surface attributes
   d. Add lighting
5. Choreography
   a. Assign motion path
   b. Do wire frame interactive pencil tests
   c. Videotape animation in wire frame only
6. Low-resolution render test
7. Final rendering of completed animation
8. Digital video layering and effects
9. Sound mixing

Storyboards

The first step in creating an animation is a good storyboard. The storyboard for the KSDK spot was created by an art director working for the television station and contains hand-drawn sketches for each shot, visually showing how the animation will develop. An important aspect of the storyboard is the treatment of transitions between shots. Note that in the KSDK storyboard, each transition is clearly indicated. After the storyboard is approved by the station management, it is shown to animation services for bidding. Services are selected by style, reputation, and price. Different services may suggest

1.

"This is Channel 5 . . ."
ID rises from under water to float above it.

2.

". . . KSDK, St. Louis."
Pulling back to reveal reflection in arch.

3.

(Music up with two horn notes)
Truck around one face of arch to the other.

4.

(Start main horn melody)
Constant motion back, right, down. Reflections
of St. Louis and people.

FIGURE 13.1

*Storyboard for KSDK station ID.
(Courtesy Post Perfect, New York,
and Station KSDK, St. Louis.)*

different ways to execute the boards. Discussions at this stage focus on interpretation and what the animation will cost to produce.

Figure 13.1 shows the proposed storyboard for KSDK's station ID.
The actual 20-second animation created for KSDK begins with a close-up of
bright reflections in the silver-colored surface of the St. Louis arch. The camera
quickly pulls back to reveal the number 5, part of the KSDK logo. It pulls
back further to include the full logo and the NBC peacock. It then reveals
that the logo is floating in front of the silver arch. The camera then arcs to
the right to reveal the right (inside) surface. We then see live video clips of
St. Louis reflected on the arch surface. As the camera pulls back further, we
find ourselves inside the number 5 again, and we see the original station logo
on a blue background. The logo remains on the screen and is keyed over the
live newscaster.

Budgeting and Preliminary Planning

At the animation service, the creative services director looks at the storyboard
and estimates how much time it will take to create the animation. Because
large postproduction facilities can take many approaches to any given assign-

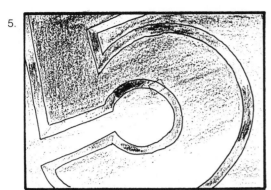

5.

"And now Channel 5 . . ."
Zoom out revealing arch, actually metal bevel
of 5. Panel #4 fits into dotted box area of this
panel.

6.

". . . Eyewitness News Update."
Continue zoom back, revealing full logo. Show
title scripts on.

7.

(End horn melody)
Logo unstacks and background wipes to ultra
black.

8.

(Rhythm track)
Logo lower third over ultra black.

FIGURE 13.1

Continued.

ment (using computer-generated 2-D or 3-D animation, digital video effects, live photography, or a combination of all), the estimator must be a skilled technician who understands how the facility can meet the needs of a particular project. The creative services director looks at the project and figures out the production sequence. Some projects use computer-generated animation; others rely on 3-D puppet animation or motion-controlled animation. The creative services director decides which technique is best for the project, considering both artistic and cost factors.

Design

After the client approves the budget, the project goes into production. Even though the storyboard has been carefully designed by the client or art director, it still may need more details added before it goes into production. Detail is often added to assist the animator, who must create the computer models and plan their motion paths. In another preliminary step, the music is carefully timed, and an animators' exposure sheet is created. The exposure sheet notes all of the variations in the music, and the animation is later shot to match the exposure sheet.

FIGURE 13.2

Workstation at Post Perfect. (Courtesy Post Perfect.)

Technical Design   Based on the requirements of the project, the creative services director makes a flowchart showing how the project will progress through the facility. Decisions are made as to how specific visual effects will be created and which aspects of the animation will use two-dimensional animation and which will use three-dimensional animation. The project is broken down into its component parts, and its course through the facility is planned in detail. Three-dimensional elements that will later be layered together using digital effects equipment are sketched in detail and given to the computer animation artist for construction.

Model Construction

After detailed discussions with the client's art director about how the animation will look—the type of surfaces objects will have, the colors, and so on—the models (also called geometry) are created with 3-D modeling software. Post Perfect uses a combination of Wavefront software (see Appendix A) and in-house software for solid modeling and animation. The software runs on an Iris minicomputer workstation from Silicon Graphics (see Figure 13.2).

The most prominent object in the KSDK spot is the aluminum arch, which identifies St. Louis. Blaine Cone, the computer modeler, begins creating the model by tracing in an artist's sketch of the arch into the computer.

> Basically, we have the flat artwork, and we digitize it on our digitizing tablet. Once the object is digitized, we extrude it [give it thickness] with the 3-D modeling software. After that we give it beveled edges with a bevel program that cuts a 45-degree angle along all the edges. This gives it nice highlights when light pans across the object. And basically that's the model. We then assign materials and textures to the surface using the Wavefront software.
>
> For the St. Louis arch, we texture mapped the metallic surface with panels, each with a brush texture look. The brush texture was created in a paint program and then mapped on to the panels. It gave it a nice effect.[3]

---

[3] Blaine Cone, computer modeler, Post Perfect, New York. Conversation with the author, Aug. 11, 1988.

The NBC peacock was created in much the same way, being first traced in from an artist's sketch. The final step in the modeling procedure is a full-screen render of each 3-D element. The full-screen render test is shown to the client for final approval.

Choreography and Interactive Wire Frame Tests

After the computer models are created and surface attributes assigned, the models are given animation motion paths. In this particular spot, the paths were developed interactively with the help of the client. Wire frame pencil tests are used to display each motion path variation. Objects are placed at different starting and ending points, and various twists and turns are tested. On slower systems, bounding boxes containing fewer data points can be used to test the movement. Later, the bounding boxes are replaced with the actual models. When the pencil tests look right, the full animation is recorded on videotape in wire frame mode for a final check (see Color Plate 12).

Low-Resolution Test Renders

Finally, the animation is test rendered at half the screen size, with every fourth video field computed. Because there are two video fields per frame, this is the same as saying every other frame is rendered. The rendered fields are recorded four times each so that the animation runs the normal length. With only half the resolution in each frame and $\frac{1}{4}$ the number of fields computed, computation time is about $\frac{1}{16}$ of what it would be normally. Lighting, colors, and surface textures are given a final check. The introduction of movement sometimes changes highlights, so these variations are watched carefully.

Full-Resolution Render to Videotape

When the low-resolution render tests are approved by the client, the animation is rendered at full resolution and then recorded on videotape. In this particular project, the master model was broken up into several elements that were each rendered separately. The model elements consisted of the station logo and NBC peacock, the right side of the arch, and the left side of the arch. In addition to these elements, the animator created other graphic elements that were added later. These elements included the soft shadow matte, used behind the station logo; a matte of the arch itself; a grid pattern, which was added to the arch to make it look more realistic; and a white amorphous shape used to soften the edges of the video images (see Color Plate 12). The master model and additional elements were each recorded separately on videotape. The elements were then combined (layered) on the ADO digital video effects system to form the final animation.

Digital Layering on the Digital Video Effects System

The final animation consists of eight layers of video, which were developed by combining many elements into each layer. One important section of the KSDK spot required several elements:

- ▸ Individual shots of the water
- ▸ A 3-D model of the left side of the arch

- ▸ The arch matte
- ▸ A shadow of the station logo

The horizontal lines in Figure 13.3 represent composites of the elements above the lines. Each composite is then used as an element of the next composite (horizontal line). The processed water was created by superimposing four different views of the river surface. Together they give the river surface reflected in the arch surface more sparkle.

Often elements are combined using electronic video keying—that is, the image from one video source is "cookie cut" to fit the positive portion of a high-contrast matte. The negative portion of the matte is then used to add a second image to the first. The result is a composite image containing two separate shots (see "Blue Screen Photography" in Chapter 12 for a related discussion).

The triangles in Figure 13.3 represent elements that are combined by using video chromakey to form the composite. For instance, the processed water was first shaped to fit the outline of the arch by keying the water to an opaque matte in the shape of the arch. The shaped water was then superimposed on the surface of the arch. (Follow the line down from the "processed water" in Figure 13.3 to where it is shaped by the arch matte and combined

FIGURE 13.3

Schematic of digital layering used for left side of arch for KSDK station ID. (Courtesy Post Perfect, New York, and Station KSDK, St. Louis.)

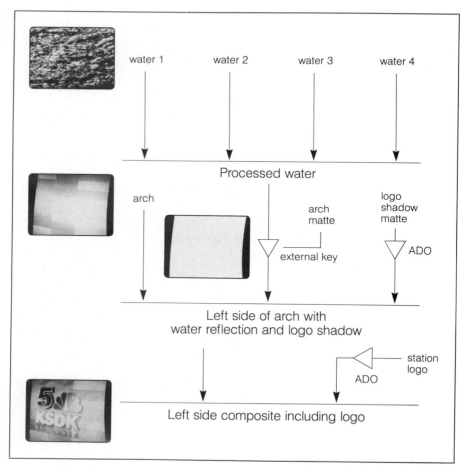

UNIT FIVE: COMPUTER GRAPHICS ANIMATION

with the other elements, including a shadow for the logo.) The actual logo was then added, and the resulting composite image, making up the left side of the arch, was later combined with the right side (not shown) to form the completed animation.

The right side of the arch contains reflections of scenes shot in and around St. Louis. Because the camera arcs to show the right (inside) surface, perspective on the video scenes had to change as the camera brought more of the right side into view—as if the images were really on the surface of the arch. Perspective changes were done with the ADO system before the images were added to the arch. The turning of the arch was scripted in the animation software. The turning of the images was done by eye to match the movement of the 3-D arch.

At the next generation, the right and left sides of the arch are combined with the help of the ADO video effects system. Note that the two sides were originally created as one 3-D model and given the same motion path. They were then rendered to separate pieces of videotape so that they could contain different reflections and embellishments. After the video overlays are added (many generations later), the 3-D model elements are reunited using the ADO system.

The KSDK spot is unique because it combines both computer animation techniques and ADO digital video effects. Three-dimensional animation and live footage were integrated using the ADO system. The spot could not have been created using the Wavefront system alone. Winkler reports that the postproduction and special effects budget for the whole package was around $75,000, which includes 3-D animation, ADO video integration, and seven different versions of the final spot. A noontime version features a brighter background and daytime scenes around St. Louis. The evening version has a darker background, with evening scenes reflected in the arch. Because the animation elements (the right and left sides of the arch, the station logo, the shadow masks) were kept separate as individual modules, they could be reused to create the different versions at relatively low cost.

SUMMARY: SKILLS OF THE COMPUTER ANIMATOR

Work done in postproduction centers is necessarily technical. As animation becomes a function of highly complex postproduction centers containing digital video effects, motion control cameras, and other special effects equipment, the artist must understand how this equipment operates in the integrated system. Dean Winkler believes that in order to get into video postproduction, the artist should have training in video or computer science, as well as strong artistic credits. The two skills are essential in this creative yet technical environment. Even though computer animation no longer requires that people learn programming, the technical video environment found in today's postproduction centers requires that the artist be comfortable with such equipment, and although programming knowledge is not required, it is still a plus. Artists who know programming often write extensions to existing software to meet the requirements of a specific modeling problem not anticipated by the original software.

As video and computer technology rapidly change, the artist must quickly recognize important trends and breakthroughs. State-of-the-art equipment is expensive, and investment in this equipment can only be done by experienced artist/engineers who understand its application to the art of video animation.

Besides technical skills, the artist should understand how traditional animators bring their stories to life, using human elements, humor, and caricature. Writing nearly 30 years ago, John Halas, a well-known British animator, begins his book on traditional animation with the following advice:

> The animator . . . must have certain qualifications both as artist and technician if he is to become successful in this form of filmmaking. He must have the cartoonist's flair for getting the essentials of character firmly established with the minimum graphic effort. He must have an eye for movement so that he can visualize how his characters should move and at the same time retain in movement the essentials of their being. He must have a strong dramatic sense so that he can develop a movement to its own graphic climax within a given shot or sequence, making it part of the larger action as it has been planned on the storyboard for the complete film. He must have a sense of mobile composition, so that he can unfold and place movement within the limits of the screen frame, and he must also have a musician's sense of timing, for much of his work will have to be animated in close synchronization with music.[4]

With today's emphasis on technology, the artist cannot overlook the roots of computer animation. We are, after all, telling stories, just as animators did when all they used were pencil, paper, and a camera. The trend toward 3-D computer-generated character animation draws heavily on the artist's sensitivity to human traits that project character and personality. Gleaming logos in space are only an initial application of computer animation. As the medium matures, it will evolve into a more expressive form. Artists will be trained in both the art and technology of computer animation.

Exercises

1. Visit a television production facility, possibly on your college campus, and observe how television special effects are added to television programs during taping. Ask if the facility has a digital video effects (DVE) generator and compare the scope of effects created with normal special effects equipment to those created with digital equipment.

2. Create a computer-generated logo animation for a student television production. Ideally, the logo will be for someone else's production. Find out what the subject of the program is and make a logo specifically for that program. Whether it be a drama, a news program, or a talk show, the logo should reflect the content of the program. Be sure to get a copy of the logo animation for your portfolio.

3. Begin reading the following computer graphics and video magazines that are directed to the video market: *Videography* (2 Park Avenue, New York,

---

[4] John Halas and Roger Manvell, *The Technique of Film Animation* (New York: Hastings House, 1959), 19.

NY 10016), *Audiovisual Communications* (50 West 23rd. Street, NY 10010-5292), *Computer Graphics World* (119 Russell Street, FOB 1112, Littleton, MA 01460), *Computer Pictures* (2 Village Square West, Clifton, NJ 07011), and *AV Video* (Hawthorne Boulevard, Suite 314, Torrance, CA 90505). These periodicals regularly carry articles on computer graphics applications in television.

Bibliography

Baldwin, Huntley. *Creating Effective TV Commercials*. Chicago: Crain Books, 1982.

Mathias, Harry, and Richard Patterson. *Electronic Cinematography*. Belmont, Calif.: Wadsworth, 1985.

Merritt, Douglas. *Television Graphics from Pencil to Pixel*. New York: Van Nostrand Reinhold, 1987.

Winkler, Dean, ed. *Special Effects with Computer Graphics*. Chicago: SIGGRAPH, 1988.

Zettl, Herbert. *Television Production Handbook*. 4th ed. Belmont, Calif.: Wadsworth, 1984.

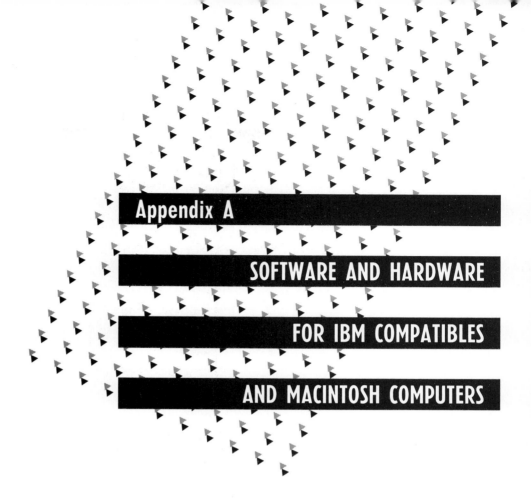

Appendix A

SOFTWARE AND HARDWARE

FOR IBM COMPATIBLES

AND MACINTOSH COMPUTERS

he following is a representative sampling of software and hardware available in the computer graphics marketplace. The authors do not endorse any of the products, nor is the list meant to be exhaustive. Use it as an initial guide. You will also want to talk to software and hardware suppliers and technical support people about the products you are considering. Be sure that the hardware and software are compatible. You may want to select the software best suited to your needs and then purchase the hardware required to run the software (see "Purchasing Graphics Software" in Chapter 1). Talk to as many people as possible with knowledge of the product and actually use the software and hardware when possible.

GRAPHICS SOFTWARE FOR MICROCOMPUTERS
(IBM COMPATIBLE)

Unless other graphics cards are listed, most of the following software supports standard graphics cards such as the CGA, VGA, EGA, and Hercules cards. Where software requires or supports special purpose graphics cards such as the Number Nine Revolution Cards, Pepper cards, TARGA cards, or Vision cards this has been indicated. Check current versions of the software for hardware compatibility.

Draw and CAD Software   Vector-based programs that create high-resolution output not limited to the pixel resolution of the screen.

AutoCAD. Standard graphics cards, Number Nine Revolution, Pepper, and other cards. Autodesk, Inc., 2320 Marinship Way, Sausalito, CA 94965. (415) 332-2344

Logo Editor. TARGA 16 and ATVista. Flamingo Graphics, 19 Bishop Allen Drive, Cambridge, MA 02139. (617) 661-1001

RIO. Draw and image/text layout system. TARGA 16, 24, 32, Vision 16, or VISTA. AT&T Graphics Software Labs, 10291 N. Meridian, Ste. 275, Indianapolis, IN 46290. (317) 844-4364

Versacad Design. Standard graphics cards, TARGA 16, Pepper, and other cards. Versacad Corporation, 2124 Main St., Huntington Beach, CA 92648. (714) 960-7720

Paint and Pixel-Based Animation Software   In addition to normal paint features such as airbrush, rotate, and perspective, many programs will digitize an image from a video camera or desktop scanner.

Brushwork. Paint program. Pansophic Systems, Inc., Graphic Products Division, 2400 Cabot Drive, Lisle, IL 60532. TARGA 16 or ATVista 4MB/10MB VMX. (708) 505-6000

Colorrix VGA Paint, EGA Paint. Rix Softworks, Inc., 18552 MacArthur Blvd., #375, Irvine, CA 92715. (714) 476-8266, (800) 345-9059

Dr. Halo III. Paint software. CGA, EGA, VGA, and Hercules. Media Cybernetics, 8484 Georgia Ave., Silver Spring, MD 20910. (301) 495-3305

Halovision. Graphics editing software. Number Nine Revolution Card, TARGA 8, 16, Pepper Card. Media Cybernetics, Inc., 8484 Georgia Ave., Silver Spring, MD 20910. (301) 495-3305

Lumena. Paint and animation software. Vision 16 and 32, Number Nine Revolution Card, or TARGA 16, 24, 32. Time Arts, Inc., 3436 Mendocino Ave., Santa Rosa, CA 95401. (707) 576-7722

NIMBLE. Two-dimensional and simulated three-dimensional animation. Pansophic Systems Inc., Graphic Products Division, 2400 Cabot Drive, Lisle, IL 60532. TARGA 16 or ATVista 4MB/10MB VMX. (708) 505-6000

TIPS. Paint software. Truevision, Inc., 7351 Shadeland Station, Ste. 100, Indianapolis, IN 46220. TARGA 8, 16, 24, 32 or ATVista. (800) 858-TRUE, (317) 841-0332

Three-Dimensional Modeling and Animation Software

Artwork/Videowork. Three-dimensional modeling and animation. Pansophic Systems, Inc., Graphic Products Division, 2400 Cabot Drive, Lisle, IL 60532. TARGA 16 or ATVista 4MB/10MB VMX. (708) 505-6000

Digital Arts. TARGA 16 or ATVista card. Requires additional graphics coprocessors. Three-dimensional modeling and animation. Digital Arts, Inc., 7050 Convoy Ct., San Diego, CA 92111. (619) 541-2055

Crystal 3D Solids Modeler. Vision 16, Number Nine Revolution Card, or TARGA 16, 24, 32. Time Arts, Inc., 3436 Mendocino Ave., Santa Rosa, CA 95401. (707) 576-7722

PictureMaker 60. Three-dimensional modeling and animation. Uses special hardware. Cubicomp Corp., 21325 Cabot Blvd., Hayward, CA 94545. (415) 887-1300

TOPAS. Three-dimensional modeling and animation. Vision 16, TARGA 16, 24, 32, or ATVista. AT&T Graphics Software Labs, 10291 N. Meridian, Ste. 275, Indianapolis, IN 46290. (317) 844-4364

Page-Layout and Design Software

PageMaker. Aldus Corp., 411 First Ave. S., Seattle, WA 98104. (206) 622-5500

Pagework. Pansophic Systems, Inc., Graphic Products Division, 2400 Cabot Drive, Lisle, IL 60532. TARGA 16 or ATVista 4MB/10MB VMX. (708) 505-6000

Publish It. Timeworks, Inc., 444 Lake Cook Rd., Deerfield, IL 60015. (312) 948-9200

Ventura Publisher. Xerox Corp., Desktop Software Division, 9745 Business Park Ave., San Diego, CA 92131. (800) 822-8221

Children's Writing & Publishing Center. The Learning Co., 6493 Kaiser Dr., Fremont, CA 94555. (415) 792-2101, (800) 852-2255

Image Digitizing and Editing Software

Aldus Snapshot. Aldus Corp., 411 First Ave. S., Seattle, WA 98104. (206) 622-5500

Imagedit. IBM Corp., 101 Paragon Dr., Montvale, NJ 07645. (800) IBM-2468

T-Scan. Videotex Systems, Inc., 8499 Greenville Ave., #205, Dallas, TX 75231. (214) 343-4500

Presentation Graphics Software

Chart-Master. Ashton-Tate, 20101 Hamilton Ave., Torrance, CA 90502-1319. (213) 329-8000

Chartwork. Pansophic Systems, Inc., Graphic Products Division, 2400 Cabot Drive, Lisle, IL 60532. TARGA 16 or ATVista 4MB/10MB VMX. (708) 505-6000

Freelance Plus. Lotus Development Corp., 55 Cambridge Parkway, Cambridge, MA 02142. (617) 577-8500

Harvard Graphics. Software Publishing Corp., 1901 Landings Drive, Mountain View, CA 94039-7210. (415) 962-8910

Lotus Graphwriter II. Lotus Development Corp., 55 Cambridge Parkway, Cambridge, MA 02142. (617) 577-8500

Microsoft Chart. Microsoft Corp., 16011 N.E. 36th Way, Box 97017, Redmond, WA 98052. (206) 882-8080, (800) 426-9400

Mirage/Autumn. Standard graphics cards, Number Nine Revolution Card, Pepper card, TARGA 16, and other cards. Zenographics, Inc., 19572 MacArthur Blvd., Ste. 250, Irvine, CA 92715. (714) 851-6352

Show Partner. Standard graphics cards and special hardware. Brightbill-Roberts & Co., Ltd., 120 E. Washington St., Ste. 421, Syracuse, NY 13202. (315) 474-3400

Starburst. Pansophic Systems, Inc., 709 Enterprise Drive, Oak Brook, IL 60521. (800) 323-7335

Videoshow. EGA and VGA with special hardware. General Parametrics Corp., 1250 Ninth St., Berkeley, CA 94710. (415) 524-3950

Image Processing

Digital Darkroom Software. This is instructional software that shows various types of image processing (see Figure 4.8). It is meant to be used with *Beyond Photography: The Digital Darkroom* by Gerard J. Holzmann (New York: Prentice-Hall, 1988). Software can be purchased from Prentice-Hall, Inc., Route 59 at Brook Hill Drive, West Nyack, NY 10995. (914) 358-8800

GRAPHICS SOFTWARE FOR MICROCOMPUTERS (MACINTOSH)

The following software will support standard color graphics cards such as the Macintosh video card (4 and 8 bits) and/or high-performance cards such as the Colorboard series from Rasterops Corp., Nu Vista, and Spectrum/24.

Draw and CAD Software

Adobe Illustrator 88. Adobe Systems, Inc., P.O. Box 7900, Mountain View, CA 94039-7900. (415) 961-4400, (800) 833-6687[1]

Aldus FreeHand. Aldus Corp., 411 First Ave. S., Seattle, WA 98104. (206) 622-5500[1]

AutoCAD. CAD program. Autodesk, Inc., 2320 Marinship Way, Sausalito, CA 94965. (415) 332-2344, (800) 223-2521

Canvas. Deneba Software, 3305 N.W. 74th Avenue, Miami, FL 33122. (305) 594-6965, (800) 622-6827[1]

Cricket Draw. Cricket Software, Inc., 40 Valley Stream Parkway, Malvern, PA 19355. (215) 251-9890[1]

DeskDraw. Zedcor, Inc., 4500 E. Speedway, #22, Tucson, AZ 85712-5305. (602) 881-8101, (800) 482-4567[1]

Drawing Table. Broderbund Software, Inc., 17 Paul Drive, San Rafael, CA 94903-2101. (415) 492-3200[1]

In-CAD. Infinite Graphics, 4611 East Lake St., Minneapolis, MN 55406. (612) 721-6283

MacDraw II. Claris Corp., P.O. Box 58168, Santa Clara, CA 95052. (408) 987-7000, (800) 334-3535[1]

SuperPaint. Contains both draw and paint features. Silicon Beach Software, Inc., PO Box 261430, San Diego, CA 92126. (619) 695-6956[1]

---

[1] Reviewed by Steve McKinstry, "Draw, Pardner," *Mac World* 6 (August 1989): 141ff.

Versacad. Versacad Corp., 2124 Main St., Huntington Beach, CA 92648. (714) 960-7720

Paint and Pixel-Based Animation Programs

DeskPaint. Zedcor, Inc., 4500 East Speedway, #22, Tucson, AZ 85712-4567. (602) 881-8101, (800) 482-4567[2]

GraphicWorks. Paint program. Mindscape, Inc., 3444 Dundee Rd., Northbrook, IL 60062. (312) 480-1948[2]

GraphistPaint II. Aba Software, Inc., 41 Great Valley Parkway, Malvern, PA 19355. (215) 644-3580, (800) 234-0230[3]

Lumena. High-end paint program due for release in mid-1990. Time Arts, Inc., 3436 Mendocino Ave., Santa Rosa, CA 95403. (707) 576-7722

MacPaint. Claris Corp., 440 Clyde Ave., Mountain View, CA 94040. (415) 960-1500, (800) 334-3535[2]

Modern Artist. Computer Friends, Inc., 14250 N.W. Science Park Dr., Portland, OR 97229. (503) 626-2291, (800) 547-3303[3]

Photon Paint. MicroIllusions, 17408 Chatsworth St., Granada Hills, CA 91344. (818) 360-3715, (800) 360-3715[3]

PixelPaint. SuperMac Technology, 295 N. Bernardo Ave., Mountain View, CA 94043. (415) 964-8884[3]

Studio/8. Paint program. Electronic Arts, PO Box 7530, San Mateo, CA 94403. (415) 571-7171, (800) 245-4525[3]

SuperPaint. Silicon Beach Software, Inc., PO Box 261430, San Diego, CA 92126. (619) 695-6956[2]

Videoworks II. Two-dimensional animation with paint capability. Macromind, Inc., 410 Townsend St., San Francisco, CA 94107. (415) 442-0200

Three-dimensional Modeling and Animation Software

Zing. 3-D modeling. Enabling Technologies, Inc., 600 S. Dearborn St., #1304, Chicago, IL 60605. (312) 427-0386, (800) 544-0629[4]

Sculpt 3D. Solid modeling. Eight-, 16-, and 32-bit frame buffers such as Truevision NuVista. Byte by Byte Corp., Arboretum Plaza II, 9442 Capital of Texas Hwy N., Ste. 150, Austin, TX 78759. (512) 343-4357

Swivel 3D. Solid modeling and animation. Paracomp, 123 Townsend St., #310, San Francisco, CA 94107. (415) 543-3848[4]

Super3D. Solid modeling and animation. Silicon Beach Software, Inc., PO Box 261430, San Diego, CA 92126. (619) 695-6956[4]

Page-Layout and Design Software

PageMaker. Aldus Corp., 4111 First Ave. S., Seattle, WA 98104. (206) 622-5500[5]

Publish It. Timeworks, Inc. 444 Lake Cook Rd., Deerfield, IL 60015. (312) 948-9200

---

[2] Reviewed by Adrian Mello, "Paint Roundup," *Mac World* 5 (September 1988): 151ff.
[3] Reviewed by Erfert Fenton, "Brushes with Color," *Mac World* 6 (May 1989): 151ff.
[4] Reviewed by David L. Peltz, "3-D Perspective," *Mac World* 5 (December 1988): 109ff.
[5] Reviewed by Jim Heid, "Page-Layout Contenders," *Mac World* 6 (April 1989): 109ff.

QuarkXpress. Quark, Inc., 300 S. Jackson, #100, Denver, CO 80209. (303) 934-2211, (800) 356-9363[5]

ReadySetGo. Letraset USA, 40 Eisenhower Dr., Paramus, NJ 07653. (201) 845-6100, (800) 526-9703[5]

Image Digitizing and Editing Software

Digital Darkroom. Silicon Beach Software, Inc., PO Box 261430, Carroll Center Rd., San Diego, CA 92126. (619) 695-6956

Image Studio. Letraset U.S.A., 40 Eisenhower Dr., Paramus, NJ 07653. (201) 845-6100, (800) 343-TYPE

Presentation Graphics Software

Aldus Persuasion. Aldus Corp., 411 First Ave. S., Seattle, WA 98104. (206) 622-5500

Cricket Presents . . . Cricket Software, Inc., 40 Valley Stream Parkway, Malvern, PA 19355. (215) 251-9890.

Microsoft Chart. Microsoft Corp., 16011 N.E. 36th Way, Box 97017, Redmond, WA 98052. (206) 882-8080, (800) 426-9400

Microsoft PowerPoint. Microsoft Corp., 16011 N.E. 36th Way, PO Box 97017, Redmond, WA 98052. (206) 882-8080, (800) 426-9400

VBS No. 5. Visual Business Systems, Lake St., Ramsey, NJ 07446. (201) 327-2526

FILE CONVERSION PROGRAMS (IBM COMPATIBLE)

Image Tools. Converts TARGA .TGA files to .GIF format. GRAFX Group, 31551 Camino Capistrano, Ste. D, San Juan Capistrano, CA 92675. (714) 240-7105

Hijaak. Text and graphics capture and conversion. Will convert between the following file formats: Amiga (.IFF files), CompuServe (.GIF), Halo (.CUT), HP Laser Jet and HP Plotter (.PCL & .PGL), Lotus (.PIC), Macintosh MacPaint (.MAC), Microsoft Paint (.MSP), PC Paintbrush (.PCX), PostScript (.PSC), Ventura DTP (.CUT), Desktop scanners (TIFF), and various FAX file formats. InSet Systems, Inc., 12 Mill Plain Rd., Danbury, CT 06811. (203) 775-5866

Metafile. Converts AutoCAD (.DXF), (Hewlett-Packard Graphics Language) HPGL, Lotus and 1-2-3 Symphony (.PIC), VideoShow (.PIC), and Zenographics (.ZGM) to .CGM files, Graphics Software Systems CGI and VDI drivers, Microsoft Windows Clipboard and .GDI, and Mirage .IMA files. Zenographics, Inc., 19752 MacArthur Blvd., Suite 250, Irvine, CA 92715. (714) 851-6352

Target. Converts TARGA 16 images to PICT2 format for use in Macintosh-based software. ABRA, 1675 Larimer St., Ste. 700, Denver, CO 80202. (303) 820-2272

T-EGA. Converts TARGA or Vision 16, .TGA, .ICB, or .PIX files into VGA, EGA, and CGA format. Videotex Systems, Inc., 8499 Greenville Ave., Ste. 205, Dallas, TX 75231. (214) 343-4500

TRUETILITIES (GIF2TGA, TRUEPS, TRUETIF, etc.). File conversion programs for .TGA files available from Truevision, Inc., 7351 Shadeland Station, Ste. 100, Indianapolis, IN 46256. (800) 858-TRUE. (317) 841-0332

MINICOMPUTER SYSTEMS

Paint and Animation

Alias/1. Three-dimensional modeling and animation. Alias Research, Inc., 210 Carnegie Center, Ste. 101, Princeton, NJ 08540. (609) 987-8686

Images II Paint System. Computer Graphics Laboratories, Inc., 405 Lexington Ave., New York, NY 10174. (212) 557-5130

Intelligent Light. Three-dimensional modeling and animation. Intelligent Light, Inc., PO Box 65, Fair Lawn, NJ 07410. (201) 794-7550

NeoVisual. Three-dimensional modeling and animation. SAS Institute, Inc., SAS Circle, Box 8000, Cary, NC 27512-8000. (919) 467-8000

Quantel Graphic Paintbox and Quantel Harry. Paint and animation. Quantel, Inc., 655 Washington Blvd., Stamford, CT 06901. (203) 348-4104

Symbolics. Three-dimensional modeling and animation. Symbolics, Inc., 8 New England Executive Park East, Burlington, MA 01803. (617) 221-1000

Vertigo. Three-dimensional modeling and animation. Cubicomp Corp., 21325 Cabot Blvd., Hayward, CA 94545. (415) 887-1300

Wavefront. Three-dimensional modeling and animation. Wavefront Technologies, 530 East Montecito St., Santa Barbara, CA 93103. (805) 962-8117

Prepress and Color Separation Systems

Crosfield Electronics. 47 Farnsworth St., Boston, MA 02210. (617) 338-2173

Scitex America Corp. 8 Oak Park Drive, Bedford, MA 01730. (617) 275-5150

Presentation Graphics

Dicomed Corp., 12000 Portland Ave., PO Box 246, Minneapolis, MN 55440-0246. (612) 885-3000

Genigraphics. Pansophic Systems, Inc., 709 Enterprise Drive, Oak Brook, IL 60521. (800) 323-7335

HARDWARE FOR THE IBM "AT" ARCHITECTURE AND MACINTOSH COMPUTERS

Graphics Cards for IBM AT Architecture. Many will digitize images from an RGB video source.

CGA/EGA/VGA Boards. Available from IBM and various third party sources.

Hercules Graphics Board. Hercules Computer Technology, 2550 Ninth St., Berkeley, CA 94710. (415) 540-0749, (800) 532-0600

TARGA and ATVista cards. TARGA cards provide either 8, 16, 24, or 32 bits per pixel at a screen resolution of 512 × 482. The ATVista card provides up to 32 bits per pixel with a maximum interlaced screen resolution of 1024 × 768. Truevision, Inc., 7351 Shadeland Station, Indianapolis, IN 46256. (317) 841-0332, (800) 858-TRUE

Revolution and Pepper Pro cards. Revolution cards provide up to 32 bits per pixel at a screen resolution of 512 × 482; the Pepper Pro 1024 provides 4, 8, or 32 bits per pixel at a screen resolution of 1024 × 768. Number Nine Computer Corporation, 725 Concord Ave., Cambridge, MA 02138. (617) 492-0999, (800) GET-NINE

Vision cards. Vision cards provide 16 or 32 bits per pixel at a screen resolution of 512 × 484. Everex Systems, Inc., 48431 Milton Drive, Fremont, CA 94538. (415) 683-2900

Graphics Boards for the Macintosh. Many will digitize images from an RGB video source.

Macintosh display adapters (4 bit and 8 bit). Available from Apple Computer, Inc., 20525 Mariani Ave., Cupertino, CA 95014. (408) 996-1010

Colorboard series. Provides 8, 24, and 32 bits of color per pixel at resolutions of 640 × 480 up to 1024 × 768. Rasterops Corp., 2500 Walsh Rd., Santa Clara, CA 95051. (408) 562-4200

NuVista 1M, 2M, and 4M. NuVista boards are identical to the ATVista boards, except that they run on the Macintosh. Truevision, Inc., 7351 Shadeland Station, Indianapolis, IN 46256. (317) 841-0332, (800) 858-TRUE

Spectrum/24. Provides 24 bits of color per pixel at resolutions of 640 × 480 or 1024 × 768. Supermac Technology, 485 Potrero Ave., Sunnyvale, CA 94086. (408) 245-2202

Monitors

NEC MultiSync analog RGB monitor (IBM and Macintosh). NEC Home Electronics, 1255 Michael Dr., Wood Dale, IL 60191. (312) 860-9500

Radius gray-scale display monitor (two-page for Macintosh desktop publishing). Radius, Inc., 1710 Fortune Dr., San Jose, CA 95131. (408) 434-1010, (800) 527-1950

Radius color monitors. Radius, Inc., 1710 Fortune Dr., San Jose, CA 95131. (408) 434-1010, (800) 527-1950

Peripherals

Apple Scanner. Apple Computer, Inc., 20525 Mariani Ave., Cupertino, CA 95041. (408) 996-1010

HP pen plotter. Hewlett-Packard Co., 3404 East Harmony Rd., Fort Collins, CO 80525. (303) 229-3800

HP Scanjet Plus desktop scanner (Apple or IBM). Hewlett-Packard Co., 19310 Pruneridge Ave., Cupertino, CA 95014. (800) 752-0900

Kurta digitizing tablet. Kurta Corp., 3007 E. Chambers, Phoenix, AZ 85017. (602) 276-5533.

Mini-Vas frame controller. Lyon-Lamb Video Animation Systems, Inc., 4531 Empire Ave., Burbank, CA 91505. (818) 843-4831

NEC Silentwriter laser printer. NEC Information Systems, Inc., 1414 Massachusetts Ave., Boxborough, MA 01719. (508) 264-8000, (800) 343-4418

PCR and QCR film recorders. AGFA Matrix Division, 1 Ramland Rd., Orangeburg, NY 10962. (914) 365-0190, (800) 876-7543

Polaroid Palette film recorder. Polaroid Corp., 575 Technology Square, Cambridge, MA 02139. (617) 577-2000, (800) 343-5000

Pro-Mavica video still camera and Sony video tape recorders. Sony Corp. of America, Sony Drive, Park Ridge, NJ 07656. (201) 930-1000

QMS Color Postscript Laser Printer. Laser Connection, 7851 Schillinger Park West, Mobile, AL 36608. (800) 523-2696, (205) 633-7223

Scanmaster color scanner. Howtek, Inc., 21 Park Ave., Hudson, NH 03051. (603) 882-5200

Summagraphics digitizing tablet. Summagraphics Corp., 60 Silvermine Rd., Seymour, CT 06483. (203) 881-5434

Superview series color monitors. Supermac Technology, 485 Potrero Ave., Sunnyvale, CA 94086. (408) 245-2202

Tektronix color thermal printer. Tektronix, Inc., Graphics Printing and Imaging, PO Box 1000, M-S 63-583, Wilsonville, OR 97070. (800) 835-6100

TT200 color thermal printer. AGFA Matrix Division, 1 Ramland Rd., Orangeburg NY 10962. (914) 365-0190, (800) 876-7543

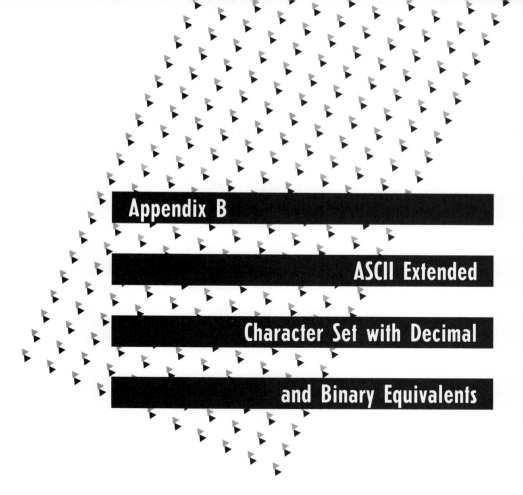

Appendix B

ASCII Extended

Character Set with Decimal

and Binary Equivalents

o see the ASCII characters on your computer screen, hold down the Alt key and type the decimal value for that character on the numeric keypad, then release the Alt key. Characters 0 through 32 will only show when using a word processing program such as Microsoft Word or WordPerfect. The extended characters begin with decimal value 128.

Decimal	Binary	Character	Decimal	Binary	Character
0	00000000		16	00010000	►
1	00000001	☺	17	00010001	◄
2	00000010	☻	18	00010010	↕
3	00000011	♥	19	00010011	‼
4	00000100	♦	20	00010100	¶
5	00000101	♣	21	00010101	§
6	00000110	♠	22	00010110	▬
7	00000111	•	23	00010111	↨
8	00001000	◘	24	00011000	↑
9	00001001	○	25	00011001	↓
10	00001010	◙	26	00011010	→
11	00001011	♂	27	00011011	←
12	00001100	♀	28	00011100	∟
13	00001101	♪	29	00011101	↔
14	00001110	♫	30	00011110	▲
15	00001111	☼	31	00011111	▼

Decimal	Binary	Character	Decimal	Binary	Character
32	00100000		89	01011001	Y
33	00100001	!	90	01011010	Z
34	00100010	"	91	01011011	[
55	00100011	#	92	01011100	\
36	00100100	$	93	01011101	]
37	00100101	%	94	01011110	^
38	00100110	&	95	01011111	
39	00100111	'	96	01100000	←
40	00101000	(	97	01100001	a
41	00101001	)	98	01100010	b
42	00101010	*	99	01100011	c
43	00101011	+	100	01100100	d
44	00101100	,	101	01100101	e
45	00101101	-	102	01100110	f
46	00101110	.	103	01100111	g
47	00101111	/	104	01101000	h
48	00110000	0	105	01101001	i
49	00110001	1	106	01101010	j
50	00110010	2	107	01101011	k
51	00110011	3	108	01101100	l
52	00110100	4	109	01101101	m
53	00110101	5	110	01101110	n
54	00110110	6	111	01101111	o
55	00110111	7	112	01110000	p
56	00111000	8	113	01110001	q
57	00111001	9	114	01110010	r
58	00111010	:	115	01110011	s
59	00111011	;	116	01110100	t
60	00111100	<	117	01110101	u
61	00111101	=	118	01110110	v
62	00111110	>	119	01110111	w
63	00111111	?	120	01111000	x
64	01000000	@	121	01111001	y
65	01000001	A	122	01111010	z
66	01000010	B	123	01111011	{
67	01000011	C	124	01111100	|
68	01000100	D	125	01111101	}
69	01000101	E	126	01111110	~
70	01000110	F	127	01111111	⌂
71	01000111	G	128	10000000	Ç
72	01001000	H	129	10000001	ü
73	01001001	I	130	10000010	é
74	01001010	J	131	10000011	â
75	01001011	K	132	10000100	ä
76	01001100	L	133	10000101	à
77	01001101	M	134	10000110	å
78	01001110	N	135	10000111	ç
79	01001111	O	136	10001000	ê
80	01010000	P	137	10001001	ë
81	01010001	Q	138	10001010	è
82	01010010	R	139	10001011	ï
83	01010011	S	140	10001100	î
84	01010100	T	141	10001101	ì
85	01010101	U	142	10001110	Ä
86	01010110	V	143	10001111	Å
87	01010111	W	144	10010000	É
88	01011000	X	145	10010001	æ

APPENDIX B

Decimal	Binary	Character	Decimal	Binary	Character
146	10010010	Æ	201	11001001	╔
147	10010011	ô	202	11001010	
148	10010100	ö	203	11001011	╦
149	10010101	ò	204	11001100	╠
150	10010110	û	205	11001101	═
151	10010111	ù	206	11001110	╬
152	10011000		207	11001111	
153	10011001	Ö	208	11010000	╨
154	10011010	Ü	209	11010001	╤
155	10011011	¢	210	11010010	
156	10011100	£	211	11010011	╙
157	10011101	¥	212	11010100	╘
158	10011110	₧	213	11010101	╒
159	10011111	ƒ	214	11010110	
160	10100000	á	215	11010111	╫
161	10100001	í	216	11011000	╪
162	10100010	ó	217	11011001	┘
163	10100011	ú	218	11011010	┌
164	10100100	ñ	219	11011011	█
165	10100101	Ñ	220	11011100	
166	10100110	ª	221	11011101	▌
167	10100111	º	222	11011110	▐
168	10101000	¿	223	11011111	▀
169	10101001	⌐	224	11100000	α
170	10101010	¬	225	11100001	ß
171	10101011	½	226	11100010	Γ
172	10101100	¼	227	11100011	π
173	10101101	¡	228	11100100	Σ
174	10101110	«	229	11100101	σ
175	10101111	»	230	11100110	µ
176	10110000	░	231	11100111	τ
177	10110001	▒	232	11101000	Φ
178	10110010	▓	233	11101001	
179	10110011	│	234	11101010	Ω
180	10110100	┤	235	11101011	δ
181	10110101	╡	236	11101100	∞
182	10110110	╢	237	11101101	φ
183	10110111	╖	238	11101110	ε
184	10111000	╕	239	11101111	∩
185	10111001	╣	240	11110000	≡
186	10111010	║	241	11110001	±
187	10111011	╗	242	11110010	≥
188	10111100	╝	243	11110011	≤
189	10111101	╜	244	11110100	⌠
190	10111110	╛	245	11110101	⌡
191	10111111	┐	246	11110110	÷
192	11000000	└	247	11110111	≈
193	11000001	┴	248	11111000	°
194	11000010	┬	249	11111001	•
195	11000011	├	250	11111010	·
196	11000100	─	251	11111011	√
197	11000101	┼	252	11111100	ⁿ
198	11000110	╞	253	11111101	²
199	11000111	╟	254	11111110	■
200	11001000	╚	255	11111111	

GLOSSARY

Add-in card Expansion card that plugs into the system board. Adds additional capabilities such as high-performance graphics, frame buffer, modem, communication ports, and connections for peripherals.

Additive primary colors Colors that when added together produce white light. The additive primary colors are red, green, and blue (see Color Plate 1). See also *subtractive primary colors*.

Algorithm A procedure or set of instructions for solving a specific problem.

Analog Something similar (or analogous) to the original. Representing data by using a continuously varying quantity, such as using electrical modulations to transmit sound. The electrical signal has a direct relationship to the pitch and volume of the original sound. See *digital*.

Analytical graphics Simple graphic representations of numeric data (e.g., bar charts) without color or typeface enhancements, usually meant for one person or a small group.

Animation exposure sheet Frame-by-frame set of instructions containing camera moves and other information for shooting an animation; also called a *dope sheet*.

Anti-aliasing Process in which stair stepping (or "jaggies") in raster displayed images is softened by averaging pixel intensity on line edges with the background (see Figure 5.19).

Applications software Program or group of related programs written for a specific task such as word processing, graphics illustration, or accounting.

Area chart A variation on the line chart, also called a mountain chart, in which the area under the line is shaded. Used to emphasize volume and change (e.g., in the national debt or cubic tons of coal) (see Figure 10.21).

Art director The person responsible for the graphic design of a publication. An art director usually has graduated from a design school and specialized in graphic arts communication; generally has significant experience in the industry at a design studio, advertising agency, or creative services department.

Artwork (1) The full-page images of type and illustration, usually mounted on illustration board, that are to be supplied to a print shop for reproduction. (2) The separate images of graphics, logotypes, or illustrations to be included in a publication.

Ascender Lowercase characters such as *k*, *t*, and *l* that extend above the body of the letter. Also, the portion of the character that extends above the body.

Aspect ratio The ratio of height to width in a motion picture frame, video screen, or 35mm slide.

Assemble editing Electronic videotape editing, which includes video, audio, and control track. Because a new control track is recorded for every edit, you cannot go back and re-edit existing material that has been assemble edited.

AT Second generation IBM microcomputer that uses an 80286 microprocessor. It runs approximately 7 to 10 times faster than the original IBM PC. The AT computer architecture is also a standard used in non-microchannel 386- and 486-level microcomputers.

Atmospheric perspective A cue to depth perception that is dependent on the amount of haze in the air. Distant objects look hazy so we assume that they are farther away.

Back light In three-point triangular lighting, the light that is behind and pointing at the subject, separating it from the background. Sometimes called rim lighting because it highlights the outline of the subject.

Bar chart A chart that uses horizontal or vertical bars (columns) as data indicators. Bar charts are useful for comparing discrete quantities of information such as yearly profits or income by age group (see Figure 10.11).

Baseline Horizontal *x* axis on a chart, just above the data labels.

Batch files Files containing a series of commands or

programs that will execute as a unit (batch process) without further input from the user. DOS batch files end in the .BAT extension (e.g., AUTOEXEC.BAT).

Batch processing The procedure whereby a program or series of programs is run in its entirety without the opportunity for user interaction until the computer has finished running the program(s).

BEFLIX Programming language developed by Ken Knowlton at Bell Telephone Laboratories in 1964, used for creating early computer animation films such as Stan VanderBeek's *Poemfield 1–8*.

Bezier curves and patches A procedure for making smooth sloping transitions between three or more points on a line or surface, with influence exerted unequally by intermediate control points (see Figure 5.18).

Binary code System of numeric notation that encodes information by expressing one of two states; in digital computers the states are either on or off. The binary system uses a string of 0's and 1's to represent quantities. For example, 10000000 equals 128 and represents the letter Ç; 01000000 equals 64 and represents the @ symbol in the extended ASCII character set.

Bindery operations A postprinting process that assembles press sheets into booklets, mailings, and so forth, and often includes folding, stapling, gluing, or combining pages printed on separate papers.

Binding Final assembly of a publication. Types of binding include saddle stitching, spiral, perfect, and case (hardcover).

Bi-packing Overlapping two pieces of film in the same printer gate for creating a double exposure. If one of the pieces of film is a traveling matte (silhouette against a clear background or vice versa), the other piece of film will only be printed where there are clear areas in the matte.

Bit Binary digit, the smallest unit of information in a binary code. Each bit is either 1 (on), or 0 (off). There are usually 8 bits in 1 byte.

Bit map Map of numeric values representing the colors and/or gray intensities for each pixel stored in computer memory.

Bit pad See *digitizing tablet*.

Black burst Signal recorded on virgin videotape to prepare it for insert editing used in single-frame animation recording; contains no picture content but supplies a sync-pulse control track.

Blue See *blueline proofs*.

Blueline proofs An assembled photographic proof of a publication produced by the printer from plate negatives. The special paper used renders the images in light blue rather than in black (or any other ink color chosen for printing), hence the name.

Blue screen photography In film production, combining foreground and background information from separate shots. For instance, an actor or object is photographed in front of a blue background; using a matte process, the blue area behind the actor is later replaced with a different background, creating a composite image.

Boolean operations In solids modeling, a means by which solids are combined to form new shapes, either by adding to or subtracting from existing shapes. Based on Boolean logic developed by British mathematician George Boole comprising three basic operations: *and, or, not*.

Boot From "bootstrap." Originally, where a computer loads its operating system; now any initialization such as starting the computer, loading software, and so forth.

Bounding box Wire frame box temporarily substituted for the actual computer model. It occupies the area normally taken by the model and speeds the process of creating a motion path.

Bubble chart A chart that shows the progression of three variables while using a two-dimensional plane. Besides the x and y variables, the third variable is represented by the diameter of each bubble.

Buffer Intermediate storage area for data waiting to be transferred between the computer and a peripheral. Can be in semiconductor memory or on a disk.

Bullet An attention getting mark, usually a solid dot in the shape of a circle or square, placed at the beginning of each of a series of sentences or paragraphs. Normally used in place of numbers when there is no special order of precedence to be communicated.

Bus Common electronic pathway for the transmission of data inside the computer.

Business graphics Graphics used in business for analysis and presentations.

Byte A series of binary digits, usually eight, that represents a character, symbol, or operation.

CAD Computer-aided design; software used by architects, engineers, and product designers in the creation of diagrams for building, equipment, products, etc.

Camera framing The positioning of the camera for good composition according to aesthetic criteria and the needs of the narrative.

Camera movements

    dolly To move the camera toward or away from the subject.

    pan To pivot the camera left or right on the tripod.

    tilt To pivot the camera up or down on the tripod.

    truck To travel with the action left or right.

    zoom To show more or less of the subject by adjusting a variable focal-length lens while the camera is operating.

Camera-ready art The photoreproducible layout of type

and graphics from which the printer makes press plates.

Cartesian coordinate system A means for plotting points in two-dimensional and three-dimensional space by setting up x, y, and z axes intersecting at right angles. The x axis runs horizontally, the y axis vertically, and the z axis travels either toward or away from the eye of the viewer, representing the three-dimensional aspect of the space (see Figure 5.1).

Cathode ray tube (CRT) Any video display device using a sealed tube, electron beam, and phosphorescent screen.

Cell Sheet of clear acetate upon which images are printed or painted for traditional animation. Each cell is punched with registration holes for purposes of alignment.

Central processing unit (CPU) Computer circuitry responsible for fetching and processing data, contains arithmetic and logical units which enable it to manipulate data according to instructions contained in the program.

CGA Color graphics adapter card. Displays 4 colors simultaneously out of a palette of 16 colors at a screen resolution of 320 × 200. See also *EGA* and *VGA*.

Character generator Dedicated computer for creating text and numbers for use in video production.

Clip art Art elements that are purchased through a subscription service and that can be used over and over without violation of copyright laws.

Clip text Text paragraphs, often anecdotes and filler used in newsletters, that are purchased through a subscription service and that can be used over and over without violation of copyright laws.

Clipping plane User-definable boundary in a three-dimensional Cartesian work space outside of which graphics will not be displayed.

Clone Lower-cost product (hardware or software) that duplicates the function of another.

Co-axal chart A chart using two or more reference scales that displays dissimilar but related data for purposes of comparison (see Figure 10.27).

Cold type Typesetting using photography (phototypesetting), first developed in the 1950s by exposing film to light shining through letter silhouettes. Compare with *hot type*, where machines, such as the Linotype, used molten lead to compose lines of type.

Colophon A paragraph that provides technical information about the design of a publication; it usually lists fonts used and paper type and manufacturer. It sometimes includes the names of the printer, binder designer, typesetter, and illustrator. *Colophon* means "finishing touch."

Color balance Adjusting video or motion picture color for proper rendition. Most color balancing is keyed to flesh tones.

Color cycling Changing the screen colors by repeatedly cycling through the colors in a look-up table. See also *color table animation*.

Color encoder Electronic device that takes separate RGB signals from the computer graphics card and a sync pulse from external sync generator and encodes them into one NTSC standard video signal.

Color map Customized colors in a look-up table saved as a special palette for a raster image, containing the red, green, blue (RGB) values for each color. Change the color map and all of the screen colors will change to match the new values in the look-up table (see Color Plate 3).

Color space Three-dimensional color model that displays hue, luminance, and saturation as separate attributes (see Color Plate 2).

Color table animation Cycling through pre-determined colors in the look-up table on a specific object or portion of the screen. See also *color cycling*.

Column chart Vertical bar chart (see Figure 10.11).

Communication design Contemporary philosophy that the purpose of design is to transmit a message; similar to and essentially derived from the architectural philosophy that form follows function. Design elements themselves are minimized and subordinate to the communication objective.

Communication styles The three basic styles of publications: informational, persuasive, and instructional.

Comprehensive layout An artist's full-color rendering of a proposed publication. Usually used by a designer to communicate the concept execution to a client. Headlines and subheads are drawn to scale in the intended font. Photographs and illustrations are shown, in position. Text may be greeked in. In computer prepress operations, a 300 DPI laser proof is usually substituted.

Computer-assisted animation Traditional animation equipment or motion control camera under the control of a computer system.

Computer-generated animation Animation created from a computer database of coordinates representing the objects in the animation. The animation does not exist outside the computer until rendered to the screen or stored on magnetic media for recording on videotape or film.

Conforming Matching the original videotape or film to preliminary edits done on an off-line editing system (video), or from a workprint (film).

Contrast The difference between light and dark areas in an image. High-contrast images show the extreme levels of white and black but lack mid values. Low contrast images show mid values but lack the extremes.

Coordinate space A two-dimensional or three-dimensional environment in which we draw designs or construct objects (see Figure 5.1).

Copy The term used for the manuscript that is to be typeset for a publication (sometimes refers to both text and illustrations).

Copyfitting Calculating the exact space copy will occupy in the publication based on the specifications.

Crop To trim the sides, top, or bottom of a photograph or illustration to eliminate extraneous portions or to achieve a more dramatic effect.

CRT See *cathode ray tube*.

Cursor Movable marker noting screen position; used to access menu items, edit text, or create images.

Cut and paste Using a sharp knife and paper adhesive to assemble (paste) type and artwork on illustration board to make a mechanical.

Cutaway In film or video production, a shot that is related to the main action but not part of the main action; sometimes used to bridge lapses in narrative continuity.

Database Systematic organization of information, as in a database of vertices used to describe computer-generated models.

Data indicators Chart elements that depict numeric values visually, such as lines or columns.

Degree of freedom In motion-control photography and animation, a direction of possible camera or subject movement, such as x, y, and z axis orientation, pans, tilts, dollys and so forth.

Depth cueing Rendering option that makes the shading of distant objects less intense so they appear farther away.

Descenders Lowercase characters such as j, y, and p that extend below the baseline of text. Also the portion of the character that extends below the baseline.

Digital (1) An electronic signal with discrete states—such as on and off. (2) A recording process that encodes analog information as numeric values representing frequency and intensity. See *analog*.

Digitize To convert analog information into digital format. Images and text must be digitized before they can be used in paint, draw, and desktop publishing programs.

Digitizing tablet Device that translates hand position into cursor position; used for drawing or tracing images into computer memory.

Dingbats Special typesetting characters or symbols; sometimes included with a font or sometimes composing a separate font. Examples include snowflake and star shapes (commonly used to construct decorative borders), male and female symbols, arrowheads, and checkmarks.

Dip switches Small switches on the system board, add-in cards, or peripherals that can be changed to select operating mode or to prepare the device for the specific operating environment of the computer.

Display The computer monitor screen. See *cathode ray tube*.

DOS Disk operating system. A collection of utility programs that enables you to format disks, copy files, and do other housekeeping chores. It provides a programming environment that resides between the computer hardware and applications programs to access computer memory, drives, printers, and so forth.

Dots per inch (DPI) A measure of resolution. Dot-matrix printers produce a resolution of around 100 DPI, laser printers 300 to 600 DPI, and professional-quality printers 1100 DPI or higher. The lower the resolution, the more discernible the dots. Above 1100 DPI a loupe or magnifying glass is needed to see the dot structure.

Draw program Vector-based computer graphics program that remembers images as a collection of vertices stored in a database. Image resolution is dependent on the output device and not on the screen resolution of the monitor.

Dummy An initial folded mock-up of a planned publication with sketched blocks indicating position of text and graphics. Often used as a planning tool in newspapers and magazines to indicate advertising and editorial space on each page.

Duotone In printing, the process of adding a second color (such as brown) to enhance a black-and-white photograph.

Ease In animation, the gradual acceleration or deceleration of camera or object movement.

Edit decision list List of shots from an off-line editing session containing beginning and ending code numbers for each shot. The decision list is used to automatically edit the original tape to match the work copy.

EGA Enhanced graphics adapter. Displays 16 colors simultaneously out of a palette of 16 colors at a screen resolution of 640 × 200, on a standard TTL color monitor. See also *CGA* and *VGA*.

8088, 80286, 80386, 80486 Family of microprocessors developed by Intel Corporation; used in MS-DOS compatible microcomputers.

Electronic keying Electronic matte technique that replaces chromakey blue areas in a scene with a second video source. Used in news, weather, and sports shows to provide illustrations behind the announcer.

Em space In typesetting, a horizontal space equal to the vertical measurement of the type. In handset type, an em space was perfectly square; in desktop publishing it is usually used when indenting to mean a space equal to the height of the type.

En space One-half an em space or one-half the height of the type.

Exploded pie Pie chart with one segment extended away

from the others for emphasis (see Figure 10.9).

EXPLOR *EX*plicitly *P*rovided 2D Patterns, *L*ocal Neighborhood *O*perations and *R*andomness. Programming language developed by Ken Knowlton at Bell Telephone Laboratories in 1970, used by Lillian Schwartz and other animators.

Fairing See *ease.*

File compression A programming technique that will store more data in the same or less space than is possible without file compression.[1] For example, file compression may replace XXXXXXXXXX with 10X to reduce the number of characters. File compression is useful when transmitting images to computer bulletin boards or when sending them to a service bureau for printing.

Fill light In photography, light used to fill in shadows created by the key light. Placed on the opposite side of the camera from the key light.

Film recorder Device that creates photographic images (usually 35mm color slides or motion picture film) from video signals or digital files.

Flat shading Shading technique that assigns a single intensity to each surface polygon of a three-dimensional object based on the relationship of the surface normal for that polygon to the direction of the light source (see Figure 5.22).

Flicker fusion In motion pictures, the ability of the eye to retain the last frame projected so that the viewer does not notice a momentary interruption in the projected image. Similar to *persistence of vision.*

Floppy disk Portable mass-storage device used to record computer information.

Flush left Type aligned with the left margin.

Flush right Type aligned with the right margin (see *justified*). Occasionally, type is set flush right and ragged left as in a caption positioned on the left side of a photograph or illustration (long text set in this way is often very difficult to read).

Font A complete set of alphanumeric characters, including capitals, lowercase, small caps, numerals, punctuation marks, and symbols (@, &, #, +, =, etc.) in a particular style. Originally, each size of type, ranging from 6 to 72 points, was considered a separate font since it had to be purchased separately. In desktop publishing, since sizes can be adjusted by computer, a font is used to describe a single style without regard to size.

Font cache A "parking place" in computer memory for special downloadable fonts used in a publication that are not readily available on the printer. Allows faster printing.

Format To prepare a computer disk (floppy or fixed) for recording data.

Four-color process The method used in printing to reproduce color photographs and illustrations. It combines dot patterns created using the primary subtractive colors of cyan, yellow, magenta, and black.

Fractals Intricate two-dimensional and three-dimensional graphic shapes created with special algorithms that branch or fragment lines into smaller and smaller parts to create shapes that duplicate the look of mountain ranges, clouds, and so forth (see Figure 5.14 and Color Plate 4).

Frame buffer Area in computer memory reserved for storing pixel data displayed on the graphics screen. The number of bits per pixel stored in the frame buffer determines the number of colors that can be displayed on the screen at one time (see Figure 4.4).

Frame controller Equipment that starts and stops the videotape recorder when it receives a signal from the animation software (see Figure 3.15). It transforms a videotape recorder capable of insert editing into a single-frame recorder.

Galleys In typesetting, copy set into long strips of type, which are then cut apart and pasted on the mechanical.

Gantt chart A chart that uses double-ended floating bars to mark the starting point and ending point of specific steps in the completion of a project (see Figure 10.24).

Gouraud shading The simplest form of smooth shading. Pixel intensities across each surface polygon are interpolated using the highest and lowest intensities for the edges of that polygon, so that the faceted surface of the object appears smooth.

Graphics coordinator Person who supervises the production of graphics within an art department or corporation.

Greeked text In developing design concepts for a publication, the space where text is to be inserted is set in illegible characters so the overall effect can be visually evaluated. In desktop publishing, when a full page or a two-page spread is shown on the screen, the text often appears as a series of gray lines, although magnification options permit fuller detail.

Grid format Intersecting guidelines at set distances used as a design tool for visual consistency when creating documents. The grid lines are not printed with the image.

Grid line See *grid format.*

Gutter The area of a publication between two facing pages where the fold or binding occurs.

H&J (hyphenation and justification) In typesetting, justification occurs when the individual lines are adjusted to fit a set line length. With unjustified type, the right-hand edge formed by the lines of text is

---

[1] *Cubit Owner's Handbook and Guide.* (Manchester, N.H.: SoftLogic Solutions), 10.

ragged. With justified type, the right-hand edge formed by the lines of text is straight, or aligned. In both cases, words at the end of a line may require hyphenation to maintain proper line length. The test of a good H&J program is the amount of unnecessary white space appearing between words and letters in the typeset text; the less unnecessary white space, the less disruptive to the reader and the better the program.

Halftone In printing, the technique of reproducing gray scale photographs or illustrations; achieved by a screening process that divides continuous tones into separate tiny dots. Within each dot, the ink can occupy 0 to 100 percent of the space, and the empty balance of the space allows the white or color paper to be exposed. Dark areas of a photograph become dots almost completely filled in; light areas have little or no ink. Tones of gray, then, are described as a percentage of black: 10 percent is very light gray, 90 percent is very dark, and 50 percent is medium.

Hanging indent A style of formatting paragraphs in which the first line is flush left and subsequent lines are indented.

Hard copy Computer output in final form: text or graphics.

Headline The title of an article, usually set in larger type.

Hidden lines Lines (representing edges) on the back surface of solid objects that should not normally be seen from the front. Removing the lines makes it easier to visualize the shape and orientation of the object (see Figure 5.21).

Hierarchical control In animation, the ordered control of segmented 3-D models like the body of a cartoon character. Hierarchies of dependent parts allow you to automatically move the hands and fingers when the upper arm is moved.

High-key lighting Lighting a scene as though it were in direct sunlight. The scene is uniformly bright with no extreme areas of darkness.

High-level language A programming language that uses English-like expressions which are then translated into machine language instructions, a series of 1's and 0's used by the computer. Pascal, BASIC, FOR-TRAN, and C are high-level languages.

High-low chart Similar to a Gantt chart, in which a given range of values is plotted as a discrete line. Found in newspapers, where it is used to chart daily stock trends (see Figure 10.25).

Hot type The process of casting type in lines using molten lead. The first automated typesetting machine was the Linotype machine, patented by Ottmar Mergenthaler in 1884. This remained the primary means of typesetting until the 1950s, when phototypesetting, or cold type, was developed.

Hot wax machine Applies a thin coating of wax to the back of galleys and illustration photostats to facilitate pasting on a mechanical. Less permanent than using rubber cement, hot wax allows easy repositioning of type and photostats.

Hue Chroma or color.

Image processing Manipulating bit-mapped images by adjusting graphic qualities such as contrast, intensity, and edge-line definition. Image-processing algorithms will increase readability of images from surveillance cameras by revealing detail not discernible before processing. Also used for special effects (see Figure 4.8).

In-betweening In animation, drawings or computer-generated animation created between key frames of action.

Incident light Light falling upon an object directly from the light source.

In house The ability to produce slides, video, newsletters, etc., on site, rather than by sending to a production service.

Initial caps Text in which the first letter of each word is a capital letter. Used to emphasize the individual words in a phrase.

Inkjet printer A printer that electronically directs ink from either one nozzle (black) or four nozzles (red, green, blue, and black) onto paper, forming color dots that make up the image.

Insert editing Recording video and/or audio information on videotape which has already been prepared with a control track.

Interactive program A program that allows user input and responds to user commands in real-time or near real-time.

Interface The boundary between computer systems or computer components that allows communication between them, as in the software interface of menu options displayed on the computer screen.

Interlace scanning In video, the procedure where even lines and then odd lines of the raster image are painted to the screen. Two scans make up each video frame. When images are interlaced, flicker is reduced.

I/O Input/output. Device used for connecting the computer to peripherals.

Joystick Graphics input device that allows the user to position the cursor by moving a lever.

Justified text Type set so that the text aligns with both margins in a straight line. It is created by adding extra space between words and letters.

Kerning Reducing the space between two individual letters: those with parallel strokes (e.g., AW), those where one letter can overhang a smaller letter (e.g., Te), and rounded letters (e.g., D and O) that give the optical illusion of additional space around them.

Key frame Extreme frame showing a key point in animation movement, such as the extreme flattened shape of a ball when it hits the ground.

Key light Principal source of illumination in three-point triangular lighting.

Keyline Another term for *mechanical.*

Kilobyte 1024 bytes of information.

Laser printer Printer that uses laser and plain paper copier technology to produce high-resolution text and graphics (see Figure 3.10).

Layout The initial design concepts for a publication showing approximate size and position of text and graphic images. It becomes the basis for instructions to the art director, typesetter, and printer for production.

Leading The space between lines of text. In general, the larger the point size, the more leading needed to assure readability. (Pronounced "ledding.")

Light pen Pointing device that is held near the monitor. It translates hand movements into cursor coordinates by noting the position of the light pen in relation to the monitor scan beam (see Figure 3.4).

Line art Illustrations and logotypes that can be reproduced without the use of halftone screening; artwork is rendered in black and white.

Line chart A chart that uses lines as data indicators. Line charts are used to show trends over time (see Figure 10.5).

Logarithmic chart A chart where the distance between values on the x or y axis becomes smaller as you move away from 0 (see Figure 10.28).

Look-up table A table of color values that determines what colors will be displayed on the screen for an image stored in a frame buffer (see Figure 4.5).

Low angle Placing the camera below the eye level of the subject.

Low-key lighting Lighting a scene for dramatic effect; sometimes called motivated lighting because the lighting is motivated by the dramatic mood of the scene.

Luminosity Scale representing brightness in a color space coordinate system (see Color Plate 2).

Machine language The series of 0's and 1's directly processed by the computer.

Map chart A chart that uses a map to show geographic data such as altitude, time zone, zip code, and country, state, or county information (see Figure 10.32).

Marquee animation Pixel-based animation that quickly turns individual pixels on and off or changes their color, similar to the lights on a Times Square billboard. See *color cycling* and *color table animation.*

Masking Related to the phi phenomenon, later images "mask" prior images, displacing them in our minds and convincing us that we are seeing a single moving image.

Matte Opaque area on clear film matching the foreground action. The matte (traveling matte in motion picture production) is printed with a separate background, leaving a hole where the foreground action can then be printed. The foreground action is printed with a reverse matte (clear area matching foreground action against opaque background), creating a composite image showing the foreground action cookie-cut into a new background (see Color Plate 11).

Mechanical The camera-ready art for a publication, consisting of illustration boards on which the type and illustrations have been pasted in position for printing.

Menu On-screen list of software options available to the user when using an interactive system.

Menu driven software Software that uses a menu rather than keyboard commands for user input.

Mezzotint A method of screening photographs that creates a grainy effect, changing the feeling from that of a straight photograph to that of a pointillist drawing.

Microcomputer Desktop or small self-contained floor-standing computer that uses a microprocessor for the CPU, such as the Motorola 68000 series or Intel 8088–80486 microprocessor.

Microprocessor Computer chip that contains all of the functions of the CPU.

Minicomputer More powerful than a microcomputer but less powerful than a mainframe; used for general business computing and computationally intensive applications such as computer animation and engineering applications.

Mismatch Break in visual continuity within a scene or between shots meant to show continuous action.

Modem (From **mo**dulate/**dem**odulate.) Device used to make digital computer signals compatible with telephone communications equipment.

Monochrome Having shades in a single hue.

Mother board Primary circuit board within a computer into which all of the computer components are plugged. Also called the *system board.*

Motion control system Mechanical equipment such as optical printers or cameras under the control of a computer.

Motion graphics Animated designs and logos used for television identifications and commercial announcements.

Motion path The path taken by objects in a computer animation, interactively assigned by the animator.

Motion preview Means by which the animator can preview motion in real time, usually in low-resolution wire frame mode. Also called *motion test.*

Mountain chart See *area chart.*

Mouse Input device that is moved over the work surface of a table for controlling cursor position.

NCGA National Computer Graphics Association.

Negatives In printing, the film reverse of the mechanicals; used to make the offset printing plates.

Normal angle Camera angle that is at eye level with the subject.

NTSC National Television Systems Committee, a trade organization that promulgates electronic standards for industry-wide compatibility.

Object definition Defining the shape and three-dimensional characteristic of a computer-generated model. Also called *defining object geometry*.

Object space See *world coordinate space*.

Off-line editing Preliminary videotape editing done on less expensive editing equipment. An editing decision list is generated from this session which is used to automatically edit the original master videotapes on the more expensive equipment.

Off-screen space In a motion picture film or video, the space just outside of view of the audience but part of the dramatic space in the scene.

180-degree rule In film or video production, keeping the camera on the same side of the action to prevent viewer disorientation after editing.

On-line editing Direct editing of the master videotapes.

Open architecture Computer designed so that third-party manufacturers can add high-performance graphics cards and other components to the computer.

Optical printer A device for creating optical effects in motion pictures; consists of a projector, camera, lenses, and related equipment.

Optical scanner See *scanner*.

Orthographic projection Displaying objects in flat perspective, showing a surface at a time, usually in three views—top, front, and side.

Output The result of a computer operation after combining or processing data, now extended to mean the result of any effort or process.

Overhead transparency A large photographic or acetate slide used with an overhead projector. Because of the open area above the transparency, presenters can progressively disclose items in a list or use a pointer to draw attention to specific items.

Page formatting In desktop publishing programs, assigning the basic specifications for publication-wide design elements: number and width of columns, margins, and type specifications.

Pagination In desktop publishing, the process of combining the text and graphics, usually in a multipage publication. Originally, simply the numbering of pages.

Painter's algorithm Ordering objects in a three-dimensional environment by adding them to the screen in sequence from back to front.

Paint program Interactive graphics program that allows the artist to draw images into the frame buffer by controlling pixel intensities or colors.

Parallel port Computer I/O port that transmits 1 byte of data at a time; usually used as a printer connection.

Pasteup Another word for *mechanical*. Also, to construct a mechanical.

Pasteup artist The person who creates a mechanical by cutting and pasting galleys and illustration photostats onto illustration board.

PC-based Software or hardware that uses a DOS-compatible microcomputer as its computing platform.

Pencil test See *motion preview*.

Pen plotter High-resolution vector-only output device that produces hard copy with a pen or pens. Used in engineering, architecture, cell animation, and draw programs.

Peripheral Device connected to and controlled by the CPU (e.g., monitors, disk drives, printers, and keyboards).

Persistence of vision The ability of the eye to hold an image for a fraction of a second beyond its duration.

Perspective Displaying objects on a two-dimensional screen so that they have apparent depth and distance.

Phi phenomenon Psychological sensation of seeing movement when none exists.

Phong shading A refinement in smooth shading where every pixel on the surface of the object is independently computed in relation to the light source so that the edges of each polygon disappear and highlights look more realistic.

Pica A unit of measure used by printers; equivalent to ⅙ of an inch. One pica consists of 12 points and is usually used to indicate column width.

Pixel (From **pic**ture **el**ement.) The smallest visual unit on the computer screen that can be modified or addressed by the graphics software.

Plates In offset lithography, the flexible metal sheets on which the publication image has been photographically imprinted. These are installed on the printing press.

Point addressable The ability to control individual pixels that make up the screen image. Graphics screens are point addressable, text-only screens are not.

Points A unit of measurement used by printers; equivalent to 1/72 of an inch. Twelve points equal 1 pica. Points are usually used to indicate the height of type (e.g., 10 point type for text, 36 point type for headlines).

Polygon A closed two-dimensional shape made up of three or more straight sides.

Postproduction Phase in the production of a videotape or film that begins after the footage has been shot; includes editing, adding special effects, and sound mixing.

PostScript Page description language developed by Adobe Systems and used in desktop publishing. Provides the ability to combine and manipulate text and graphics.

Prepress The process of preparing a publication for printing.

Presentation graphics Business graphics used in sales, training, and management meetings that have been enhanced with better typefaces, artwork, and shaded color backgrounds.

Presenter A person who uses presentation graphics, usually the author of the material, who provides basic data to the graphics coordinator for visual embellishment.

Press proof One of the first sheets of the publication off the press; used for final checking of color balance, dot alignment, and ink coverage.

Program Set of instructions enabling a computer to perform a specific task.

Progressive-disclosure slides A series of slides that reveals an additional item in a list of items a slide at a time (see Figure 10.7).

Pseudocolor Assigning false colors to an image by manipulating the values in a color look-up table. Pseudocolors can be assigned arbitrarily or by specific reference to contrast ratios or luminance values as in image processing.

PS/2 Third generation IBM microcomputer. Uses special add-in cards that are compatible with its microchannel bus architecture.

Quadratic surfaces Object surfaces created by mathematical means rather than being built from individual polygons.

RAM Random access memory. Computer semiconductor memory accessible by the CPU for storage and retrieval of data and programs. Random access memory is volatile. When the computer is turned off the memory is erased.

Raster Video scan pattern where horizontal lines are scanned from top to bottom to create the image.

Raster image Image created on a raster monitor.

Raster monitor A type of monitor that displays images as a series of horizontal lines painted on the screen by an electron beam scanning the screen a line at a time from top to bottom twice every frame, 30 frames per second.

Ray tracing A rendering procedure in which each ray of light falling on a scene is "traced" back from the observer to its origin. Rays that pass through or bounce off objects are calculated accordingly (see Color Plate 5).

Real-time 1) Computer systems that respond immediately to requests for information or action. 2) Images that are generated at a rate which matches or exceeds the video refresh rate of 30 images per second, so that action looks natural.

Reflective light Light that bounces off the subject.

Rendering Making a three-dimensional computer-generated object appear solid by shading its surface according to the location of a predetermined light sources.

Render test In computer animation, test made of individual frames to check surface highlights, texture maps, and other effects, usually at less than full resolution.

Resolution Measure of sharpness of an image on a monitor or output device.

Retouching Changes to a photograph or illustration to add or tone down highlights, eliminate or add visual features, or adjust colors.

Reverse Artwork that is the conversion of whites to blacks and blacks to whites. Also, to make a negative print of the positive (e.g., to make ordinarily black type white on a black background).

Reverse type White type on a black or solid dark background.

RGB Red, green, blue. Primary colors used in the HLS (hue, luminosity, saturation) color space. Also used when referring to color additive process.

ROM Read only memory. Data burned into computer semiconductor chips that contain information used over and over again, such as instructions for the computer Power On Systems Test (POST) or for creating screen text characters.

Rule-based systems Modeling and animation systems that use physical, biological, and behavioral laws to control the movement and "behavior" of objects, such as the movement of waves hitting the beach or the gentle flow of a dancer's dress (see Figure 12.10).

Rules In typography, lines placed in the publication. Rules are normally measured in point sizes (1, 2, 3, etc.); the thinnest is called a hairline rule.

Run-length encoding A way of compressing the space needed to store pixel-based images. Adjacent pixels with the same color value are recorded as a group instead of individually.

Running heads Part of a publication that is repeated on every page; may include the publication name (magazines) or part and chapter titles (books). For example, "Glossary" is the running head on this page.

Saddle stitching A method of binding publications in which a staple is inserted in the fold.

Saturation A scale corresponding to the amount of gray or vividness in a hue (see Color Plate 2).

Scan in The process of converting art, photographs, or text into digital format.

Scanner An input device that digitizes continuous tone images, line drawings, and text for use in computer programs.

Scatter chart A chart that plots a grouping of individual points. A tight grouping indicates more correlation and a loose grouping indicates less correlation.

Scene In film or video, a group of related shots.

Screen shooter Cone-like device connected to an instant camera at one end that can be held against a CRT screen for photographing images.

Screen space Area of view in front of a motion picture or video camera. It can be as wide as the universe (as in the opening scene of *Star Wars*) or as intimate as the smallest detail on a flower bud.

Sequence In film or video, a group of related scenes.

Serial port I/O device that transmits data serially, 1 bit at a time. Commonly used for computer peripherals such as data tablets and mice.

Service bureau A company that sells production services, such as presentation graphics slides, or technical services, such as slide and animation recording.

Shaft encoder Device that measures camera movement for each degree of freedom and transmits that data to a computer.

Shape editor Used in draw programs, shape editors modify existing shapes by selectively changing their dimensions.

Shot In film and video production, beginning when the camera is turned on until it is turned off. The piece of film or videotape resulting from this operation.

SIGGRAPH Special Interest Group on Computer Graphics, of the Association for Computing Machinery.

Signature In printing, a large sheet of paper that when folded becomes four, or a multiple of four, pages of a publication.

Silhouette A photograph or illustration in which the background has been eliminated. In cut-and-paste operations this is achieved by masking the shape of the subject and shooting the negative twice in pre-press. In desktop publishing the silhouette process can often be accomplished in the drawing program.

Silhouette halftone A photograph in which the subject is rendered in normal gray scales, or in color, and the background is white. Sometimes a border rule or solid tint is used to replace the white space so the final art has a geometric shape.

Slit scan Special effects technique used with motion control cameras in which an opaque sheet with an open slit is placed over a backlit line drawing. Individual frames are recorded as the slit is moved across the drawing.

Small caps A special font of capital letters that are smaller than regular capital letters. Used most often in subheadlines, chart headings, and in text to indicate A.M., P.M., A.D., B.C., etc.

Smooth shading See *Gouraud* and *Phong shading*.

SMPTE Society of Motion Picture and Television Engineers.

SMPTE time code A series of numbers recorded on videotape marking off hours, minutes, seconds, and frames. Developed by the SMPTE to provide frame-accurate editing capability.

Soft copy Text or graphics displayed on the computer monitor.

Software Computer programs.

Solids modeling Using graphic primitives such as cubes, cones, spheres, and cylinders that are then combined or subtracted to form three-dimensional shapes.

Spatial resolution Screen resolution. Number of pixels used horizontally and vertically to depict an image.

Speccing Defining design specifications for presentation graphics and printed material, such as color, font style, font size, and other technical details.

Spec copy In publication design, annotating copy to indicate (specify) the typeface, size, column width, and other requirements for the typesetter.

Sprite User-defined animated pixel-based figure that is implemented with hardware chips or with programming techniques.

Steelpoint engraving Originally, the process of engraving on steel that produced very fine lines. Now any artwork that replicates the same look.

Step chart A bar chart with no space between the individual columns (see Figure 10.16).

Storyboard Preliminary set of drawings that visualizes individual shots in a film or graphics presentation.

Style sheets Predefined templates that specify page layout, fonts, and page design elements for desktop publishing programs.

Stylus Drawing implement connected to a digitizing tablet for selecting menu items or creating images.

Subhead In publication design, a title of a section that is usually set in larger or bolder type.

Subtractive primary colors Color pigments that when added together produce black. The subtractive primary colors are yellow, magenta, and cyan. *See* also *additive primary colors.*

Surface normal Line perpendicular to the surface of a polygon.

Surprinting Superimposing text on top of a photograph or printing a second color on top of another.

Sync Synchronization. In video, keeping the video scanning in cameras, monitors, and recorders in electronic step with each other. In film; keeping the picture and track in proper relationship.

Sync generator Generates horizontal, vertical, blanking, and subcarrier signals that when combined with the composite RGB signals from the color encoder provide a stable and color-accurate image.

System unit Housing surrounding the system board and related components.

Tabular A word chart that organizes data in columns (see Table 10.1).

Taper See *ease.*

Texture mapping Conforming a pixel image to the surface contours of a three-dimensional computer-generated object so that the object looks more realistic.

Thermal printer An output device which receives raster image data and uses a heat bar to transfer color (cyan, yellow, and magenta) from ink sheets onto paper.

3-D net chart Computer-generated presentation graphics chart having three variables that take the form of a wire frame mesh (see Figure 10.31).

Throughput Total operating efficiency of a computer system, including processor speed, bus speed, and disk access time.

Thumbnail A small sketch of a page layout used to explore design alternatives.

Tic marks Reference lines next to each numeric value on the x or y axis.

Tight, not touching (TNT) Kerning type to reduce letter spacing to an absolute minimum. Most often used in headlines and subheads.

Tint An area of color or gray used as a design element, usually expressed as a percent of the solid. For example, a 10 percent tint is a very light gray and, when it includes text or art, requires surprinting for legibility; a 90 percent tint is a very dark gray and requires a reverse for legibility.

Tracking ball An input device similar to a mouse except that the ball that normally is in contact with a table surface is turned up so that it can be moved with your hand.

Transformation Manipulations such as translation, scaling, rotation, and perspective; applied to an image database.

Translation Moving an object along one of the axes, left or right, up or down, or in or out.

Traveling matte See *matte*.

TTL Transistor to Transistor Logic. As in a TTL digital monitor.

Typesetter A person or computer program that does typesetting.

Typographer A typesetter or compositor, or a type designer.

Unjustified Text that is set so that the right side is not aligned with the margin; sometimes called ragged right. More informal than justified text.

Vector A line created in a draw program that is defined by its x, y, and z coordinates.

Vector display A monitor that displays images by drawing line segments from one point to the next rather than as a raster of horizontal lines.

Velox Screened photostat containing the dot pattern used to reproduce continuous tone photographs. It is used for placing photographs on mechanicals so that the printer shoots the page as line art.

VGA Video graphics array graphics card. Operates at a resolution of 640 × 480 and displays 256 simultaneous colors out of a palette of 262,144. See also *CGA* and *EGA*.

Video layering Videotape compositing process that allows independent x and y axis movement and perspective control of video sources.

Video still camera Still camera that uses a solid state video array to capture the image and then records the image on a 2-inch floppy disk inside the camera.

Voxel (for volume element) Similar to pixels that define two-dimensional raster images, voxels define three-dimensional objects by using 3-D building blocks called volumetric primitives that are the smallest divisible unit of the object.

Wash drawing Originally, a brushwork illustration made with diluted India ink or watercolor so that, in addition to black and white, it has varying shades of gray. Now, any illustration that replicates this style. Reproduced in printing with halftones, not line art.

Western perspective Traditional system of perspective developed in the Italian Renaissance in which parallel lines will converge to a vanishing point at infinity. Also called linear perspective and photographic perspective.

White space The part of a page in which there is no type or artwork. Sometimes called negative space, it is an important element in page design.

Wire frame Simple line representations of three-dimensional objects that may or may not have hidden lines removed.

Wire frame animation test A motion test done in wire frame to check timing and movement.

Word A sequence of binary digits (bits) treated as one unit. Words can be 4, 8, 16, or 32 bits long, depending on the capabilities of the computer system.

Word chart Chart with text only, no graphics.

Work-alike Computer designed to function like a name-brand computer and run the same software. See also *clone*.

Workstation Computer and related input and output peripherals used by one person, as in a graphics workstation.

World coordinate space Three-dimensional workspace in Cartesian coordinate system where objects are created and interact.

WYSIWYG Acronym for What You See Is What You Get. Describes the situation where a computer monitor displays actual (or near actual) fonts, formatted text, and graphics as they will appear in printed output.

XT Expanded Technology. The original IBM PC with a hard drive and two additional expansion slots.

z-buffer Computer memory reserved for sorting three-dimensional objects in the object space, front to back, and displaying them as they would appear in a three-dimensional environment.

INDEX